W9-DEE-296

The Political Cartoon

Also by **Charles Press:**

*When One Third of a City Moves to the Suburbs, A Report
   on the Grand Rapids Metropolitan Area*
Main Street Politics
The American Political Process (with Charles Adrian)
Governing Urban America (with Charles Adrian)
American Politics Reappraised (with Charles Adrian)
Democracy in Urban America (co-editor with Oliver P. Williams)
Democracy in the Fifty States (co-editor with Oliver P. Williams)
Empathy and Ideology (co-editor with Alan Arian)
State and Community Governments in the Federal System
   (with Kenneth VerBurg)

**Frontispiece.   Mischa   Richter: The   Senator   weather   vane.
See page 338.**

The Political Cartoon

Charles Press

Rutherford • Madison • Teaneck
Fairleigh Dickinson University Press
London and Toronto : Associated University Presses

© 1981 by Associated University Presses, Inc.

Associated University Presses, Inc. ·
4 Cornwall Drive
East Brunswick, N.J. 08816

Associated University Presses Ltd
69 Fleet Street
London EC4Y 1EU, England

Associated University Presses
Toronto M5E 1A7, Canada

Library of Congress Cataloging in Publication Data

Press, Charles
    The political cartoon.

    Bibliography: p.
    1. Political cartoons–History. 2. Wit and Humor,
Pictorial. 3. United States–Politics and Government–
Caricatures and cartoons. 4. American wit and humor,
Pictorial. I. Title.
NC1763.P66P73   741.5'793   76-2309
ISBN 0-8386-1901-0

PRINTED IN THE UNITED STATES OF AMERICA

To Nance

Contents

Acknowledgments

Finishing a book is somehow like closing a door. The book, for better or worse, is done; there's not much left to do about it but brace yourself for the just criticisms and thank those whose aid has been invaluable. The latter task is a very pleasant one. So this I now do.

I wish to acknowledge support from persons at Michigan State University: Dean Gwen Andrew of the College of Social Science who awarded me a Development grant to defray a major share of manuscript preparation costs, Charles Cnudde, Chairperson of the Department of Political Science who made released time from teaching available to me at crucial stages, and to the University Research Committee for awarding me All University Research grants over a period of four years. Also I very much want to acknowledge typing assistance that I received from Katherine Lehman and Iris Richardson and other department secretaries, who indeed will be puzzling out and typing clean copy of this preface shortly after I finish it. I also wish to thank Dan Preston of University College Learning Research Center for letting me use his camera and teaching me how to take decent pictures of the cartoons and being ever ready with useful advice on why the slides or prints didn't turn out as they were supposed to.

Several persons in their discussions with me helped me greatly in gaining more understanding of the subject. Roy Matthews of the Department of Humanities became a close friend through our mutual interest. Arthur Poinier and Draper Hill, editorial cartoonists of the Detroit *News,* brought insights too numerous to acknowledge, as did Peter Marzio of the Smithsonian Institution. I also learned from the students in my two undergraduate seminars on political cartoons who challenged my vagaries on the subject.

Finally I thank my wife for encouragement and for putting up with all those tedious side trips to used bookstores, flea markets, and antique shops looking through the art or humor sections for those outsize volumes that might turn out to be — collections of political cartoons!

Thank you all. But for the errors of fact and judgment in this book, you have to blame —

Charles Press
East Lansing

The Political Cartoon

1
The Political Cartoon

This is a book about the political cartoon — which some readers will, I hope, recognize is written in the same fine, balanced, and judicious style of that art form itself.

A political cartoon is worth looking at just because it is enjoyable to stick pins into fools and villains or to watch others doing it. It also provides important data for the students of politics. The cartoonist is part of that linking process which connects the general public and its political leaders — a give-and-take rough and tumble out of which comes what the pollsters call public opinion.

First, let me distinguish the political cartoon from other types of graphic art in which an artist comments on current events. I adapt to my own use the categories already worked out by Alan Dunn, himself a cartoonist of considerable merit.[1]

Types of Cartoons

All forms of the graphic art of comment are alike in that they muse upon the ridiculous and the incongruous in life. They may be based on fantasy, incongruity, and surprise, or they may hone ridicule and satire into a sharp-edged weapon. But the repeated theme in all such art is the contrast between reality and the ideal, between aspiration and practice, between what is and what could be. The novelist William Makepeace Thackeray, who began as a cartoonist, illustrates the point with a mild satire on Louis XIV, who was known in life as "Le Grand Monarque."

Cartoons differ in purpose, whether they seek to amuse, as does *comic art*; make life more bearable, as does the *social cartoon*; or bring order through governmental action, as does the successful *political cartoon*. But all distinctions in this field, as in most others, get a little hazy at the boundaries. It is like trying to decide where the nose leaves off and the rest of the face begins. I suspect that ear, nose, and throat specialists probably handle the problem in the same way that I am going to — by doing the best they can, and then making some rather arbitrary decisions. So I begin by admitting that some drawings may fit into more than one category — or at least it is hard to

11

1.   William Makepeace Thackeray : Louis XIV, Ca. 1845.

decide which. But most cartoons, I think, can be sorted into one of Dunn's three boxes: comic art, the social cartoon, or the political cartoon.

Dunn's typology is useful because it is based on the artist's purpose, rather than on his or her subject. Comic art is the most innocent form of cartoon comment. The artist's goal is simple entertainment in a weary world. This kind of art tries for a humorous and good-humoured observation on daily life and problems, varying in technique from the subtleties of pratfall art of the old-style comic strips in which all characters in the last box went "plop!" (Chic Young's "Dumb Dora" and "Rodney Rockett") to what may be called the newer, more refined and respectable comedy (Chic Young's "Blondie"). The earlier slapstick of "Mutt and Jeff" and "Jiggs and Maggie" was related to vaudeville and burlesque and all the gaudy racetrack plaids and big bow ties of Bobby Clark and Bert Lahr; the latter type is more domestic and homey situation comedy. The funnies, as their name suggests, have been the natural home for comic art.

A second type of cartoon is that of social comment, with a little more cutting edge added to the purely comic. For that, they call the artist a humorist rather than a comic. In such cartoons the artist aspires to comment of a sort about daily life and its problems. His or her main purpose is to bring on the wry smile of recognition — hopefully to make life and its irritations a little easier to take. The contrast with comic art is similar to that between the innocent foolery of a Robert Benchley or Stephen Leacock piece and the humorous comment with a little more bite found in Mark Twain or Ring Lardner. In graphic art, social comment flourishes in the *New Yorker* cartoon, from Peter Arno to Helen Hokinson, though some of the comics, such as "Peanuts" or "Beetle Bailey," mix in doses of social comment. Alan Dunn, a master of social-comment form, describes such art as follows: "[it] encompasses the entire scope of the human society's activities, from pollution to pills — from technology to the desire to believe in little green men with pointed heads — and, by the use of contrast, exaggeration or stark reality, it conveys to the viewer *the absurdity of going too far out in either our dreams or our fears*" (emphasis added).

So far so good, but complications begin to rear up. Dunn argues that the social-comment cartoon, by the artist's design, has a more objective viewpoint than the political cartoon. The political cartoon, he says, is comment championing a specific political faction or point of view. A 1933 cartoon by Robert Day showing a coal miner who looks up and says "For gosh sakes, here comes Mrs. Roosevelt" is, by his definition, social comment on the incongruities of life rather than political comment, since even though the subject is a political actor, no partisan line is being peddled. The same is true of Dunn's own cartoon of a very upper-class couple at a war rally during the World War II alliance with the Soviet Union, "It's the Internationale; if you don't know the words, just mumble." Both cartoons are of the wry, grin-and-bear-it category.[2] But when we move over to vintage "Little Orphan Annie," or some of past and current "Lil Abner," we are getting a slightly more acerbic and partisan comment by the artist mixed in with entertainment and social comment. When we move to Herblock and Oliphant, even with their heavy helpings of humor, we have arrived at the political cartoon.

The political cartoon, then, is defined by this social cartoonist, Alan Dunn, as a subcategory, perhaps even an abased or bastard type, since embedded in it is a nasty, partisan comment upon a current event. It seeks to do more than amuse or make one sigh out a "Well, that's life"; it tries to influence the viewer to a particular viewpoint and predispose him or her to a particular action.

For the most part, the cartoons this book is about fit this category of opinion huckstering, but so do a good many cartoons that I will arbitrarily call cartoons of social comment. I do not intend to deal much with cartoons that seek to influence their viewers on moral matters in the style of the pictorial sermons of William Hogarth, whose familiar prints include those contrasting thoroughfares "Beer Street" and "Gin Lane," or in the style of such series as "The Harlot's Progress," "The Rake's Progress," "Marriage à la Mode," and "Industry and Idleness." These are great cartoons, and maybe even great political ones. They certainly are a long shot from the typical Peter Arno or Whitney Darrow, if only because of the earnestness the artists has mixed in with the amusement. They would fit into the political category if attempt at influencing the viewer were the only differentiating factor. But it is not.

These I rule out with a flourish because political cartoons, as I see it, need to have an implicit appeal to do something political. This is what makes them partisan, not the ties to any political party or grouping. The cartoon can encourage action on a social question, but the solution to the problem must somehow involve putting lighted matches under politicians and getting them off their duffs. Hogarth's social cartoons appeal rather for individual moral action (i.e., "be more like the industrious apprentice, you clod!"). So too do George Cruikshank's in favor of prohibition, as in our day do the fine religious cartoons by the artist Howard Brodie. The logic of my position means, I suppose, that I will have to chuck all those editorial cartoons against drunken and reckless driving, since they frequently call not for political action but for the self-reform of drunks. But then, on reflection, so be it. Their omission does not break my heart.

Also I exclude those staid, representational, nicely shaded drawings of a politician framed in a big box, an idea borrowed from the sports pages, which show the kindly,

2. **William Hogarth : Gin Lane. 1751.**

photogenic gentleman posed full face, with funny cartoon vignettes and copy surrounding him depicting his career from the time he won his first agate in a neighborhood game of marbles. These kinds of cartoon were more popular before the camera and photoengraving were invented, but they are still found in local papers and hanging on the walls of local politicos.

But definitely left in are those caricatures of politicians which often wickedly pirate in a partisan message. I am thinking of David Levine and Renan Lurie, and their able predecessor Max Beerbohm, who, if for nothing else, should have been knighted for his "Gladstone in Heaven series." These I shall not part with.

Left in also are the cartoon arguments over such moral-political questions as legalizing abortion or marijuana, since these appeal for political action. This is a hollow victory, since offhand I can remember only a few particularly good political cartoons about either subject.

On the next point I will be even less consistent. I want to take a broad and generous view on the question of timeliness. The political cartoon does not have to be journalism. Most political cartoons are a form of journalistic comment designed to

3. Max Beerbohm : Gladstone in Heaven. II. The same evening Mr. Gladstone addresses a mass meeting of Angels. He pays an eloquent and graceful tribute to God. 1892.

influence viewers with regard to specific political events of the day, just as the editorial usually tries to. This is indeed part of Dunn's classification scheme, but he does not develop the levels of generality — which leads to some question of what should be considered a political cartoon.

One step removed from a specific political event are Hogarth's series of four prints, "The Election," drawn with the 1752 election in mind with no specific geographic locale identified. Rather, Hogarth aims for a composite of political horrors, just as Charles Dickens did later in *Pickwick Papers* in his description of the election of a member in the "ancient loyal and patriotic borough of Eatanswell". As one ponders Hogarth's picture of the dying suffragist and the idiot voter with a bib, both led to the polls by political manipulators, or watches the purchaser of votes as he appears here and there throughout the series, a sermon comes through. While it may not favor either of the partisan groups pictured, it certainly projects a message that could be, and was, used by later partisan critics of English elections.[3] So it stays in, and to legitimize it I will call it and others like it a "political cartoon of the nonspecific mode."*

At a more diffuse level of generality are drawings such as Goya's in *The Disasters of War* (Fig. 78) or Käthe Kollwitz on war and poverty,[4] or the Victorian cartoonist John Tenniel's last cartoon, "Peace." It showed Father Time pleading with Mars to pull up his chariot. Each of these is political comment with a message, though in each case, the tie to particular political events is even more tenuous than in Hogarth.

In future references to this type of political cartoon, for the sake of brevity I shall drop the last four words of the descriptive term.

15

4.   William Hogarth : The Polling. 1754.

Goya's drawings relate to Napoleon's invasion of Spain in 1810, but their message is a moving plea against war itself; Kollwitz draws for Germans of the 1920s and early 1930s, but her message has a broader humane appeal that applies wherever people go hungry to bed; while the "Peace" drawing of Tenniel or in today's editorial cartoon may refer to the latest war but unfortunately would seemingly have been appropriate and relevant at any time in the past sixty centuries or more — and perhaps into the immediate or foreseeable future for about the same span of time.

The difficulty with cartoons at this level of generality is that they are so often bad cartoons, bad because the message says very little beyond that the cartoonists put themselves on record as being for virtue. The price tag is left off. It makes one feel very moral to be lined up with the saints against political corruption and for political purity, but what about the difficult cases? Does Tenniel's plea for peace mean that one stands by, whistling "Blest be the tie that binds" in the face of warlike acts directed by a Hitler? Do we give the Charles Street Meeting House back to Massasoit? It is much safer to stay up there on the pedestal throwing first stones and pitching the sermon in generalities.

All of these, nevertheless, I class as political cartoons, since they are drawings with a partisan message for viewers about what they should think or do politically. To summarize, a political cartoon need not be wholly journalism. It need not have a specific historical event tied to its tail like a tin can.

One other minor matter troubles those who would study the political cartoon. Some such cartoons are classed as art with a capital A, and are carefully preserved with the toenail cuttings of Henry Wadsworth Longfellow, while the rest of their day are

16

dismissed as transient and artistically worthless. Ralph E. Shikes, in an excellent work *The Indignant Eye,* subtitled *the Artist as Social Critic in Prints and Drawings from the Fifteenth Century to Picasso,* isolates those political works which he feels are really artistic, and presents them for the benefit of those of us who can appreciate art.[5] Shikes's book is splendidly printed and put together, with illustrations and discussion of many artists not fully represented in any other source that I know of.

In common with other commentators on Social Art, Shikes has a soft spot for the revolutionaries. Not all the great artists he features, of course, are seditious rebels, though seemingly the more truly artistic they are, the more they tend to be so, while those who lean to the philistines seem to demonstrate the fact by settling for only being desperately unhappy with the sins of the polity, economy, and society that they partially adorn.

Thus I conclude that a leading characteristic of the Great Art Political may be that the artist forcibly reject the social, political, and economic system that he or she actually lives in. One notes how Al Capp plummeted from "Great Political and Social Critic and Artist" to cartoonist hack after he shifted his politics to the right. Aside from this genuinely significant characteristic, the political cartoons by artists with a capital A seem to me pretty much like the ruck of political cartoons by artists with a small a. Some of both kinds are good cartoons that are long remembered, and some of both kinds stink. (I display a personal prejudice in feeling that arty art that does not come off is worse, but in fairness to the seriously artistic with a message, I should note that daily newspapers do still publish political cartoons on such subjects as April 15th's being the day when Good Old John Q. Public has to pay up on his income tax, doggone it!)

Now that I have sorted out the main types of cartoons, at least to my own satisfaction, let us turn to looking at cartoons and the question of what makes a good cartoon.

What Makes a Good Political Cartoon?

The problem of defining what a good cartoon is, is like that of defining justice for the court system, health for the medical profession, or the public interest. It is impossible to say precisely what the supreme good looks like, even though almost everyone pays lip service to it. Fortunately, it is a good deal less difficult to identify the bad eggs. One may hazard the guess that swinging a baseball bat in the vicinity of the accused's head or hitting him with a rubber hose that leaves no marks, in order to try to gain a clear picture of what happened at the scene of the crime, does not fall within what most would define as the optimum operation of a just legal system. So we screen out the obviously bad and within the basket of what is left lies the good, we hope.

Some disagreement will surely exist even about what is left. At best, only a rough consensus exists about the really first-rate, because tastes and experiences differ. Not everyone likes Beethoven or even Handel, though it is as hard to imagine them classed as second-raters as leaving Hank Aaron or Babe Ruth off the upper half of lists of baseball aficionados. Cartoon art may just be a little trickier than baseball. In one generation, George du Maurier is in; in the next, he is on the remainder table. But even those who are downgraded for the moment always get at least an honorable mention whenever one reviews their period. What the people who lived then considered great political cartoons has to be given some decent niche, even when the art looks bad and the sentiment is fragrant or moldy in the view of later generations.

5. Charles L. Bartholomew (Bart). What the Senate thinks. House — What do you think of that little popularity contest of mine? Senate — Nice lot of weather we're having, isn't it? February 15, 1902. **Minneapolis** *Journal.*

Again, there is more complete agreement over the negative — over "The Lost Chord" or "September Morn" or Edgar Wallace. So in describing what a good cartoon is, I shall concentrate on what makes a really rotten one, just the way court procedures rule out actions inappropriate to a reasonable system of justice.

A good political cartoon is not distinguished by trite artistry, by what has been called correspondence-school art, which has an artistic formula or cliché for every time you draw a hat or nose or foot. At one time the style of drawing found in the Bart cartoon was possibly thought of as artistic chic. Now it seems quaint and trite. But this does not imply that better artistry can save a bad cartoon. Artistic excellence is only secondary to a cartoon's main purpose. It can only be supplementary. A short review of the editorial cartoons appearing in daily newspapers should be enough to convince most observers that producing a good cartoon requires a good deal more than expertise in drawing. If one looks at the carefully drawn originals of uninspired cartoons, this point is even more forcefully hammered home. Pure representational art down to the last buttonhole is not necessary for a good cartoon. Not even excellent likeness in caricature always is. Good cartoons may even have that abomination, labels, to tell you who President Eisenhower is supposed to be. It might be supposed that one may tentatively grant that the greater the artist's skill, the wider the range of conditions he may present. But even this is not very helpful, because the political cartoon puts more stress on ideas presented in a striking way than on artistry. A childish scrawl or what pretends to be so, as in the Max Beerbohm drawing of Gladstone, may pack a good deal more political punch than the neatest airbrush job. The latter may turn out to be like a beautiful woman with no brains, no wit, and no personality.

So my first conclusion is that artistry is supplementary and contributory rather than central. Already good political cartoons are helped by skillful presentation of material, but cartoons with blah messages require more than artistic merit to make them worth any attention at all.

One may go even further. Sometimes the artistry gets in the way of a good idea; the technique becomes the excuse for the drawing and the idea gets lost. I present no examples. I just conclude that the major element of a good cartoon lies not in the artistry of the cartoonist, though artistic presentation may help get the cartoon across. It also helps if the cartoonist is not an artistic cliché-monger.

Even worse than a dead, empty, prettified likeness is a picture that rings phony in its message. An allegory is always false on the surface. Franklin Roosevelt is shown juggling knives. This is OK, since a cartoon is really an exaggeration to get at an underlying truth. But the misrepresentation of everyday life has to be believable because it presents an underlying truth — one more true than the facts themselves. The creation can not be one the artist knows is essentially a lie. If it is, it often shouts the fact to its viewers, and it is a dead elephant.

Some artists have developed to an unusual degree the normal capacity all of us have for self-delusion. Somehow they can hide the fact of their own posturing from themselves. They have perhaps done it so long that they need outside help to recognize the falsity of their work. Some never seem to understand why what they create does not stimulate the admiration they would like to have. But it is a hopeful fact of life that no one very much likes false emotion once he or she recognizes it, or, perhaps I should say, he or she can only get to like it if it is presented in the form of camp parody.

Much political humbug is space filler — what has been described as the crusade against the man-eating shark. The emotion as well as the ethics of the political message is a misrepresentation, either because the artist is drawing by demand of someone else, is expressing a faddish view he or she feels will please an audience of phonies, or is afraid to say what he or she really means or thinks.

Sometimes artists produce this class of bad cartoons because they have run dry. They may not be able to think of much to say that day or, like all humans facing deadlines, they may just have had a bad day. Sometimes an artist may be faced with a topic about which he or she feels it a duty to say something, and it is not easy to work up new enthusiasms. Armistice or Veterans' Day, despite all of its tragic and heartbreaking significance, comes to mind. It is hard to keep crying me a river year after year, because after a while the tears become forced and it shows in the cartoon.

Especially dangerous are those treatments which are appeals to high idealism or exaggerated moral purity. They lie along that dangerous boundary line that separates the genuine from the false, and so may invite the opposite response from the one intended — some form of vulgar feedback such as a yawn or a deep belch or a horse laugh.

To summarize, in a good cartoon the aroma of genuine sentiment seems to be floating about in the air somewhere, instead of the more pungent stink of false emotion or false political morality covered with cheap perfume. Viewers will detect the latter and, whether they react negatively or just ho hum, will frequently, without knowing why, reject work that they sense lacks basic integrity.

When we move from the level of the political message to the imagery with which the cartoonist packages the idea, we are probably coming closest to what makes a really good cartoon. After all, Jack the Ripper was probably sincere, and was even a consummate craftsman, and so are a good many of those dreadful educational lecturers one hears, if one is not careful, on public broadcast radio. What distinguishes a Herblock from others is not the sincere liberalism of his message. A good many of the cartooning profession share his often simple-minded sentiments. What makes him great is how he puts that message across. The cartoonist has to present his idea to the viewer in some way that will be striking, forceful, or amusing, or all three. Again we can spot the negative more easily than the positive.

Cartoonist Clare Briggs, in giving hints on how to draw comic cartoons, begins and spends most of his book on *the idea,* which is his term for the imagery that clothes the message. In rechecking this work, I find that for the best advice ever given to him he credits someone named Foster Coates, Briggs's all-wise editor. Coates, Briggs reports, always said : "Never be satisfied with the first idea that occurs to you. Cast it aside and think of another. Then cast the second aside, and the third; and keep up this process of elimination until you are sure you have the best idea possible on that particular subject." What Briggs calls attention to is that the obvious idea is the one that occurs to a good many people almost right away.[6] That is why it is called trite.

Editor and Publisher illustrated this point in 1966 with perhaps some little cruelty to political cartoonists. The week's big news happened to be a counterrevolutionary uprising in Communist China. The magazine published the work of six cartoonists, including some very good ones. All six showed a dragon biting its tail.[7] So the first point about imagery is that it should not be ordinary but should have an element of novelty and surprise. While no one can give the formula for sparkling originality, the reverse has its own smell of staleness that all can recognize. We have all absorbed too much of the card game among the Great Powers, the old-time cartoon figures such as Uncle Sam instructing small-minded politicians, or the grave with the headstone marked for the unpopular issue. As William Murrell, one of the great critics of political cartoons, wrote about war cartoons : "Take the dozens of cartoons in which the shade of Napoleon says to Hitler, 'I tried that too!', and those in which Uncle Sam seizes a musket or beats a sword out on an anvil, and hoariest of all — those in which history appears as an aged man with a flowing beard and a large open book. Let us have no more of them, even though it will cost a little more cerebration."[8]

All of these were once fresh and original imagery. Now, unless they have a new twist, they are dreadfully boring. Parenthetically, less of a sin is committed when a cartoonist resurrects an old idea that only a few of those who muck around with cartoons will recognize or know of. Every so often someone adapts an old idea from one of the masters, with few the wiser or much injured by the borrowing.

But since cartoonists on modern newspapers are forced to meet rigorous deadlines, every artist deserves to be forgiven some triteness. As Fischetti suggests, three good ideas a week are not bad, and these three are what separates the real cartoonists from what he reports his colleague Bill Mauldin calls the pants pressers in the business.[9]

We turn next to those negatives in respect to imagery which lead to wrecking the impact of the message. Not only do fancy artistic practices sometimes make it difficult for the viewer to understand what the political message is supposed to be about, but the viewer may also stumble over the imagery. The allusions may be too complex, elaborate, or obscure. They may also get too involved. One is tempted to say that the trick of a good cartoon is to cut out unnecessary detail. The Communist *Daily Worker* artist Robert Minor (Fig. 11), for example, began drawing with a fat black crayon so he would be forced to omit detail from his picture and would thus maximize its impact. In the same way David Low developed power as he moved from the fusty representativeness of his then famous Australian cartoons for the Sydney *Bulletin* to his more striking, modern style of imagery. Each is a little imaginative drama, but the second has the gas pedal down to the floor.

6. **David Low : The Raven. 1915. Sydney** *Bulletin.*

7. David Low : The Angels of Peace Descend upon Belgium. June 10, 1940. London *Evening Standard.* **By permission of the trustees of the Low Estate and the London** *Evening Standard.*

Because cartoons are visual, it is especially important that this element be exploited to the fullest. Some cartoons give a visual jolt as the eye is led through the drawing to the hidden kicker. Some artists impressed with the fact that cartoons are visual comment, want to go all the way and eliminate all the words in cartoons. John Chase, the New Orleans cartoonist, omits all captions in an attempt to simplify, simplify, simplify. But this impulse to starkness can also have its negative aspect. Sometimes a caption is worth 1,000 pictures, since it helps by quickly unraveling the picture puzzle. What is Herblock's one-word drawing on hysteria all about, without the caption? So rather than stating the rule positively as "use simple imagery," it seems useful to come back to the negative. A good cartoon does not contain *unnecessary* complications in its imagery or its title, and the good cartoonist does not make too inaccurate an estimate most of the time about what is unnecessary imagery or words.

8.   Herblock : "Fire!" June 1949. The Washington *Post* — from *The Herblock Book* (Beacon Press, 1952.)

A related point is that the imagery should not get too complicated, because the artist may run the danger of saying more than he or she wants to say. John Tenniel, the Victorian cartoonist, made sure that he was not stuck with just one image for Britain. He created a circus of types to fit many moods and situations : Britannia, the British lion, John Bull, and even Mrs. John Bull complete with daughters. Added to these were the Queen or prime minister, who also on occasion stood in for that nebulous entity the nation. Thus Victorian Britain might sometimes be like a lion, but it was not lionlike in every respect or all the time.

In the opinion of some, one other element seems to make a good cartoon: the subject that inspired it must have lasting importance. This helps in understanding the cartoon a decade or so later on, but it argues more — that the artists who live in interesting times have the advantage, since the times will inspire their best work. I have reluctantly come to share this view, even with some reservations. Certainly David Low in his defiance of Hitler is greater and more memorable than David Low on the subject of Jix (Sir William Joynson-Hicks) or on the labor leader J. H. Thomas in tux — two of the more perishable, though no doubt lovable political memories of the English nineteen-twenties, whom Low preserved in ink. But the other side of this argument is also worth noticing. Great events have inspired some horrible cartoon fizzles, and, with all their flimsiness, the amusing antics of Jix and Thomas are preferable to many of the ponderous presentations of World War II by less-gifted practitioners. Which is a way of saying that great cartoons get drawn by great cartoonists.

But one can go a little further. Gillray's "Sin, Death and the Devil" is viewed by his biographer, Draper Hill, as "one of the most daring satires ever published."[10] Yet to me it is a fairly dead creation. The cartoon is based on the rumor that Pitt, with the Queen's influence, had had Thurlow dismissed as Chancellor by the perhaps demented George III. The drawing depicts a topless Queen Charlotte as "the Snakey Sorceress that sat Fast by Hell's Gate" in Milton's *Paradise Lost.* (The cartoon is·a takeoff on a Hogarth painting of the Milton scene.) Pitt is portrayed by the artist as the flattering figure of Death as he fights off a critic, Thurlow, who presumably is complimented by being portrayed as Sin. With more justification than Victoria later, the Queen might have dropped the hint "We are not amused." As a matter of fact she did, for all the good it did her.

9. James Gillray : Sin, Death, and the Devil. June 9, 1792.

The Gillray cartoon gives me the same feeling I might get watching a rabbit blasted apart with a Howitzer. If the artist brings up the big artillery, he or she must have a reason for firing it, more than just showing off or having a test run of the equipment. A great cartoon has to latch somehow onto a theme or even political cause that makes more of the event than manufacturing a transitory irritation with one's queen. As I look at the cartoons I regard as great, I find that somehow they twist the trivial into a shape that makes it of lasting significance. John T. McCutcheon's "The Mysterious Stranger" does more than say *Missouri for the first time in about forty years went Republican in 1904.* It seems to me to say that the last-ditch-never-forget-bitterness of the Civil War is over - finally. Robert Minor's World War I comment, "at last a perfect soldier!", is the final assessment for me of the military, and, I might add, the bureaucratic mind. Bill Mauldin's "Just Gimme a Coupla' Aspirin" sums up the state of mind of the reluctant, but murderously effective, civilian soldier. I find in other great cartoons the same summarizing of a conclusion about an event and about life itself: Herblock's "Fire," Thomas Nast's "Who Stole the People's Money?" (Fig. 154), or Opper's "Willie and his Poppa" series (Fig. 168). Sometimes there is no one cartoon but a whole series, as in Daumier (Fig. 30), F. A. Opper, or Homer Davenport (Fig. 119), or in the more recent work of Oliphant (Figs. 208-210). So we come back to square one. A great cartoon can not be trite, even when inspired by a trite event; it has somehow to twist its subject matter into a statement that lasts beyond the event to generalize from it into comment applicable to many times and seasons.

10. John McCutcheon : The Mysterious Stranger. 1904. Chicago *Tribune.* Reprinted, courtesy of the Chicago *Tribune.*

11. Robert Minor : Army Medical Examiner : "At last a perfect soldier." 1915.
The Masses.

At least the second last word, as a kind of summary, should be left to a great practicing cartoonist. Herblock writes: "The question of what's a good cartoon and what is not is something that's up to you. I've often heard formulas for what these things ought to be, but I've never heard one that applied in all cases. There are many cartoonists with many styles of drawing; there are humorous cartoons and others that are stark and dramatic — some with many words and some with none. I've seen outstanding examples in all styles; and along with others in this business, I can only mumble that a good cartoon is a good cartoon."[11]

And for the last word, here is the formula of what these things ought (not) to be, a formula that applies in all cases: *A good political cartoon does not treat a trite subject as trivial, has a political message that does not obviously ring false,* and *is not presented with trite imagery or artistry.* With a formula like that as a guide, how can any political cartoonist who can read miss? In addition, if the cartoonists have some artistic talent, that should make it all the easier to be successful unless they let their technique get in the way and succumb to the temptation of showing off; succumb that is, in a way that does not amuse or stir us. Now, is all that clear?

12. Bill Mauldin : "Just gimme a coupla Aspirin. I already got a Purple Heart."
1944. Drawings copyrighted 1944, renewed 1972, Bill Mauldin, reproduced by
courtesy of Bill Mauldin.

What It's All About

Since we now know what we are not looking for, I digress again to point out a few of
the obvious problems of trying to find out the meaning of political cartoons. Even
when the cartoonist has done a good job we may miss his or her point after the event he
or she portrays recedes into history.

Here is a well-known political print by James Gillray. It is dated June 26, 1803.
James Gillray (1757-1815) was the first popular political cartoonist, and he is
recognized as a genius even by those who loathe him. But what does this, one of his
famous cartoons, mean? Hazard a guess.

"My little friend Grildrig, you have made a most admirable
panegyric upon Yourself and Country, but from what I can
gather from your own relation & the answers I have with
much pains wringed & extorted from you, I cannot but conclude you to be, one of the most pernicious, little odious
reptiles that nature ever suffer'd to crawl upon the surface
of the Earth."

13.   James Gillray : The King of Brobdingnag, and Gulliver. June 26, 1803.

Fortunately there are two commentaries to tell us about this Gillray print, one of the advantages of studying prints of artistic geniuses of over a hundred years back. The first was written in 1851 by Thomas Wright.[12] The second is found in one of the eleven volumes published by the British Museum, which give fairly complete descriptions for some ten thousand prints issued in England before 1832.[13]

In this case the explanation is relatively easy. On our own we can hardly fail to grasp the source of the imagery, since the title tells us the idea is lifted from *Gulliver's Travels*, which is still part of our cultural heritage (perhaps only for the next generation, thanks to Walt Disney). The persons portrayed, the erudite sources tell us, are Napoleon and George III, except that in this case that old authoritarian devil whose exploits dominate our own Declaration of Independence is the hero; and our nation's benefactor, who was at this instant peddling the Louisiana Territory to Thomas Jefferson, is Gillray's villain. Napoleon at this time was threatening England with an invasion. George III is shown breathing ridicule on the upstart dictator. The message is that Napoleon is a pigmy, to be held in contempt by all true Englishmen rather than feared. The cartoon breathes fiery patriotism. Gillray's biographer, Draper Hill, notes that the greater the danger of invasion, the smaller Napoleon came to be drawn by Gillray.[14] If so, this cartoon must therefore represent a moment of extreme peril.

This drawing illustrates the problem of analyzing a political cartoon from another time and place. Cartoons are usually journalistic comment and may be based on a current event a good deal more obscure than this one — an event that is really remembered only by the historians, and sometimes only by the specialists. Many of Gillray's prints, also very good, refer as did "Sin, Death and the Devil" to such minor political happenings, and so the books of explanations are a necessity. Commonly, no one has bothered to write them about cartoons produced since 1832.

The second problem is that the imagery used may no longer be familiar, if it ever was. The eighteenth- and nineteenth-century cartoonists favored the classics, and historical and literary metaphors, since these were the common heritage of their cultured viewers. The first American cartoon shows a man in a toga sitting on a cloud in the sky, looking at another man on the ground, who is kneeling in prayer next to a team of horses and a wagon stuck in the mud. The man in the sky, the explainers tell us, is the God Hercules who, like Mama in the ads, always said, "God helps him who helps himself." Everybody knows what Hercules said. The message is directed at the thirteen colonies and suggests how they should deal with the Indian problem. In his later and better cartoon of 1754, "Unite or Die," Franklin has improved considerably. One gets the point even if he or she has forgotten that old wives' tale which says that a snake joined before sundown will grow together again and keep living.

14.   Benjamin Franklin : Hercules. 1747. *Plain Truth.*

Today our standards have dropped a little, as far as classical allusions are concerned. The audience is middlebrow. There are more topical asides to the pop culture that the mass viewers share with the artist. The Ponderosa of Bonanza, the miniskirt or frisbee or other fads and fashions, the lyrics of a popular song, and even a phrase or scene from a best-selling novel have all found their way into political cartoons. But will viewers ten years from now be able to understand what streaking or trashing is without help from the social historians? There will inevitably be a dropping-off of comprehension, and in some cases one hopes so.

A third problem is that the caricatures may also no longer be recognized. Everyone can tell who Franklin D. Roosevelt is in those old New Deal cartoons, at least everyone interested enough to look at them. But does Henry Wallace or Henry Morgenthau register? How long will Senator Sam Ervin and his eyebrows last now that he's back in North Carolina chewing tarheels?

Finally, the whole process is complicated further when the cartoon is from a foreign nation with whose politics you are unfamiliar or perhaps couldn't care less, as, say, with the domestic politics of Denmark or Sweden. Such cartoons may be real side busters, or breathtaking in their incisiveness, if only one knew what they were all about. But one should not surrender to despair. Some cartoons transcend even these difficulties, as this anonymous German drawing from a Socialist newspaper shows. The cartoon makes sense even before you know that Michel is the name for the symbolic peasant and that the title translates as "Michel and his Protector."

15. **Anonymous German : Michel und sein Beschützer. 1902. Stuttgart,** *Der Wahre Jacob.*

There is no avoiding fully difficulties such as these. When they are great, they kill all but the most obviously lively and humorous cartoon. By time one reads a long description in small print about the cast of characters and the event, or gets a friend to translate the *Kobenhaunske Skilte,* the cartoon has quietly expired. What looked interesting and inviting is now only just a little more titillating than a diagram for putting together a lawn swing for your wife's mother.

What's Available

One other major problem plagues those who would appreciate political cartoons of any day but their own. The difficulty is in finding them. There are really only three sources. The obvious is the original publication, either as a print, a cut in a magazine or newspaper, or, more rarely, in books. The British Museum has a fine collection of colored prints if you can afford the air fare. The only complete, unmutilated file of the American magazine *Puck,* I am told, is at the New York Historical Society offices, where it is carefully guarded and permitted to peek out only now and again into the pages of *American Heritage.* Original newspaper publications present the same problem involving travel, with the additional hazard of the yellowed papers crumbling in your hands after you arrive. All of this going to original sources presents two further difficulties : It is often difficult to get good copies made by Xerox, etcetera, at the library, and the librarians show an almost unanimous reluctance to let strangers check out serials. A related difficulty is that original sources lead you down many interesting side alleys, and you read the other beguiling stories and features in the newspaper or magazine. The tracing down of cartoons in original sources is not impossible — just difficult and time consuming. One is thus driven to reprints of cartoons in either a weekly magazine or a newspaper of the period, as, for example, in the *New York Times'* "News in Review" section of former times, the *Literary Digest,* or *Editor and Publisher.* All of these present the same problems, except that with magazines the quality of paper is better. The best solution is to find cartoons in book collections.

But the preservation of cartoons in a handy and usable form between the covers of a book is hit and miss. Some political cartoonists understand this and strive to insure that suceeding generations will not be culturally deprived. By my count, the variations of David Low between covers are some thirty plus. (His colleague Norman Lindsay, of Australia days on the Sidney *Bulletin,* described the young Low as "ruthlessly determined to get on."). But a great deal of the reproduction of cartoons in books is by fluke. Three-time Pulitzer Prize winner Edmund Duffy has no book collection of his work that I am aware of, while the St. Joseph (Mo.) *News Press* in 1916 issued a collection of their relatively little-known artist Hanny. They did not, unfortunately, identify him by his Christian name, so I cannot convey that added bit of important information to you.

Book collections are going to be an incomplete sample of a cartoonist's work, which may be good or bad, but in compensation they are also likely to be better technically, since book paper is usually better than newsprint. Color may disappear and cartoons will sometimes be drastically reduced in size, but on the whole, book production has technical superiority over the original.

Even what collections there are, are uneven. Some are put together as "a history of our times." Usually this is the favorite way of presenting work by a single cartoonist. It requires including some less-than-inspiring efforts in order to nail down every significant historical event that occurred from the sinking of the Titanic to the introduction of the Turkey Trot. Herblock does it best by presenting books at several-year intervals and presenting cartoons and comment by subject rather than, like so many corpses all laid out in a row, in chronological order.

31

A variation is the collection of the work of many cartoonists on a single theme, as, for example, an instructive survey of varied views of cartoonists on the subject of the prohibition menace or pollution or of Vice-President John Nance Garner, all of which have been so covered. No one cartoonist usually gets much exposure in such works, and sometimes silly cartoons that pad out the work are dragged in because they happen to be on the right subject.

When collections span a single year, it may be a considerably haphazard choice of year. Selection of year seems to be related to the economic cycle, so that some of these collections probably appeared only when there was money to be wasted in tax write-offs.

Also available since 1973 are annual collections with three or four cartoons by each of the nation's major cartoonists. The editor of these collections has been Charles Brooks, editorial cartoonist for the Birmingham *News*.[15]

Best, perhaps, are the collections by a single cartoonist of his lifetime work, with selection made by the cartoonist himself, as in the case of books by Daniel Fitzpatrick, "Ding" Darling, and Vaughn Shoemaker. These are, of course, a painfully small sample in terms of an artist's total output. A political cartoonist such as Fitzpatrick, who created one cartoon every day for 30 or so years, produced some 14,000-plus published political cartoons. "The best" gets crammed into some 238 pages and represents presumably that 1.7% part of his output which is most memorable. But seventeen out of every thousand cartoons gives a taste anyhow.

Also available are a pitifully few autobiographies. Besides that of David Low, the best one by far, there are those of John McCutcheon, Bill Mauldin, Art Young, and one by Walt McDougall that does not include even one reprinted cartoon. Also there are excellent biographies of such famous figures as Thomas Nast, George Cruikshank, and James Gillray, and some articles about others.

Finally, and this is perhaps the most galling roadblock of all, even collections devoted exclusively to the political cartoon — for example, the collection *LBJ Lampooned* — may omit the name of the cartoonist who drew the picture, as if he were a menial who did the sweep-up chores for the person whose name adorns the cover.[16] One also learns that some artists, on order of their employers or through excessive modesty, have left their work unsigned, or use a cryptic squiggle or bug that is difficult for anyone but a pharmacist to decipher, particularly if the drawing has been reduced in size and reprinted in the *Literary Digest* of 1926.

A Closing Note

With all these difficulties, you may wish to close the book up here and go study Egyptian belly dancers for the far more clear-cut, and perhaps less complicated, political messages they project. Some cartoons you will never understand, and neither will I or anyone else, anymore. Others will not be worth the effort to try to understand them. If, however, you have not given up at this point, let us move on, because there is indeed a great deal you will both understand and enjoy that is worth looking at. And sometimes you can kid yourself into believing that a little obscurity adds extra spice to the enterprise.

2
Technology and the Political Cartoon

A number of students of cartoons trace the first caricatures back to the prehistoric caves. The first known political caricature seems to have been done 3,000 years back — a portrait of the founder of the Sun God religion, King Akhnaton of Egypt, father-in-law of King Tut(ankhamen). Caricaturelike distortion in drawings crops up from time to time thereafter, as in the features of the people dancing around on Greek vases, some of whom are clearly of the ruling class, in early Roman graffiti, and at Pompeii, in a drawing ridiculing Alexamenos, an early Christian. Caricature flourishes in the gargoyle statues of medieval churches and is found in sketches by Leonardo da Vinci. But all of these outcroppings appear as almost accidental.[1]

The birth of caricature as a conscious method seems, by common consent, to have taken place in Rome in the late 1500s. G. B. Della Porta drew humans as animals, and a few years later, around 1600, Roman artists Annibale and Agostino Carracci, who with their cousin Lodovico were founders of an Academy school, began turning out in abundance caricatures of fellow citizens. The drawings were at first done as jokes, for relaxation. Then, because of their popularity, they became a lucrative artistic sideline. Some argue that caricature got its name from the Carracci, though other scholars have made small reputations by disagreeing.

The first political cartoons date from the Reformation; those reproduced for a large audience appear to have been the anonymous woodcuts in a series of tracts published in Florence during the 1490s. For the next two hundred and fifty years political drawings appeared in pamphlets, books, and broadsides, but such political propaganda remained unwedded to caricature.

The introduction of such drawings into England occurred in the early 1700s and received a mighty push forward with the publication by Arthur Pond in 1737 of a book of twenty-five Italian and a few French prints in caricature style. The first significant English caricaturist, despite his disclaimers, was William Hogarth. (See especially his drawing of 1763 of that libertarian hero and fraud, John Wilkes.)

33

But it was not Hogarth who really introduced caricature to political conflict in the merger that gave rise to the modern political cartoon. For in about 1750 in England, George, later Marquess of Townshend, a dilettante artist and aristocrat, began privately circulating cute little caricature cards that, in verse and comic art, attacked his political enemies and colleagues. One shows Pitt in the role of playright whose play is rejected by the King. Townshend soon dropped regular cartooning and went on to a distinguished public career — second in command to Wolfe at Quebec and a governor general of Ireland. Others in time took up his innovation. From the 1770s on, political caricature was alive and squalling, with no letup since. It blossomed in England in the eighteenth-century print, the nineteenth-century magazine cartoon, and the twentieth-century editorial cartoon of the newspapers. In other democratic nations the time periods varied, but the progression (or regression) from print to magazine to newspaper was similar.

Technology's Imperatives

The above is a telescoped version of the standard history of the political cartoon, but it fails to emphasize what seems to me to be the most important element of that history. This is, how great the impact of technology was on the way the political cartoon would be drawn and on the independence of the cartoonist.

Let us start at the beginning. The development of the printing press brought the cartoon to life.[2] Before then an artist's drawing, when political, suffered from two handicaps. It would be seen by only a few people, as a scrawl on a wall or a few scratches on a paper passed around among a few friends as a private joke. Also such drawings, or even more elaborate ones in the form of stained-glass windows, statuary, or paintings, could be killed dead by destroying the original. Even as late as the 1930s, when Diego Rivera put Lenin in a mural in Rockefeller Center in New York City, paint remover could be and was smeared on the wall by the owners, in what was interpreted by some as a mark of disapproval of the artist's political message. But the Rockefellers throve after methods of reproduction were well developed. Rivera's Lenin had already been photographed in color and would appear in many art books alongside the gruesome story. But numerous kings, popes and other ecclesiastics, knights, two-bit squires, and judges could consider themselves luckier. They throve before technology had perfected such subversive reproduction techniques. Occasionally, we may assume, they took advantage of this fact by stomping out some perhaps classic expressions of artistic political criticism directed against them.

So, with the invention and continued improvement of printing processes, the security of those in charge altered. From this point on, it was, as it has been expressed by a now almost-forgotten sports-oriented president, a different ball game.

The imperative of technology in respect to printed cartoons seems to me to have set four specific goals : (1) to increase the output, that is, the potential press run, (2) to reproduce drawings more quickly, (3) to reproduce drawings more cheaply, and (4) to reproduce drawings with accuracy, including reproduction of shadings and color. This fourth imperative, that of artistic accuracy, is the least important and was, as we shall observe, sacrificed from time to time, as it is today, to the imperatives of mass production, speed, and economy.

Nevertheless, all four imperatives were attacked with what can only be viewed as admirable dispatch. In the early 1430s German goldsmiths had begun experiments with engraving in metal as others had begun making woodcuts. About 1436 Johann

Gutenberg invented movable type and made improvements for the now-useful printing press. By the time 450 years had passed, the technical problems listed above were solved reasonably well, and with another 50 years refinements were added that made color reproductions of even very delicate art possible, on a mass basis and at relatively low cost for moderate press runs.

The impact of this technical improvement process on the artist as a critic of his times seems to me to have had four effects: (1) it set the upper limits on the number of openings available for those wishing to make a living as political cartoon critics, (2) it determined what would be the mass outlet for an artist's political output, that is, the potential audience for the cartoons, (3) it affected the artist's independence in making political comments and critical judgments, and (4) it determined the artistic limitations the artist would have to accept if he or she wanted work reproduced for a mass audience.

At this point I should insert a caveat. The political cartoon has always been an aesthetic achievement only by accident. Its purpose is propaganda, not art. Its audience has usually been the politically active rather than those concerned about artistic values. Sometimes this has meant appeals to the relatively less-educated masses. Political cartoonists thus gravitated to those techniques which promised, first, longer press runs per cut and, second, relatively speedy and less-costly reproduction. Often in the process artistic values and even accuracy in reproduction were sacrificed. Today, for aesthetic reasons a small clique of artists continue to do etchings and engravings on expensive papers while the mass of political cartoons are reproduced by high-speed presses on wood pulp that after a few months cracks and turns yellow. The same two tracks of artists and political cartoonists existed throughout the history of pictorial reproduction. Most students are concerned to trace the history of aesthetic reproduction; we need not here be bothered much with its problems but rather will concentrate on the development of the processes that made the mass-produced political cartoon possible and on the effect these processes had on the way the political cartoonist could express himself or herself.[3]

An easy way to trace out the effects of technology is to go back over the history of the political cartoon, spotting the highlights of technical development and noting some of their significant effects on the dominant cartoonists of the period. The process I shall describe can not be viewed as one of steady progress by all artists on all fronts or in all nations at the same time. Historical periods can not always be so neatly marked off, because some men and women, and especially some artists, exhibit a contrariness in refusing to adapt immediately to improvements. Others forge ahead and invent or adopt new techniques. There are overlaps and even some throwbacks and regressions to a more primitive technology. New technical advances require retooling, abandonment of sunk investments, and the assumption of new costs for both the established publisher and the artist. Both financial and artistic risks are involved. Some, especially the young, are ready for the trumpet call, but others, especially the established artist and craftsman, may respond less willingly and with less enthusiasm. They do not see why what worked in the past fairly well cannot continue to work for them. John Tenniel insisted that his drawings continue to be hacked out of woodblocks by hand a good ten to fifteen years after the easier process of reproduction, photoengraving, had been perfected. He perhaps recognized that the wood-engraving process, as practiced by the cutter Swain, thickened his rather finely drawn lines and resulted in a bold black-and-white cartoon. Thomas Nast, whose later cartoons were produced by photoengraving, seems, according to one biographer, J. Chal Vinson, to have lost artistic forcefulness thereby, since these drawings seem finer of line and somehow more tentative than his earlier dark and bold wood engravings.

The story begins with the cartoon attached to a pamphlet or heading a broadside. The political possibilities of this kind of mass-produced cartoon first became apparent on a wide scale to the Lutherans in the 1520s, when they made up their minds that it was their God-given duty to chuck out the Pope. The devilishness of the papacy could be graphically illustrated, and these little woodcuts made an eye-catching piece to put on the covers of weighty and significant pamphlets, or they could be put just inside, in what was logically called the frontispiece. The Hollanders fighting for freedom from Spain in another authoritarian society, and the Puritans attacking Charles I in the 1640s, borrowed and effectively used this snappy technique to lighten their soggy prose. This combination of art and argument evolved rather quickly into the single-page broadsheet that could be posted in prominent places. The early ones were cut as one block, but the prose lengthened with the use of movable type. The picture attracted attention and the full argument appeared below.

16.   Lucas Cranach : Birth of the Papacy. 1545.

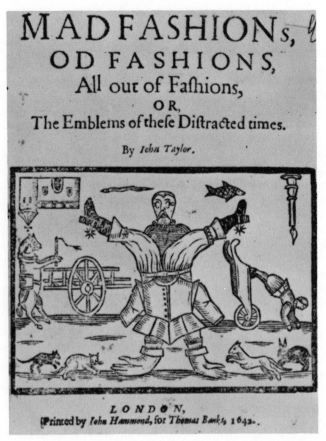

17. Puritan (pro-Cromwell) print on a John Taylor Pamphlet : *Mad Fashions, Odd Fashions. All out of Fashions,* **or** *The Emblems of these Distracted Times.* **1641.**

To modern eyes these early drawings before 1700 seem filled with involved and no doubt deeply bitter and cutting allegory, some of which escapes us but other aspects of which are about as subtle as being hit on the head with a twirling rolling pin. It is hard for us to make the effort to understand, but in their day the drawings had an impact not too different from that of the underground comic book among that part of our society which perhaps shies away when faced with pages of unbroken type. The drawing was read and studied as carefully and laboriously as was the extended verbiage to which it was the cartoon's fate to be eternally attached. The viewers appreciated the effort and perhaps thrilled at the novelty of actually owning a drawing.

They had good reason to value this product. Both woodcuts and etchings were somewhat hard and painstaking work and were relatively costly. These woodcuts printed from raised lines had to be gouged out laboriously. They were a form of relief printing in which the raised lines were inked and printed just as type is. The grain of the wood ran parallel with the face of the block from left to right. After 1500 the intaglio process was available. In this the ink was forced into lines that were incised in a soft copper plate. The surface was then wiped and when dampened paper was pressed down on the cut, the ink in the grooves printed on the paper. These grooves could either be cut by hand into the copper, which made it a line engraving or dry cut, or be etched in by acid. This process required covering the metal with a film of black varnish and lightly scratching through the film with a needle. When dropped into acid, the scratched parts would etch. Later the film, called a ground, would be wiped off. Drypoint and etching could be combined, if the artist wished, on the same plate. In the next century further refinements included sprinkling exposed parts of the copper plate with acid-resistant resin to give a speckled, or mezzotint, or aquatint effect.

Each process had drawbacks and each had advantages. The drawbacks of woodcut were in the area of the quality of the print produced, at least so the practitioners between 1500 and 1700 felt. The drawbacks of the etching or metal engraving were that the process itself was more expensive overall. Albrecht Dürer, for example, charged four-and-a-half times more for his etchings than for his woodcut prints. Here are some direct comparisons in respect to preparation: copper was a good deal more expensive than wood, copper was easier to work than wood, and etching and even metal engravings were felt to permit a more flowing line than the carved woodcut. On the other hand, most printing advantages were with the woodcut. It could be printed with movable type, whereas intaglio required a separate press run and a slower process. Wood stood up better and therefore, at least through 1700, resulted in longer press runs.

From 1500 on, the use of the woodcut for artistic work declined steadily. Increasingly, the main artists came to prefer etching combined with drypoint engraving. These dominated in books and in the quality print-sellers' market that began to develop about 1550. Meanwhile, the woodcut in its artistic decline came to dominate the market for cheap reproductions — the chapbook and the political fly sheets prepared for the masses. Much political art between 1500 and 1700 fell under the heading of hackwork and is found in woodcuts.

The effect on the politically inclined artist of having to bend to the imperatives of the technology circa 1550 was multiple. He had a mass audience as he had not had before printing, but it was one still relatively limited by modern standards. His cuts would last for probably less than 1,000 imprints. The big increase in circulation came because an artist's work would be preserved and passed from hand to hand or pasted up on a wall. The actual audience was considerably greater than press runs suggest. Given the kind of work involved, inevitably all of the artists were male, I find no female artists in those early days.

Artistically, the political artist had to avoid two problems: being so fancy in his draftsmanship that the printers and those paying for press runs would rebel, and false starts. Cartoon reproduction involved enough investment of time and effort that one did not lightly sketch off a drawing; both the artist and his backers were looking for sure-fire propaganda and that, I suggest, often meant unsubtle artistry and imagery.

The political restraints were even greater than the artistic ones. First of all, the number of appointments for the political artist was limited, and those who controlled them were not likely to be of a judicious temperament. Those who gathered together the capital investment for production of political art from circa 1500 to 1650 were intense partisans who tended to see political events from a very finely honed point of view. The well-reasoned "on the one hand and then on the other hand" type of political comment was not universally desired, but even less so was political art that slapped at the enemy with gentle laughing satire and so seemed to give some credence to his action or motives. Art that called a spade a spade and drew the enemy as a tool of Satan seemed to hit the nail exactly on the head; the freshness of such imagery seemed never to pale in those serious-minded times. If the artist were heart and soul with the revolutionary movement or the counterrevolution, all was well. Knowing something of artists and their chafing under orthodoxy, we would anticipate some friction, heartbreak, and even explosions.

By 1700 technology turned another corner. Presses were improved in design but, even more important, ways had been found to lengthen the press runs of copper plates by deepening the etched lines by drypoint cuts. A plate could last up to 1,500 copies. By the 1700s printing had become a well-established commercial trade, and presses were now produced cheaply enough so that the political artist no longer had to look around for a revolutionary movement to get his work before the public. Private printers interested in commercial gain would perform the service. In such conditions more widespread production of political prints began. Because they were etchings, they were divorced from the printed page and sold separately.

The breakthrough for the political and social print occurred in England in 1710. A great number of amateur political prints, relatively speaking, were produced spontaneously about the affair involving the Reverend Henry Sacheverall, whose high-Tory sermons favoring the Queen were considered seditious and scurrilous by a Whig-dominated Commons. The Commons showed its displeasure by impeaching him, and the battle was on. These cartoons may be of great interest to historians, but few are reproduced today, either because most subsequent historians have been Whigs or because the cartoons themselves do not seem to have been very well done. What these political prints portended was the commercial possibilities associated with widespread print sales.

It was print seller Thomas Bowles, whose shop was at the St. Paul's churchyard, who early sensed these commercial possibilities and encouraged a variety of artists to try their hand at illustrating. Most of his prints were, however, cheap and badly produced woodcuts and most were nonpolitical. Then, in the early 1720s England was rocked with a commercial speculation similar to the Florida real estate gamble of the 1920s, in which boom was followed by bust. These brought a new outpouring of prints. The most notable of these South Sea Bubble prints, as they were called, were two etchings by twenty-three-year-old William Hogarth. Soon, in order to raise money for himself and his bride, he began producing sets of exceptional prints commenting on the social conditions and customs of his age. By 1730 Hogarth was lobbying for effective copyright laws to protect the cartoonist-creator. Shortly he won that battle. Very quickly, Hogarth dominated the upper-class commercial print market. He has continued to dominate his age artistically in terms of the prints he produced, in the judgment of most of those who have looked since at the prints of the period. But also available in this period were an increasing number of etchings whose quality fell below Hogarth's and whose content may be characterized as often vulgar and coarse. These were beginning to reach out through dealers to a middle-class and even lower-class market, the same market the early news sheets were striving to reach and to please.

Hogarth's prints, as noted, were mainly social criticism and were largely representational in artistic style. Arthur Pond had introduced the English to Italian and French caricature in 1737. Townsend wedded the caricature touch with political art in the 1750s, and this, stimulated by the day's political events, unleashed the political print for its golden age. It was not until the 1770s that James Gillray began his magnificent production of scurrilous and seditious political prints. Another notable

18.   From Arthur Pond's collection of Italian and French caricatures 1737-39.

producer of the day was Thomas Rowlandson, a friend of Gillray's and a high liver, whether commenting socially or politically. Some of his productions can be secured today from those booksellers who advertise titles such as *The Erotic Works of ---*, and in Rowlandson's case the advertising does not overstate the content.

Hogarth, Gillray, and Rowlandson were all masters. I can not, even though it is irrelevant to this work, neglect to comment on the absolute beauty mixed with an endearing ugliness of Rowlandson's social satire, as found in Dr. Syntax or the English

19. William Hogarth : John Wilkes, Esq. 1763.

"Dance of Death" series. He captures Fielding's *Tom Jones*'s mood in its most magnificent charm and outrageousness. His political prints are less charming, perhaps because he seems to have regarded them as hackwork.[6] The one reproduced here shows the liberal politician Charles Fox beheaded ("as he should have been").

The period of the social and political print in England and France closed, in terms of mood, about 1830 with the last of William Heath's (Paul Pry) prints and, in actual fact, about twenty years later with the last of John Doyle's (HB) more refined and Victorian-like prints. In America, however, Currier and Ives continued to grind out their lithographs through the early 1870s.

The impact of the technical developments on the English artists who produced the eighteenth-century political print was varied. Press runs advanced to about 1,500

20.   George Townshend : The Distressed Statesman. 1761.

21.   Thomas Rowlandson : The Political Hydra, December 26, 1788.

before the copper began to wear down or mash apart. But the prints could be produced within a few days. There was even time for water coloring by hand to give the production some added zing. Also, the artist finally came into his own as a person, rather than being just an adjunct of a political movement or an anonymous hack. Print sellers were on the lookout for clever young men whose work would sell, and an artist might even set up his own press, as Hogarth did. Quick production made it possible to bring out a steady flow of prints, and while each might be limited in its press run, their combined impact, at one or two a week, began to approach that of a system of mass production by 1790.[7] The fad of the aristocracy of collecting portfolios of prints for leisurely viewing later by the refined further increased the artist's appreciative audience.

As the century progressed, the artistic quality of political art improved. Etching encouraged a freedom of line like that of the pen drawing. Engraving or gouging permitted varying the width of line but inhibited its freedom to weave about and double back without effort. Finally, the etching process was not so difficult that the artist and etcher necessarily had to be different persons in order to get quick production. The artist could, if he wished, control the process at least up to the press run. After that he might still be at the mercy of printers, but some, like Hogarth, supervised even this aspect, thus fulfilling the artist's dream of having total control of technical production of his work. He was in effect a free agent, not needing to be guided artistically by a political faction or a commercial publisher.[8]

One of the remarkable aspects of this half century was the large number of amateurs who got into the business of producing one or more political prints. Anyone who wanted to produce one needed only to sketch out his idea for an artist or, even better, he might do the full drawing and dig up an engraver or etcher to produce it for a limited run. Seldom have so many of the public themselves had the opportunity to try their hand at being cartoonist-critics.

It was, given the technology of the day, a period of freedom to comment politically. Effective libel laws were not to arrive until the early 1800s. In between was a period of inviting liberty and even license, heightened by the astonishing political events of England's losing a revolutionary war with its American colonies, of the French deposing the feudal heirs of the absolutist Louis XIV in a bloody uprising, and of a Napoleon who seemed destined to bring liberalism to other benighted nations of Europe. In England it was a period in which an authoritarian system was seemingly on the run, with the landed aristocrats perhaps as inevitably doomed as Marie Antoinette. Add to this a King who flitted, or perhaps one should more kindly say stumbled, in and out of lunacy over a twenty-five-year period. It was a period made to order for the artist freed by technology from any restraints especially political ones, except those self-imposed or those imposed by the print processes. Some artists look back, as David Low did, with nostalgia to this as a golden age. I incline to share the Victorian view that it was a peculiarly barbarous one.

In this period of opportunity the cartoonists went wild. Draper Hill, James Gillray's sympathetic biographer, describes him as follows: "Gillray seems to have had all the manners of a hungry cat in mid-spring, an irresponsibility which must have been one of his chief attractions. Confined like a circus panther, he was a provider of dangerous entertainment. *Sin, Death and the Devil* could never have been carried through to publication by anyone who possessed the inhibitive machinery which normally governs civilized conduct."[9]

The next stage of political cartoon production was in the weekly magazine. The technological developments began to arrive in bunches. Thomas Bewick in the 1790s

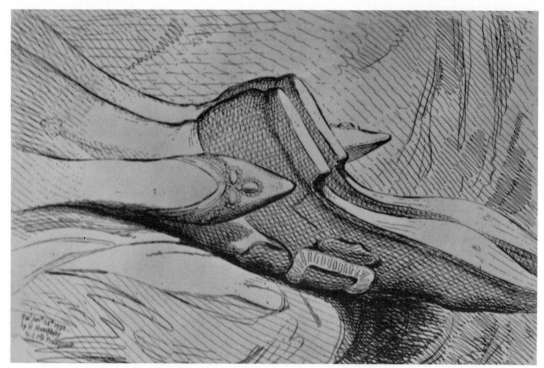

22.   James Gillray : Fashionable Contrasts, January 24, 1792.

had discovered new possibilities for wood engraving. His technique of engraving in boxwood used the end grain to cut into. These blocks stood up to long press runs while at the same time providing a material that was not impossible to work with. Because the blocks were now cross sections of the boxwood tree, they were smaller and had to be joined together. Less happily, someone thought up the idea of assigning these parts to a number of engravers so that all could work on a drawing at once to speed up the cutting. The pieces were rejoined for the press run. Note the light joint lines in many Victorian cuts in *Punch* and other magazines of this period.

An additional process of production was also invented. Around 1796 Aloys Senefelder, a Bavarian, introduced lithography. This was a form of printing in which the artist drew on limestone with a grease pencil. Ink was then rolled on and, when the stone was washed, it stuck to the grease but not to the rest of the stone. The image could then be printed. This process also was suitable for long press runs.

Finally, there were notable improvements in paper manufacture, and in 1815 the *Times* of London replaced its hand press with one driven by steam. The stage was set for a new form of mass production of political art. While these processes each achieved the goal of increasing the possible runs, none as yet permitted daily reproduction of cartoons to follow news breaks. The result was that, as the market for the print died out, that of the weekly magazine was born. No longer did production occur when the spirit moved the artist. A system of commissioning cartoons from various artists developed, followed by recruitment of staff artists to meet the weekly deadline. In

France, Charles Philipon in 1830 began his series of magazines and newspapers that featured political comment but turned to social comment when artists like Philipon himself or his star cartoonist, Honoré Daumier, were put in jail by the authoritarian regime of Louis Philippe. The French adopted lithography. They avoided the problem of separate lithograph and type-copy press runs by a process of transferring the lithograph from stone to metal plate and etching. Critics say the process spoiled the quality of much of Daumier's earlier work; artistry was sacrificed to the imperatives of lengthening press runs and quick production.

In England, perhaps because it was the Victorian age, the boxwood engraving was preferred. Only a few artists used lithography during the nineteenth century: HB (John Doyle) in his prints between 1828 and 1851, and Tom Merry in *St Stephens Magazine* in the 1880s. A number of English magazines attempted to copy Philipon's French success before one finally caught on. The most notable first effort was *Figaro in London* (1831-38), with woodcut editorial cartoons by Robert Seymour. In 1841 *Punch,* subtitled *The London Charivari,* was begun. By December 1842 Bradbury and Evans took business control, put the journal on a sound financial basis, and it prospered. It also used boxwood engravings and developed a cartoon style that dominated the political cartoons of the Victorian age and those of the magazine itself up to 1945. It was a long reign.

In America, from Jackson through Lincoln, the Currier and Ives colored lithographs of horse races, steamboats, and trains have received some attention from later generations. The firm's political output was small. The struggling magazine weeklies, none of which really established itself before about 1855, printed woodcuts but only began really to flourish from the Civil War on.

During the Civil War Thomas Nast's rather overdrawn and overblown Victorian panoramas in *Harpers Weekly* led Lincoln to describe him as the North's best recruiting sergeant. If so, it adds one more telling detail to the story of the conduct of the war by the Union: the Northern artists appeared to be no better than the Northern generals. In any case, within a few years after the end of the conflict Nast simplified and vastly improved his style (he was inspired by John Tenniel of *Punch*) and he began the powerful series of wood-engraved cartoons for which he is still known, and which incidentally skyrocketed the circulation of *Harpers Weekly.* Other popular magazines followed. Joseph Keppler founded *Puck* in 1877, and subsequent rivals emerged; *Judge* (1881) and *Life* (1883). Each recruited some of Keppler's cartoon talent, along with new faces, to compete with him.

The impact of technology on political cartoonists during the Victorian Age, the period of magazine production, went in sometimes similar, and sometimes different directions, depending upon the print process adopted. Both lithography and the new wood engraving could be used to increase press runs and both permitted reproduction within a relatively short time after receipt of the drawing, that is, within two or three days. Artists of the 1800s had a real opportunity to capture a mass audience.

Artistically, the effect diverged. The lithograph could be used to produce a fuzzy but fluid line and shadows showing a whole range of gradations. A genius such as Daumier demonstrated that it could be a deeply biting line and a lively one as well. In inept hands, such as I am afraid most of us class HB's, the drawings tended to blur together. If there were disadvantages, they were the ones of the artist's having to draw directly on the stone, having to draw in reverse and, until the camera obscura process of reflecting images was devised, having to draw precisely to the size to be printed. Until the lithographic process was improved about mid-century, something was also lost in artistic quality. An added difficulty was that the artist had to lug around heavy stones, which invited accidents to himself or to his drawing.

Judging by the cartoons produced, the wood engraving was similar in its effect on artistic freedom to that of the Victorian corset in molding the feminine form to its light whims. It did, however, result in a nice, black, heavy-lined print. Such drawings many of the day considered especially suitable for dignified political comment. In this it paralleled, or perhaps even inspired, what has been called the Grand Rapids style of furniture manufacture. The wood engraving was produced in stiff, black lines. Even worse, the engravings were generally done by somebody other than the artist. Worse yet, the block might be cut into four or six pieces and each one be done by a different engraver, each following the artist's lines and sometimes perhaps having less than a full appreciation of what the completed design would be like when joined with its mates. Sir John Tenniel of *Punch* reports: "Although case hardened in a sense, I have never the courage to open the [*Punch*] packet, I always leave it to my sister, who opens it and hands it across to me, when I just take a glance at it and receive my weekly pang." Nevertheless, it should not be forgotten that a number of great cartoonists such as Nast, and Tenniel himself, channeled great political force through the wood engraving.

The effect of both wood engraving and lithography on the artist's independence was, however, similar. Both, because they made political cartooning big business, pushed the cartoonist toward the position of mouthpiece for the publication in which his work appeared. On *Punch* this was institutionalized by having the subject and message of the major political cartoon decided upon each week at the staff dinner. Tenniel, a mild conservative, dutifully produced the messages agreed upon by the mildly liberal *Punch* table. Nor were liberal journals notably different. Philipon did not see it as his business to publish the political comment of the pro-Louis Philippe faction. Joseph Keppler, Jr., wrote a ringing tribute to his father's desire as an artist to state his own views. But *Puck* had editorial conferences on cartoons, and other *Puck* artists had no such freedom. Among the more famous cartoons of *Puck* was that against the Republican nominee of 1884, James G. Blaine, titled "**Phryne** Before the Chicago Tribunal," more generally called "The Tattooed Man." It was drawn by Bernard Gillam, who was a Republican who drew Democratic cartoons for Keppler and *Puck* until he was offered the opportunity to draw, without financial loss, Republican cartoons for the Republican journal *Judge*. He took that opportunity.

A few artists tried to buck this relationship. Thomas Nast fought with *Harpers Weekly* when they refused to print a number of his cartoons. The management's patience finally gave out in 1885 and there was a parting of the ways. *Harpers* continued to exist, but Nast quietly faded from the scene until he had to write pathetic letters to magazine editors (who referred to him as "the late great") pointing out that he was still alive. Walt McDougall, a veteran of this period in American cartooning and on the *Graphic* staff and later on Pulitzer's newspaper, *The World*, was more practical minded. In listing the attributes of a political cartoonist in his autobiography, he observed that he should have that "curious elasticity of mind that permits him to make cartoons for either party without doing violence to his own opinions." Most cartoonists of that day appear to have gone the **McDougall** route.

In defense of the magazine owners, from the Harper brothers to *Punch*'s Bradbury and Evans, one may note that beginning a journal in the 1800s was both a risky financial investment and a partisan commitment. For journalists or cartoonists who disagreed greatly with the publisher's views, there were competing journals with different views. The owner, in his own journal, felt that he had more right to state his political views than did his writers or cartoonists. Cartoonists who felt otherwise could still assume the risk of starting their own journals, as had such artists as Philipon and Joseph Keppler, and as Thomas Nast in America and Harry Furniss in England had tried to do and failed.

The last technological advance made the daily editorial cartoon a possibility for newspapers, even very small ones. This was the invention of photoengraving, and its adoption in daily newspapers between 1885 and 1900. Art work could be done frontwards, photographed, and transferred to a plate at any size preferred. The messy and meticulous work of engraving, etching, or lithographing was finished. No middleman stood between artist and pressman. If a plate was damaged, another could be made. Within an hour or two of receipt of the drawing, the presses could be whirling out the printed cartoon.

The impact of this change was to make the cartoon in the daily newspaper first a novelty and then a necessity. In the 1890s daily comics began in America and so, too, did the daily editorial cartoon right next to the newspaper masthead. The first such cartoonist in England appears to have been F. Carruthers Gould. Walt McDougall claimed that honor for himself in America, and he very likely deserves it.

The Hearst and Pulitzer circulation wars led to raiding of the political magazines for artistic talent, and they, like the print before them, began to falter and fail. Hearst's most valuable catch was Fred Opper, who left *Puck* to draw for the then radical William Randolph Hearst the excellent "ABC of Trusts" and "Willie and His Poppa" series. Later he set a trend that was to be followed by many newspaper artists of his day: he moved from the less lucrative political cartoon to the comic page. By the end of World War I, artists were moving directly to the big money — comic art without a waystop on the editorial page. In this period and since, a number of major political cartoonists appeared in America who used the artistic freedom of the photo-engraving to great advantage.

The first impact of photoengraving, however, was to open up to budding political cartoonists a vast minor league of newspapers in middle-sized cities. On these cartoonists could get their start, since every paper with any pretensions had to have its own cartoonist.

Newspaper demands, with their daily deadlines and mass audience, also helped to wake up the art of political cartooning. In England the reinvigoration of the cartoon from the stodginess it had fallen into under the leadership of the heirs of John Tenniel was begun by Will Dyson in Edwardian times, but was fully achieved by David Low, who arrived in post-World War I England from New Zealand. In America, Walt McDougall was among the first to sense that the newspaper cartoon had to be both simple in artistic form and aimed at an audience more familiar with Casey at the Bat than with Shakespeare. McDougall also took note of how Pulitzer complimented him and put him on the permanent payroll because his first drawing was simply drawn and so went through a press run of 30,000 without getting clogged up with ink.

A further technological development was the cardboard matting of lead cuts. The mats could be cheaply and quickly distributed by mail and within less than an hour be recast as lead cuts.

Paradoxically, the last technological change widened the cartoonist's mass audience but steadily reduced the number of cartoonists who would reach it. The first effect of photoengraving, was, as noted, to create many staff newspaper jobs. But the period of newspaper mergers was in full swing by 1915 and the number of cartoonist positions shrank. After rapid syndication became possible in the between-war period, middle-sized city papers dropped their staff political cartoonist and ran the stars. By the early 1970s there were perhaps 150 working editorial cartoonists in America. Fewer than ten of these were widely syndicated. The rest had the audience of their own daily papers with an occasional reprint in the news magazines and in *Editor and Publisher*, but no longer in the Sunday New York *Times* News in Review section, since it had gone arty and op-ed. The same narrowing process held true in England. The

London newspapers developed national circulations and so the concentration there was even more intense.

The artisic impact of photoengraving was to free the style of the artist, with this one drawback. As David Low discovered when he arrived in England, his cartoons could be reduced to one-column smudges. He insisted upon, and initially was given, a full half page for his work. Others, especially in reprints, have been less happily dealt with by space-conscious editors. In one other way the artistic quality of the cartoon declined. Mass circulation meant cheap newsprint. No longer would cartoons be reverently produced on good paper with no printing on the reverse, as they once had been in the limited-circulation journals, such as *Punch*, that were aimed at the middle- and upper-middle-class market. Now wood pulp that turned yellow and brittle in time was good enough. Chafing at the restriction, David Low had some of his work privately printed with paper, ink, and impressions to meet his dream specifications. Most political cartoonists could only hope to see their work republished in book form or, what was more common, they could adapt their drawings for maximum artistic impact when printed on cheap paper.

The photoengraving also had a clear effect on a cartoonist's independence. They initially became the mouthpiece for a daily newspaper and were expected to harmonize their work with that of the editorial writers. As on *Punch,* the cartoonists attended editorial board meetings and, in a give-and-take process, were assigned cartoon subjects and had their ideas approved before finishing up. This is the position most staff cartoonists are in today. Most find themselves able to work in this sort of an arrangement without undue friction, since they are frequently in sympathy with their paper's stand. Others, such as Rollin Kirby, moved on through several papers until they found a comfortable niche, or like Robert Minor, quit the profession altogether. But more on this later.

A second kind of relationship has grown up for the stars. Like those whose local fame makes them a clear circulation asset to their papers, the stars developed a leverage from being widely syndicated. David Low illustrates the first. He rocked the profession when, as a price for moving over to the Beaverbrook newspapers, he asked for and got complete editorial independence. He thus attacked his employer's policies at will and even continued to caricature Lord Beaverbrook and his publisher cronies in his cartoons. Perhaps the American artist tied to a single paper who came closest to this degree of independence was Daniel Fitzpatrick of the St. Louis *Post Dispatch*. The formula he worked out with his editors was that he could refuse to draw on a particular subject, and the newspaper's editor could exercise the right to refuse to print a particular cartoon. On few occasions were either of these rights exercised, most notably when Fitzpatrick refused to support Alfred Landon in 1936.

Syndication and its circulation bonanza after World War II also made a greater degree of independence possible for a handful of political cartoonists. Since they were clearly not home talent, they could be put in the category of the opinionated and syndicated columnist, with all the independence and quirks this lofty station generally implies. Some papers liked the prestige of carrying one top cartoonist. Others mixed the bag. Thus the cartoons of a variety of artists would be printed on occasion and if some readers penned nasty letters about the content of any one of them, editors could shrug their shoulders and say they were trying to show all sides of the issues. The result was a degree of freedom within bounds. If a cartoonist was too independent, or perhaps too bitter in his views, he or she could possibly lose newspaper customers. In the Vietnam period the degree of independence permitted sharply increased. That it will not remain so seems probable.

I have tried to give a historical overview in terms of how technology affected the quality, both artistic and critical, of political-cartoon comment. One conclusion that emerges is that the constraints or freedoms of one day cannot necessarily be transferred to another. The constraints that technology has placed on today's cartoonist are the result of being able to create mass-circulation newspapers with widespread syndication, not those that faced Gillray in Georgian England.

The imperatives of technology were four: (1) increase length of press runs, (2) reproduce more quickly, (3) reproduce more cheaply, and (4) reproduce more accurately. The working toward these goals determined the number of cartoonists who would be employed, the artist's potential audience, the artistic techniques he or she could use, and his or her independence as political critic.

The technology of today's America, which has made syndication possible, has reduced the number of cartoon critics just as it has artists and critics in the other mass media — freed them, on the whole, in terms of artistic technique, created a mass audience for them, and given them a high degree of independence.

I have not yet alluded to a second technological impact and it would perhaps be well to do so here. The question is this: Is anybody still looking at political cartoons?

Technology has not affected the political cartoon alone. It has also created for it a myriad of competitors in movies, radio, comic books, and television. It has encouraged education, at least to the level of progressive school literacy. And so on the surface it seems that the political cartoon no longer has the influence it had in the England of *Punch* or the America of *Harpers Weekly* and *Puck*, where Nast and Keppler from 1868 through 1892 set the campaign themes for presidential elections.

But the political cartoon remains what is has always been throughout its history — *critical comment aimed at the fairly bright*, that group of society which the sociologist Scott Greer notes manages most of society's affairs. Through this political stratum of activists and opinion leaders, the cartoonist hopes to reach down even into the mass. Thus today the political cartoon no longer dominates, as it did in the days of widespread and admitted illiteracy. The net impact of the political cartoon today continues to be its ability to join with other media critics in creating a climate of opinion or consensus among that politically attentive segment by peddling assumptions about the conditions and problems facing the society, their nature and even sometimes their solution. That audience can now be assured of getting to know fairly well, through the magic of syndication, the thoughts and moods of the very cream of the cartoonist profession.

In today's society of PR image-making for politicians, the cartoonist has an added advantage. Political caricature exposes for all to see the character and personality of our politicians. They try to answer for us that haunting political question — "What is X really like?"

3
Analysis of Cartoons

Some romanticize cartoonists as staunch friends of freedom. This is like saying that the shillelagh is always swung in support of democracy. Sometimes it is and sometimes it is not. To state it otherwise, some awfully devilish and even bitingly funny cartoons have been drawn to defend totalitarian systems or authoritarian positions. It is more important to us to reflect upon the kind of roles the political cartoonists play and then pick out those we think are democracy's friends.

In this chapter I argue that cartoonists whether operating in a totalitarian, authoritarian, or democratic system, accept the job of saving time and effort for citizens. They do this by offering judgments, by making some kind of sense for citizens out of what those who run the government are up to. Their guiding star through the political wasteland, is not, I argue, a set of political ideas that the cartoonist holds. When the chips are down, it is rather human beings — some community that he or she treasures.

Those Who Guard the Guardians

Whatever the government, average citizens have neither the time nor the requisite specialized knowledge to follow what is going on. What they desperately want is someone they can trust to interpret governmental actions for them — intermediaries between the politicians and public officials who run the government and the public who pay the bills and reap benefits or get it in the neck. Such critics help reduce information costs for all of us. We are deeply involved in our own important affairs: career, family, the rosebushes, pro-games on TV, and all sorts of other significant absurdities. We have very, very little time left over for government and politics, unless it happens to be our hobby or livelihood. And rightly so. According to older rationalistic or idealistic models of how democracy works, we should feel guilty about this — but this is moonshine. Humans can not operate that way. Even if we tried to understand all the details of the making or closing up of income tax loopholes, the regulation of morticians, or how social security is put together, all of which may have a marked effect on our life styles or even life chances, we would have trouble sandwiching in ten minutes for meals and sleep, with very little time left over for other pleasures or for getting a living. And this leaves out keeping tabs on all the great and little issues like what is stirring the viscera of members of the U.N. General Assembly, or such a weighty matter as how well the local sheriff is handling the county road-patrol fleet.

It is not just information that we want — all of us get more information than we can absorb. What we yearn for is interpreters who seem to make sense of things that are and will be important to us. They are especially useful when things are not going well and we don't know why. We turn either to critics of the government whom we trust because we share their points of view, or to many critics with many different vantages. Somehow their combined efforts in informing us about what it all means will, hopefully, keep the politicians money-honest and their policies to some degree reasonable.

The information the critic provides is naturally selective. He or she is a finger-pointer about what we should pay attention to. He or she winnows out and attempts to assess what is really significant. Just focusing attention so that items get on the public agenda is a useful service, even if the critic has no more idea of a solution to the problems raised than we do.

These critics not only interpret specific policies and politicians to those publics which pay attention to them, but they also project a judgment about the system itself — whether it should be regarded as legitimate and deserving of loyalty or not. This matter of judgment of the system is the critic's assessment of its social justice — of whether the way status, power, and material benefits are divided and may be achieved in a society is acceptable or not in its main features.

In democracies especially, critics provide a way of channeling back opinions from the public as well as absorbing feedback from the public officials. Out of this process of interaction, I believe, may come a consensus sometimes called public opinion if enough people share it. The consensus is not wholly a creation of officials, critics, or the general public, but is the result of interaction of all three. Such consensus is not inevitable.

In totalitarian systems the critics are official and, as such, subservient to the rulers. Almost immediately on taking power, dictators crush whatever independence critics have had. The new leaders create the office of propaganda ministry and institutionalize the critics as part of their governing apparatus and so pay homage to the critics' importance as legitimizers of the system.

In democracies, though, many of the critics are independent and they tend to dominate this communication process as their own. Politicians and officials may try to horn in through TV and radio speeches, press conferences, newsletters, public statements, and even public appearances in shopping centres. All this politician contact with the public is to try to capture a hold on public opinion the way that Franklin Roosevelt did in his fireside chats or that Winston Churchill did during the blitz. Very few democratic politicians succeed in this bypass of the critics, because the critics follow them around, commenting on what the politicians are up to as soon as they go off the air or ride off around the corner.

On the other side of the equation, various attentive publics in democracies also try to bypass the critics and go directly to the politicians. They push themselves forward to let politicians know directly what they want or believe. Angry mothers object to school bussing, or groups use the techniques of lobbying or spontaneous meat-boycotts or rioting. These groups are helped in getting views across by such indicators of opinion as polls and elections. But all of this occasional hubbub from the public does not dispense with the critics, who, whether self-appointed or institutionally expected to so perform, dominate the day-by-day interaction and linkages between politico and J. Q. Public.

The cartoonist, it should be noted, has a special advantage among the babbling army of critics. They can sugarcoat their messages by stuffing them into a little allegorical drama, so that if they are skillful, their points slide down easily, and don't get stuck in the craw as the printed word sometimes does. They can also insinuate relatively subtle cues and hints as signals of what they think, and thus sometimes say what others dare not.

The Totalitarian Cartoon Critic

In an absolutist system, the governors seek the illusionary goal of complete control over everything political, social, and economic. In respect to the political cartoon, they achieve it almost completely, because the cartoon needs to be mass produced and that requires at the very least a small printing press, a very risky piece of heavy equipment to keep hidden under the basement stairs in a police state. The scrawl on the wall, or the drawing passed from hand to hand the way the caricature of a teacher goes quietly around a class, is the only other outlet for the cartoonist. Both are clearly ineffective and, in a police state system, perhaps even foolhardy. Far more useful for criticizing the system is the political joke passed surreptitiously by word of mouth.

A few exceptions prove the rule. A cartoon captioned "USA: We Christened Her Peace" is an anti-Communist one that was mass produced in Communist Czechoslovakia. It depicted all of the major leaders of the Czech Communist government of 1950 paying homage to the U.S. and toasting her efforts for peace. Its publication required the kind of antics made familiar by the Mission Impossible or the Watergate wiretapper crowds. Shortly after J. Molin (Porcupine), one of the most popular Communist cartoonists, left for a summer holiday, this cartoon was delivered to his paper. It was drawn in his familiar style with his signature attached and no one there gave it a second look. It was duly reproduced and the presses were whirring before anyone took a closer look. One copy of the newspaper got to London and the cartoon was reproduced in the *Daily Telegraph*. Other free-world journals, including *Life*, also printed it. By such a risky, Scarlet Pimpernel kind of gesture, an anti-government cartoon was indeed mass produced in a totalitarian system — once. Molin, incidentally, was able to prove his complete innocence of possible criticism of his betters to the satisfaction of the party apparatus.

Those who have studied cartoons in the Soviet system report that they portray images of the outside world for Soviet citizen consumption that are as virulent as are Soviet words when things are not going exactly right for the crimson tide. Note, for example, the image projected for Soviet citizens of the leaders of foreign nations, such as the apelike features of General George Marshall, author of the plan that bears his name.[1] The cartoon was produced to honor his being awarded a Nobel Peace prize. The cartoon dramas on internal affairs are, on the other hand, patterned on the style of the old-fashioned McGuffey Readers. They gently underline the virtues of proper citizens with the subtlety of an efficient Sunday school teacher. Sometimes, regretfully, they touch upon minor backsliding. The Soviet citizen is taught not to spit on the floor in the grandiose subway stations, and mild jibes are aimed at such enemies of the system as lazy slackers, drunkards, and inefficient minor functionaries. In this way the Soviet cartoon channels irritations of citizens into safe outlets and against safe targets. Totalitarian rulers in cartoons get presented as heroic and are tied to any image of the past that is admired, much as General Foods associates outstanding baseball players and other professional athletes with its breakfast food containers.[2]

23.   Kukryniksky : The Nobel Peace Prize. November 4, 1953. *Pravda.* **Reprinted with permission from Michael M. Milenkovitch,** *The View from Red Square.*

The Nazis used similar propaganda techniques, except that cartoons for internal consumption stressed the image of the Jew as an untouchable and unspeakable enemy and the Aryan a local apostle dedicated to spreading sweetness and light.[3] The message being projected by both kinds of cartoons is that the totalitarian system is the only legitimate one in the world, and to think otherwise is unthinkable. The system rulers never let up in manufacturing a synthetic public opinion through their mouthpieces, or in discouraging a contrary one. Thus, while the critic remains the major interpreter of governmental actions, he is a stooge who has sold out.

The Authoritarian Cartoonist Critic

A system is authoritarian when an establishment retains strong formal control of political offices and of the top slots in the economic and status hierarchies but no longer has complete control over the critics of its acts. The critics project an idealistic, sentimental, or even sour-grapes defection from the system, often accepted by a good many who are beneficiaries of the actions of the governing group. The Establishment's moral legitimacy is undercut. The mass of the people can thus be led to take an independent course that will isolate the formal leaders.

Colonial systems fit this pattern very well when the division between mass and imperialist governors is rubbed raw by differences in race or ethnic background. But the same thing happens in traditional societies where the authority of the rulers is undermined by contact with the outside world, as happened, for example, with the Sultan of Turkey after World War I and the Shah of Iran of post-World War II.

A significant fact is that, when aspects of a controlled system come under severe criticism, the formal leaders are almost always on a no-win course, in spite of their status, wealth, or military power. Things have already gone too far. They can lash out against and shut off some criticism, but they will be ineffective in the long run. The box cannot be closed up again. Nothing the leaders do will help matters very much, or be approved of as right by their critics. Every action or inaction will result in a confrontation and the radicalizing of the masses, and will increase their sympathy for any martyrs who get injured or killed, and increase their opposition to the formal rulers. Perhaps the only effective defense the oligarchy can use is successful repression, and this is not a viable alternative, either because of the oligarchs' inefficiency or because of their lack of confidence and belief in their own cause. They eventually must give in — gracefully, as the landed aristocracy did in England in 1832, or in astonishment at violent overthrow, as has been the fate of French oligarchies in several similar circumstances.

What makes defeat inevitable is that comment that begins as criticism of specific government policies usually balloons rather quickly into a questioning of the legitimacy of the system itself. The mass base provides sufficient foundation for mounting an effective anti-government campaign when the output of revolutionary printing presses exists side-by-side with attempts at suppression. Luther's questioning of the papacy that led to a revolutionary break was the first occasion in which cartoons were widely produced for such a fight. The struggles of Holland for freedom from Spain produced more cartoons, and the Puritan challenge to Charles I in 1641 introduced the political cartoon as a weapon into England. Our own revolution of 1776 repeated the same process, from questioning the wisdom of specific policies, through incidents like the Boston Massacre, to the final break. Paul Revere's cartoon on that event is a typical, flamboyant criticism of authoritarian rule. It is reproduced as figure 62.

In authoritarian systems the political cartoon reaches its full glory. The role of self-sacrificing martyr for the people, a role that can give life new meaning and zest to a rather dreary existence, is attractive to certain types. The self-selected critic who embraces this heroic part in a great historic drama sees himself or herself facing a tyranny that can be painted in bold colors as evil and Satanic. Jefferson's description of that devil George III in our Declaration of Independence, as compared to the blundering reality, suggests the flights of poetic fancy that are possible. But that distortion and misrepresentation do enter the anti-government propaganda effort should not blind us to the fact that the revolutionaries of 1776, and most others who have fought authoritarian systems, were essentially correct. Those governing systems were kaput morally and politically, and required drastic changes to survive. The old system of redistributing the benefits of status, power, and material resources was archaic for new times. The cartoon by George Cruikshank attacks privilege in the English system of George IV as it stumbled toward reform or revolution in 1832.

24.   George Cruikshank : Poor Bull and his Burden. 1819.

To recapitulate, several factors contribute to the attractiveness of the revolutionary role in an authoritarian system. The risks in joining the anti-government faction are genuine, and so can give meaning to humdrum lives. Opposition is only in part dramatic play-acting. Occasionally, as in the IRA or the Stern gang or the Bangladesh partisans, rebels are caught and tortured, or languish in prison, or have their property confiscated, or find their careers ruined, or are even executed, assassinated, or blown up. This adds to the excitement felt by the survivors. Every such movement against an authoritarian system — from that of American Labor from the 1880s to the Civil Rights marchers against Selma — has had its genuine martyrs. Some, indeed, were the critics who fought with pen and cartoon.

But the second fact is equally important. Opposition is not hopeless, as it is in a totalitarian system. It will very likely eventually lead to payoffs. Where the formal leaders have thus far lost control, "We shall overcome" is a simple statement of fact. New ways will be found, peacefully or with violence, to distribute the political power that goes with office, the status that flows from social position, and the material benefits that the system produces. Success is possible on the idealistic level, but also on the practical level; the surviving critics of the old society are likely to become the heroes and formal leaders of the new one. Parenthetically, one observes that occasionally those critics and activists who have died in the struggle, still believing in its purity, may have been the luckiest ones. The troubles at the Dublin prison in 1916, which resulted in the hanging of 15 patriots, are a far nobler and more admirable thing to contemplate than the antics at the Dail of today, which provide all the idealistic inspiration of a Monday-night session at the Wyoming State House. The survivors have to face the petty political squabbling and maneuvering for personal advantage and the seemingly inevitable domination by what new critics may come to describe as Green Tories. The old spirit is dead, unless one can find it again in the clear presence of a menacing foe, such as that surrounding tiny Israel, or in a new struggle in the north, as in Ulster. Only then can a measure of revolutionary fervor and selfless commitment be revived.

Contrary to what one might suppose, the loyalists are the ones who have trouble not the critics of oligarchy, expressing themselves in the mass media. Cartoonists fighting authoritarian oligarchies, or those imagining that they are doing so, generally receive the greatest attention from the people of their times, as well as from later students. Cartoons defending the oligarchy are usually scarce, because the appeal of the political cartoon is generally to the masses and the masses do not receive pro-government propaganda gracefully. M. Dorothy George thus describes the situation in respect to the Puritan conflicts in 1640: "Royalist prints are rare and generally cautious: prints voiced the then dominant opinion in London; they did not lend themselves like ballads (which are predominantly Royalist) to clandestine production and sale." Haines Halsey notes that, out of 150 English prints of the 1760s and 1770s, only three can be found that favored George III against the American colonies. The pattern found by Victor Alba in prerevolutionary Mexico is the same; prints were overwhelmingly critical of the authoritarian government.[4]

Some of the best cartoons that we shall subsequently review spring from this kind of anti-authoritarian conflict over special privilege. It is indeed the authoritarian critic who makes observers think that most cartoonists are natural democrats. These cartoonists seem to be natural democrats, busy creating an embryonic public opinion that will redistribute a society's political, social, and economic benefits for the greater benefit of the masses.

The Democratic Cartoonist Critic

Sometimes critics looking for a more romantic role than the humdrum one facing them in a democracy are tempted to act as if they were fighting an entrenched and evil authoritarian oligarchy. Thus we have the incongruous situation of self-styled underground cartoonists flaying their democratic environment in publications that can be purchased at any corner capitalist newstand. The critics must pretend to believe, somehow, that they have wrenched the privilege to criticize from an unwilling and devilish authoritarian oligarchy. They can then assume it with a flourish and seemingly at great personal risk. This is posturing, and it deserves the same cheers one gives to acrobats who perform with a net.

In fact, the role of critic is built into the democratic system and is protected by effective constitutional guarantees as well as social habits of one kind or another. The important point, one not to be missed, is that democratic governments not only tolerate criticism, but they institutionalize it in such practices as the election, the press conference, the TV talk show, or the editorial page with its cartoons. An assumption of democracy is that government cannot remain democratic without permitting the existence of such critics, independent of the government itself. So England knights as acerbic a cartoon critic as David Low (plus five others), and the United States awards Pulitzer Prizes to some of the most biting cartoon critics of its institutions.

These legal and social underpinnings perhaps rest on a hope that most such critics will conclude that they are among the fortunate few in history who are permitted to live under a relatively free system, and that they will voluntarily conclude that such a system, on balance, deserves their loyalty. But if they seem to have loftier standards and ideals, to march to a different drum, this is their own business. They may, if they wish, present images of the democratic system and its leaders reminiscent of Beowulf's view of Grendel, as told later in the mead hall.

At any rate, this is the independent critics role in a democracy: they are expected to criticize leaders and their policies so that everyone else can get a glimmer of what's going on. By sending up trial balloons they feed back mass reactions. The result should be peaceful change. Only in time of war do democratic critics come close to being government mouthpieces, and not even then, it seems, when the war is limited, questionable, and long, as was the Vietnam effort.

Reviewing the history of our democracy, one could, I think with justice, conclude that its institutionalized critics have performed reasonably well, given the level of weakness and culpability that seems to be the lot of any institution connected with human beings. While the role of democratic critic looks commonplace and sometimes less than inspiring, the critics perform as valuable a service for free government as do the mass of politicians and lobbyists whom democracy's beneficiaries also sometimes scorn as two-bit incompetents and chiselers.

It will be my thesis, maintained I hope consistently throughout this work, that the role of democratic politician and that of cartoon critic who is voluntarily loyal to our system are often grossly and unfairly maligned in our culture. They are roles that, I venture to add, give more commendable service to the cause of human decency than playing the Red Shadow, in Sigmund Romberg operatic style, against the imagined oligarchs of today's precious democratic governments. This has been indeed a somehow unpopular view to espouse in recent times, and so I can feel properly ennobled and beleaguered in assuming it.

The Essence of the Political Cartoon

Many observers see the political essence of a cartoon as a matter of ideology — the critic is born as or develops into a little liberal or a little conservative. In the discussion that follows I shall suggest that trying to fit critics into neat categories of liberal and conservative, as people commonly do, soon leads to all types of corkscrew reasoning, because this is not the way the critics or other people act. They get inconsistent and squirm around out of those ideological boxes. They are not so faithful a priesthood of the holy creed as true believers might desire.

It was that eminent philosopher Dwight D. Eisenhower who tried to straighten out some of these ideological inconsistencies when he announced that he was a liberal in social matters but a conservative in economic ones. Students have discovered that the blue-collar workers, on the other hand, seem to be liberal on economic matters but conservative on social issues. Others of us find other matters on which we can go off on a tangent and agree with one or the other, or neither, as on foreign policy or race relations or civil liberties. At some points, according to the currently fashionable definitions, we are liberals and at other conservatives. Sometimes the sides even switch fairly fast on the same issue, as on whether the presidential office verges too close to a dictatorship, once a conservative battle cry against FDR and later seemingly a liberal one against Richard Nixon.

The problem with all of this ideologizing is that it treats political-issue stances as if they were arrived at on some windswept hill after much communing with one's maker. But what Eisenhower was perhaps saying was that he identified with the suburban, button-down-collar, organization man and his way of living life, while the blue-collar worker was trying to tell Democratic politicos that he doesn't like the new politics because he thinks it doesn't identify enough with the blue-collar ethnic family and its problems. *Both are describing that spot we usually call home.* The focus in both cases is a community of fellow spirits that they value and, if I may be permitted a rather flowery and elaborate term, even cherish. It is the life style and life chances of this grouping that are all-important, not the set of ideas that for the moment is handy for their protection.

Earlier I talked about whether a critic or an individual considers the system to be legitimate and worthy of support, or whether he or she views it as something evil and illegitimate that should be destroyed or at least radically changed. Central to this judgment, I now argue, is the answer the viewer gives to this question: Are those I identify with benefited as they should be by the present distribution of status, wealth, and power? That's what they mean when they ask: Is the system just?

Radicals from left or right pretend to answer questions of distributive justice with slogans and vague phrases such as "all power to the people," or to "the natural aristocracy," or "the common man," or some other ethereal formulation. But when one looks closer, the common man or natural aristocrat or spearhead for the proletariat that they extol has the teeth markings and toe prints of some very specific types of individuals. They turn out to be very uncommon men (or women) indeed, who are readily distinguishable from all of the rest of downtrodden humanity. If distinguished in no other way, they are generally a grouping that finds the critic or cartoonist one of their membership. They are what critics really mean when they think "home folks."

Finding out who this select community is from looking at cartoons is not always so easy as one might suppose. This is because cartoonists, like most social critics, spend more time attacking, and so emphasizing the negative, than painting inspiring pictures of the positive. The rulers can be portrayed as monsters or fools or weaklings or something else that one should deplore, and the rules can be shown to result in atrocities or failures or disasters or worse. It is more awkward and mawkish, particularly to modern tastes, to bare one's secret heart. But in a series of cartoons, even those that only criticize, artists are likely to give some clue as to whom they see as the pure in heart and spirit, who is really living the good life, *whom society is really very lucky to have around to pick up the pieces.*

The cartoon by Jules Feiffer "Scratch the crowd who want to impeach the president" follows a standard pattern of exaggerated ridicule of those who, in the artist's eyes, are living the unlovely or the bad life and nevertheless are rewarded for it. It differs only in the special bite the artist puts in it. But Feiffer's effort can readily be reversed with dialogue something as follows (as you read along, try to imagine who is speaking, what he or she probably looks and acts like):

25.   Jules Feiffer : "Scratch the Crowd — " April 14, ca. 1973. *The Village Voice.*
Reprinted by permission of Jules Feiffer.

> Scratch the crowd who defend the President
> And you find the type who still believe in narrow patriotism
> And still think we were right to fight in Vietnam
> And who are trying to stop racial integration by attacking
>   bussing,
> And who want to deny abortion on demand.
> So when we attack the President,
> It's not Nixon we attack
> It's those know-nothings who love their country too much,
> The bigots who don't want their children bussed around,
> And the puritans who won't let us abort when we want,
> And all those others who won't buy our free style of life.
> Strengthen the office of the Presidency and you strengthen good
>   old-fashioned repression.

Actually, that is not a very good reversal, since I probably toned it down too much and left out too much of the vinegar.

But from it and the original cartoon you get a pretty clear idea of whom Feiffer does not like, and I hope I've shown that you can get some hint of the kind of secular-minded, swinging singles that he might sort of like to see given a little more social recognition. Perhaps it would have been easier if I had said right out what he has taken pains to deny: Feiffer has a soft spot for the Bernard types he has so often portrayed, and is possibly one himself.

We also get a notion of what is eating Feiffer. It is that social and political benefits are still being withheld from this cherished salt of the Bronx. With some further redistribution of social status, it is possible that Feiffer's inner compass might swing him around from being uptight, and he might become a pillar of society rather than its caustic critic. Then again, we may never live to see it quite the way he'd like it.

Being unaware of the inner compass can lead to some glaring misconceptions about a cartoonist, based on a cursory view of his or her work. One can find, for example, numerous descriptions of the Victorian cartoonist John Tenniel that characterize his pen as always full of sweet, reasonable cross-hatches and placid poses, feet akimbo. This is as if the Bengal Tiger, or his comments on Ireland, Abraham Lincoln, or anarchists had never been put down on woodblock. Tenniel can be quite bitter with those who attack his vision of a world ruled by right and proper English gentlemen. Perhaps we can more profitably say that Tenniel was always full of a Will Rogers kind of dignified amiableness in respect to certain subjects of the realm, a kind of "I never met a man I didn't like, except for those who deserved not to be liked."

26. John Tenniel: The Irish Tempest! Caliban (Rory of the Hills). "This island's Mine, by Sycorax my mother, which thou takest from me." — Shakespeare. March 19, 1870. *Punch.*

Just to be sure that Feiffer is not a fluke, let us try it one more time. By chance, J. N. "Ding" Darling's Pulitzer Prize-winner of 1924 is almost the reverse of Jules Feiffer's

27. Jay N. "Ding" Darling: In the Good Old U.S.A. (Pulitzer Prize 1924) Des Moines *Register*

effort of fifty years later. Darling is defending what he sees as a cherished type under siege from some mutations in man's evolutionary process — sports that surfaced in the roaring twenties and seem to him of questionable value. Darling poses it as a question of morality, which is always the best way: The constrast between self-discipline and self-indulgent hedonism. But basic to Darling's viewpoint is the community he cherishes, that of family, church, and business all rolled together, the way it gets served up in self-employed, small-town America. What Darling's opinions later were, about his small-town printer's helper named Warren G., are not reported.

One may be tempted to conclude that these inner loyalties are mainly derived from childhood experience. Darling was born in a northern Michigan village, the son of a

Congregational minister. Feiffer was not. But this early experience seems to be only part of what turns out a cartoonist critic. The experiences he or she has between eighteen and twenty are perhaps equally or more significant, since that is when one finds or makes a place for himself or herself in the world. Even later experiences may be important. A social convulsion, such as a war or depression, or even a private one such as a personal tragedy or divorce, may change one's vision of what makes home. Few react more strongly than those who see themselves spurned, not by enemies but by former friends.

My point then has been that cartoonists, like other critics, look at politics from a vantage point. This is true whether they draw in a totalitarian, authoritarian, or democratic context. A loyalty fires their comment, and that special loyalty is less to a set of ideas than to the community of individuals that the cartoonist thinks needs nurture.

One additional point needs to be emphasized: popular critics, especially cartoonists, have to be timely in their choice of cherished communities. Those who are too offbeat in their preferences either find themselves confined to a small audience or have to find a way to ally themselves with more widely cherished groups of their day. Artists who grimly paddle upstream against the assumptions of their day and its favored groups may not be swamped or even wholly deflected, but their output will bear the marks of struggle and loneliness and, likely, some compromise with the preferences of the mass audience. In some cases such dislocations have caused once-great artists to falter and their work to lose force. It takes dedicated critics to speak their piece to an unsympathetic or indifferent audience, and an unusually sympathetic mass publisher to keep printing it. I will suggest at a later point that lack of timeliness was the fate that befell Thomas Nast in the period following his campaign against Tweed. After twenty years, the community he had been defending was no longer out there. The cheering stopped. He found himself through as a political cartoonist when a comparatively young man of forty-five. He never did regain his foothold.

The Three Elements of Political Cartoons

A political cartoonist uses three tricks to sell his vision of the cream of society, and these are what I will call the elements of the cartoon. One is the picture of reality that artists present to us as the essence of truth. They are showing what is happening to their cherished community. A second is a message, sometimes very sketchily implied, as to what they recommend ought to be done on behalf of the deserving. Finally, through artistic technique and allegorical imagery, the artist creates a mood telling us how we should feel over what is happening — amused, chagrined, or any one of the pedal stops up to outrage. The division here is one of head, heart, and gut or, if you prefer, cognitive, normative, and affective or, alternatively, is, ought, and feel or, perhaps even better, intellect, conscience, and emotion.

One would think that being timely is enough to make a cartoonist memorable, since that quality clearly strengthens the appeal of the intellectual and moral elements of the cartoons. But all of us have viewed cartoons whose loyalties we can share if we can only stifle our yawns and keep awake while paging through them. They can be as dull as carbon on pistons or as what interests those tropical fish that swim round and round in dentists' offices. All of us have also come across cleverly done caricatures whose basic political message we regard as approaching distilled wickedness. But we can't quite look the other way, or avoid admiring, or even get those pictures out of our mind. Perhaps some boundaries exist as to how far we can be entertained by what repels us or bored by what we adore, but for most of us broad limits of tolerance seem to exist, within which we may, unlike Victoria, be amused. This is a way of saying that I reluctantly conclude that it is not only whom he or she defends but the way the artist does it emotionally that brings fame to a cartoonist.

But before we go any further on this important emotional element, let us look first at the intellectual or realistic aspect, and then the moral component.

The Picture of Reality

Cartoonists claim to be peddling truth. What they portray may be an imaginary situation in allegory or a figure greatly distorted by caricature, but to the artists this is the essence of what is actually happening. They are faithful to reality rather than merely painting the surface features or what is literally to be seen. They are trying to show how the world really is so you can gauge its effect on the salt of the earth.

David Low in *Ye Madde Designer* gives an excellent discussion of this distinction in talking about caricature and what he called Karicature with a capital K. He notes that if you look into either side of a spoon you get a distortion of your face. This is what much meaningless caricature or, more appropriately, what he called "Karicature" achieves — distortion just for the sake of showing the artist's cleverness. But real caricature, he argues, distorts in order to hammer home what the artist regards as the essential truth about an individual. At one point, Low says, the caricature may in fact look more like the person he or she really is than he or she does.[5] Do you want to read over that again?

The formula of cartoon presentation can frequently be summed up as, "They say — I say," "They say it's this way — but I say," or such variations as "Don't let them kid you, here's how it really works," or "He may look to you like ..., but behind the mask this is what he's really like." One of the best of modern cartoonists, Bill Sanders, thus pulls the mask off the Nixon Administration during Watergate. All of the above sentences suggest muckraking exposé. But cartoonists can also use the technique to glorify the humdrum politician. In place of warts and hickies, we are shown a knight in shining armor stabbing some loathsome dragons. And who is to say that, sometimes at least, that image is not closer to the real truth than what the camera shows?

What artists are giving us is their assumptions about reality. They begin by selecting facts — what I will call a condition — that they think have good or bad effects. They are saying that these are the main elements of the situation. — how it should be looked at. The elements that seem important come from two sources. The community they wish to protect, preserve, or nourish to full bloom suggests most of them. But the rest are events the cartoonist finds it difficult or impossible to deny. Let us look at each in turn.

Most cartoons present as reality what artists really expected to find before they began looking or, even more commonly, they looked through current events and found some for instances, to illustrate how right their underlying assumptions really are. The community they are defending so predisposes them. The current events are used as window dressing to establish the validity of his or her assumptions about how life should be lived. Thus a cartoonist viewing student riots on campus in the late sixties could portray the reality of trashing as the result of the repressive and foolish rules, made *in loco parentis,* to stifle college youth. Another cartoonist might see the same events as the outgrowth of permissiveness in family-rearing practices. These are the elements of reality each stresses, and in the process the cartoonist's message is

28. **Bill Sanders : After an exhaustive investigation I find this elephant trunk acting independently and of its own accord, guilty of ..." 1972. Milwaukee** *Journal.*

already half formed. Each in their mind's eye is predisposed to see according to the kind of social community that they feel it desirable to nourish.

But sooner or later some events pop up that do not quite fit. And they won't go away. They may be handled by shifting focus slightly but, if this is done too often, as if it were an addiction, such shifts can in time lead to a radical change of assumptions. The community isn't being defended anymore. Wars have this property.

A calamity such as the Great Depression is also hard to keep hidden around the corner, and even the peccadillos of President Harding, previously alluded to, or those of the entourage of President Nixon, have caused a shift in some people's assumptions about what reality is like. Among the more heartening of such shifts appears to be the picture of reality held by whites about blacks. It was not difficult to find shuffling Sambos or crazy, dancing watermelon-eaters in the political cartoons of just a few generations ago. Presumably, behavior contrary to that picture of reality has jarred that previous image out of focus.

To summarize: the first element of the cartoon is the picture of reality presented. The artist points to a condition whose impact is in his or her opinion good or bad and tells you that this is what he or she thinks is really happening. Just calling attention is an important selective function of the cartoonist critic. But behind this interpretation of reality, guiding the pen, is the hint of the community the cartoonist cherishes.

A political cartoon is supposed to beam out a specific message that political leaders or government officials can do something about. That is the way political cartoons were defined in chapter 1. This message grows out of concern for the cherished community and so becomes the moral justification of the cartoon production.

But the problem of finding these beamed-out messages is a good deal more difficult than the lighthearted definition of chapter 1 suggests. Some cartoons fall into place neatly. They take the condition portrayed and build a message right out of it. They single out a problem, tell you who the villain is, and then tell you what should be done about it. John Tenniel's famous cartoon for *Punch* about the Sepoy Mutiny of 1857, "The British Lion's Vengeance on the Bengal Tiger," left neither Britons nor Indians in doubt about what the problem was, who was being hurt who should not be, and Tenniel's recipe for political action.

29.   John Tenniel: The British Lion's Vengeance on the Bengal Tiger. August 22, 1857. *Punch.*

The artist can even build out of the picture of reality a very basic message, one that says plainly whether the system is really legitimate. Revolutionary cartoonists specialize in atrocity pictures for this purpose. Among the most famous is Honoré Daumier's "Rue Transmonain le 15 Avril, 1834," which pretends to be a realistic portrayal of a home destroyed by royal troops — I say *pretends* because, unlike a photograph, which might blur the real horror, Daumier's picture stages the scene for maximum emotional impact. The conclusion that a system that results in these horrors is illegitimate is not too great a leap for most of us to make, especially if we share the artist's identification with decent lower-middle-class types.

30.   Honoré Daumier: Rue Transmonain, Avril 15, 1834. September 1834.

But most cartoons, including most by Tenniel, are more gossamerlike. When one reaches out to grab hold of their message, it isn't all there. The artists do not get very much beyond pointing to a condition worth one's attention and giving nebulous hints about its causes. By this I mean that they single out an event or related set of events that have, in their opinion, a favourable or, more generally, an unfavourable result on their cherished group. They say "That's bad, isn't it?" They may not even imply very distinctly who or what to blame (which would then make it a *problem* that possibly could be solved) and may still be a couple of hundred miles away from suggesting what is to be done (how to reach a solution). John Tenniel again provides an illustration. His most famous cartoon, "Dropping the Pilot," is perhaps the world's most widely recognized political cartoon — so much so that it has become a cartoon cliché. It shows young Kaiser Wilhelm II dismissing Chancellor Otto Bismarck, the architect of the modern German state. One can sympathize with each of the principals in this drama and perhaps with the reasons each feels justify his behaviour: age must make way for youth, but youth can go too fast; sluggish experience faces impetuous energy; prudence looks at innovation. Is the effect of the event good or bad for the world or, more narrowly, for Victorian England? The cartoonist doesn't precisely say. To me the cartoon suggests a mood of uneasiness that Tenniel's gentlemanly conservatives of Victorian days felt in the face of uncertainty and unpredictable consequences. They didn't like sudden changes. If so, their prejudice was in this case amply justified by subsequent events. If a clear-cut judgment about what reality means is this hard to detect, then finding the answer to the question "What to be done?" is even more elusive. The Tenniel cartoon is a prophecy, or a warning mixed with resignation: The message may really be "That's life," or perhaps "Brace yourself," or "Get ready for trouble," or some other bit of comment suitable for passengers on a plane that is possibly, but maybe not, on its way to a crash landing. It deals with events we can not do much about anyway, but must somehow or other accept.

31.   John Tenniel : Dropping the Pilot. March 29, 1890. *Punch.*

Cartoons that have explicit messages operate at two levels. Most commonly, the message is directed at a specific law or ruler or beneficiary of present arrangements. The messages vary all the way from "Whatever you do, don't vote for McGovern" to "Drunken drivers should get jail terms," or any one of the large variety of practical alternatives for improvement that are generally trotted out. These kinds of specific comment are by artists who most of the time live in the day-to-day world of the rest of us. They see events that they're not sure aren't menacing, problems they suspect they know the causes of, and solutions or actions they at least want to see tried.

The second kind of message is about those more weighty matters of the legitimacy of the whole system and the methods to be used to preserve or replace it. The most explicit cartoons, such as those of the Bengal Tiger or "Uncle Sam Needs You" type, usually state their message on these great topics quite clearly. In these cases the system was proclaimed to be legitimate and the use of ultimate force to protect it was recommended. This does not necessarily mean that the artists have no criticism of the administration in power or of the distribution of wealth, power, or status in their societies. But on balance they plump heavily in support of the system. One does not need to ask J. M. Flagg's familiar finger-pointing Uncle Sam of the poster what he thinks about the legitimacy of "the good old U.S.A."

If all cartoons were this crystal clear, we could sort them out into the kind of table produced below and neatly put their creators on pins for display. This categorization, incidentally, does not drop them into the six slots according to whether they are "left" or "right," liberal or conservative, in ideology; some of both inclinations will be found in each and every box since political action of all types proceeds from both. It sorts them out by goals, and methods to achieve those goals — positions arrived at by concluding how their cherished group is being treated at this point in time.

A totalitarian apologist in modern times is generally a mouthpiece for a feudal, Fascist, or Communist state, a military junta, or any other of the rag-tag dictatorships, from that of Napoleon on, that claim to be bringing heaven to earth by jamming it down people's throats. A revolutionary will represent similar groups. The difference is that revolutionaries are on the outside kicking the door to get in. Both speak for groupings under a state of siege.

Terrorists generally can't hope to win by outright confrontation and so use guerrilla tactics. They exist in a zone of turbulence, whether the terror is dished out by the government in various forms of physical and mental harassment of their enemies, through a 007 bag of dirty tricks, or by energetic critics of the government who utilize such techniques as kidnappings, bomb-throwing into crowds, or other refinements of violent intimidation. The sorry and dreadful events of Northern Ireland, which are seemingly endless, are, I think, exceptional in their duration. Commonly such events lead more quickly to a revolutionary struggle, as in South Vietnam, or to a temporary repression of conflict as in Greece, Uruguay, or Nazi Germany, or Algeria, Czechoslovakia, or Yugoslavia, depending on whether the government or anti-government terrorist bands in the end win out.

The box reserved for the politicians is a familiar one in democratic systems, but that of the radical reformers is less frequently recognized and is especially interesting, though wearing on the other democrats. The latter are persons who regard the system of distribution as illegitimate, but who are still willing to use democratic methods to change it. The struggles over clericalism in France in the twenties and thirties were fueled by such firebrands. Those who brought about the Great Reform Bill of 1832 in England and who, through this and the repeal of the Corn Laws, deposed a landed aristocracy, seem to me to fit in this category. The radical reformers can create a great

TABLE 3.1

METHODS SEEN AS REQUIRED	GOALS FOR THE CHERISHED GROUP	
	Status Quo or Moderate Change*	Radical Change**
Naked Force	Totalitarian Apologist	Revolutionary
Force Mixed with Intimidation	Government-Sponsored Terrorism	Anti-Government Terrorism
Influencing Opinion Following Democratic Rules of Procedure	Politician	Radical Reformer

*The system of distributive justice and its rulers should be regarded as legitimate.
**The system of distributive justice and its rulers should be regarded as illegitimate.

deal of commotion and instability, which deceives some citizens into believing that they live in a time of violent revolutionary activity where it is best to hide the Bible under the bed each night. Romantic thrills abound in the breasts of youthful attackers and middle-aged defenders of the status quo. But when the dust begins to clear, the radical reformers, often much to their own chagrin, find new places in democratic society and tacitly make their peace with it. Our own day has had an abundant supply of occupants for this radical reformist box. Such reformers seem to me to be struggling to replace our present business-corporation-technician-dominated society by one that is dominated by government-technician type. Both seem to be organization men or women more like each other than like the independent entrepreneur of a long-bygone day.

Two difficulties plague us when we try to fit cartoonists into this supposedly neat schema. One is that while the boxes may make good analytical sense, artists are not usually obliging enough to tack labels on themselves or on each and every cartoon they draw that tells whether they want to overthrow the rulers by force or are just mildly joshing them. Sometimes we can get a pretty fair notion about how legitimate they think the system is, but the methods they recommend are a little blurry. Only the most care-free of journalists, after all, print explicit diagrams on how to put together Molotov cocktails that can always be depended upon to explode at just the right time. And even these might reach for their nearest attorney if you were to interpret this action as implying that they are seeking to preserve or replace the system by some form of illegal violence or intimidation.

A second difficulty, so noted, is that whatever message there is in a cartoon is generally at the level of immediate tactics concerning the administration in power rather than about grand strategy and basic concerns. Preserving or destroying the system may be the basic goal hiding in the top rear end of the minds of some cartoonists, but most of us, including most cartoonists, live day-to-day. We have to remember to take the garbage out along with pondering about who is to blame for Michigan's latest Rose Bowl loss, and never quite get around to settling the big, basic, constitutional issues. The "what's to be done?" is more frequently about the next short step as we stumble along, rather than a road map of the $341^1/_4$ miles ahead. Some cartoonists, like the rest of us, have only a vague idea of where they will be next Sunday afternoon.

But all is not lost. Even where cartoonists fail to state their moral recommendations explicitly, they may be implied in the other elements of the cartoon, especially in the mood of civility the cartoon projects. Whatever we look at in the cartoon may shout out implied messages about how cherished groupings are being treated.

The Mood of Civility: Imagery and Artistry

An artist will often criticize other communities than his or her own. Whether the cartoonist recognizes their right to existence or attacks them destructively is the basis of the mood of civility his or her cartoons project. This mood tells us pretty clearly how the artist feels and how he or she thinks we should feel about the system and almost certainly about the administration in power. The artist projects this mood through the imagery and artistry he or she uses.

An artist's imagery is found in the choice of setting, the characters and their costumes that he or she puts on stage, and the situation portrayed. These give the opportunity to present a wide variety of symbolic images and even stereotypes. They are the most striking part of the cartoon. I want to touch on each of these briefly, and their potentialities for projecting a message.

First, take a look at the setting and characters. If one dresses the president up as a knight, the purpose is generally to make him look somewhat comic or a little ridiculous, but one may seriously be trying to show the presidents true nobility. In 1933 FDR was so portrayed. The possible costume changes are endless, but the one most favoured today is some form of modern realistic dress, showing politicians as they normally appear or as they would appear in an occupation such as airplane pilot or plumber.

The presentation of character allows for particularly subtle hints. Teddy Roosevelt decked out as Napoleon is suggestive. Herblock quite appropriately offered Nixon one free shave in a cartoon the day after the president won the 1968 election. Characters whom Herblock tends to be critical of are plastered all over with cues suggesting they flock together with hoboes and tramps. An additional technique employed by many artists is to present character contrasts; the inept contrasted to the skilled was used by Darling in a cartoon showing an insouciant FDR decked out as a ship captain, at the helm and directing an experienced hand to change the direction of the compass since FDR didn't want the boat to go that way. The sailor man gives a broad hint to the kind of old-fashioned characters that inhabit Darling's valued community and to their good, solid attributes.

The choice of situation provides all sorts of opportunities for hints. Violent action may suggest humor or menace or a dozen other moods. Equally promising may be the possibilities in the situation, especially of the slightly daring or even taboo. Art Young, appropriately from his stance, drew the American newspaper profession as working maidens in a house of ill repute Batchelor used the same image to depict European Wars in 1936. Most situations adopted are a good deal less gamey.

How much does the imagery used buttress the message? It is frequently the tip-off to the major message in the cartoon, whether the artist consciously means it to be or not.

In the choice of images the artist often clearly says what his or her position is with regard to the system. The artist is projecting an emotional mood, and whether he or she cultivates those virtues of civility appropriate to democratic decision-making or is encouraging more animal-like approaches to conflict resolution is strongly hinted at. The artist projects the mood of civility that he or she considers appropriate to the times

32.   Art Young : The Newspaper — House of Prostitution. December 1912. *The Masses.*

and to the subject matter, given the way his or her valued community is being treated.

Especially with symbols, the cartoonist produces images that tell everyone in the system, leader and public, what they themselves are like. In later chapters, we shall examine how the symbols of John Bull and Uncle Sam changed in terms of the artist's views of the system. Especially revealing is how a cartoonist portrays the citizens themselves. George Grosz projected a pessimistic-destructive image of Weimar German society, its rulers, its junkers, and its citizens — one that placed them on a par with blown-up photos of the kind of creatures that swim around in a drop of water. Hitler's cartoonists streamlined this image back into the form of the knight errant on a white horse, with Aryan blood corpuscles percolating through him. It is such pictorial stereotyping that gives tone to a society, and in this process cartoonists excel; their cues can rarely be matched by verbal descriptions.

An interesting symbol, it is claimed, was fashioned in the USSR underground. In 1971 a Czech artist named Petr Sadecky said he smuggled out of Russia some underground comic strips prepared in the neighborhood of Kiev University.[6] The heroine of these strips is Octobriana, whom the news stories droolingly described as a half-dressed, busty, Soviet sexpot who pranced around Russia righting wrongs, acting like superwoman, or perhaps one should say *superperson.* Her name suggested the Revolution, and on her forehead was a red star. Not only did the strips reek of sex; they also seldom missed the opportunity for scenes of sadistic violence.

Some specialists on Russia challenged the authenticity of the drawings. But one,

33.   George Grosz : The Voice of the People Is the Voice of God. 1920. Estate of George Grosz, Princeton, N.J.

Abraham Bromberg, noted that, while the reliability of these specific cartoons might remain in question until confirmed independently, certainly the underground revolt against Soviet prudery was a genuine event.

Challenges to the legitimacy of the system in its different sectors are, I think, related. When one is breaking or defying political rules, those who do the same in the social or economic community are allies, whether they know it or not. The observation is borne out in the imagery of underground or revolutionary cartoons as well as "exploitation" movies designed for black audiences. In them one finds a great deal of obscenity, pornography, and violence. One finds taboo subjects often openly dealt with, Henry Miller style. Lighthearted horrors are a big joke, as are debaucheries or perversions. The decencies of society must be treated with disrespect and the artist seeks them out for some attention. Violence and open expression of hatred are glorified, personal vilification is cultivated, and vulgarity is striven for. All these reinforce the message that the system is rotten in its every aspect and all of its rules are to be spat on. Good manners and any sign of good breeding become the taboo of the revolutionary cartoon. Since the symbol Octobriana fits this pattern, she does not appear to be an altogether friendly portrayal.

Patriotic or sacred and religious symbols are, of course, held up by underground and revolutionary movements for open contempt as well as the symbols of any other

Establishment organization or institution. The Boy Scouts and the capitalist press are libeled, while enemies of society such as criminals, saboteurs, or foreign foes are glorified as the politically oppressed. Atrocities against the ordinary citizen by the monster leaders are sought out. It is, in effect, an upside-down world designed to discredit the middle-class view of morality that dominates most stable societies. Thus Octobriana, the anti-Soviet sexpot with a name mocking the Revolution and a symbolic red star on her forehead, could well be the heroine of Russian underground cell intellectuals. The attack on prudery is a political attack. In the same way, Aubrey Beardsley's decadent art in the magazine *The Yellow Book* in the early 1890s signaled a crack in the stability of the Victorian political as well as social system. Sensing this, the *Punch* artist E. T. Reed drew Britannia as she would be portrayed by Beardsley.

34.   E.T. Reed : Britannia à la Beardsley, by Our "Yellow" Decadent. Ca. 1892. *Punch.*

The tip-off in all this, as noted previously, is the stereotyped images that get presented. What does the artist's way of presenting them say the leaders and public of a society are like? The underground, where Jan Faust published a cartoon of a General with a dead baby for a medal, illustrates such sentiment. During the Vietnam war, the Weimar Republic, and certainly the Georgian age of Gillray, this kind of presentation of the rottenness of society was thought by many to be justified.

One should recognize that the reverse is also true. The more supportive of the system the political message is, the more likely it is to be presented with dignified imagery. Such symbols as flag, motherhood, and family will receive the respect they are deemed to deserve. This is true of totalitarian cartoons as well as those of, say, Victorian England.

Taste in morals is always to some degree a matter of context. What shocked the Victorians was accepted without comment before and since. But some forms of human brutalization seem always beyond the bounds of decency — especially the knowing exploitation of one person by another. To such events the destructive satirist is attracted like flies to a garbage pail.

One may also take heart about democracies. Democratic artists most of the time accept the presence of alternative communities without seeking to destroy them. That a skeptical kind of imagery, with a friendly, rough questioning of leaders, is the most common in democracies seems to me a healthy sign. It shatters indiscriminately the sick self-hatred of the revolutionary imagery that must destroy the system and the sick self-hatred of those who must adulate in imagery a political system designed and operated by fallible human beings. Imagery always goes overboard when artists treat those they consider as enemies beyond the pale, or heroes, as far, above the rest of us. Civility, by definition, requires that differences never be allowed to get so intense. When democratic artists show bad blood, it is as they paint pictures of the system's enemies in time of crisis. In such imagery standards of civility may be thrown in the waste-basket, especially when the nation is at war. The enemy may be portrayed as a great beast.

The same projection of message, one supposes, should be reflected in artistic technique, that is, drawing style. A little more slippage creeps into this relationship. Perhaps a shocking message may gain more viewers at one point in history, if it is presented in a more conservative dress. One thinks of Art Young, the conservative turned radical and his drawings during the Republican twenties. Instead of the slashing lines or brooding blacks and streaky grays that often characterize radical cartoons, someone once suggested, many of Young's black-and-white anti-capitalist cartoons, like the one noted earlier in this chapter, looked as if Young had been scared at age ten by a medieval woodcut. There have also been those with a modernist artistic style who peddle a fairly cozy system-supporting line.

Nevertheless, for most artists some tendency does exist to harmonize drawing techniques with content. In the rigidly loyalist Victorian age, style leaned heavily to the dignified representational, and presentation was static and with the lines properly falling into their appropriate crosshatch ranks. As comment moves toward greater questioning of the system, cartoons also become more caricaturelike, veering even to the grotesque among the radically disaffected. Outright ugliness may be cultivated, a slapdash technique may be nurtured, and dramatic effects in color, action, perspective, and form striven for. A vigorous active line will, of course, be stressed over the more staid and dignified style.

Since cartooning, even of a political sort, is an attention-getting art, one cannot press this aspect of artistic technique too far. Style in harmony with message remains a relative matter, but the general tendency is to combine a lively art with a lively message. At the extremes of bigoted patriotism and open subversiveness, the expectations I have described are most clear. At the skeptical center there is more variation, but the broad mass of democratic cartoonists tend to choose a loose comic-strip form that can project some deference mixed with irreverence.

The combination of imagery and artistic technique creates an emotional mood that gives a cartoonist's message its real impact and power. This mood can imply that a radical overthrow of the system is justified, or that at any cost the system must be preserved. In democratic societies it more commonly implies that the administration has been up to its usual incompetencies but that with a little good sense and goodwill the matter will be partly straightened out. Maybe.

Political Cartoons — A Shorthand Typology

The combined impact of imagery and artistry in a projected mood, and even of picture of reality and message, can be put in shorthand form. The historian W. A. Coupe, in one of the most enlightening essays on the subject, isolated three general classes of political cartoon: the descriptive, laughing satirical, and destructive satirical.[7] The classification is based on the artist's purpose. The last two are distinguished by whether the incongruity the artist points to between real and ideal, which is at the heart of all satire, is presented in a humorous and playful way or in a way that projects hatred and loathing.

The descriptive cartoon appears to be almost neutral in that the cartoonist is saying little more than "this is the way it is." But such a cartoon seems to me often to add this very relevant political comment, that the main variables in the situation can probably not be changed much by political activity. John Tenniel's "Dropping the Pilot" as noted, can be so interpreted. My conclusion is that a descriptive job is useful to convey a suggestion of fatalism, especially when it dwells on those tragic flaws which are built into all individuals or nations, which must be accepted as the mysterious givens of life. I am, of course, suggesting that descriptive cartoons are especially suited to the expression of status quo viewpoints.

The descriptive kind of cartoon category may also, I think, be expanded to include political cartoons whose primary purpose seems to be only a light moment of entertainment. In the 1830s HB portrayed the prime minister asleep in the midst of a parliamentary discussion. He thus suggested an appeal to a common humanity in all of us, and is suggesting that the prime minister, despite his exalted position, is fallible and human just like the rest of us. Essentially this is system supporting. Almost every cartoonist has drawn one or two of these on a mellow day.

Most political cartoons in democracies are of the laughing-satire type. They accept the legitimacy of those they criticize. Some thus doubt that their criticism can do much good. We do know that their political targets frequently collect the cartoons and display them on their walls. The cartoons are aimed at reform of administration rather than destruction of the system. They are a corrective in keeping politicians honest without chastising them severely. A kind of chaffing tone, with some bite, suggests the message "You have these faults and we wish you would reform, but whether you do or do not, we will still support and perhaps even like you." This comes close to the portrayal of individuals in great humanist art, as in Chaucer's Prologue or in Shakespeare and Dickens. It gives politicians a little of the business, but leaves few festering wounds. One gets overtones of the attitude expressed in the phrase "You are punished by, rather than for, your sins." The trick that the best cartoonists manage is to keep the laughter up so high that they can slice unusually deep. As one put it, the subjects of the rapierlike attacks do not know what happened until they turn their heads. Herblock cartoons especially fit this merry mood, as when he drew Republican Senators as comic but somewhat sinister undertakers of social welfare or civil rights programs.

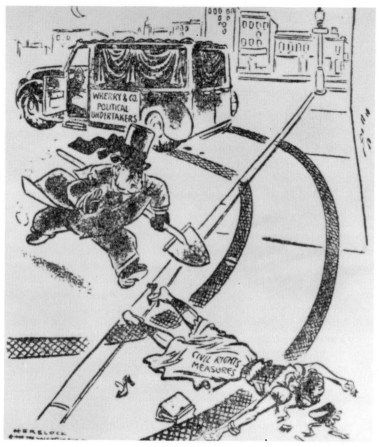

35. Herblock: "Tsk Tsk! Another Suicide." March 1949. The Washington *Post* from *The Herblock Book* (**Beacon Press, 1952**).

I would also add, as a variant of this type of cartoon, drawings that are somewhat more serious but are critical in about the same measure as laughing satire, such as some of Daniel Fitzpatrick's efforts. They do not seem to me different enough to justify setting up a separate category.

Destructive satire is distinguished from laughing satire not only in that the drawing is meant to be cruel and to hurt, but in that the message says unmistakably "These creatures that I criticize are not human; they should not be allowed to exist." When one begins to draw one's opponents as apes or as capitalists with dollar signs or radicals with wild looks and bombs, one starts in the direction of this kind of satire, but it can still be all in good fun, somewhat like the way the fiendish villain is depicted in melodrama. The real stab comes when the artist truely means that there is little or no hope for redemption for the society or for the immediate political targets, and the hate shines through, uncontrolled and slightly insane. The message then is "It is a rotten world, and it is every man for himself." George Grosz's drawings of the German Junker have, and not, I think, surprisingly, much more of this quality than even the USSR drawings on the Wall Street stereotype. The type is naturally favored by those who favor violent solutions to the problems of rulership. It was also characteristic of cartoons of World War I by the Allies against the Germans, such as those by the Englishman E. J. Sullivan (Fig. 92) and the American W. A. Rogers (Fig. 98).

To this list I add an additional type of drawing: the glorifying. This makes a god of the subject. It is hard to get away with in our cynical times. Examples are those

36. Homer Davenport : Uncle Sam : "He's good enough for me." 1904. New York *Evening Mail.*

wartime pictures of Edith Cavell-type nurses and the various idealizations of the radical working man, the tiller of the soil, or good old what's his name, the noble (and perhaps a little stupid) martyr to the cause. These kinds of cartoons fade fast, almost as soon as one can imagine the subject off screen, picking his nose. The only really successful political cartoons of this type I can think of offhand are Homer Davenport on TR, "He's good enough for me," or more artistically, Ben Shahn's "Sacco and Vanzetti" poster. The Davenport served as a very successful campaign document. But it was effectively parodied by Charles Macauley, who showed a coy TR in 1912 slapping the shoulder of candidate Theodore Roosevelt. (For another see Fig. 139) The work by Shahn, because it mixed in some humanizing realism, far outlasted more stilted glorification efforts on the same subject, such as, for example, that by Art Young.

These types of approach can be related to the message projected, using the legitimacy scheme outlined previously, but one should allow for shifts of position by artists as the community they defend fares. The descriptive and laughing satire are drawn when the cartoonist supports in general the current distribution of power, status, and material resources, or at least does not expect very much change for the better. Destructive satire is reserved for when the system's legitimacy is in question or has been decided in the negative, or when the artist is attacking what he or she regards as a particularly virulent enemy of the system or of the way of life he or she cherishes. It is the approach most favored by revolutionaries of the right or left. Destructive satire, however, may also be used against a society's enemies by one who defends the system. All types of critics unfortunately try the heroic from time to time, especially when a leader goes on to that great election campaign in the sky.

An artist may favor one or another type of cartoon and over time try all of them. Most democratic political cartoons are laughing or serious satire, or descriptive and entertaining. But when a cherished group comes under attack, bitterness can creep in, as "Ding" Darling's farm-sale cartoon illustrates so well.

The most difficult position to draw from is that of radical reformer who works within the system's rules and is looking for the appropriate style of presentation. No approach quite fits. At the height of the Black urban riots Jules Feiffer drew Lyndon Johnson in a way that he felt he had struck a devastating blow, one that once and for all nailed LBJ to the wall. Only the next day, when he opened his mail, there, to his dismay, was his target requesting the original.[8] On occasion those in favor of radical reform within the system have crossed the line into destructive violence. More frequently their efforts at destructive criticism are treated by targets as laughing satire. But David Low ruefully reports that in his case this was not always true of the target's friends and supporters. They resented his darts directed at their favorite.[9]

A Closing Note

The central role of the political cartoonist is, like that of other critics, to form a communication link between the governors and the governed. The artist's message are an assessment of how things are going and, more basically, whether the distribution of benefits in a society is morally defensible.

The guiding values in making this assessment, I suggested, was not a well-thought-out political ideology, but rather a community within the body politic that the cartoonist felt to be especially worthy of receiving benefits in the society. The assessment is transmitted in three ways: the picture of reality that suggests the effects

37. Jay "Ding" Darling : The Situation on the Farms. 1932. Des Moines *Register.*

of present events on the favored community, the specific message that suggests what should be done, and — through artistry and imagery — a mood of civility that suggests how the viewer should feel. The mood of civility projected perhaps most clearly states the whole case the cartoonist is presenting. For shorthand purposes in this book, I will use W. A. Coupe's categories to describe the projected mood: descriptive, laughing satire, and destructive satire with my addition of the heroic or glorifying.

4
Defenders of the Establishment

When a political system is regarded as legitimate by its citizens, they strongly support its leaders, accept as proper the way they are recruited, and generally support the way social, economic, and political benefits are distributed within the nation. When it was believed that God had especially selected the kings to rule, the distribution of status, power, and wealth that accompanied His regal system was accepted as right and just, even by many of the deprived. When this idea was put out on the curb for the rubbish packer, the arrangements for distributing social benefits also came to be regarded as questionable and finally as indefensible and illegitimate.

The Victorian Age in England had a system that was extremely stable, one in which acceptance of rulers and distribution of benefits seem to have been generally upheld by its citizens. This is true even though there were groups like the Chartists and reformers like Charles Dickens. Most of the public appear to have regarded the system as good and capable of improvement rather than one whose basic character was in question. The period of Victorian rule from 1837 through 1901 was thus one of basic stability amidst change, in contrast to the Georgian period that preceded it, characterized by instability.

This acceptance of the system could have been the result of brainwashed ignorance on the part of those groups least benefited, or it might have been a result of the rise in benefits across the whole system so that all citizens felt a degree of improvement; or it might have been from undue optimism about the possibilities for reform of the worst conditions, or the result of the dethronement of one ruling class and the takeover by another; or it might have been that England and her empire were at the crest of their power. All of these were characteristics of the Victorian age at its prime and they no doubt contributed to the sense of legitimacy that appears to have emerged in the public opinion of this period.

I argued earlier that cartoonists are part of the opinion-formation process of a democracy. Logically, then, the Victorian cartoonists should have shared this sense of legitimacy and shown it by beaming messages of support of the system with a style and mood reenforcing notions of stability. It is this cartoonist output we examine.

The Victorian Age

A few brief refreshers on Victorian history are in order. It was, as noted, an age of basic stability, but perhaps equally significant is that it followed an age of instability and chaos on which the major battles had been over system legitimacy. Beginning with the loss of a colonial war in America, the position of the monarchy of George III was never completely secure. The French Revolution and the ideas of republicanism it encouraged, followed by the wars of Napoleon, further encouraged political restlessness and talk of revolution. The actions of the self-indulgent George IV and of the landed aristocracy, who in the generation that followed Napoleon's defeat in 1815 burned themselves out in high living, added to the sense of crisis.

Through 1830 the tradition of mercilessly flaying the political, social, and economic system was the order of the day among journalists, and especially among cartoon print makers. One of the last of this breed, Paul Pry (William Heath) shows Prime Minister Wellington with his aide, Peel, giving John Bull a bolus or bitter pill (Irish emancipation) with all the delicacy and refinement that generally characterized the Georgian print. The vulgarity, violence, and hint of bowel trouble portrayed all fit the imagery we would anticipate in times of instability.

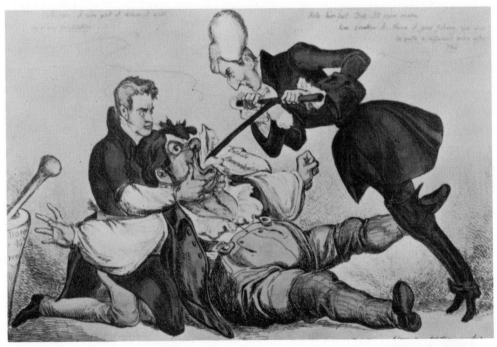

38.   William Heath (Paul Pry): Dr. Arthur and his Man Bob Giving John Bull a Bolus. April 1829.

While the Georgian age was one of conflict and challenge, it was also one of false starts and political stagnation. Only at its close did reform begin with the bill for Irish Catholic suffrage in 1829 (a move pilloried in the Heath cartoon). The Victorian age, in contrast, was also one of conflict, but not over the system — over its administration. It was nevertheless, or perhaps therefore, one of continued reform, by which I mean a marked redistribution of power, status, and economic resources. The battles of the previous age were brought to fruition without violent revolution. In 1832 the Great Reform Bill eliminated many of the rotten boroughs and effectively cut back the power of the landed aristocracy in the House in favor of the new middle-class manufacturers. In 1833 slavery in the empire was abolished. By 1834 the East India Company lost its trading monopoly and in 1835 municipal corporations were reformed and made elective. In 1837 Victoria became Queen. Her accession was greeted as a welcome change from the dissolute or mildly ineffective monarchs who had preceded her.

Under Victoria, the process of democratization continued. Her age was also one of slow retreat from the exercise of monarchical prerogatives as well as those of the nobility, and a strengthening of those of Commons. This process had begun in 1832 when William IV played with the idea of creating new peers to get the Reform Bill through the House of Lords, thus weakening its potential veto. Victoria was the last British monarch to dismiss a prime minister whose party held a majority of Commons, and this occurred early in her reign. More and more during her reign the monarch took on ceremonial functions but, as Bagehot noted, doggedly retained the important right to be consulted.

Another great redistribution of power came with the repeal in 1846 of the tariff on grain, the corn laws, and the adoption of free trade. Again the privileges of the landed aristocrat were removed, it was claimed for the general benefit of the citizens. In 1848 the Chartist agitation to further expand the electorate fizzled out. But this reform, which extended the vote to members of the working class, was adopted twenty years later by a Conservative government in 1867.

The point to be remembered is that Britain was the most advanced democracy of its time among large European nations. If its citizens felt a sense of pride and legitimacy, that opinion was not extorted under authoritarian conditions.

These political gains were accompanied by an expanding industrial system that at first brought all the miseries described by Dickens and others, but also brought, side-by-side, tremendous opportunities. Many did rise, and in time most of society felt the influence of the new prosperity.

It was also an age in which the British Empire flourished and expanded. Britons again faced a two-sided opportunity for improvement and potential for misery in the armies of the Empire. After the Crimean war, the purchase of commissions was eliminated. One could rise, but one took continued risks. In no year of Victoria's 64-year reign was England ever free of some type of border clash and some killing of its soldiers. The Army, and especially the Navy, were always required, with the Empire's steady expansion of territory reaching a peak in 1897.

But not only did England lead politically, technologically, commercially, and as a great power; it also led the world in pure science, culminating in 1859 with the devastating research of Charles Darwin. Symbolic of such leadership in the sciences is the fact that Greenwich mean time is named for the observatory in a village suburb of London.

But there were also the disenchanted, those who mounted challenges to the legitimacy of this grand pyramiding of power, wealth, and talent. A few, like the

Chartists, were internal, but they clamored for entrance into, rather than the destruction of, this Grand System. The severest challengers were largely external, and they directed their blows at the Empire. The Indians revolted in 1857, and the Irish early began their campaign of terrorism that has continued to last night's newspaper. The English Act of Union with Ireland in 1800 was designed to bring the two nations together, just as Wales and Scotland had become an integral part of Great Britain. But the barriers proved to be too great. One was religion, and it is a barrier that has never been bridged, despite a continued series of compromise measures during the Victorian age, ending with Gladstone's unsuccessful proposal for Irish Home Rule. A second barrier was economic. An English aristocracy that had lost ground at home continued to control Irish land through absentee ownership. Compromises were offered here, too, but without real success. In the end the Irish plunked for destruction of the empire system.

So, if it was an age of stability and legitimacy, it was not an age of tranquillity or of stagnation. Bitter conflict, domestic and foreign, was as characteristic of the Victorian age as of the Georgian that preceded it. Not only was agitation for a redistribution of society's prizes not diminished, but much genuine redistribution occurred. Yet all of this happened within a legal framework accepted by the British citizens. It is this attitude and the cartoonists' contribution to and interaction with it that I examine next.

Cartoonists and Stability

The Victorian age was ushered in with a new type of cartoon criticism. Biting and destructive satire was cut out, so far as domestic politics were concerned. Laughing satire, descriptive, and even heroic cartoons, all presented in a gentlemanly way, were in. This trend was true not only of content but of imagery and artistry as well. All harmonized with the overriding cartoon message: "This is a system that deserves your support."

The remarkable fact is that we can date the introduction of the new mode of criticism by a single cartoon and the subsequent work of a single cartoonist. He was of the middle class, with solid respectability, and so preferred to remain anonymous in his day, and perhaps this is significant since it suggests the ambivalent status accorded the cartoon art in Georgian times. He remained incognito for twenty years, signing his prints HB, which was presumably a double decker of his real initials, J.D. for John Doyle, though how this works out really escapes me. He is better known for his descendents than for his Irish ancestors. His son, Richard Doyle, became a political cartoonist for *Punch* and designed its famous cover, while a grandson, Sir Arthur Conan Doyle, wrote the detective stories about Sherlock Holmes.

John Doyle was an Irish Catholic and a miniature portrait painter. He was born in 1797 and emigrated to England in the 1820s, a fact of some significance for both the content and the style of his comment. His line was to preach tolerance and understanding and what he regarded as sensible reform. He was liberal enough to favor Irish emancipation and the Reform Bill of 1832, but he did not vent his spleen on those who opposed him.

Doyle's style in his first cartoon, "The Apparition," reflected his difference in approach from what was then current. The print was less exciting or violent than the usual Georgian print. Lithography fuzzed the sharp line associated with etching. The drawing gives a feeling of sketchiness and tentative statement, with an absence of bold black splotches. The figures are slightly elongated, awkward, and wooden. The action is arrested and static. The characters are all in costume proper to their exalted station, including that in which the late George Canning, the ghost, is draped. This and other HB prints, despite their artistic weakness, occasionally drop into the kind of Norman Rockwell realism that is found on *Saturday Evening Post* covers of the 1920s and 1930s. Doyle was indeed a friendly fellow, even though his cartoon artistry was, perhaps purposely, severely limited.

39.   John Doyle (H.B.) : The Apparition. March 1829.

His first cartoon was appropriately on Irish emancipation. He shows the ghost of the wise Canning gently chiding Wellington and Peel and their colleagues for not having joined him earlier in giving the Irish the vote. It is dated March 1829, three years before the Reform Bill and eight years before Victoria's accession. It was printed one month before the Paul Pry print of the bolus, which suggests that the two currents in public opinion jogged along side by side.

It appears that Doyle both sensed and helped stimulate a new mood of civility. Within three years the Doyle style was to dominate the market. Heath's output dropped to no prints and he appears to have been driven to another trade. The more violent style of the Georgians still crops up in some of the political drawings in *Punch* during its first two years, as late as 1841-43, but it is like the last firecrackers late at night on July 4. After John Leech and Richard Doyle took over the large political cut in *Punch*, civility came on with a rush.

What, then, characterizes the content message of the new style as we enter the age of legitimacy? In tone, it is forbearance with fellow citizens with whom one differs. It is as if people became fed up with political and social controversy as a substitute for concrete reforms. My own preferred HB cartoon is "For Auld Lang Syne," which shows a reconciliation between John Bull and the Duke of Wellington after the Duke had abandoned his opposition to the Great Reform Bill. The Duke is receiving at home in slippers and nightcap. The Duke: "Ha, my old Friend! This kindness was unexpected. Why, they told me that you were quite turned against me." John Bull: "What, I turned against *you*? Why see, we have had some differences of late and I am an obstinate old fellow although not so unreasonable as some people would make me out." Etcetera, etcetera, ending with "but come, cheer up, they say you live too low, and think too much about these D--d Politics."

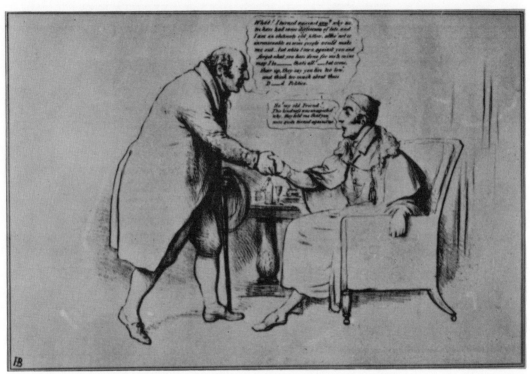

40.   John Doyle (H.B.) : "For Auld Lang Syne." December 28, 1831.

One notes that HB presents a different John Bull from the brandy-faced, ruby-nosed clod of the Heath cartoon. Here is a man of modest substance, one who has seen hard work and modestly prospered. His foremost traits seem to be bluffness, doggedness, and honest perseverance, traits not unlike those of the independent small shopkeeper. In a moment I shall trace the development of the image of John Bull through the Victorian cartoon. It seems clear that, to HB, the salt of the earth were just those hardworking, respectable types.

We note also in HB a kindlier treatment of royalty. William IV is portrayed as human in his faults as well as his virtues, rather than as a monster. He is dressed in a simple business suit and top hat, just like all the other gentlemen of the day. He is distinguished only by a single decoration on his coat, a signal to the reader that this simple bourgeois is really their king. In a cartoon, when the king's support for the

Reform Bill appeared to be faltering, William is presented as quizzically staring at a wall on which is painted "Reform Bill!" He asks, "Can that mean me?" Instead of cutting satire, HB adopts the more genteel humor of the pun. One is moved to sympathy for a man who happens to be king and is trying to do his best with limited talents. Such a view is consistent with a constitutional monarchy as found in the spirit of the coming age. That it should have flowed from someone who experienced the vagaries and vulgarities of the Georges is a tribute to HB's sensitivity to the potential of the future, and perhaps to his own innate kindness.

41. John Doyle (H.B.) : Handwriting upon the Wall. May 26, 1831.

Let me next subject some of HB's cartoons to closer analysis. In two of his works I have described the political event and the message, a message that, one notes, in both cases favors reform despite the gentle tones in which it is presented. The cartoons also do not hesitate sadly and gently to chide those who obstruct reform. But it is in the underlying assumptions that the presentation differs from the Georgian. HB's cartoons suggest that politics is not of life-and-death importance, that wounds can be healed and bygones be bygones. They imply that obstruction is more likely due to ignorance than to bad faith or unforgivable corruptness. They suggest that political enemies have more in common than immediate differences, since all are part of the same nation. The break between Ireland and England has not yet taken place. This message appropriately is transmitted with a mixture of the descriptive and gentle laughing satire. The artistic style and analogies used harmonize with the message.

The other fact that separates the HB prints from predecessors is that HB's either tend to represent a political scene descriptively as it probably took place, with at best only slight embellishment, or they use a domesticated analogy from the life of the country squire. Overall this means that the prints are genteel enough to be shown to children, should they ever be interested in such tame drawings.

Later generations find it hard to account for HB's popularity, because his artistry is so staid and wooden. In early Victorian times, nine volumes of 917 prints were issued. Only one brief collection of his works has been published since, and these are not in color.[1] It is not difficult to see why the tameness of HB is so easily dismissed. My own case is illustrative. In the last weeks of a summer in London, I visited an Islington bookstore and noticed a few prints for sale. I conceived the notion of buying them as gifts for political science colleagues, plus a few for myself. This began my interest in political prints and cartoons. I purchased the Paul Pry bolus cartoon at once, but only reluctantly bought "The Apparition" by HB, and did so only because no other cartoons were available. I assumed that I could give it to someone, if I could not find prints for sale elsewhere. I seem to remember also that it was priced below the more exciting Paul Pry's, and at the time I thought rightly so.

HB's immediate impact was no doubt the result of his good manners, a trait then largely absent from fifty years of English political prints. Up until then the cartoon critic was supposed to aspire to getting a reaction similar to that achieved by hitting the reader across the face with a slimy, wet, snapping alligator. HB did not compromise his political position but eschewed such confrontation. He preferred to present what a nameless someone of a later age has described as a low profile. A few other HB cartoons suggest how he developed this approach and still maintained something of a critical attitude. For example, in a cartoon "The Way to Bamboozle John Bull," John Bull is giving vent to hollow laughter at a dinner with the Whig ministers at which new taxes of 1834 are under discussion. A drawing less full of sweetness and light, "It's No Go," shows an exasperated John Bull as a squire with a stick making John Russell return the apples he has stolen from the tree, a reference to a changed clause in the 1832 Reform Bill that HB interpreted as restricting the electorate more than the original version. John Bull has the same look in his eye as the farmer would have for the neighbor boy caught in this act — a look of firmness and determination to see justice done, but not a call for the eternal damnation of those he opposes.

The HB drawings had their own growing audience, but the habits of the Georgian age persisted and only gradually disappeared. The last separately printed and mass-produced prints in the old style were a series by HB's publisher, McLean. These were illustrated by Robert Seymour, the talented artist whose curse it is to be remembered for only two facts: that Dickens was recruited to write a story line for his sporting prints, and that Seymour committed suicide before that project, known as *The Pickwick Papers*, was well under way. Seymour's earlier political prints for McLean show the same slashing style as Heath's and others'. It appears that between 1829 and perhaps 1833 the demand for both types of prints coincides. But at that point a decline in the Georgian style sets in with no mistake. Robert Seymour's drawings for a new journal, *Figaro in London*, are the first real editorial cartoons as we have come to know them. They are still reformist, but they are simple and dramatic, with a punch. They lasted but two short years, from 1832 to 1834, after which Seymour was replaced by Robert Cruikshank. The last of the radical prints, those of Charles Grant, were privately printed in a crude style. They document atrocities against the laboring man. They are difficult and artistically unattractive, characterized by heavy blacks, caricature to the point of the grotesque, with long perorations by each of the many characters on stage, and heavy allegory. It is the end of a dying breed, the Georgian print.

The death of the separately produced print can be laid to the possibilities presented for magazine mass-produced art. But three facts suggest that this does not account for the change of style: (1) HB stuck to prints and remained popular, so much so that the London *Times* devoted part of its columns each month to a descriptive resumé of his newly issued work. He successfully continued to publish prints through 1851, long after the market for other political prints had disappeared; (2) the first mass-produced magazine in France was in the Georgian style, *Le Caricature*, edited by Philipon, hence one would assume that the same style might prove popular in England as well. This was the assumption of the editors of the many short-lived journals of the thirties, and the emphasis is on the words *short-lived*; (3) *Punch*, which was subtitled *The London Charivari*, after a Philipon successor, began with a radical program but with an editorial announcement that it would strive for civility in its columns. Nevertheless, its artistic output was uneven. Many of its early artists combined atrocious artistry with clumsy polemic, Hammerton's work providing a major exception. During this period of uncertainty, the firm was sold to a firm of businessmen — printers Bradbury and Evans. Within a short time *Punch* cartoons began to reflect the HB blend of good taste and increasingly mild liberalism. It is to the *Punch* political cuts that we turn next.

42.   Robert J. Hammerton : Capital and Labour. July 29, 1843. *Punch.*

The Punch Cartoons

Punch brought the big cut to Britain — a full-page, black-and-white drawing with no printing on the back, just like a print. It came to be regarded by the staff as an attempt to crystallize each week an opinion on "the week's chief idea, situation or event, ...truthfully representative of the best prevailing feeling of the nation, of its soundest common sense, and of its most deliberate judgment — a judgment possibly to be revised in the light of subsequent experience, but at the moment of its publication seriously formed, albeit humorously set down and portrayed."[2] The significant point is that the big cut was almost from the beginning a cartoon thought up by the whole staff at its weekly dinner after considerable discussion. Then it was drawn by the artist.

In the first three years of *Punch* a total of ten artists was used. By 1844 one of these, John Leech, was joined by Richard Doyle, HB's son, and these two drew all but a few cartoons through 1850. The artistic talent improved, but the style stayed loose. In 1850 Richard Doyle resigned over the magazine's anti-Catholicism, and John Tenniel, later the illustrator of *Alice in Wonderland*, took his place. Tenniel and Leech drew

43.   John Leech : The Poor Man's Friend. February 22, 1845. *Punch.*

the cartoon until Leech's death in 1864. After that Tenniel continued alone, with only a few substitutes from time to time, through 1901. A second cartoon was drawn by Linley Sambourne from the 1880s on. The succession of *Punch* cartoonists after Sambourne included L. Raven-Hill, F. H. Townsend, and Bernard Partridge, the latter of whom ended the line in 1945. Thus artistic production of the cartoon for a hundred years was concentrated in a few hands and the product maintained a striking sameness in style and content through all those years. Tenniel's cartoons were sharp and wooden and matter-of-fact, with some improvement in artistry over HB's.

In content, the early *Punch* cartoons, particularly those of Hammerton, were radical criticism of the distribution of economic benefits. Both Tenniel and Leech drew cartoons such as those expressing sympathy with the poor seamstress caught in the toils of an expanding capitalistic system. But as Susan and Asa Briggs note, a Leech cartoon of the later fifties shows a different kind of seamstress, one dreaming of the ball Cinderella style.[3] By then the system of distribution was less at issue.

In later years of the nineteenth century the distribution of honor and wealth within England is also taken pretty much for granted in Tenniel's work, as befits a system that deals out rewards on merit. One of the remarkable facts is how few of Tenniel's cartoons show even mildly unfavorable conditions as the result of system rules or leader action. The effects of incompetence in Crimea are an exception. More cartoons praise advances or deal with how enemies of the system are to be handled.

Women's righters are continuously denigrated and strikers are advised not to destroy the commercial goose that lays the golden eggs. Anarchists are regarded as madmen who are outside the accepted society. The problem raised by the Chartists, and the Bright proposal to extend the ballot to the working class, are portrayed in *Punch* as creating a Frankenstein monster, but in time they are reluctantly agreed to. One might argue that both impulses were probably reasonable — extension of the suffrage did in the end destroy the Victorian middle-class society, but not to have given in gracefully would also have brought destruction. Aside from these issues, the

44.   James Gillray : John Bull Taking a Luncheon, or British Cooks Cramming Old Grumble Gizzard with Good Cheer. October 24, 1798.

90

content of the cartoons concentrates heavily on foreign affairs and in these matters, *Punch* assumed, all sensible Englishmen were in agreement about the value of Empire.

To demonstrate how the HB mode of criticism took hold on *Punch* and later on its rivals, I will examine the imaginative handling in *Punch* cartoons of three symbols for the nation: John Bull, Britannia, and the British Lion. Each tells us how Englishmen in this age of legitimacy came to view themselves.

45. George Woodward and Thomas Rowlandson : The Head of the Family in Good Humour. 1809.

We begin with John Bull. The first views are by Gillray in 1798 (John Bull Taking a Luncheon) and George Woodward and Thomas Rowlandson in 1809 (The Head of the Family). George Cruikshank in 1814 (Peace and Plenty) draws a similar John Bull. One can see where Paul Pry in 1829 got his model. The crude and foul-mouthed clod of the lower classes who is gulping down his food of battleships is the same bleary-eyed, loud-mouthed oaf whom William Heath had portrayed getting a bolus. He is made to be the butt of other's jokes and schemes. Rowlandson and George Cruikshank present the same bloated, blotched, and unhealthy figure. With HB, John Bull loses his hangover and moves up the social scale to the honest, self-employed and self-sufficient, small merchant or village squire. He now has a no-nonsense air about him. In the early cartoons in *Punch* in 1841, John Bull, if anything, slides down a bit socially, and takes on the slow-burn look of the old-time movie star who specialized in that art form — was he really named Edward, no Edgar, Kennedy? But as the years move on, John Bull gets on. By the sixties he has become the bluff, commonsensical successful merchant and businessman, no longer a rounder but thoroughly domesticated, occasionally even presented with a Mrs. Bull in tow. He is a man of substance, a little old-fashioned, but one who can be trusted, practical and bustling.

46.   Archibald S. Henning : The Modern Ceres. February 26, 1842. *Punch.*

The change in Britannia is even more startling. Two of the early *Punch* cartoons by different artists show two versions of a haggish shrew. One by the first *Punch* artist, Archibald Henning, is reprinted here. Again, under Leech and later Tenniel, Britannia becomes more matronly, more rounded in her curves under those Roman togas, and ten thousand percent more awe inspiring. When angry, she is a majestic but beautiful woman, not to be crossed. For grand occasions she can be wheeled out for the proper ceremonial touch. In all, she has risen to a fine and noble ethereal plane in just a short span of years.

The rise of the lion to nobility is even more rapid, but his climb can be placed almost exclusively at John Tenniel's door. The lion of even Leech is a butt, a comic figure who gets his nose tweaked and looks motheaten and a little smelly. Tenniel shows his possibilities in one of the first *Punch* cartoons he signed, the British lion grieving over the death of the Duke of Wellington. In 1854 another lion is shown chomping to get at the Russians in the Crimea. But the full magnificence of the noble

47.   John Tenniel : Sir Rowland LeGrand. March 19, 1864. *Punch.*

beast bursts forth only in the famous 1857 Sepoy Rebellion cartoon (Fig. 29). When an Englishman opened to that center spread, a thrill shot through him. This was indeed an image to aspire and live up to. It is perhaps symptomatic of our own condition that center spreads now serve different artistic purposes.

That such images were not the exclusive line of *Punch* is shown in the drawings in its most vigorous magazine competitors — William Proctor and William Bowcher in the conservative-oriented *Judy*; the more critical Matt Morgan, whose best work was done in the aptly named *Tomahawk:* and Tom Merry in St. Stephen's *Review*. All use the same symbolic figures. The same sturdy John Bull, dignified Britannia, and splendid king of the beasts are surrogate for the British nation and its people in their works too. These journals were among those to dominate the cartoon market and they all shared a high-minded image of their nation and its destiny, just as, generations before, print makers had shared less-honored images.[4] Even the Socialist drawings of the children's-book artist Walter Crane, as late as 1896 borrowed this high-flown imagery.

The handling of royalty follows the same pattern, except that Victoria checkmated the cartoonists from her middle age on. The first *Punch* drawings portray a girl in her early twenties in all her innocence, with all goodwill for her subjects, always ready to encourage self-improvement. With the coming of Albert, there is some chaffing at his bustling activities, but by the 1850s Victoria and her spouse have arrived as valuable stage properties, well suited for patting on their heads the children in hospital beds or coal miners, and assuring one and all of the nation's genuine interest in them and their welfare. Let me add that this is no small service to a nation, as *Punch* and others discovered when the Queen retreated into seclusion at Albert's death in 1861. At this

48. John Leech : Ridiculous Exhibition; or Yankee-Noodle Putting His Head into the British Lion's Mouth. May 2, 1846. *Punch.*

49.   John Tenniel : September XIV, MDCCCLII. October 2, 1852. *Punch.*

point Victoria disappears from the *Punch* cartoon until the middle seventies. By this time, as was commented on by the artists themselves, it was difficult to catch the right spark of ennobling presence and harmonize it with the reality of a somewhat pathetic, strong-willed but still admirable, little old lady. But the *Punch* artists tried hard to create someone to be properly revered, as did the cartoonists of the competing journals. No one succeeded very well.

50.   John Proctor : The Great Eclipse of 1868. August 28, 1868. *Judy.*

The HB touch was also preserved for the nation's political leaders. All are accorded honor because all have a station in the legitimate polity. Like HB, the artists, of course, had their separate preferences on policy and individuals, but no legitimate politician was outside the pale. *Punch* was at the beginning particularly harsh with Lord Brougham and John Bright, but with the growing influence of William Makepeace Thackeray and John Leech at its table and the death of Douglas Jerrold in 1857, the journal moved to a more mildly critical position. Politically the cartoonists favored Gladstone and all of his heavenly works, except for some reservations about his

51. Walter Crane : From *Cartoons for the Cause,* **1896.**

foreign policy. *Judy* in the same way reverenced Disraeli and took every opportunity of pointing out how W.E.G.'s foolishness got the nation into difficulties, particularly with its foreign enemies.

In the art of both journals there is a gentleness with the loyal opposition that flows back directly to HB. Domestic political opponents were no longer treated as creatures of Satan, but as misguided and often amusing in their wrongheadedness, and as fellow Englishmen.

Cartoonists began to favor drawings of their own political heroes in the medieval armor of knights. The heroic style was presented and accepted with a deadpan seriousness incongruous in our day.

97

52.   John Tenniel : The Queen's Year! January 16, 1897. *Punch.*

But laughing satire also was used effectively, even on one's heroes, but always on one's domestic opponents. In a number of his best-known works, Tenniel gives Disraeli a playful cuffing in a manner largely unknown to Gillray. Tenniel, as a gentlemanly kind of in-house joke, parodies his own drawing of the Peri from his "serious" illustrations for *Lalla Rookh.* This Persian angel, excluded from Paradise until penance is accomplished, is made to represent Disraeli at that moment when he achieves the prime minister's office for the first time. Another illustrates Disraeli's remark about Darwin to the effect that he, with wings attached, is on the side of the angels rather than the apes. A third salutes a winking Disraeli sphinx on the acquisition of Suez Canal shares. In "Pas de Deux," Disraeli and Salisbury are in a ridiculous Gilbert and Sullivan ballet step after the Congress of Vienna's "Peace with Honor" treaty. Nor was *Punch* above twitting Gladstone — for example, in the waiter scene in which John Bull grumbles about humble pie. Yesterday and again today, Gladstone, the waiter, answers, "Yes, sir — No, sir — That were GENEVA humble

53.   John Tenniel : The Broken Covenant. "We cannot close this book and say we
will look into it no more." Mr. Gladstone's Speech, April 27. May 9, 1885. *Punch.*

pie, sir. This is BERLIN humble pie, sir!!" A particularly delicious cartoon is that in
which Disraeli and Gladstone comment on each other's recently published literary
works. Gladstone: "Hmm, Flippant." Disraeli: "Ha! Prosy!" All of these take on the
tone of gentlemanly joshing with a little bite underneath.

In general *Judy* was less skillful and more heavy-handed in dealing with the
opposition, but it still had its occasional light touches. Proctor shows Gladstone as a
cross-legged veteran beggar titled "An Old Crimean Hero — Out of Place," selling
Bulgarian atrocity stories. Another *Judy* cartoon shows him playing Hamlet with
soulful gestures in the "I did love you once" scene, with the pope cast as Ophelia.

But all was not sweetness and light as in HB. The same gentle treatment was not
accorded either domestic or foreign enemies of the system. Here the artists achieve a

54.   John Tenniel : Paradise and the Peri. February 28, 1874. *Punch.*

more biting and sometimes even destructive satire. Mob rule personified, or Anarchy, was dealt with by a stern Britannia armed occasionally with a cat-o'-nine-tails. Law and order must be preserved. As L. Percy Curtis, Jr., illustrates, the Irish in Tenniel's drawings became progressively more like apes as their outbreaks of terrorism increased.[5] A different but also unattractive presentation was accorded the cigar-chewing, upstart Yankee by Leech (review Fig. 48) and also Tenniel. In 1860 the characteristics were transferred to Lincoln (with cigar removed). As late as 1909 an American, William S. Walsh, was still steamed enough over Tenniel's Civil War cartoons, especially the one in which Lincoln is portrayed as a treed coon, to write a book denouncing them.[6]

Other nations were usually presented in terms of what might be called their

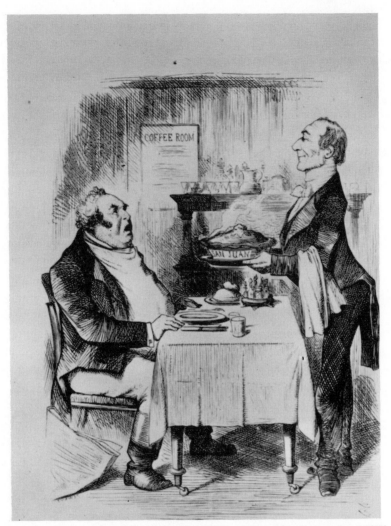

55. John Tenniel : "Humble Pie." Mr. Bull. "Humble pie again, William! — You gave me that yesterday!" Headwater. "Yes, sir — No, sir — That were GENEVA humble pie, sir. This is BERLIN humble pie, sir!!" November 9, 1872. *Punch*.

stereotype stage characters in melodrama as presented to an English music-hall audience. Napoleon III was often the dapper but occasionally menacing Frenchman, as in the revolting "Eagle in Love," in which Eugénie clips his claws. Russia is Nicholas with all his uniformed pomp, or the clumsy bear who can injure. Germany perhaps comes off best as the thick-headed Dutch boy who grows really menacing only in the nineties.

But interestingly, every nation also had its more admirable side to be appealed to. Perhaps *Punch* took to heart Palmerston's famous axiom: "Britain has no permanent friends, we have no permanent enemies, we only have permanent interests...." Every

56.   John Tenniel : The Eagle in Love. February 5, 1853. *Punch.*

nation, even opponents such as the Irish, has his good and noble "feminine" self along with a baser "masculine" self. Just as John Bull is the practical Sancho for Britannia's high-minded Quixote, so the Irish ape or bomb-thrower is tied like a Siamese twin to noble, grieving Hibernia, or the tobacco-chewing Yankee to the inspiring, if always somewhat soulful clinging vine called Columbia. The feminine contingents in effect perform as lifelong and long-suffering helpmates of their often revolting spouses; except, of course, for John Bull and Britannia, where both partners have different but admirable sets of character traits. This permits *Punch* to call a nation to account one week and then, a week later, appeal to its better national self, which one hopes exists in all of us, and extend the olive branch of tolerance. Thus one can practice both a little realpolitik and highmindedness. Both the stern disciplinarian and the understanding sympathy for error harmonize with the superior moral role that the

British see themselves playing on the world stage. From this knowledge Englishmen may derive an inner satisfaction that a special position is only Britain's due as she dutifully assumes the leadership of the world of the nineteenth century. It is the burden of responsibility that the great civilizer of the less fortunate must cheerfully bear.

How Representative Is Punch?

How can I be sure that the cartoons I have described were representative of Victorian opinion? Let me first marshall some of the evidence to the contrary. *Punch* was a magazine designed especially for the upper-middle and middle classes. Its readership was far from the greatest of its day. Thackeray at the time pointed out that there were a number of working-class journals with far larger circulations. How then can what *Punch* published be regarded as representative of more than a very selective opinion?

The same can also be said of HB. For a time his cartoons were in vogue, perhaps through 1837 and the accession of Victoria. Soon, because of their lack of sparkle, their popularity declined, though he continued to find a market for their publication through 1851. They too were drawn for a select audience of the middle and upper-middle class who read the *Times* and could afford such productions. Their press run was even more limited than that of *Punch*.

Yet this selective audience in that society was not all disadvantageous. We note that HB, *Punch*, and also *Judy* had the ear of those who held social, economic, and political power and set the tone of Victorian society. At least one end of the interaction process was securely nailed down. Whether *Punch* cartoons reached the broad masses below the lower middle class is in doubt; that all of these artists reached the groups that formed the ruling elite can not be seriously questioned. What they reached, however, was, until 1867, the most important segment of the electorate.

Second, they reached those in this broad public most concerned with social and political questions and most likely to influence the leaders — the politically effective. Leaders of the established parties and even of the Chartists were from this stratum — the group that can be called the fairly bright middle class. This status group determined the political trends of Victorian society. It had ties upward as well as down into the working class. In a democracy, as Aristotle observed, it is this stratum that gives substance to state policy. In Victorian England it counted a good deal more politically than did the far more numerous nonvoting working class. Public policy was in harmony with the views of *Punch* and its sister journals on basic matters, and it appears that these journals reflected rather accurately the mood of the middle classes.

We can also deduce one further piece of evidence of this influence. No contrary cartoon output existed for fifty years. The Georgian type of cartoon disappeared by the early 1840s and did not surface again until the nineties. When a more mocking cartoon did reappear then, it came in the rather timid efforts of Cynicus (J. Martin Anderson). We know of no such political cartoons in the mass media, nor have underground cartoons of this sort been unearthed during the heart of Victorian times. What we find in *Punch*'s competitors is an imitation of *Punch*. It is as difficult to find even a mildly subversive cartoon at the height of the Victorian age as to find one in the gentle HB style at the height of the Georgian period. At the same time, what was in harmony with this mood of gentlemanly tolerance flourished. While the lively Georgian print died out completely as a commercial venture by 1832-34, HB, even while uninspiring in artistic technique, could survive and make a good living for twenty more years, itself an indication of his acceptance by dominant public opinion.

Finally, we have the evidence of the lives of cartoonists themselves. The Georgian cartoonists were characterized by lives filled not infrequently with the tragedy of alcoholism, insanity, suicide, and poverty. Their biographies read like a text book in personal or social disorganization. With the advent of HB, cartooning becomes the trade of respectable gentlemen, so much so that one of the talented, William Newman, was used widely in *Punch* but, because of his lower-class manners, was never invited to join the table. He emigrated to America, where he continued with some success to produce ungentlemanly political satire. With the advent of the Victorian age, the artists and the communities they cherished had shifted. Cartoonists were no longer marginal men, but a new breed accepted in polite society.

All of these facts suggest that the message of the Victorian cartoon had a distinctive mood of its own that was indeed supported by the dominant public opinion of the day. In few periods of modern history has there been such a harmony of views in the midst of conflict. With all its unattractiveness and under-the-surface miseries, all of its artistic bad taste as symbolized in the awe-inspiring, awful Royal Albert Memorial, a system that could inspire this spirit of loyalty under democratic forms should still receive some twinge of admiration from us moderns.

Stable Systems in Modern Democracies

Perhaps a more interesting question is whether a legitimate polity, society, and economy can exist in modern times, where critics seem bent on making reputations by moralizing every hurt (Max Weber's phrase), no matter how inconsequential. My question of course assumes a democratic society. That a kind of paean of legitimacy wafted out of China, when TV crews visited it with President Richard Nixon, seems unquestionable. Those smiling faces at the airports, those men and women sweeping the streets with branches, those earnest students — all seemed to see themselves as part of a system to which loyalty should be freely accorded. They all had religion. But China is in fact a tightly controlled totalitarian system, a closed one living in isolation, which has only recently stamped out serious revolutionary conflicts that went to the point of civil war and ended in the mysterious disappearance and death of its leader's chosen successor. The question rephrased is: Can legitimacy by sustained in modern democratic nations?

I believe that I can illustrate legitimacy in other societies besides that of Victorian England. For the period since the Civil War and up until Vietnam, the United States seems to have had such a society. Such too were the systems of other former British colonies, Canada, Australia, and New Zealand, and while language creates a barrier for examining cartoons, so too, probably, were Switzerland, the low countries, and Scandinavia.

In the cartoons of these nations, until recently, one finds an honoring of national symbols and leaders side by side with arguments for redistributive justice in respect to the working class or oppressed minorities, but few bitter-end struggles or the kind of mindless baiting of rulers that characterized Georgian England or the Weimar Republic. What distinguished these modern democracies from Victorian England was the healthy doses of ungentlemanly skepticism commonly present in the comments of its critics. There was less worshipfulness in cartoons and a trifle more wholesome vulgarity, and more laughing satire — a mood that is a little more human and less uplifted. I would argue that it is a mood healthier and more appropriate for a democracy than the tendency of Victorian times to confuse the system with the realm of the heavenly hosts.

But since 1964, in most democracies, the mood has clearly changed, with attacks on the system and its leaders and its rules of distribution becoming more bitter and more destructive. In the underground press at the height of Vietnam, and sometimes slopping over into the traditional media, there appeared attacks whose tone was one of high condemnation not unlike what is found in the Georgian print. At a less intense level, it became faddish in the mass media freely to attack what was the old Establishment. Whoever still thinks it has been easier in the last decade to defend Wall Street or General Motors than to attack them seems to me to lack a certain quality of insight. Yet we may possibly be heading for a new period of redistribution of benefits similar to 1832, with controversy becoming more muted and politics regaining some measure of civility. One hopes so.

The Victorian System: A Closing Note

I have tried to show a system whose legitimacy was freely supported by the public opinion of its citizens, in this case that of nineteenth-century Britain. Despite the continued presence of conflict and some very practical redistribution of benefits, there was an underlying mood of self-satisfaction and self-approval, as evidenced by its cartoons. The nation was viewed as moving upward rather than in decline.

This was reflected in the stock figures representing the nation, but also in the more humane handling of fellow citizens with whom the cartoonist might on occasion disagree. Playful satire, with an occasional rapierlike sting, replaced the meat-axe approach to political comment. My own opinion is that this mood produced some great satire and some great cartoons — a good many indeed that should be as lovingly collected as the colorful prints of an earlier day.

The fiercest cartoons, and the ones most nearly approaching the earlier tradition, were those portraying this beloved system's enemies, foreign and sometimes domestic. Few reached the revolting depth of Gillray, who portrays "sans coulottes" eating other Frenchmen's flesh, nor did they completely damn most of their enemies to Hell. Nevertheless, many were portrayals that the hero who was singled out would not necessarily care to place among the studio portraits on the shawl draped over the living-room piano for the edification of the offspring or visitors. For a few of these, *Punch* even earned a ban in a foreign nation for a period; for others, only an undying hate. From the Irish they received perhaps the most sincere tribute, imitation and an attempt to erase the hated image with different and more noble presentations of the Irish patriot in the Time of Troubles.

For the student of trends in public opinion, the case of HB presents special interest. He caught and portrayed the new Victorian mood perhaps a half-dozen-or-more years before it became general: one year before George IV had for the last time indulged himself in whatever took his fancy at the moment, that is to say, died; three years before the Reform Bill; and eight years before Victoria demonstrated what royalty could contribute to a self-approving but earnestly striving-to-improve nation. As late as the beginning of *Punch* in 1841, hangovers of the old style of drawing were still about, but not for long. To suggest that HB wholly created the mood would be folly. To suggest that he contributed nothing to its creation would likewise be silly. He appears to have found in himself this new tolerance, and by testing (note his insistence on preserving anonymity) he found the attitude shared in others.

Alternatively, we may imagine what would happen if John Tenniel found an accommodating medium and attempted to portray the Sepoy lion in the *Punch* or *Private Eye* of the 1970s. It would be like trying to revive the lady's bustle — no, that just might be possible — like trying to revive the hand-crank auto. The artist cannot create the mood in a mass journal when the makings are not there. He or she can only test and see what the response is, and then supplement and encourage.

I next discussed the question of whether such cartoons were representative of Victorian opinion and concluded that they were. I finally examined the question of whether, given current internal struggles and the widespread influence of mass media such as television, democracies could again create systems widely regarded by citizens as legitimate. I optimistically and fearlessly concluded that they could, and even that they very well might again soon.

Legitimacy in Other Systems

I have defined authoritarianism as a system ripe for conflict over legitimacy — that is, a system held together by force of dubious power. The old elite still control many of the institutional leadership posts, but they are under attack from other groups and not wholly able to suppress dissent. Even more important, some of its own members, usually the young heirs, doubt the legitimacy of the system from which they benefit, and so either defect, are half-hearted in its defense, or go in for thinly veiled types of self-destruction. We have already noted that such systems seem to produce few cartoonist defenders. I reserve till the next chapter their attackers.

The case of the totalitarian system, as previously noted, is the reverse. Almost the first step a totalitarian government takes is to exercise complete control over the mass media. It is now the media's job to proclaim the legitimacy of the new system. The instances we have of totalitarian cartoons suggest that they devote their full efforts to that end.

Surprisingly, there are few Nazi cartoons that survive in collected form. Despite the cluck-clucking among social scientists about Herr Goebbels's early experiments in propaganda and mass brainwashing, no one appears to have thought it important to collect the Nazi cartoons or study how the Nazi cartoonists portrayed Hitler, his enemies, or the German people. About the only extensive collection available was one put out in England at the beginning of World War II and it deals only with Nazi comment on the English.[7] It includes both written attacks and cartoons, and emphasizes, of course, external rather than internal German politics. The hated figure of the Jew is coupled with everyone — with John Bull, that meddling governess called Miss Britannia, the British imperialist in India and Palestine, and even the leaders of the established Christian church. Direct attacks are made on the loose morality, the hypocrisy, and the duplicity of the English. A few cartoons contrasting the Jewish and the Aryan are reprinted by E. H. Gombrich, and a provocative analysis of Nazi propaganda with a few cartoons among the illustrations is found in Kinser and Kleinman.[8]

In respect to the Soviet system, students, and some propelled by other motives, have done better. An excellent analysis by Michael Milenkovitch reprints and discusses political cartoons, while that of Nelson presents a mixture of social and political cartoons. Two other collections, by Peter Tempest and Rodger Swearington, concentrate solely on social and humorous cartoons.[9] In addition, there is available one collection of political "comic"-book cartoons from The People's Republic of China.[10] If the cartoon output of other totalitarian nations has been collected, I am not aware of the fact. My comments then will of necessity be concentrated primarily on Soviet Russian cartoons.

The freedom granted a cartoonist in a totalitarian system varies with the times, but some small measure of choice must always be permitted. No system can completely stamp out creativity. But as has been noticed in other contexts, what can be called a difference in degree finally becomes a difference in kind, since free choice is so systematically restricted. Much of what is produced in totalitarian cartoons has a phony ring characteristic of propaganda art. It is melodrama complete with heroes and heroines and twirly-moustached villains.

Totalitarian cartoonists, like other artists, can be expected to elaborate their work where some freedom is possible. You might suppose that a major area for such experimentation would be in the artistic presentation rather than the content.

What strikes one about the general run of totalitarian cartoons, especially those

57. **B. Efimov: Like a Miner. January 1, 1960.** *Pravda.* **Reprinted with permission from Michael M. Milenkovitch,** *The View from Red Square.*

concerning internal matters, is that even in the choice of technique the artist appears to be somewhat limited. The totalitarian rulers are perhaps intuitively aware that technique is suggestive of message. Thus, until Khrushchev, the Soviet cartoonist was not even permitted to portray the USSR rulers. When this was finally allowed, the drawings were representational, sometimes an accurate portrayal, but more often what could be called a romanticized realism, that is, similar to the way Jesus Christ is presented in Sunday School bulletins. This style is deemed the only one appropriate for revered subjects. The present example shows Khrushchev.

58. Soviet Cartoon : "This fellow has dangerous thoughts, sir!" "What did he say?" "We grabbed him before he could say anything." Ca. 1947. *Krokodil.* Reprinted with permission from William Nelson, *Out of the Crocodile's Mouth.*

The cartoon produced here from *Krokodil* shows how artistic technique varies when the subject changes. It portrays an American policeman and judge with the slap-dash irreverence we expect in humor magazine cartoons, but there, standing in the middle of this melange, is a heroic figure representing truth and beauty and whatsoever, who looks as if he just stepped out of "Steve Canyon." A more artistic, and evidently a favorite way of using the two styles is by contrasting pictures — the Soviet system in romantic representational, the foreign one with biting caricature. The contrast of the two riders brings down to center stage again the familiar Knight like figure contrasted with the humorously drawn broken-down U.S. nag. (with atomic bomb head).

59. M. Abramov : The Socialist Steed and the Capitalist Nag. September 1960. *In the Name of Peace.* **Reprinted with permission from Michael M. Milenkovitch,** *The View from Red Square.*

As one would expect, the Chinese comic book, which is largely about people's heroes down at the Commune level, follows the same style and is drawn much like what our parents used to recommend to us as educational comic books. To emphasize the glorious seriousness of the works, the speeches are not placed in balloons for easier reading by the comrades, but are printed separately below, which I suppose gives them an additional dignity.

The romantic representational is especially evident in cartoons about Soviet matters produced for home consumption. Those chosen by Peter Tempest, for the Society for Cultural Relations with the USSR, are the blandest collection. Most of these cartoons have the style and the humor of a *Punch* two-liner he-and-she cartoon of the 1920s. There is a quaintness and an old-fashioned style about them, which lends a certain charm. While they lack the sophisticated technique of the *New Yorker* or modern *Punch* cartoon, their style seems peculiarly appropriate to the subject matter, because these are laughing satire of an aristocracy indulgently criticizing the lower orders, reminiscent of those horrible *Punch* "servantgalisms." This is as close as one can come to questioning legitimacy. They poke gentle fun at various home-based problems, but perhaps even this is a great step toward freedom in a totalitarian system. The inefficient or thoughtless or lazy could be portrayed as saboteurs and enemies of the people instead of as fellow human beings and comrades with a few failings to be gently but firmly corrected. But, unless I misread from the sample available, I conclude that the cartoon of self-criticism requires a degree of artistic restraint. The caricature and artistic presentation must project a notion of good fun and avoid the savage and the cynical. The idea is to be a small safety valve, not an invitation to redesign the boiler.

But all is not lost. Soviet cartoonists are capable of modern techniques, and an outlet is provided for their most imaginative artistic experimentation. What remains is the cartoon of vigorous attack on the nation's enemies who menace the system from outside. It is in attacks on the world's democracies that the artist has free rein to experiment in artistry, if not content. These cartoons are in a style that could be found in the most sophisticated modern-humor magazine or on an American editorial page. Artistically the work moves toward what can be described as a more skeptical and biting tone, almost without exception. The Soviet artist has found the zoo he may caricature freely, and almost all the wraps are off.

When one looks at content, the cartoons of system glorification and of self-criticism for home consumption offer few surprises. But two interesting facts emerge in the cartoons directed against foreign enemies. I use as examples those of the *Krokodil* collection directed against America.

One is struck first by the surface familiarity with the American milieu. Since this is the only area in which artists can be creative, they rise to the challenge and set high standards of professionalism. Glib knowledgeability, ironically, becomes a must in the anti-foreign and particularly the anti-American cartoon. Having no other target on which to exercise their imaginative skills, the cartoonists appear to devote more attention to the enemy than the enemy does to Russia. This also lends an air of plausibility to the criticism. Walt Disney and Walter Winchell, Chicago gangsterism or HUAC, and many American politicians become part of the educated Soviet citizens's fund of information. While this knowledgeability often reveals itself as without real depth and subject to embarrassing kinds of error, it is nevertheless impressive. It appears that the average Soviet citizen knows a good deal more about the surface events of our society than we know about his or hers. American cartoonists would be hard pressed in the reverse situation. Few, for example, could be very sure how to draw a downtown Moscow street one block away from Red Square so that it looked reasonably accurate. Most would just draw in a few squiggles to represent those Kremlin turrets.

The second aspect of these cartoons is that they have a much greater-than-average amount of what may be described as sledgehammer humor. It is no only that we find that the jokes of another nation, just as those of another time, are difficult to comprehend. If this were so, the charm of many of the self-criticism cartoons would escape us, as would also the occasional flashes of wit in some of the anti-American ones. Rather, it is that we are faced with humor manufactured by formula, in the Milton Berle or Bob Hope tradition, but with a difference. The reason the cartoons are not funny is that, as with all formula work, the artist is tempted to strain too hard. They have the stink of the nonhumorous type of person who divines that jokes are often based on insults, and thus concludes that all insults are jokes.

A Closing Note

The political cartoonist in a totalitarian system is of necessity what cartoonist Don Hesse of the St. Louis *Globe Democrat* aptly describes as an egg walker. He or she is there to justify the system. While this position seems similar to the one voluntarily assumed by John Tenniel, it is really much more circumscribed. Always a sacred cow

110

is nosing about, and each is a large one at which the cartoonist cannot poke even light fun. He or she can only really let go at the foreign enemies, and even here is circumscribed by the political formula.

Within these limits some interesting and even striking work has been produced. But I conclude that a totalitarian political cartoonist, like the writer for the old TV situation comedy, can never really be completely out of chains, and I suggest that their work shows that they know it too.

Whether this continual beating the drums for the legitimacy of the glorious system is completely effective is to be doubted. When the revolutionary spirit approaches religious ecstasy, as it presently appears to do in the Chinese boondocks, one can believe that peasants do indeed sit up all night on trains reading and wearing out these comic-book melodramas, just as Nebiolo and Wilkinson describe them as doing. But when the glow wears off and the first signs of hangover become apparent, an unexpressed but stubborn resistence to the system may develop. While postwar Germany, Italy, and Japan had some nests of the prewar fascist ideologies, most of the citizens appear to have shed the old ideological systems as if they were worn-out overcoats. The bad seeds nurtured so carefully in the Nazi schools of the thirties sprouted into something else. Neither legitimacy sold by force nor propaganda could stand up to the rude comment characteristic of open democratic societies. And so it is my heretic hope and hypothesis that this may also be true with other totalitarian systems after they crash, whether they be of the right or left.

5
Attackers of the Establishment

Successful revolt in a totalitarian system takes the form of intrigue swirling around the conflicting ambitions of a palace elite, especially perhaps involving the military against the civilian leaders. When there is a crisis of succession, these tensions are fought out a little more in the open. Otherwise, resistance generally is hidden and hopeless.

Attacks on legitimacy do occur in democratic systems, but usually they also are ineffective, unless the nation is deeply divided or faces a deep crisis. The division between two racial, ethnic, or religious groups or between classes can bring the sweats. When a democracy, particularly a young one, experiences the loss of a war, severe economic crisis through depression or inflation, or some deeply dividing issue that focuses the latent splits, as the Dreyfus case did for the 26-year-old Republic of France, a crisis of legitimacy may be recognized. But democracies are generally tougher than their critics suppose. Crises of legitimacy have been ridden out; even civil wars have been healed over. Moralized hurts have been cauterized.

It is the authoritarian system that is made to order for crises of legitimacy and the inability of its leaders to be wholly repressive or democratic makes them inviting targets. Crises of any kind can be escalated into crises of legitimacy, and so such crises are endemic to authoritarian systems. Cartoonists have played a generally admirable role in these struggles.

The Revolutionary Strategy

Every system of distributing rewards has built-in deprivations and pain for someone. Someone will get hurt when there are promotions on the job, grades given in school, cheerleaders chosen, or merit badges awarded by the neighborhood Boy Scout troop. Administrators or leaders in every system can be expected to be lax or lazy occasionally and to make mistakes based on enthusiasms or antagonisms or lack of alertness or just plain dumbness. All systems that are "manned" by humans or animals are given to some error.

These pains and deprivations are accepted just as long as the moral justification underlying the system of distribution of rewards is widely enough accepted by enough people to make challenge seem wrong, ineffective, or even dangerous. The position of the Negro in American society for many years was justified by whites because it was claimed that Negroes were inherently inferior in intelligence and perhaps in morals. For many years that assumption was tacitly unchallenged even by Negroes themselves. The washouts from medical school accepted their lot as a rule, because the system of judging candidates was thought to be reasonable and generally administered fairly. The occasional injustice was not seen as the fault of the system but of administration.

But sometimes pains are not accepted, but are viewed as basic injustices. This, as noted earlier, is what the sociologist Max Weber called the moralization of hurts. When disadvantages or deprivations are seen as no longer justifiable on a moral basis, they are regarded as unfair and the stage is set for reform or revolution.

If these pains and hurts are seen as flowing from some correctable administration of the rules, they can be handled by reform, that is, by adjustments in the system rules. In effect, the good faith of leaders and the moral justification of the system continue to be accepted.

But a deeper challenge is one that says the whole system of distribution is based on an unjust principle and therefore a fair parceling out of rewards can never occur. Such a challenge to legitimacy argues that the moral justification for the distribution must be rooted out and destroyed and a new one put in its place, or, as is sometimes argued, the system of former days reinstituted. The groupings who should be favored are not being rewarded.

A notion about inevitable progress sometimes makes us forget that all systems are subject to this kind of questioning. The systems of distribution proposed by Socialism and Communism are challenged by those who claim unjust hurts, and in utopian community experiments even systems set up by Christian pacifists and anarchists have been smashed as unjust. All systems have the seeds of their human corruption built in, as their performance demonstrates whenever they have been tried. All have produced subversives, that is, citizens whose experience was such that they felt justified in venting hatred on the system and trying to destroy it.

The strategy of the revolutionary cartoonist is not, of course, to inspire love and loyalty to the system but to instill hatred and subversion. The cartoonist-saboteur of the system must vividly demonstrate that the present social, political, and economic leaders are not justified in receiving the benefits they get. It is not enough just to show them receiving high honor, riches, and power. The cartoonist must inspire hate and envy by showing that leaders are moral degenerates who are undeserving of what they receive from the system; that they, too, recognize that they have gotten their benefits by unjust and corrupt means. To do this effectively the system leaders must be portrayed as monsters. They must be shown as planning persecution or hurts out of cold-hearted indifference or sheer sadism, not out of absent-minded incompetence.

The other side of the coin is to dramatize atrocities created by these monsters. Those deprived must be seen as innocents being mashed apart or gunned down, as inhumanely ground up into hamburger by the system.

The subversive cartoonist is also required to attack all of the norms of the system. He or she must show contempt of such rules by encouraging people to break them in every way, while at the same time insisting, when it is to his or her advantage to do so, that those who believe in those rules must follow them to the letter. The artist must continually shout that those who are in power are being unjust, even by the rules they claim to believe in. This attack on accepted rules spills over into all the areas to which society's rules apply: relations between or among the sexes; relations between parent and child; and education, religion, and the economy, as well as government. All such rules in some way specify the distribution of power, wealth, and honor, and so they must all be attacked and ridiculed if the system is to be destroyed. A handy way for the revolutionary cartoonist to show contempt for rules is by denigrating every symbol or institution of the society from the National Anthem to the Campfire Girls. The flag used as a pants patch provides a titillating example. Sacred symbols are especially inviting. This is why revolutionary attack so quickly falls to the level of the blasphemous, the scatological, and the pornographic.

Here is one of the earliest revolutionary cartoons by Honoré Daumier. In one drawing he manages to combine all of these elements: a monster king, an exploited people, and an evil system of rules. He draws the king, Louis Philippe, as the Gargantua of Rabelais. He is shown calmly gobbling up the best of the French nation. The cartoon looks harmless enough but it netted Daumier a jail term of six months and a fine. The reaction of the king is so bitter because his regal throne is drawn as a commode with bodily functions going forward full blast. With this cartoon Daumier earned his wings — or perhaps spurs would be a more appropriate descriptive term.

It is also helpful if the revolutionary can create new symbols for the revolution. Often these are abstract, such as the swastika or the clenched fist. Sometimes they are a special kind of dress. All are supposed to symbolize somehow the justification for the

60.   Honoré Daumier : Gargantua, 1831, *Charivari.*

proposed redistribution of benefits. It was a sure aim that led young blacks to attack bitterly the "Rastus image," which has symbolized the past moral justification for the distribution of social, political, and economic benefits that Negroes received from the Civil War to recent times. In place of the Negro was inserted the Black, dressed in the new and startling Afro hair styles, beards, fancy robes, and African jewelry, all of which, while phony, were in fact truly ennobling. The new costume symbolized that blacks now thought of themselves differently, and that they expected whites in society to do so also. This symbolizing of their new status has been concurrent with a redistribution of social benefits in their favor. Other such symbolizations through costume, as, for example, that of the bloomer girl of mid-nineteenth-century America, have been resisted for some seventy or more years before a significant redistribution of social, political, and economic benefits began to occur. But Virginia Slims had its finger on the right pulse; and a look at styles of dress suggests "You've come a long way, baby" in styles of behavior as well. The patronizing endearment "baby," however, suggests that maybe the women's rights movement still has a little way to go.

The revolutionary cartoonists will be most effective if they can create new symbols at two levels. On one level the symbols of revolution should be ennobling. They are fine for wheeling on stage occasionally, but something of a bore to live with over an extended period of close contact. A second type of more human symbol, gives the followers someone to identify with. Revolutionaries, often lacking a sense of humor, can achieve the noble type of symbol more easily than the human one. Usually the best they can do in creating a humanizing symbol is to produce the kind of warm-hearted "common people" who always stood around at the end of Frank Capra pictures misty-eyed and blinking when Jimmy Stewart or Gary Cooper refused to jump off buildings or end their filibusters in the U.S. Senate.

In what follows I will attempt to show how cartoonists have functioned as revolutionary-critics. Creating hated images seems made to order for them. But one note of caution must be entered. The theory of public opinion I outlined earlier suggests that cartoonists interact with an audience. They will be influenced by it as well as influencing it. The artists I discuss here were not closet cartoonists exhumed by cognoscenti of a later day. All were part of the swirl of events of their times. Most had run-ins with the local police of their day and some had to flee their nations. All were struggling to produce drawings that would inspire men to action, and all in fact did.

Previously the tribulations of the pope at the time of Luther, and of Charles I, who could not keep his head, were touched upon. These were authoritarian "systems" that succumbed to revolution. Each provides a full complement of monster and atrocity cartoons.

Instead of returning to them, I move on, for an illustration of the revolutionary cartoonist in action, to some excellent examples from our own home-grown revolutions — that of the thirteen colonies against England in 1776 and that of eleven states in 1860.

American Revolutionary Cartoons

Before the Stamp Act in 1765, William Murrell reports that American cartoons dealt mainly with dissensions within the colonies. How to handle the Indians was a major focus of conflict, with Benjamin Franklin having the honor not only of being thought to have designed the first colonial cartoon in 1747 but also of being the subject of the first concentrated cartoon ridicule.[1] Both concern his humane but firm stand on the problem of Indian skirmishes.

Franklin's best-known print, "Join or die," the snake cut in eight parts that must be joined before sundown or die, was produced in 1765 as a warning that the colonies must stand united. It was used against the Indians, the Stamp Act, and, later, in the Revolution. As will be noted in chapter 8, the snake was used for a short time as a symbol of union. As Murrell points out, by 1770 a better revolutionary symbol was found when the Boston *Advertiser* substituted the Goddess Minerva for Britannia on its masthead. By degrees Minerva changed into the sublime Goddess Columbia, and we were off and running.

In the wild stage of revolutionary activity, other more blood-curdling symbols were trotted out. One was on the famous front page of William Bradford's Pennsylvania *Journal and Weekly Advertiser*, which was set up with reversed slugs in a tombstone design. The bold black type said that the journal was expiring, murdered by the monstrous Stamp Act. To emphasize the death's-head mood, an imitation stamp with skull and crossbones was affixed to the corner.

Other colonial cartoons for this period are relatively rare. Many revolutionary cartoons were in fact made in England itself or in Holland. Some were pirated by colonial printers. These tended to be high-flown allegory featuring the Goddess Liberty and the like.

An attack directly on the symbol of Britain appears to have been first produced in Britain in 1768, but it was given wide circulation by Franklin and was printed on all of his stationery. A number of writers attribute it to him, though it is not clear that he did indeed design it. It gets down to the business of real atrocity-mongering of shock and horror, the stock-in-trade of all revolutionists. A battered Britannia is shown to have slipped off the top of the world. The colonies — her arms, and legs — are hacked off. Her ships have broomsticks for masts, a sign that they are for sale. Other warnings of disaster and ruin are scattered around wherever there is any unused space in the drawing. To later generations the picture appears perhaps a trifle overdrawn. But for revolutionaries, revolution is a serious business, one hard to overdo once you've been bitten and the sedition bug is swimming around in the bloodstream. It feels very satisfying to hack up the symbol of the enemy.

61. **Benjamin Franklin : The Colonies Reduced. August 1768.**

Colonial times provide one very good atrocity print as well, a colored print engraved by the Paul Revere who also rendered other services to the cause. Murrell prints a plaintive letter by Henry Pelham dated March 29, 1770, claiming (probably correctly) that Revere pirated this famous drawing from Mr. Pelham.

It is titled "The Bloody Massacre Perpetuated in King Street, BOSTON, on March 5, 1770 by a Party of the 29th REGT." It is the atrocity cartoon par excellence. Its full color features liberal splashes of bloody red. The scene is stage-managed to call forth proper expressions of horror. The attack, as anyone can see, was unprovoked. A line of dirty redcoats, their monstrous commander waving his sword to cheer them on, is firing volley after volley into a peaceful crowd on Boston Common — men and women who just happen to be gathered there for a reasonable discussion about the growing tensions between colony and mother country. Not a one is in any way belligerent. Some are gesturing to the British to hold fire, some have hands clasped in prayer or have their hands meekly at their sides, or are trying to support the wounded. No one has even a rock, a stick, or anything like that. No one is jeering. They are all defenseless, peaceful, orderly, and gentle. Symbolically, a dog stands idly center front, pausing in wagging its tail. But the artist indulges himself a little. One of the buildings is renamed "Butcher's Hall," a telling and subtle stroke indeed. Below the drawing is a poem whose thoughtful message ends with "Keen Execrations on this place inscribed,/shall reach a Judge who never can be bribed." Then the poet solemnly lists the five killed and the six wounded (two mortally). The innocents are slaughtered by monsters; this is a moralized hurt if ever there was one. Such is the cartoon message, and a more effective one for stirring up hatred of the British is difficult to imagine.

62. Paul Revere (and Henry Pelham?): The Bloody Massacre Perpetrated in King Street, Boston — 1770.

Colonial art is limited in both quantity and quality, and we shall examine such American prints later in more detail, so we leave these revolutionary artists at this point. But before turning away from the Georgian print altogether, we should remark one that shows how James Gillray in England at about the same time handled a similar theme — the inhumanity of the rulers backed by the military. In his "A March to the Bank," Gillray, with a good deal more artistry than Revere, distills the inhumanity of stolidly marching soldiers who follow a leader who prances over the bodies of the citizenry. It is not difficult to imagine the feelings of revolutionary restlessness of the mob, pictured waiting for someone to throw the first brick. Incidentally, I saw the prancing figure of this print reproduced in a poster prepared by one of the more erudite of the rioters during one of the student demonstrations of the 1960s.

63. James Gillray : A March to the Bank. August 22, 1787.

The American Civil War produced one superior cartoonist and I do not refer to Thomas Nast, who at that time was the General Burnside to this man's Robert E. Lee. The cartoonist I mean was a Baltimore dentist with Southern sympathies, Adalbert Volck. His work was done in copperplate etching for individually circulated underground prints. We tend to forget that the Confederate insurrection was a revolutionary movement.

Volck emptied all his intense loathing for Lincoln and the North into a series of haunting creations. In the process he provided a memorable series of revolutionary cartoons. His drawings are, of course, chock full of allegorical allusions and all of the other nonsense prized by his contemporaries, but they are distinguished in three ways.

118

64.   Adalbert Volck : Writing the Emancipation Proclamation. October 1862.

His ideology was simple hate. The prints reverberate with his passionate repugnance for the North. The attack focuses mainly on Lincoln as the symbol of the nation. The cartoons picture him as a secret Negro (under the veil), as a devil urged on by other demons, and all of the other paraphernalia associated with a good dying curse. They call to mind the emblematic prints directed by Luther against the pope. In comparison, American Revolutionary War prints are pallid.

Second, Volck did not depend on allegory alone for imagery. The faces he draws are not attempts at displaying the outside features, but the rotten inner souls of his subjects. Abraham Lincoln is pictured over and over with careful and loving attention to what Volck regarded as his innate depravity. These are not prints that Mary Todd would collect to frame for the hall outside Abraham's office.

Third, Volck's artistic style, like that of most outstanding cartoonists, was original, and a clear break from that of his contemporaries. You do not have to look twice to know you are looking at a Volck. He emphasizes white space and lines and thus begins to reach toward the bold black-and-white impact drawings later popularized by Nast. But neither Nast nor any other American of the period drew quite as Volck did. His drawings jump out of the page with double artistic force, given the fusty Civil War art that surrounds them.

Volck had to flee to England during the war but, with the stick-to-itiveness that characterized everything about him, he had his work smuggled back into the Union through Copperhead sources. When the war ended, he returned to Baltimore to his old trade of painless dentistry. There he died in 1910.

One hopes that the dental profession gained as talented a recruit as political cartooning lost.

Honoré Daumier: Hopeful Revolutionary

For variety, and also because several excellent and perceptive studies exist, we turn next to a professional revolutionary: the French cartoonist Honoré Daumier.[2] At times he was able to portray the revolutionary spirit with great bitterness and effectiveness. But more often he was squelched and had to pirate in his message. Either way he was murderously efficient. His cartoons never lacked the spirit of ready criticism against injustice and he never ceased in his attacks on the rulers, the rules, or the atrocities that he felt automatically flowed from the system.

Honoré Daumier spent his life longing for a French Republic while he spent his days undercutting authoritarian systems he considered hopelessly illegitimate. Perhaps fortunately, this old puritan did not live to enjoy republican governing for too long. It is a more satisfying life to live where the fizz is, and even to make real sacrifices as Daumier did. The revolution, like most other dreams, always seems to fall into the wrong hands.

A number of commentators on Daumier's work emphasize his hopefulness about man's potential and his own sweet nature. Daumier falls easily into the category of optimistic radical and revolutionary — the kind more motivated by generosity than by hatred, by hope than by despair. The temperaments of such men incline them to pacifism and anarchy, since it seems to them that if only the old institutional chains that bind can be struck off, humans could emerge free. These new men would not be partly liberated as Daumier saw that he himself was, but would leave behind the prison of traditional religions, of old class and status hierarchies, and of poverty and inherited wealth. They would live in a world where all would share equally in political power, honor, and wealth.

Thus, for Daumier, the salt of the earth is of two types. One is the common working-class man who like himself had modest tastes and pleasures. The other is no man or woman, no group yet living, but the new liberated type of human being — the kind of person he himself would more fully have been if not inhibited by those in his society with inherited power, wealth, and status. These hopes were symbolized by that untouchable and sacred female — Republican France.

What would such new human beings be like? Secularists undoubtedly, but also puritans, in their willingness to work for the sake of the work alone, rather than just for the reward. Self-expression would be for the common good, would replace the old self-serving desire for power, wealth, or status. One can almost hear that old roundhead battle cry, "From each according to his abilities, to each according to his needs." Curiously enough though, Daumier was not himself completely liberated. He wanted women to be the helpmates of their men. But their secondary status is not for reasons of erotic control, which strikes me as cold comfort for both sorts of the female sex. Rather, much of the ascetic attitude to sex is found swimming around inside this revolutionary.

The revolutionary in Daumier came to a boil when as a young man in his early twenties he joined and became the artistic star of the group of artists that worked for Philipon's series of journals. This was in the early 1830s, when it became clear that the new king, Louis Philippe, had little intention of fulfilling the promise of the new constitution.

Philipon's major contribution to this effort was as editor and guiding spirit. His contribution to its art was a drawing of four parts. One showed the King, Louis Philippe, full face, with each successive drawing more like a pear and fourth being a pear. Pear was slang for simpleton. The drawing has been widely reprinted, but perhaps never often enough. The artist was charged, and in his defense he asked the court to point to the picture in which Philippe disappeared and the pear began, or vice versa. While the joke was good, the judge did not want to get it. It earned Philipon a fine and a jail term.

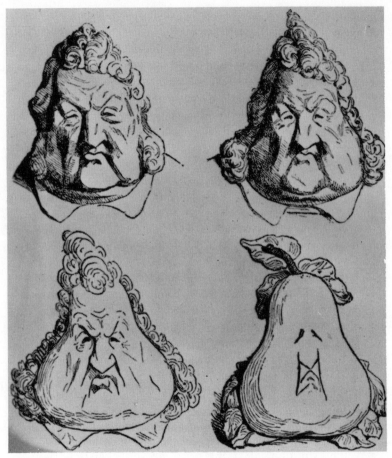

65.   Charles Philipon : The Pear. Ca. 1831. *Charivari.*

Daumier also contributed to the series of pear cartoons, most in the spirit of laughing satire, but some like Gargantua, which echoes this theme, more biting. Daumier's period in jail inspired him to create more destructively satiric cartoons against the system, but he was artist enough to mix these with a bitter, cold-blooded satire. One such cartoon shows Louis Philippe at the funeral of the liberal patriot Lafayette. The suggestion of a smirk is on the king's face as he stands hypocritically

121

mourning with folded hands and downcast eyes. Another, called "The Legislative Paunch," is a bitter but laughing, cold-blooded attack on the national assembly.

66.   Honoré Daumier : "Now that Lafayette's dead!... it's your turn." June 1834. *Charivari.*

Daumier seemed more at home with bitter destructive satire as Louis Philippe vigorously suppressed minor uprisings and set about muzzling critics in the press and legislature. The crisis year was 1834. In "Rue Transmonain" Daumier as already noted vividly pictured the atrocity of a police raid against suspected revolutionists. In "You have the floor, explain yourself," he shows the monster judges making a mockery of justice in a trial of gagged republicans. Another shows the inhuman pear shaped king in a jail cell, permitting the release of a prisoner now that he has expired. Another jail scene shows a still resistant and quite nobly portrayed prisoner outfacing his guard, with Daumier's wholehearted approval evident. As in revolutionary cartoons generally, the criminal is the hero and the jailer the criminal. Another cartoon glorified freedom of the press, before which tyrants cower.

Daumier continued this attack, along with other artists of Philipon's journals, until the September Laws of 1835, which effectively silenced the system's critics. A bitter closing comment is of Louis Philippe as clown, dropping the curtain and announcing "The farce is ended."

With repression Daumier worked out a different kind of attack. In common with other revolutionaries, he turned to the cartoon of social criticism or of comic art. Some commentators argue that he had trouble adapting and was always restless in his new role as comic artist and social critic. What is patently clear is that whenever the lid was even slightly off, he immediately returned to political cartooning. Nevertheless, even his comic art packed a political wallop for the establishment.

First, at Philipon's suggestion, he adapted from a current play the character of Robert Macaire, a caricature of the bourgeois man of the time of Louis Philippe. Macaire and his friend Bertram symbolized all of the shoddiness of the period. He was a living example of how wrong the system of distribution of social benefits was. Macaire was a promoter with the moral aspirations of those who today peddle upset stomach remedies on TV or operate adult book stores. The beauty of the character for Daumier's purposes was that he could be cast in a different role in each cartoon. In one he was a con-man Bible salesman, in another a doctor. In this way Daumier could work his way through the Establishment, passing out bouquets as he went along.

67.   Honoré Daumier : Patent for the invention (of the wheelbarrow) 3 million. August 19. 1839. *Charivari.*

Other cartoons concentrated on revered professions and businessmen and their cupidity. Today a number of collections have been made of these cartoons, as, for example, of doctors handling patients, masters with their pupils, politicians, and so on. All of these cartoons preach the same message: something is basically rotten with this system.

Henri Mondor, in his introduction to one such collection on doctors and medicine, makes a telling point. He writes: "When Daumier attacked doctors, he was thus attacking one of the flanks of the opposing army. According to him, they were all profiteers, mouthers of garrulous clichés, and mountebanks. He does not seem to have heard of the work of such men as Pinel...."[3] Mondor then lists by name the group of bourgeois medical men of France who were in fact just then systematically upgrading the medical profession and making possible the large step forward in medical science that reached full fruition in the twentieth century. Yet all Daumier could see and report on were the system's quacks. This is not because he was wholly blind but because he was a revolutionary out to discredit the system, or so at least it looks to me.

If Daumier was critical of businessmen, doctors, and teachers for their money grubbing, his bitterest jibes were expressed for those whose duty it was to administer the system's basic rules — its judges and lawyers. In one, a lawyer is explaining to a potential client that he lacks the most important evidence — evidence of money. To a heartbroken working-class woman with a young boy, a legal monster is explaining that while it is true that the case was lost, she had the pleasure of hearing him argue it. In such social-criticism cartoons the political message about the system is not difficult to discern, nor is the mood projected the usual lighthearted one about minor human faults.

68. **Honoré Daumier : Man of Justice — "It's true. You lost your case, but you had the pleasure of hearing me plead it." 1848.**

69.   Honoré Daumier : Ratapoil. Ca. 1848.

With Louis Philippe's overthrow in 1848, Daumier becomes the defender of the fledgling republic. On the one hand, cartoons ask why anyone would think it too ill to survive. Other, more typical cartoons warn of the potential danger to it in a typical Daumier way. He creates a Louis Napoleon supporter whom he calls Ratapoil (Ratskin), and then endows him with the physical characteristics of his mentor as well as all of his sleazy and nasty qualities of political opportunism. It is the platonic technique of painting the state as the man writ large. When Napoleon declared himself emperor in 1851, Daumier relapsed back into social subjects and political subjects not overtly critical of the regime. In the middle sixties he began a series of political cartoons about the growing might of Prussia and of the uncertainties of war and the balance of power in Europe. These were warnings against the kind of military adventure that did in fact end in the Franco-Prussian war and the defeat of France in 1870.

70.   Honoré Daumier : Peace is as strong as the Chinese at the Hippodrome, 1867.

This last period of freedom brings out of Daumier some of his bitterest cartoons. He seems to be trying to hammer home the lessons of his life. He drew the devastation of France as the logical outcome of feudal monarchy and its pursuit of glory. The inevitable atrocities could be laid squarely at the empire's door. His most acid comments are reserved for the established order; in contrast were his idealization of the sacred Republic and of the spirit of rationalism as symbolized by Voltaire.

71. Honoré Daumier : "I wanted to throw it at him and I muddied myself."
1869.

The lifetime output of Daumier thus faithfully fits the mold of a professional revolutionary. In times of relative freedom or in times of suppression, he continues to portray the system leaders as monsters. He exploits and cries out against outrages, and cries out from his heart. There is no phony ring about these cartoons.

The pattern is that of attack, attack, and attack again. Daumier's enemies are the leaders of the old system: monarchists, the clerics, and the economic opportunists, including those who claim to be professionals. Their inhuman qualities are sometimes touched on subtly, sometimes brutally. The atrocities are political murders, war and corruption, exploitation of the poor, hardheartedness to those below them on the social scale, and the bitter fruits of the system of justice. The heroes are two — Voltaire and the chaste feminine image of the Republic, whose assigned chores vary from turning out discredited ministers to suckling the young. He attacks the symbols and institutions of the old system most magnificently in the Napoleonic eagle nailed to the book, or in the cartoon of the corrupted legislative body with its bellylike curves, or in those of justice, and, with extreme effectiveness, in the Macaire series.

But Daumier also deserves a hard second look for his defects. What is false about the revolutionary, even one such as Daumier, is that he is unrelenting and therefore sometimes more inhuman than those he attacks. He does not see it as his job to give the

127

system or anyone in it an even break. He has declared war and winning is everything. Could Louis Philippe's monarchy have evolved into a constitutional one, as was occurring in Britain under the gross Georges III and IV? If so, in France it would have to do so under the barrage of a group of idealistic cartoonists who had early decided that such an outcome was impossible. In place of reform, they held up a romantic ideal of a new system based on man's wonderful potential. The kings and emperors are now gone and France still waits.

This stance of unrelenting criticism carries with it an unwillingness to allow people to be human, a peculiar thing to say about Daumier, who could paint human foibles so well. Mondor writes, "It is hard to excuse him [Daumier] for so constantly denouncing a certain inhuman frigidity in the face of suffering, but never admitting the heroic abnegation, kindness, and charity practiced by men far too modest to boast of their good deeds." Daumier sits as a puritan in judgment, and no supporter of the system was spared. And so, with all his generosity and humanity toward the lower orders, he could not create a believable revolutionary-hero type, since to be human was to be corrupt. Only the icy old rationalism of a Voltaire was the fit companion for that puritanical figure — Republican France. His heroes sadly seem to be only statues on pedestals.

The Mexican Revolutionists

Victor Alba examined the cartoons of Mexico in the hundred-year period from 1860 through 1960.[4] His discussion is well worth looking over for the light it throws on the process I have been describing.

In 1823 Mexico had freed itself from the political dominance of Spain, but by 1860 it still had the strong social and economic ties of a former colony. A series of revolutions by adventurers culminated in Napoleon III's efforts to place Maximilian on the Mexican throne as emperor. The ensuing revolution succeeded, but attempts by Juarez to set up a constitutional democracy failed. Out of this chaos finally emerged, in 1876, a military dictator, Diaz. At first Diaz was regarded as a liberal reformer, but increasingly this proved to be an illusion. His self-serving regime was finally overthrown in 1911 and Madero, the leader of the reformers and parenthetically an alumnus of the University of California, took control. Disputes among revolutionaries, who besides himself included such colorful figures as Huerta, Zapata, and Pancho Villa, encouraged a continual chaos. In 1913 Madero was deposed and murdered by soldiers. After a period of further fighting, Carranza took control in 1914. His government proclaimed a constitution in 1917, which brought extensive changes. Church and state were disentangled, Spanish clerics in the Mexican Catholic hierarchy were replaced by Mexicans, some large land holdings were broken up and redistributed, and the silver mines were nationalized. In addition, foreign control was weakened. In 1920 Carranza was assassinated.

The next twenty years were a test of strength between new and old forces to determine whether the revolution would stick. It was evolutionary change, with the possibility always of slipping into a dictatorship of the extreme right or left. Governing was punctuated by assassination — the antics of generals, a bickering clergy, and many of the other unlovely phenomena that make up the North American stereotype of Latin American politics. But throughout the period, the hold of the upper classes on the status, political power, and wealth of the society slipped, and that of the middle classes grew stronger. In the Cardenas regime of the late thirties, the earlier reforms were consolidated, foreign holdings of oil and other resources were socialized, and

Mexico began to pop up occasionally on lists of "democratic systems" prepared by political scientists.[5]

Cartoons reflect this history. In the period between 1860 and 1910, Alba finds the classic type of revolutionary cartoon. The monsters, as crudely portrayed in the revolutionary cartoons, were three: the priest, the general, and the economic exploiter. The latter included the Spanish landholder and businessman as well as the American imperialist. These were presented with all the subtlety and refinement that one would expect would bring the response of contempt or hatred for society's social, political, economic, and religious leaders. Alba presents several such illustrations. From Shikes's discussion we get even more vivid cartoon illustrations of the

72.   José Guadalupe Posada : Revolutionary Calavera. 1910.

129

inhumanity of such leaders and the atrocities it was claimed they committed.[6]

The leading Mexican political cartoonist of the prerevolutionary period was José Guadalupe Posada (1851-1913). He specialized in a type of cartoon called calaveras, which were drawings of dance-of-death skeletons that acted out his satirical comments on society. These were published as penny prints. Shikes states that "Posada's flippant skeletons were often pictured dancing, drinking, running over pedestrians with their bicycles, attired in the latest foolish fashion." Other Posada drawings feature little devils doing other horrid little tricks, but the skeleton drawings were the most popular. Could an artist more plainly state that the society in which he lived was a dying one and beyond saving? Was there a less subtle way than to show it as a world of disembodied skeletons.

73.   Mexican Cartoon : The Knife (Charro). 1879.

Artists also emphasized the monsterlike qualities of leaders. One drawing, entitled "Calavera Huertista," combines skeleton and monster. Shikes sums it up very well: "The strong-arm President, Huerta, is portrayed as a revolting spider, crawling with maggots, holding the bones of his victims." Such cartoons are interspersed with atrocity scenes in their gory details. Posada did one of a laborer without food for his family, another of a young man being forcibly impressed into someone's army, and one of a peasant hanged by landowners.[7]

The revolutionary artists did not neglect to glorify their cause. As Alba points out, Posada and others were able to achieve that most difficult of symbols, a revolutionary hero who was also human. The figure was the Charro, the peasant on horseback, a representation related somewhat to the American cowboy and not too far removed from the swashbuckling freebooter or outlaw. The Charro was drawn with wide-brimmed hat and was portrayed as acting in a flamboyant and free style. He lived on the edge of society, Robin Hood style. He was a good deal more earthy than the movie version of O. Henry's Cisco Kid. He was a symbol the peasants could identify with, and one can do so even today, at least on a movie screen. Posada, especially, also kept alive the tradition of revolution with scenes of its past. These were cartoons of straight glorification in a matter-of-fact, representational style, unlike the caricature and satiric imagery of his calaveras. We see battles between revolutionaries and governmental troops or revolutionary leaders bravely facing governmental firing squads.

To summarize, the art of Mexico before the revolution of 1910-1917 fits the revolutionary pattern of (1) portraying political, social, economic, and religious leaders as monsters, (2) portraying the society and its distribution of benefits as decaying rotten, (3) portraying the masses as subjects of atrocities, and (4) glorifying revolutionary leaders and incidents. Also, one should note, every enemy of the Establishment, including criminals or society's rejects, received sympathetic treatment.

After the revolution of 1910-1917 through its successful consolidation at about the time of World War II, cartoons took what can perhaps best be described as a revolutionary nostalgic turn. Artists remind viewers of these past glories and atrocities. A fresco of 1940 by José Clement Orozco is reprinted by Shikes and shows captured revolutionaries forced to dig their own graves. Orozco does not present a view of how the revolutionaries treated their captives, since this would not be an atrocity but just desert for the opportunistic renegades who served the government. Some of this is particularly questionable revolutionary nostalgia, since it is by those who largely missed the revolution. This mood is captured in a cartoon of 1945 that shows a monster pursuing "poor Juan and wife" in a way that positively breathes revolutionary fire. The let-down comes when one discovers that the Mexican peasant Juan and his wife are being pursued by "the demons of the black market, the high cost of living, and graft," all no doubt despicable in their own way, but perhaps a little overdrawn. Along with this kind of art were the traditional personal attacks on political leaders, plus a less vitriolic version of the attacks on the leaders of the prerevolutionary society.

With the revolutionary reforms accepted under Cardenas and his successors, Shikes noted a slackening of political art. Alba is perhaps more perceptive. He points out that the most popular modern cartoonist, Quezada, was not a revolutionary. Rather, Quezada identified with the modern regime and saw his role as teaching Mexicans how to behave properly in the new postrevolutionary society that was in process of building. The president of the state was no longer considered an appropriate subject of cartoon satire, though word-of-mouth jokes about him were still popular. The cartoonists' targets now were the gauche new rich and the swashbuckling male chauvinist, who was not, incidentally, too far removed in style and expression from the old Charro hero of the prerevolution. Quezada mildly ridicules the hangover of these old roughnecks and their customs, prejudices, and taboos as what gets in the way of building the new industrialized Mexico. Quezada's teaching is social satire, a good deal funnier but with some of the same qualities and purposes as the output of the now hopefully defunct charm schools of a former day. He is the cartoonist defending what he regards as a legitimate system in the process of becoming, and so we come full circ' to another topic.

The Pessimistic Revolutionary: George Grosz

Earlier I noted that there is some tendency among intellectuals to romanticize the political cartoonist as always a fighter for freedom. Seldom is such glorification less deserved than when it is accorded to those such as the talented Weimar cartoonist George Grosz, whose aim it was to destroy a democracy. After bitterly attacking a fragile and wounded German democratic system with every nasty potrayal he could think of, Grosz got out just in time, just before people began to be marched off to the concentration camps. But though he had performed as a good Spartacist militant, he did not flee to the Soviet East, whose system he and other Communists had wished to substitute for Weimar. He went West for sanctuary, to another democracy, that of America, where he lived almost twenty years until a few months before his death, when he returned to Germany.

I am reminded of Toscanini's tribute to the composer Richard Strauss. He said something like "To your art, I take off my hat. To your politics, I put on my hat ten times again."

Weimar history is tragically brief. In 1918, with the war lost, a successful revolution was mounted against the Kaiser. The Socialists took control but were challenged by the militants of the left, who wished to institute a wholesale housecleaning of the old system, and those of the right who wished to apply similar methods to different targets. An attempted revolution in 1919 by the Spartacists, who despite the romantic name were the German Communist party, was suppressed and their leaders, Rosa Luxemburg and Karl Liebknecht, were murdered by soldiers while being taken to prison. The Social Democrats continued to hold tenuous control while being attacked by both left and right revolutionaries. The Nazi Putsch of 1923, like the Spartacist before it, was successfully suppressed, except that their leaders got to prison and then out again in a few years. By the middle twenties, with political turmoil still characteristic of the system, Marshall von Hindenburg was elected president, with limited powers. Among the most important was the power to appoint a chancellor. Hindenburg in the beginning followed the parliamentary majorities. In this period the economy was beginning to recover and it looked as if the democratic system had a prayer, despite its bitter critics. The depression of 1929 blighted that hope; the Nazi party grew stronger. In 1932, with Socialist help, Hindenburg was reelected, but in early 1933 he caved in and appointed Adolf Hitler chancellor. The Weimar Republic was dead. The Nazis had the power to kill it, but so too had that other party that had made the Nazi alternative an attractive one to many Germans, and I do not mean the Social Democratic party.

The two sets of revolutionaries, Nazi and Communist, followed the same techniques, from attempted armed overthrow to discrediting the system rules and its leaders while out of power and, in the case of the Nazis, the use of concentration camp when in power. Had the Spartacists won out, perhaps they would have treated Socialists and Nazis with similar tenderness.

The Nazi cartoonists found their tasks easy — they identified the Weimar leaders of the social, economic, and political system as Jews or those unwittingly manipulated by Jews. To the Aryan German, their appeal was that such a distribution of benefits was unjust and deplorable because it was un-German. Any system of rules that resulted in such clear injustice, they argued, must be scrapped. Their cartoons emphasized the moral depravity of Weimar culture. They contrasted disgusting money grubbing, caricatured Jews with sweet, pure, and brave blondes. Atrocity pictures showed Jewish lechers about to molest these pure maidens. Bill Kinser and Neil Klienman, in a study of the symbolic underpinning of Nazism, note its affinity to the previously revered myth of the Germanic knight, pure and chivalrous in the best Wagnerian style, acting heroically in a setting complete with castles, the faithful maiden, and evil, mishapen dwarfs.[8] They note that the German factories were built to resemble medieval castles, how the heroic Nazi leaders were photographed from below with stiff uniforms or shirts with reflecting planes reminiscent of medieval armor, and how the Jew was cast as the malevolent, hunchback dwarf gaining momentarily an upper hand over the hero by casting smarmy spells. It takes little effort for democrats to feel a shudder of revulsion when viewing Nazi cartoons.

But for the Communist Spartacists it is somehow different. Their defenders take us back to the shopworn rationalizations of the defenders of the late Senator Joseph McCarthy: "While I do not approve of their methods, their goals are certainly praiseworthy," which is in fact so much flummery. So we see George Grosz at his devastating best attempting in every way he can to show that a group of political leaders trying to build a democratic society were poisonous and rotten men undeserving of loyalty and support. The typical citizen is portrayed as a grubby German burgher who smokes his cigar and hums, self-satisfied, to himself while his Hausfrau meekly plays and sings "Heilige Nacht." Monsters, murderers, and sexual perverts are portrayed as holding the high places in the Social Democratic Party government and in the military and in industry. Church leaders are shown to be sadistic animals. Atrocities abound in Grosz's work. Men, women, and children are murdered or left to wither away just as the fat, ugly leaders of the system willed it. People are drawn as gross, with transparent clothes so that the sexual organs can look revolting. Almost every open window in a building, it seems, shows a murder or rape going on. No form of sexual irregularity or violence was to be passed by if it could be used against the Social Democrats or their faltering democratic system.

Daumier was an optimistic revolutionary inspired by generosity, while Grosz, clearly, is a pessimistic one inspired by hatred. Grosz has no ideal man because he loathed all humans, without regard to sex, color, or creed. Life itself is Hell, and the whole of mankind must be punished for doing him the disservice of permitting him to be born. In the end, it was not only the traditional creeds that were false; so too were the anti-traditional. The only value was self-expression, so that one may spew out the hatred one feels. Grosz thus seems to me essentially a nihilist revolutionary.

A similar view of the rottenness of German society is found in other artists of the time, as, for example, in the wood block prints of Franz Masereel. One from his collection *Die Stadt* shows the wonders of German civilization. As your eye travels along it comes to a girl being raped. In his woodcut drawings, unlike those of Grosz, the heroic agitator is conjured up for one's admiration and one senses the presence of the optimistic revolutionary.

74. George Grosz : "God's visible blessing rests upon us." 1922. Estate of George Grosz, Princeton, N.J.

Käthe Kollwitz was also part of this community, since she too was a radical and a pacifist. In fact, she did a woodcut memorializing Liebknecht's death. But she is not of the Grosz breed of Communist, if in fact she was one at all. To her credit, she loved her victims too much to use them the way escaped convicts do hostage children. Her posters for bread for the German children were atrocity pictures, but not distortions of reality twisted to wound; rather, they were and still are deeply moving human documents, which speak of the inhumanity of human to human in any system. The spirit of genuine tragedy pervades her more characteristic work, which portrays the widows of war and the mothers of dead soldiers. It is not a moralized hurt tied to a particular system, but a general protest against the deprivations and horrors suffered by all humanity as long as war continues. Only the truly monstrous can reject that work.

It is not astonishing to learn that her life too was tragic. Her husband, a doctor, and she worked with the poor in the Berlin slums. They stayed on after Hitler, to protect and help others, when they could, like Grosz, have fled Nazi Germany. She and her husband faced the point of Nazi interrogation, one step from the concentration camp or the alternative suicide they had planned. She was not taking cheap shots at those trying to build a democratic Germany. But let us return to Grosz.

An interesting fact emerges from review of such revolutionaries in a democracy. It is that their art can hit even more devastatingly below the belt than political cartoons directed against authoritarian systems, or at least so it seems. Perhaps this is, in part, because authoritarian systems, while clumsy, are often partially successful in suppression, at least until the lid blows off. Democracies also harass revolutionaries, but the harassment is tamer. Attempts were made legally to suppress Grosz's books and he was involved in lawsuits. But his greatest danger was his involvement in the same kind of street-corner incidents that also characterized the experience of many young Nazis of his day. He might easily have been murdered among such associates.

However, I think the major reason for the intense venom is otherwise. The pessimistic revolutionary in a democratic society lives something of the life of a cheat. It is not only that he enjoys the fruits of a system he is trying to undermine. At base his nastiness is more horrible — it seems to rest on self-rejection. Grosz, for example, does not really seem to have much hope for the system that would follow revolution. The revolutionary like Daumier, fighting an authoritarian system, has a cause and a hope for a new world that will be better and that he is contributing to. He can be slashingly bitter against the system, but still identify himself with other humans. A critic like Grosz cannot seem to really believe in this new world or anyone who might be in it, including himself. He does not expect to find a place in any world except by consciously deceiving himself, as a pathetic Grosz tried to do when he attempted after 1930 to play the role of crass American. Revolutionaries like Grosz are really most at home in decadence, and they come to enjoy their own despair — taking hope only in the destruction of all humanity with, they think, themselves included. But when the chips are down, if they are like George Grosz, they maybe draw back. Grosz came to believe only in nothingness, and this, his most recent biographer argues, he tried to hide even from himself.[9] But eventually he forced himself to portray it artistically in his late paintings as an empty hole painted into the pictures.

Some observers see democracies of our day as sick, just as Weimar was. Great Britain, they note, is puffing hard and has passed its peak, while America has had what some think is a series of paralyzing strokes called Vietnam and Watergate. Both nations have inspired some social and political criticism similar to that of Grosz and of Georgian England. From English art, I reproduce a current view of Britannia, which states rather starkly Ralph Steadman's view of the nation's situation. In America some cartoons have reached the same level of spiteful malevolence. As in Georgian England, it has become far-out mod to be acid. For its true distillation, one needs to look at the underground cartoon. For a considerably more watered-down version, one might review the political cartoons of college newspapers from around 1968-1972. At that time they favored bitter critics who still believed strongly in democratic methods. In the college newspaper I am most familiar with, the Michigan State University *News*, I found two artists featured during that period: Paul Conrad of the Los Angeles *Times* and, less frequently, Tom Darcy of *Newsday*. As the seventies progressed and student editors changed, Darcy disappeared, to be replaced by Oliphant, which suggests the shifting mood even on campus. At the same time either I am changing or Conrad is, because very often I find myself cheering as I flip over to what student editors fondly

regard as their Op-Ed page. Maybe our ex-president has done what he promised —
brought us all together again.

75. Ralph Steadman : (Britannia). 1972. Manchester *Guardian*. **Reprinted by permission of Ralph Steadman.**

A Closing Note

Attacking the system for the purpose of undermining its legitimacy has predictable risks in a totalitarian system. It is the unpredictability of the authoritarian system that permits genuine heroics. It is the lack of serious risk for such antics in a democracy that merits contempt.

The revolutionary technique follows a predictable routine: to paint the social (including religious), political, and economic leaders as inhuman monsters while conjuring up pictures of the atrocities that flow from their malevolence. The rules and symbols of that system are to be regarded with contempt at every opportunity, while those who oppose it, domestic or foreign, are to be feted as heroes.

The true heroes are those who struggle for freedom in an authoritarian

76. Tom Darcy : "Good News ... we've turned the corner in Vietnam." 1969. *Newsday.*

environment. Honoré Daumier deserves honor as an artist and a democrat, whether or not one agreed with his romanticized versions of the green pastures. The despicable are those who, whatever their rationalization, devote their talents to undermining and destroying one of the rare moments of precious freedom that mankind has thus far experienced. Talented political cartoonists have been among both groups — unfortunately.

6
Wartime Cartoons: Democracy's Dark Side

Moving anti-war cartoons date from before the birth of medieval woodcuts and continue up to the present. Some are clearly pacifist; others only cry out that humanity must find a way to stop the horror and pain of war. Outstanding examples are worth knowing and pondering even if you conclude, as I shall here, that wars are likely to continue for some time, as long as some national leaders can reasonably decide that it is possible to gain benefits for a nation by war, or to change the distribution of power, status, or wealth to their advantage. It is with cartoons treating war as a dehumanizing condition that this chapter begins.

But the bulk of the chapter is about the way wars create dilemmas for cartoonist critics in democracies. Wars circumscribe independent comment, especially in authoritarian and democratic systems. Rather than stating criticism from the vantage point of their own preferred groupings, cartoonists, like other critics, are pushed in the direction of supporting an ideological nationalist line. That they do not always comply is also noted. I close the chapter with a review of some of the assumptions American cartoonists have held about the causes of war, from the Spanish American war in 1890 through World War II. Because Vietnam was such a convulsion, I leave a fuller examination of cartoonist viewpoints on it for another book — preferably one by someone else.

The Horror of War

In our day, with the Vietnam experience just behind us, the costs of war — human, material, and moral — loom large. The greatest recent loss, perhaps, has been in our sense of our government's legitimacy. The time before Vietnam seems like an era of sweet innocence and confidence. We know what a Belgian poet, quoted by Barbara

Tuchman in *The Proud Tower*, means. He dedicated his World War I book "with emotion, to the man I used to be." In that mood, we can with a good deal of sympathy review briefly a few outstanding anti-war cartoons.

Many of the best anti-war drawings are simple illustrations of war's events. They touch on one or another of the brutalizations caused by war with a horrible matter-of-factness. They·portray the essence of that horror for all humans, on whatever side.

One can begin with the experiences and work of Jacques Callot. He was born in Lorraine in 1592. His early work was a series of heroic engravings of Ferdinand de Medici of Florence, exalting the ruler's good works and military victories. Callot also produced traditional, sacred, and aristocratic subjects, suitable for an artist of the court. On the death of his patron he returned to Lorraine and did military maps of battlefields for Louis XIII. But in the maneuverings between Cardinal Richelieu and Charles IV, Callot's home area became the battlefield. Out of these experiences at age 40 came a new and sobering look at warfare. Callot's series of 24 small etchings he called *The Small and Large Miseries and Disasters of War*. They are now more simply and aptly titled *The Miseries of War*. The etchings themselves are small and have an air of charm about them until on looks closely at the subject matter. They begin with "The Enlisting of Troops" and moving on through such scenes as "Pillaging a Farm," "The Strappado," "The Hangman's Tree," "Dying on the Streets," and end with the bitter "Distribution of Rewards" where the wounded veterans are discarded by society. Two years after completing them, Callot was dead. His comment lives on, as succinct as was General Sherman's on the same subject, but Callot's amplifies with a great deal more detail.

The Spanish painter, Goya, had a similar experience and in his last years poured out his loathing of war in a series of etchings, *The Disasters of War*. They were not published until long after his death. The events portrayed were inspired by the invasion of his native Spain in 1810 by Napoleon's armies and the deadly guerrilla warfare waged against the invaders by the whole society. But like Callot, Goya does not take sides but concentrates on what monsters war has made of all who participate, including his fellow Spaniards.

Modern artists whose drawings most nearly capture this spirit seem to have come mainly out of the experience of World War I — two Frenchmen, Forain and Steinlen and two Weimar German artists, Otto Dix and Käthe Kollwitz. I reproduce drawings

77. Jacques Callot : *The Miseries of War,* **The Hanging Tree.** 1630.

78. Francisco Goya : Disasters of War — 5. The Women Give Courage and Are Like Wild Beasts. 1812.

by the two whose work is closer to the cartoon than pure art. Forain was a French partisan during World War I, but was deeply moved by the human cost of war. In "Milestone" he shows the corpses of German and French soldiers who gave their lives over the capture of an insignificant milestone marker at Verdun. Steinlen presents soldiers on their way to the front. Otto Dix is more surrealistic in style. Using a nightmarish technique, Dix showed the individual dread and terror of a man recognizing that he was wounded. Kollwitz focuses on the grief of survivors: parents, widows, and fatherless children.

79. Jean Louis Forain : The Milestone : Verdun. 1916.

80.   Alex Steinlen : "Don't worry, we won't." 1915.

Perhaps less forceful but nevertheless haunting are drawings by two American political cartoonists. Cesare's little German boy looking in wonder at an iron cross catches a poignancy that is difficult to shake off, while Darling's is indigenous Americana.

81.   Oscar Cesare : Christmas Cheer, 1915. New York *Sun*.

**82. Jay N. "Ding" Darling : Those on the Home Front Are Not Casual. 1943.
Des Moines** *Register.*

The Other Side of War

The argument against war's brutality and devastation has led the simple-minded or the hopeful to assume that no nation or its citizens ever win or can hope to win any war. But this is regrettably nonsense. The rules still work differently. Some individuals and some nations have emerged from some wars with increased power, wealth, and honor, and these benefits may not soon be taken from them. There are spoils of war and America, like all other great and many small nations, has at one time or another participated in them. We need only reel off names of nations recently involved in successfully fought wars to demonstrate that wars have their payoffs — Angola, India with Bangladesh, the two Chinas, Chile and other nations with civil wars, the USSR and Poland, Czechoslovakia and Hungary, etcetera, etcetera, etcetera.

War, as the case of Israel illustrates, may end up to be the price for survival as a nation, and this has inspired some moving cartoons. Among the great are those by Englishmen faced with overwhelming odds against survival. Gillray on Napoleon has already been shown in chapter 1. Superior, to my mind, are David Low's, as the British prepared for the expected invasion of the Nazis.

83. David Low : "Very well, alone." June 18, 1940. London *Evening Standard.* By permission of the trustees of the Low estate and the London *Evening Standard.*

Many idealistic young men of England in the 1930s took the Oxford Oath against all wars, and David Low was in sympathy with their view. But when England was faced a few years later with a rampaging Hitler, most Oxford oathers, without any other compulsion, concluded that some things are worse than war, and so too did Low. War has been, and may again be the necessary price for the survival of freedom. The point is made in a brooding cartoon by Félicien Rops, an artist more generally admired for his portrayals of a decadent semi-pornography. The two-headed Austrian eagle over Poland is the victor over liberty. The message of the cartoon does not seem to me to be one of peaceful resignation or pacifism.

143

84.   Félicien Rops : Order Reigns in Warsaw. 1863.

Despite war's horrors, until we stumble into a way of creating a world in which disagreements over the distribution of power, status, and wealth can be settled by diplomacy and other forms of peaceful bargaining, war will be with us. So, too, will pro-war cartoons. Most nations, for the moment at least, prefer the risks involved in occasional wars to the more painful sacrifices that world law and government would require, and most of their citizens, including cartoonists, find this a fact of everyday life that they have to accept. Cartoonists will continue to portray the ultimate horrors of war, but only a few will carry through on the pacifist logic of such convictions when the caissons start rolling along toward a specific war.

The further experiences of some anti-war cartoonists is instructive. Forain and Steinlen fought with the French with their pens during World War I. Otto Dix, who along with "Wounded," drew other of the more moving anti-war illustrations in the twenties, was drafted into the Wehrmacht in the thirties, at age 53. He reluctantly fought with the Nazis until captured by the French. Käthe Kollwitz, whose pacifism and war grief flow from her prints, lost a son, Peter, in World War I, and again a grandson, Peter, with the Nazi army on the Russian front in World War II.

Most other cartoonists in effect enlist for the duration, and so it is best to get about the business of examining the stances cartoonists take as war comes.

Totalitarian Nations at War

Predictably, a totalitarian government channels and dominates the overt expression of internal opinion, and especially so in war, I suppose. Cartoon comment in a totalitarian nation, is orchestrated to fit each stage of conflict — muted, or brought to a feverish pitch of intensity, as the official line decrees. The only consistent theme acceptable is a jingoistic one, and so inevitably the regime's cartoonists play changes on that tune. The villains of these pieces are painted in the grossest of black and the regime leaders are always pure white and heroic. *Life*'s coverage of Soviet cartoons on Hitler sums up the attitude neatly, "devoted to one purpose: the ridicule of an enemy too loathsome to be adequately ridiculed in words."[1] The Hitlerites were not treated as brainless fools but as vermin. The reverse compliment was no doubt paid the Soviets by the Nazis.

So much for predictable totalitarian cartoon response to war. It is more interesting, I think, to observe how their cartoonists get trapped by the official line. We turn to Soviet cartoons. Because of the shortage of reprinted wartime cartoons, I will

85. N. Lisogorsky: "But Traveller, it won't work." January 1, 1961. *Pravda.* **Reprinted with permission from Michael M. Milenkovitch,** *The View from Red Square.*

145

concentrate on what has rightfully been called *cold* warfare, noting the kind of ideological logic that goes into its cartoon production. It is not, I think, very different in its assumptions from the wartime output. Cartoons from the books on Soviet cartoons previously noted, particularly those of Nelson and Milenkovitch, will be cited.[3]

The political cartoons of Milenkovitch's study, produced during the early period of cold war, reflect Marxist assumptions reinforced by the bitter Soviet experience of Nazi invasion. The official assumptions are two: capitalistic imperialism is the cause of wars, and Nazism is the ultimate form of capitalism. These basic assumptions have not been changed easily by new events or by logic. They lead to a predictable conclusion: any war against the Soviet Union must be started by fascists.

The Soviet cartoons thus quite easily identified their postwar opponents, the American and Western European capitalist nations, with Nazism. The symbolism over

86. **B. Efimov: In their "Image." August 23, 1949.** *Pravda.* **Reprinted with permission from Michael M. Milenkovitch,** *The View from Red Square.*

and over stresses the identification of the West and Nazism, as in a cartoon where Hitler's face is composed of the names Adenauer, Brandt, and Strauss, or when Vice-President Johnson of the Kennedy years is shown picking up Nazi refuse. The swastika and dollar and pound signs are used interchangeably as the symbols of imperialistic capitalism, with the high Nazi-type military hats serving as a symbol for its military aspect. The message is that capitalists make war as naturally as rabbits make lots of little rabbits.

The patriotic cartoons, also predictably, show smiling but firm *young* Socialists facing down the tired, greedy, *old* capitalists, as for example, Eisenhower reaching for Cuba and being stopped by a cleaned-up Castro.

Perhaps the clearest picture of the way the assumptions get in the way is in the treatment of Tito at the time of his astonishing break with the Soviets. For a full year after Stalin's denunciation of him on June 28, 1948, Milenkovitch says that no Soviet cartoon appeared in *Pravda* on this topic. Then the famous cartoonist Efinov, a wartime friend of David Low, faced up to the subject that was rocking the Communist world. He portrayed the straying Yugoslav as a Nazi worshiper, leaving ambiguous for the moment what caused this conversion to what the Soviets regarded as an ultimate form of capitalism. An explicit tie of Tito to American capitalism is also made in several cartoons, usually with a small Tito portrayed as a lackey of Uncle Sam.

To our eyes, the tie of Tito to Hitler so soon after his own bitter battles with the Nazis during World War II seems the height of purposeful falsification. More outrageous is the claim for his conversion to American capitalism. So it may have been. Efinov and his colleagues may have whipped out these claims about Tito, tongue in cheek, knowing they were the Big Lie. But a second explanation also is possible. The Marxist official assumption then held with the intensity of orthodox religious truth was that capitalism is always the root cause of war. While events such as the disaffection of a Communist state may raise doubts about this assumption, it is perhaps more comfortable for Marxists to interpret the crisis by raising questions about the troublemaker. Either there are other causes of conflict and the sacred writings are questionable on this important point, or Tito was a secret capitalist Judas all along. If one avoids the trauma of questioning basic assumptions, which is a common human trait of both capitalists and Marxists, the explanation for Tito's defection logically follows.

The taboo in a totalitarian system of any public questioning of basic assumptions is what keeps its official-line cartoons so vapid. Despite their occasional cleverness and even at times great wit, the cartoons tend to have a frozen-in-ice quality. Events must often be outrageously twisted to fit into the pattern of assumptions. This is not to say that these assumptions may not be changed, but this is generally done only from the top and after much hand-wringing. Stalin was, in fact, denounced as a bloodthirsty tyrant and, to at least my astonishment, the official recognition of this obvious fact made the whole system shudder and tremble. Everyone but perhaps Bernard Shaw or the Webbs seems to have discerned the fact some years previously.

The Nazi tie to an ideology was similarly crippling, especially during the war, one would suppose. With the Nazi totalitarians, the root cause of war was, of course, the scheming of Jews, especially against the Fatherland and the Aryan race. Variations on themes by Mendelssohn or Rothschild also had their limitations. The Anglican church, as noted, along with many other organizations or people, including a cartoonist with the German name of Shoemaker, had to be painted as Jew inspired or else the assumption be amended. The choice was an easy one. Besides such embarrassments, a good many potentially valuable citizens were sacrificed to this lunacy.

The authoritarian nation flirting with or entering war presents a situation of a little more interest. If the governmental leaders are prudent and successful, cartoon comment seems often to play a surprisingly supportive role; even some of the regime's internal critics will be voluntarily supportive. Thus the carefully planned and victorious moves of Bismarck against Austria and then France were patriotically applauded by assorted former critics such as drew in the journal *Kladderadatsch*.[4] Perhaps this was because Bismarck's goal was to strengthen the German nation by adding to its power, wealth, and honor. For that all good Germans could be

87.   Paul Hadol : The Vulture. 1871.

appreciative, even, one suspects, those who wanted a change of distribution of benefits and a change of regime.

The picture is different, though, if the war starts to go badly for an authoritarian government, as was the case with Germany in World War I and the France of Louis Napoleon against Bismarck in 1870. The initial reaction of an ill-informed citizenry to the war may be naive enthusiasm. Later the government may attempt to force consent, but if the events move to defeat or stagnation, the criticism of the old leaders is likely to become bitter and intense; and this intensity is likely to carry over for a long period after peace. (Defeated totalitarian nations, if Nazi Germany and Fascist Italy are examples, seem not to suffer this lingering bitterness.)

A losing war is the crisis of legitimacy for an authoritarian government, which it frequently does not survive. The inherent horror of war and the losses suffered, seemingly for nothing, touch off a revulsion of the old regime and the social forces that supported it. In the France of 1870 public opinion, led by critics including especially the political cartoonists, swung, through shock, from sharply favorable to, to sharply against every leader of the former authoritarian regime. The bitterness seems to have known no bounds as to good taste or human decency. One is reminded of George Grosz drawings of the Weimar Republic. Both pursue every vestige of the

88.   Honoré Daumier : Those Who Are About to Die. ... 1870.

authoritarian system; the nobility, the military and the clerics. They demand their extermination. Some of the collected cartoon output from the 1870 period in France is now readily available, but I should like to note especially a few of the cartoons of the more humane Honoré Daumier.

As war approached in 1870, the pro-government cartoons by Napoleon supporters proclaimed and predicted an easy victory.[5] The assumptions were those of a magnificent emperor who would easily conquer the stupid, blockheaded Germans. In this period Daumier was much more restrained, and he remained obliquely skeptical. His political work warned against the strength of Prussia and uncertainties of war. He mocks the reluctance to disarm on the part of all nations and openly wonders about the possibility of a peace balanced on bayonet points. He shudders over the German needle gun used so successfully in Austria. When war arrived, Daumier remained a patriot to the nation, if not the regime. He salutes in his cartoons, with heartbreaking resignation, those who are about to die for France, not just for the regime, in the battles gainst the Germans. He seems to me to hope for a victorious outcome. But the war went badly and for Daumier the lid became loosened and finally fell off. Out came bitter political cartoons. What then was Daumier's cartoon comment as war destroyed the empire in 1870? The themes were three.

The first was of intense sadness for the state of France. A second was sardonic relief

89.   Honoré Daumier : France, Prometheus and the Vulture, 1871.

150

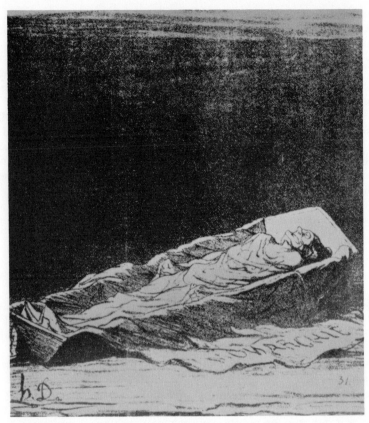

90. Honoré Daumier : And During All This Time They Kept on Saying He Never Felt Better. 1872.

in being rid of a pretentious and dangerous adventurer who was an enemy of the Republic. Daumier expressed his feelings simply and directly in a bitter antimonarchial and anticlerical attack. His most moving cartoon features monarchy in a coffin and the most amusing Voltaire thumbing his nose at mud-flinging clerics. A third theme expresses hope by glorifying the maiden, republican France. At the same time he now attacks the Germans and Bismarck for defiling the Republican dream. No prints glorify the commune and the internal split it represents. Only sadness is expressed for a nation turned upon itself in civil war. He hopes for a free France.

As time went on, Daumier had the same grave misgivings, tinged with bitterness, that were generally experienced by reformist idealists. France remained republican rather than becoming authoritarian or totalitarian. But because France strove to be a democratic republic, many aspects of the old regime could not be swept away. The clerics crept back and soon assumed much of their former status in full regalia. The wire-puller of Louis Philippe and Napoleon III, Adolphe Thiers, came back to power as President of the Republic. But at least there was a republic and somehow it would survive, if only because of the lack of unity among monarchists. Daumier could only express a mixture of hope and helpless anger. The bitter showdown between the

151

aristocratic forces questioning the republic's legitimacy and those who hoped to eliminate the old regime was 27 years away in the Dreyfus case, long after Daumier had drawn his last cartoon.

Thus in an authoritarian system criticism may be muted up to the point of disaster in war. But following such disaster comes a citizen sense of exploitation by feckless leaders. Cartoonists may express such revulsion. A surge of hatred of the former ruling elite may result in a split between those who would remove every vestige of the old regime immediately and those who would salvage and even reestablish it if they but could. In between are those who would attempt to domesticate all such feudal remains into the new democratic system. Just as in France in 1870, so too the German Weimar Republic of the 1920s faced such an internal split through its existence. I suggest that accommodation was, incidentally, the route an authoritarian England wisely took in 1688 and 1832, but not in 1660, when the less pragmatic Puritans were calling the shots. Authoritarian systems, failing, do not easily remove the poisons — at least, so their cartoonists seem to suggest.

Democracies at War

In democracies, public opinion will usually, but not always, favor avoidance of war, but will vigorously support the government if the nation gets involved against a threatening foe. The initial reaction is likely to be trust of government and a general adoption of the official line voluntarily by cartoonists and other critics.

A glance at democratic cartoons during small wars, however, suggests that even an established and effective democracy cannot handle well a long war against a second-rate foe, especially if it picked the fight itself. Such wars, it seems, must be waged quickly as border clashes or small mutinies and ended with a certain amount of flourish, as if to justify the rightness of the national cause. A prolonged guerrilla war leads to doubts, and a crisis of legitimacy for the democratic regime. It is the spark needed to fire a movement that begins calling for an internal redistribution of political, social, and economic power. This will usually not be enough to fuel a revolution, but it can cause a few earth-moving convulsions.

It is not only the cartoonist's reaction to the U.S. campaign in the Vietnam war that suggests this conclusion. The trying experience of France in Algeria, and of Great Britain in the Boer War, her struggles with Ireland, and even the semi-democratic Britain in her struggle with the American colonists in 1776, all point the same direction. Democracies can fight prolonged wars only for survival, because war is not highly approved of or treated lightly by a sizable number of their citizens. Citizens tend to disapprove of fighting prolonged wars with lesser foes for glory or amusement or spoils or other small triumphs and its cartoonists soon reflect this view. The result usually is a sapping of the regime's moral credibility and the whole-hearted support the government receives from its own citizens or critics. (An exception may possibly be wars advertised as forestalling conquest, for example, Israel at Suez.) A democratic nation can survive the discomforts of small wars badly fought, but the roller-coaster ride of wrenches and jolts is not a pleasant experience for anyone.

Britain provides an excellent example of a democracy that has permitted wide freedom to its internal critics as it plowed through a long history of major and minor warfare, and so I use it to illustrate some cartoonists' stances toward war.

Enthusiastic pro-war opinion that emerged as romantic and idealistic patriotism was the initial stance in England from 1850 through the slaughter of World War I, judging by much cartoon comment. This view of war stressed idealistic benefits, both personal and national, while dismissing the costs of war as minimal or irrelevant. John Leech in his Crimean War drawing catches this mood. It seems to suggest that goodness, truth, bravery, and morality are all on the Empire side. So too, it may perceptively be discerned, is God. Little "illfare" can therefore come; only welfare. This is of course essentially a naive and adolescent view and one with built-in tragedy. Even the John Leech cartoon shows a few tearstained faces.

91. John Leech : Enthusiasm of Paterfamilias, on Reading the Report of the Grand Charge of British Cavalry at Balaklava. November 25, 1854. *Punch.*

The World War I British cartoons at the time of Britain's entry stress these high-minded themes. The obverse of such cartoons is to paint the enemy as devils as in the cartoons of E. J. Sullivan. As the war ground on through its first year, British cartoonists began turning out atrocity pictures. I include here one cartoon by the Australian Norman Lindsay. We are inclined to view such with disdain, as self-serving, forgetting the shock that total war was to a generation that believed in the inevitable progress toward peace and democracy and the performance of the British system. The atrocity cartoons are not lovely, but they were motivated initially by a civilized impulse. Only later did it dawn on Britons that neither side had a monopoly on committing atrocities.

A different stance, resignation, came to the English population at large as the result of the World War I horrors. They accepted involvement in war in what may be called the realistic, or perhaps one should say the resigned pro-war position. As World War I

92.   Edmund J. Sullivan : Jack the Giant Killer, Dedicated to the King of the
Belgians. 1916. *The Kaiser's Garland.*

ground on, this stance became the common one. Most of the glory gets dissipated. The
Bairnsfather cartoons of World War I, (e.g. "If you knows a better 'ole") were among
the first modern British cartoons I know of to state this theme with some clarity,
though it is implicit in much of Kipling's war poetry of an earlier date and of course is
the central core of Bill Mauldin's superlative war drawings (Fig. 12).

93. Norman Lindsay: Onward Christian Soldiers. 1916. Sidney (Australia) *Bulletin.*

Real Anti-war cartoons are a feature of the post-war disillusion. Those which we find published during wars are of long drawn-out wars with small nations. They are often obliquely critical, as in the Gould comment on the Boer War.

94. Will Dyson : Wonders of Science. 1916.

Earlier I suggested that citizens in democracies, and probably citizens in most nations, could they but express themselves, commonly oppose wars, unless they believe they are wars of defense. American public opinion, as judged by its cartoonists, seems to have reflected all of the above stances toward war. Crucial to these citizens' reactions has been America's isolation which shaped their assumptions about the causes of war, and it is to this subject I turn next. I caution, however, that we are looking at assumptions of men of goodwill, though at times, and for some cartoonists, they seem remarkably like some of those held by the technical experts of the day who specialize in the study of war and international relations.

95. Francis C. Gould : A.D. 1920. Mr. Chamberlain — Good morning, Arthur, any news? Have they caught DeWet yet? Mr. Balfour : No, not yet; but I hear he's surrounded. December 18, 1900. The Westminster *Gazette*.

America and War: 1898-1945

The role of public opinion in forming democratic policy gives us the opportunity to examine cartoons for clues of how assumptions about war and its causes change under the impact of events. Such assumptions are not easily changed even in democracies. New experience is likely to be the most effective teacher. We can, I think, safely assume that the assumptions are easier to change in a democracy than in authoritarian or totalitarian systems. Because it is a mechanism for changing such assumptions, free speech is deemed worth the difficulties it creates.

To methodically explore the shifts of American opinion toward war as reflected in its cartoons would require selecting random samples of these cartoons, classifying the images cartoonists create of the regimes' leaders and opponents for the messages they convey, and looking for messages and assumptions directly stated or implied. This kind of survey of cartoons will not be attempted here. What I do attempt is impressionistic rather than methodical. I will depend on cartoons that have survived in reasonably accessible form, and use particularly drawings that we are told were at the time widely applauded. When possible, I will present cartoons from several artists on the same topic, trying to find a variety on the liberal-conservative continuum. Unless otherwise specified, the cartoons I use will be by the artists involved in drawing for the mass market of opinion.

Like most nations America was born in a war. The significant fact is that it was a war that many Americans regarded as against a feudal king and his satraps, and that notion seems to have remained in America's consciousness. In the cartoons of *Puck* and *Judge* in the 1880s and in Nast's major anti-war cartoon, this assumption emerges — kings are the cause of wars.

Americans appear to have gone into the Spanish American War of 1898-1900 with the enthusiasm of naive patriots. There were a few mass-media critics of the war and, as far as cartoons were concerned, they seemed to be concentrated in one mass-media source — the upper-middle-class magazine *Life*. E. W. Kemble, William Walker, and F. T. Richards all drew anti-war cartoons. Most of the mass-media cartoonists were critics who were supporters of the war, and many were at the level of *Judge's* balanced view of the enemy, expressed in Grant Hamilton's portrayal on the cover as an ape with bloody paws.

Both supporters and opponents of the war, interestingly, seemed to accept the same assumptions about the causes of war. The opponents stressed that Uncle Sam was misled by European feudal fads and railed against the war as they did against American debutantes who married European titles. The supporters could portray the war as the striking-off of feudal Spanish chains in Cuba, Hawaii, and the Philippines.

What John Hay called a splendid little war ended with a quick and easy victory and an embarrassing market basket of spoils. America had defeated one of Europe's oldest feudal monarchies without too much effort and had established itself in fact as well as official pronouncements as the dominant nation of the Western Hemisphere, just as James Monroe had so long ago proclaimed that it was. The anti-feudal assumption already held was confirmed by the war. Even worse, it led to a feeling that democracies seemingly could or would do little wrong. The self-congratulatory mood of manifest destiny bloomed further under Theodore Roosevelt as the nation acquired the Panama Canal and settled a war between the Russian and Japanese empires. Democracy seemed to pay off.

This assumption underlies the work of cartoonists as World War I unfolded. War is made necessary by the machinations of corrupt and archaic feudal monarchs. Such outmoded feudal leaders seek war because they glory in the pomp of military splendor and aggrandizement, or else they are prone to excesses and saber-rattling that inadvertently leads to war. The root cause of war thus is political, in that feudal monarchs and self-proclaimed Emperors vie with each other for the spoils of empire, in a manner suited to the Middle Ages or to Graustark or Zenda, but not to modern times. The solution of the problem of war is to replace an outdated feudalism with modern democracy, with self-rule and self-determination in those nations ready for it. It is now overlooked, but this was the moral rationale of William Randolph Hearst, then a socialist radical. He favored a war with feudal Spain to liberate Cuba's subjugated freedom fighters. And, of course, the war also harmonized with the very practical goal of increasing newspaper circulation. To summarize: no kings, no wars.

In the early stages of World War I, most Americans assumed that the people of other nations should themselves overthrow kings, if they wanted to be free. Most wanted the job of replacing feudal monarchs done without U.S. involvement, beyond the raising of a few cheers.

96.   Luther Bradley : The Seat of the Trouble. May 29, 1916. Chicago *Daily News.*

In the cartoons of the prewar period, and even as war began, the anti-feudal stance is general. Luther Bradley makes a neat allusion to impacted crowns that need pulling out. He further speculates whether a war easily begun can be stopped so easily.

97.   Luther Bradley : The Self-Starter Worked All Right. September 15, 1914. **Chicago** *Daily News.*

A change in assumptions begins as Britain and France's danger of going under becomes more apparent. The shift in American cartoon comment is from one of treating all feudal monarchies as the root cause of war to that of focusing on one type of feudal monarchy as a diseased menace — a kind of special nagging and virulent strain. That type was the Prussian one, in which military pomp and glory and realpolitik Bismarck style were said to be honed to the finest edge and to be the guiding principle of the regime. Junkerism was claimed to have indoctrinated the formerly benign German system with the virus of arrogance, as exemplified in "Deutschland, Deutschland über Alles." W. A. Rogers catches both the trappings of German militarism and the prehistoric survival theme in one such cartoon.

This new theme was elaborated over and over in the image of German Kultur, borrowed especially from the democratic cartoonist Louis Raemaekers of neutral Holland. His impact on Americans seems incredible. I count ten or more articles on

98.   W.A. Rogers : A Survival of the Dark Ages. January 1917. New York *Herald.*

Louis Raemaekers in American popular magazines between 1915 and 1918. He was hired by Hearst, made a whirlwind trip to America in 1918, and was consistently treated with lionizing reverence in America. He looks today like a dreadful atrocity-monger par excellence. Nothing was too monstrous for him to believe about the Germans. But what he drew with such deep emotion and heavy religious symbolism seems now to have been drawn for cheap effect. Partly, he was a nineteenth-century liberal reacting in disbelief. We are less easily shocked. It is, perhaps, because we have become as brutalized in waging war as any culture that ever existed. But there is more. I incline to the opinion expressed by an anonymous Englishman in the London *Times* of 1916, that these atrocity cartoons also had something very childish about them, "as if the Kaiser and the Crown Prince belonged to nursery stories rather than to real life."[6] But Raemakers, with his simple-minded bogeyman stories, had an impact on American cartoonists.

99. Louis Raemaekers : My Son, Belgium, 1914. "Ah! was your boy among the twelve this morning? Then you'll find him among this lot." 1914.

The argument was that not only the monarch but his henchmen trained in the system of Prussian militarism had created a vast inhuman army of Wagnerian monsters and Huns. Some critics saw as peculiarly barbarous a mixture of modern German science and the spirit of the Goths who had vandalized Rome.

Luther Bradley of the Chicago *Daily News* has been described by William Murrell and others as the only major anti-war cartoonist up until his death in 1917. He never buys the pacifist line, though he shows no love for Germans. His view is still "a plague on both your houses." He shows extreme sympathy for small nations such as Greece and Rumania, which he paints as victims in a European culture turned barbaric. But he condemns British feudalistic high-handedness as well as German. His refusal to give up an earlier underlying assumption leads him to argue that the United States has no stake in a conflict in which the world's last monarchs are being liquidated by each other. An examination of his book of cartoons, published in 1917,

100.   Oscar Cesare : The Octopus. 1915. New York *Sun*.

162

shows a preparedness theme throughout, with at least one directly anti-pacifist cartoon included. Bradley's is a classic isolationist and nationalist stance. Despite, or perhaps because of his long previous residence in Australia, he concludes that the fate of Britain and France do not justify the United States in becoming involved in a World War to save them.

The underlying assumption accepted by both Oscar Cesare (New York *Sun*) and W. A. Rogers (New York *Herald*) and even by Boardman Robinson is that Germany is a special case of feudalism akin to an inflamed appendix, and this assumption gradually leads them to the opposite conclusion from Bradley's. All of these were outstanding liberal cartoonists; two had contributed to the *Masses*. Rather than opposing royalty or militarism in general, they single out the German system of Schrecklichkeit as being particularly reprehensible. "The Octopus," by Cesare, represented here, suggests the result of such militarism on United States interests. England as John Bull and France as Joan of Arc are occasionally criticized but generally are heroically presented fighting off this prehistoric throwback. The German image they present emphasizes a medievalism gone crazy in a modern world: helmet with the spear on top, high military boots and goose step, the clanking medals, the pointed-up moustache and menacing cape. The Cesare cartoons, which date from 1916, combine a clear isolationist tendency with the message that war was begun and continued by the Kaiser and the system of military self-aggrandizement he created. The latter message comes through more and more strongly in the imagery, and finally it dominates.

101.   Boardman Robinson : Untitled. 1915.

W. A. Rogers's book was published in 1917 but contains cartoons before this date. It is more outspoken in its criticism of the German Junker. His early work is a justification for American involvement on the side of the world's other large-scale democracies: Britain and France. He, more than Cesare, limits the cause of war to a distorted and rather awful militarism of Germany alone, and he plays his major variations on this theme, painting atrocities with unsubtle comment that is meant to be devastating, but more often than not comes off to later generations as not too far from the villain tying Pauline to the railroad track. The intensity of feelings is shown in the Rehse cartoon that associates the candidacy of Charles Evans Hughes for President in 1916 with German militarism. A less-well-known cartoonist, Hanny (St. Joseph, Mo., *News Press*), in 1916 presents a clumsier picture of the isolationist theme, with occasional slaps in England, much pro-preparedness and anti-pacifist argument,

102.   W.A. Rogers : Another Case of Wiping Hands on the American Flag. 1916.
New York *Herald*.

but with Germany, when presented, coming out negatively.[7] An additional source is the books of "Ding" Darling, which reprint his early cartoons. His Kaiser is sometimes silly more than murderous, but the same argument on the irrelevancy of feudalism and the stupidity of militarism is also seldom absent.[8]

When America enters the war, it is on the basis of the new argument. President Woodrow Wilson changed his mind about the war and expressed the new theme that America had the duty to help make the world safe for democracy, which German feudalism, gone mad, was preventing. Once this last concentration of feudal debris was cleared away, he argued, a League of Nations could handle whatever minor disputes might arise among the world's happy, democratically governed peoples.

Rogers and other cartoonists present a patriotic front voluntarily that would do the dynasty of Ivan the Terrible credit. No soldiers have ever been quite so noble and, one is tempted to add, mindless — and that, pray God, no Americans will ever be again.

To summarize: the generalized assumption of these mass media cartoonists before World War I seems to have been that wars were caused by obsolete royal nonsense, or worse. The unfolding of the wars causes leading cartoonists to embrace the conclusions that Germany is an extreme and probably the last case of this type of medievalism, and that the faltering democracies must be saved from this particular form of militaristic Prussian imperialism.

103.   G.W. Rehse : Carrying the Banner, 1916. St. Paul *Pioneer Press.*

104.   W. A. Rogers : To France! 1917. New York *Herald*.

This theme is to some extent found in the drawings of the war's most severe cartoon critics, in the *Masses*. A John Sloan cartoon, in which the devil in a card game with St. Peter wins "with 4 kings," squarely hits the anti-monarchy theme. The famous Robert Minor cartoon (Fig. 11) is one of the best statements ever drawn against militarism — albeit not German militarism alone, but all types. It implies, as few cartoons have done, that war is only a game like chess, to be played among a few generals and political leaders, with the masses being mainly pawns. But the *Masses* also sounded a different note: that war had an economic cause, that it was the result of capitalism gone amuck. The Art Young cartoon "Having Their Fling," for which he was brought to trial, is based on this assumption (Fig. 121). All of capitalism's lackeys dance to the tune of war. It is a theme that does not, for a generation, enter into the mass-produced cartoon market.

Postwar cartooning reflected President Wilson's experiences in treaty-making and

America's general unhappiness with the results of the war to make the world safe for democracies. No one was satisfied with the result. The assumption quite naturally shifts from one condemning wars as the result of Prussianism or even feudalism to one that concludes that world wars and most colonial wars too are the result of the scheming balance-of-power politicians and diplomats of Europe, democratic or otherwise. All are concerned only with imperialistic spoils. I suppose that this classifies as a cultural assumption. Clemenceau is presented as desiring only vindictive revenge and German territory, while Lloyd George is a wicked man, full of shrewdness and duplicity, whose only aim is the selfish one of preserving the British Empire and its interests. In such a wicked world only Americans are painted as holding ideals above selfish interest. As late as the thirties this theme continued to appear. War debts unpaid became the symbol of American disgust with Europe's wicked power politics. The Kellogg-Briand Peace Pact of 1928 was the high tide of American soupy idealism about itself. It hoped to abolish aggression by wolves by having everyone who turned up in sheep's clothing sign an agreement. Most American cartoonists seemed determined to accept the supposition that their nation was the innocent but pure country boy come to the wicked big city. One of the great American cartoons, by Batchelor (Fig. 125), was drawn just as isolationism came under attack and was waning. It captures this view with startling bluntness and suggests Sandburg's painted women of Chicago, under the gaslights, luring the farm boy. Another, typical of Chicago *Tribune* school of art, plays directly on the theme that innocence and democracy were like chastity; they must be protected from contamination in a wicked European world.

105.   Carey Orr : The Only Way We Can Save Her. 1939. Reprinted courtesy of the Chicago *Tribune*.

To this wicked world were added in the thirties the machinations of capitalist munition makers, an idea borrowed from radical sources. This is an early suggestion of the economic argument for war in the mass media. These cartoons suggest that capitalists cause wars because they are imperialistic war profiteers. Other writers have noted that such ideas particularly took hold in German-American areas still smarting under the super-patriotism and ethnic discrimination of World War I days.

Not all cartoon opinion of the twenties took the simple isolationist tack. Rollin Kirby had the heretical thought that the United States should have joined the League of Nations, and he kept repeating that notion along with other heresies and even won a Pulitzer Prize with it. He also dared to put faith in organizations such as a World Court, but he was swimming against the tide of dominant opinion, which probably thought of itself as pacifist but was sure it was pure and isolationist. He shares an affinity with the upper-middle-class cartoonists of *Life* in 1898. Kirby's cartoons seem to me to suggest a kind of obliqueness and hesitancy on this subject, but perhaps I read into them what wasn't there.

At what point and how did the mainstream American assumptions begin to change? I suggest that that shift came with Hitler. More important, what was the basis for a new set of assumptions or guiding principles?

In 1934 the Nazi party began amalgamating its position. Hindenburg had done his bit by appointing Hitler Chancellor of Germany and dying. The book-burnings and

106.   Rollin Kirby : I sympathize deeply with you, Madam, but I cannot associate with you. 1921. New York *World*.

Jew-baiting and other intimidations had begun. Opposition within Germany was still occurring, but was being methodically eliminated as Hitler announced such projects as banning decadent art, increasing the population by sending women back to the kitchen and nearby bedroom, and organizing youth corps from what resulted. At this point a *Nazi* publishing house issued two collectons of anti-Hitler cartoons collected from world newspaper sources. The purpose of these really astonishing productions, according to the German text, was to demonstrate how much attention even those who hated him were paying to the Führer. Ernst Hanfstaengl, their editor, must have been a remarkable salesman to have sold the other Nazis this line. He also was one of the early defectors from Nazi Germany. It is his second volume of 1934 I used for illustration.[9]

American cartoonists who were represented in the Hanfstaengl volume included Herblock, Daniel Fitzpatrick, Rollin Kirby, Vaughn Shoemaker, and perhaps the most outspoken critic of Hitler at this early point, Jerry Doyle.

Hitler in 1934 did not jar the old assumptions about European machinations. In the beginning, American cartoonists adopted a "laugh him off" approach. A mainly psychological explanation of his antics appears in these 1933 and 1934 American cartoons. Most Americans drew him as a freak who had somehow momentarily gotten

107.   Cecil Jensen : A Unanimous Election. 1934. Chicago *Daily News.*

in power. They are not sure whether he is a clown or a befuddled crank with dingbats in his belfry, but do not seem to believe that he will last or that he presents a real menace. Whether clown or mental freak, the assumption about Hitler is the same: out there in Europe is a world full of nuts to be avoided. Among such portrayals is that by Cecil Jensen, which makes Hitler look like a second Charles Chaplin. At this stage Vaughn Shoemaker, who was to become one of the most effective Hitler critics, presents Hitler as a screwy prankster or village clod on a par with Woody Woodpecker, setting off mischievous fireworks. Shoemaker even gets the swastika backwards, as do several other American artists in this collection. Others present Hitler as a puffed-up little man who is strutting about like an operetta comic while his betters moan and groan and the responsibles in Germany, for example, Hindenberg, hang their heads in shame. The message is that Europe's responsible leaders are to blame for allowing this pitiful neurotic to gain power, even for just a little while, but it will probably soon be over.

Herblock drew Hitler as a steamroller, which has some suggestion of a threat, and Fitzpatrick showed him trying to fill Hindenberg's big shoes. While both present Hitler with faces more menacing than not, neither has as yet given full vent to his uneasiness.

108. Vaughn Shoemaker : Starting the Fireworks. April 26, 1932. Chicago *Daily News.*

170

But not all American cartoonists brushed Hitler aside as an accidental nuisance or just a potential threat, even at this early stage. Hitler's clear-cut anti-libertarian, reactionary, and nationalistic acts suggest an economic assumption to Jerry Doyle. He presents a series of Hitler-as-a-puppet cartoons, suggesting that the real powers behind him are wire-pullers of industrial cartels and the military. At the same time, he begins to sense an independent evil political force, and draws Hitler as the leading actor of a famous statuary group.

109.   Jerry Doyle : "We believe he (Hitler) is guided by a voice on high in shaping Germany's destiny" — Rudolf Hess. June 27, 1934. Philadelphia *Record*. Reprinted courtesy Jerry Doyle.

The assumption that some of these same cartoonists moved toward in the next few years, and soon made explicit, is the Doyle one. Some begin to portray Hitler and his Fascism as an outgrowth of imperialistic capitalism, leading a counterattack on depression-inspired progressivism. It is this economic interpretation of the war that increasingly dominates one wing of interventionist comment. A variant is the recognition that the fear of Bolshevism has created something far beyond, and different from a virulent form of capitalism. Fitzpatrick with his rolling swastika machine, which symbolizes modern industrialism, combined with Nazi cold-blooded efficiency seems to me to catch this new mood. (I present a wartime Fitzpatrick here because of its magnificence.)

171

110.   Jerry Doyle : "I saved the Reich." August 20, 1934. Philadelphia *Record.*

A second set of interventionist assumptions comes to be based more on a political than an economic analysis. Wars, it says, are caused by gangsters and adventurers. This seems to me to characterize the later work of Shoemaker, Darling, and other economically conservative cartoonists. It assumes that wars result from abuse of power, but the view has become a little more sophisticated. It holds that aggressors, whether capitalist or Communist, come from many sources as the opportunity presents itself, but mainly occur where internal democratic checks are absent. To use a homey analogy, they portray the need as for a cop on the corner. Typical of Shoemaker's prewar warnings is "Path of Appeasement." The guiding assumption of such comment is that political piracy will eventually affect everyone in the world and it is to everyone's interest to stop it. It was, in fact, a favorite view of such League of Nations advocates as W. A. Rogers during the First World War and as the Second World War progressed, and again led to the conclusion that a stronger form of international cooperation was desirable. The weakness of international action, from Japan's invasion of Manchuria through Mussolini in Ethiopia and Hitler in Europe, is the lesson hammered home in such cartoons. Without really thinking it through, these critics assumed that some sort of political police force and international organization has to be formed to stop international criminals.

After Pearl Harbor isolationism joins these two types of interventionist view to work hand in hand for victory. Batchellor's two Pearl Harbor Day cartoons provide an example; the first is a "stay-out-of-war" death's head; the second is a reaction to the

172

111.   Daniel Fitzpatrick : From the Baltic to the Black. August 24, 1941. St. Louis *Post Dispatch.*

news and is now for winning.

As the war goes on there is a blending about what causes war — the lack of a world policeman to stop the greedy or the misguided. The economic-determinist assumption seems to fade out (particularly after the Nazi-Soviet pact). In its place is a realistic assumption that every society, including the international one, will have a share of criminals.

There is also a new maturity about why we fight. Bill Mauldin more than anyone else catches and hammers home the point that warlike policing of a neighborhood is a dirty business, but one someone has to take care of. His aspirin cartoon (Fig. 12) is typical. His soldiers have a resigned heroism without heroics, or at least display reverse heroics. Viewers perhaps need to be reminded that while these dirty and unshaven GI's were kind to children and dogs, they were murderously effective as soldiers and killers of the enemy. The popularity of Mauldin cartoons suggests that Americans had grown up a little.

The psychological assumption continued to be favored by some unreconstructed isolationists, some of whom perhaps despaired of ever creating an effective world

112.   Vaughn Shoemaker : Blow upon Blow. 1939. Chicago *Daily News.*

organization or a police force attached to it. They preferred to treat Hitler and Japan's
rulers as special cases of neurotic nuts who came to power by accident and would
probably never get such an opportunity again. This view emphasized the illogic of
most of the world out there and supported the war only because we now were attacked
and in it. Implicit is an assumption of American superiority. The Parrish cartoon from
the Chicago *Tribune* presents this view sharply. A series by Reg Manning of Little
Itchy, which shows the Japanese as funny little men and the European war as a
terrytoon comedy, harmonizes with this kind of psychological analysis.

But the dominant assumption that survived the war seems to have been the one
mentioned, that its cause was political. This assumption moved a Vandenburg from
decades of isolationism to trying to help build an international political order. It traces
wars to aggressors and finds safety in international security. The cold war in Greece
and Turkey, and Korea, and the events leading up to Vietnam reinforced this
assumption in the postwar period, for it seemed to most that a nation need not be
capitalistic or be led by psychological crackpots, to be imperialistic or to resort to
international gangsterism.

113. Joseph Parrish : Some Day They'll Come Crawling Back to Her. 1947.
Reprinted courtesy of the Chicago *Tribune.*

The unfolding of the Vietnam war brings a shock to this major American assumption. The early view was that the military action was a police action, an act of selfless mutual security to stop aggressors. It comes to be questioned as the staggering costs it demands and the kind of status quo it required America to defend become apparent. The poverty of have-not nations becomes part of the equation. As things go badly with each additional escalation, all of the old assumptions of the isolationists begin to turn up in cartoons, often seriatim in the same cartoonist. One theme is that America became involved in the war because of its own miscalculating leaders and then that these are power-mad rulers. The war was no longer portrayed as a policing of aggression but an internal civil war, which America could not disentangle herself from because of the false pride of its presidents. The psychological-quirk theory akin to the Hitler crackpot assumption gets widely applied to the executive. Interestingly, the cartoon comparison of presidents and medieval feudal kings becomes common. The National Security Council, CIA, and Chiefs of Staff become the equivalent of Prussian militarism, Dr. Strangelove fashion. Finally, the economic assumption of the anti-capitalists also resurfaced with full force. War was the result of Fascism.

The assumption most generally accepted as the root of disasters after the smoke began to clear is one I am less sure about. It was, I believe, the political one: that even in a democracy, power concentrated in a chief executive without sufficient democratic

114.   Reg Manning : Hon. Trap Veery Success — 1943. Arizona *Republic*.

checks would inevitably be abused. Whatever the justification for policing gangsters, a land war in Asia without strong allies was not the shrewdest way of going about it.

In this brief review of wartime cartoons in the American democracy, three themes occur: an economic assumption that wars stem from the sins of capitalism; a psychological one, stemming from special unexplained quirks of leaders; and one that attributes war to an absence of political checks on power-hungry individuals or nations. The last seems to form the basis for consensus at each point in history, whether wars are blamed on feudal monarchs, Prussian militarism, European capitalists, cranks, or our own leaders.

In time, events change the underlying assumptions into new shapes. Rather than being twisted and distorted so that at all costs the original assumptions may remain intact, they are reformulated to fit new cases. This seems to be a major advantage of democracy as well as a significant characteristic of it. Cartoonists contribute strength to this system by interacting with public opinion, criticizing and questioning the acts of leaders, and influencing and reflecting the formation of new explanatory assumptions.

115.   Paul Szep : "We are not going to send American Boys 9,000 or 10,000 miles to do what Asian boys ought to be doing for themselves." Lyndon Johnson (1964 Campaign). February 24, 1968. Boston *Globe.*

A Closing Note

War is a highly unpleasant and risky business. Individuals find that they are willy-nilly drawn into it as their nations are. Only two groups in the world can really exert much influence toward control of war or its avoidance: the political leaders of a few large nations and, occasionally, the citizens of democratic nations.

The leaders of totalitarian and authoritarian nations can be expected to attempt to control and guide the public opinion of their citizenry in every practicable way. They will strive to protect the assumptions of their leadership groups as to what causes war and, if necessary, twist events to fit these assumptions. Democratic leaders are likely to try to do the same, but less successfully, since in democratic systems citizens themselves and special critics participate in the trial-and-error analysis of the problems of war and its prevention. Cartoonists, as critics of their government leaders, along with other critics, are part of this effort to shape and reflect opinion and, hopefully, contribute to the control or avoidance of future war. In democratic nations they inevitably get caught in the tension between critical comment and what is the darker side of democratic comment — uncritically parroting a national line.

7

The Working Political Cartoonist

Political cartoonists would rather be right about what is happening that anything else. They like to dig out old cartoons to show that events evolved just as they had them pegged, that Hitler was a menace all along, that Coolidge prosperity was a fake, that you can't trust the Communists or Nixon either. They then feel that they are truly fulfilling their function as critics and shapers of public opinion. They are on top of the formation of opinion. They are aiding the groupings they feel should be helped.

But it takes more than the gift of prophecy to fulfill this role. Like all of us, the political cartoonist is not completely freewheeling. The professional aspects of the job put some constraints on the carrying out of his or her opinion-shaping function, and it is these constraints that I examine here.

Pros versus Amateurs: The Restraints

As in all fields, in cartooning the professionals are in a different league from the talented amateurs. It is not just that they have superior skills, either artistic or imaginative, though in both they are likely to more than hold their own. The pros differ mainly in that they have to make a living out of their calling, and that demand shapes what they can do. They accept some restraints from others and some they impose on themselves. With both they have to make their peace in a way that the free-floating amateur never does.

One set of restraints is artistic: the deadline. Professionals develop a pride in turning out a competent piece of work on demand. Like pros in other fields, they have earned their rank, often by undergoing a sometimes painful initiation process to develop this ability. Like the teacher, they have done the equivalent of teaching eight o'clock classes; like the policeman, they have had their share of pounding lonely midnight beats; like the soldier, they have maintained their cool under fire. Amateurs can draw as their whims dictate and can even turn out sloppy work if they wish; the pros have reputations to live up to. They have to do work artistically acceptable to themselves while meeting deadlines and conditions set by others.

The second set of restraints is likely to be the more important: those on the freedom to comment as they please. Professionals have to find a formula that lets them maintain their personal integrity while having their work appear in outlets controlled by others. This means somehow coming to terms, whether one works for an Establishment or an anti-Establishment publication.

Art Young, a self-proclaimed radical and crusader against the pay toilet and other, more serious injustices, has stated the case for complete freedom as clearly as anyone: "As a choice between accepting the political judgment of the average newspaper owner and my own judgment as to what was best for my country and the future of mankind, I voted in favor of myself. I'd make up my mind, and follow through. But the difficulty ahead was the small demand for my point of view in the editorial offices of successful newspapers and magazines.[1]"

Some, of course, are more fortunate. They share their publishers' views, and so can go pretty much their own way. Herbert Johnson, in the introduction to a collection of cartoons that had appeared over the years in the *Saturday Evening Post*, stated: "Because the notion widely persists that all editorial cartoonists are given their subjects, it may be proper to record that cartoons here presented are my own subject, idea and execution and express my own views."[2] No doubt other cartoonists would concur, both on radical and on conservative journals.

Another way out is to draw cartoons that avoid offending anyone and, in effect, give up your freedom to comment. *Time*, in its story on John Milton Morris, the syndicated Associated Press cartoonist of the late nineteen-fifties, said, "he draws his syndicated editorial page cartoons as he parts his hair: right down the middle . . . [they] either delicately straddle current controversies or join all mankind in approving mother love and condemning sin." But even Morris, they added, occasionally "knocks out a vicious cartoon on some pet peeve or political devil, exhibits it around the office, tears it up and, refreshed in spirit, returns to the job of producing six inoffensive cartoons a week."[3]

Others, such as Dorman H. Smith, who was syndicated for years by NEA, revel in their entertainment protential and so feel less obliged to do more than drift along with the tide. Smith had been a Hearst cartoonist on the Chicago *Herald American* and was popular because of his good-humored comment on politics. In his introduction to Smith's book of cartoons, "Ding" Darling wrote with considerable truth but with something less than a happy style:

> No one who has ever known the author can ever entertain a thought that he had any other objective than to good naturedly help the reader to a pungent appreciation of human problems which beset him.[4]

Smith's syndicated cartoons during and after World War II continued the tradition of offending only the extremes, while, with a slight conservative leaning, they presented politics as an entertaining game. They were made to order for the small city daily that wanted no trouble with anyone — especially bill-paying advertisers.

In democracies, most cartoonists have worked out arrangements with their publishers that fall between the extremes of complete freedom and no-comment cartoons. Those in other political systems are sometimes less fortunate.

In this chapter I shall concentrate on these two aspects of being a working political cartoonist: the problems of artistic and personal integrity facing the pro. The carrot as well as the stick, rewards as well as restraints, are a part of the picture. Again I divide the discussion by type of political system within which the cartoonist works: totalitarian, authoritarian, or democratic.

The professional opportunities for the political cartoonist operating against a totalitarian regime are nil as long as he stays in the Old Country. A few cartoonists have learned their trade and then fled. The opposite case is the more tragic: that of the working cartoonists whose nation goes totalitarian. When Germany became Nazi in the thirties, and other nations were absorbed by it, a few political cartoonists fled to the West. But most were from conquered nations, not from the mother country. Only George Grosz comes to mind, and he had little choice but to leave, and he ceased drawing cartoons when he arrived in America. Arthur Szyk fled Poland to do effective anti-Nazi cartoons for *Colliers*, *PM*, and *Coronet*. Victor Weiss (Vicky) left Hungary and became a cartoonist for the London *Standard*; Edward Valtman left Estonia to become a political cartoonist for the Hartford *Times* and won a Pulitzer Prize.

116.   Arthur Szyk : A Madman's Dream. 1940. Reprinted by permission of G.P. Putnam's Sons from *The New Order* by Arthur Szyk. Copyright 1941 by Arthur Szyk.

But some stayed, and some of these made peace with the Nazis. Olaf Gulbrandson, one of the truly great prewar cartoonists, had as a young Swede emigrated to Germany. Though initially he ridiculed Hitler, he stayed after the Nazis took power and drew Nazi propaganda in *Simplicissmus*. The same was true of such pre-Nazi greats as Karl Arnold and E. Thony. T. H. Heine also stayed, but he gave up drawing political cartoons. Heinrich Kley, whose political cartoon output was never high, seems just to have disappeared into the landscape.

As noted earlier, the totalitarian cartoonist is supposed to manufacture propaganda for the system the way a cow does milk. Like a good productive cow, he or she is fed the best green grass. All goes well, just as long as he or she doesn't get infected with some loathsome disease like democracy.

As early as 1933 *The Literary Digest* was proclaiming that "the Muscovite caricaturist enjoys an unheard of independence." But when you looked closely at the copy and the proffered illustrations, you find the same old freedom "to ridicule the errors of application," that is, the freedom to critize the non-Stahkonovites and other shirkers. This is the same freedom any warden will extend to a trusty eager to get along in the world: freedom to squeal on the other inmates.[5]

The fact is that totalitarian cartoonists live relatively high on the leviathan. Famous political cartoonists, such as Boris Efimov in the Soviet Union, were given the same status during World War II as England gave David Low, or America, Bill Mauldin. Since the Soviet humor cartoons in *Krokodil* are signed, one assumes that these cartoonists also are able to build up a following and reap the rewards in standard of living generally accorded a professional in the Soviet society.

A further indication that the trade offers significant payoffs for the totalitarian cartoonist is that one of the most popular, Kukryniksy, was really a team: Kuprianov, Krylov, and Sokolov. They met while students at the Moscow Art Institute and began illustrating books together. Their first political work appeared in *Pravda* in 1933, and told the story of a railway journey in which they caricatured inefficient officials. The cartoons that followed are a group project similar to the output of the writers and gag men who put together the old Jack Benny radio and TV shows. And they didn't do too badly. In 1942, *Life* reports, they won the annual Joseph Stalin prize for the best political cartoons. But they (voluntarily) gave it back to the government to buy a tank.[6]

But perhaps the best evidence of luxury treatment is that we have really no example of a cartoonist who defected from an established totalitarian system the way run-of-the-mill skaters and ballet dancers commonly do. Nor can I recall one who, once in the system of producing cartoons, was purged for deviation from the line. One can conclude that totalitarian cartoonists appear to be a fairly docile lot, not unlike the more productive inmates of a well-run animal farm. They are recruited from among the pliant, are fed well, and they then chirp or grunt properly on demand.

The Authoritarian Professional

In many ways the authoritarian cartoonist opposing the system he or she lives under is the most interesting of all political cartoonists. At least he or she is the one who gets the ink, and I have been as guilty, perhaps, in this regard as many others.

This type of political critic lives a precarious existence, because the rules on what can be gotten away with are not clear. He or she always risks the possibility of censorship, or worse; it is an uncertainty that encourages caution mixed with boldness. After all, no one can predict when the revolution might succeed until it does. Nor can anyone predict quite when the axe may fall.

The professional can make what one may call the Daumier or Posada choice. When the lid is suddenly clamped tighter, they draw cartoons of social comment that have a strain of political relevance. As conditions change to more freedom and the system begins to wobble a little they may return to sharp political criticism.

This kind of life looks very romantic when viewed from a distance, especially a distance of time. In point of fact, few men or women are up to the sacrifices required of this precarious role, a role not unlike that of the professional criminal. Take a look at anti-authoritarian cartoonists. Some few gave up after an initial burst and turned to pure art or social cartoons. Others, like Goya, did their work in secret, hopefully for some future generation. It would never be published while they lived. But only a very few can survive professionally as political cartoonists. Look at the brilliant group of half-a-dozen first-rate artists recruited by Philipon between 1830 and 1835. Only Daumier returned to political art in 1848. J. J. Grandville and Garvani had found social art their calling, and the rest had drifted off somewhere or died.

About authoritarian political cartoonists who support the system, there is little to say. Like other artists, they may have done outstanding work. None, in fact, comes to mind, either because it is difficult to establish a reputation for independent comment in this role, or because they aren't very popular to begin with and their audience is happy to forget them, or because they are so few in number.

The Democratic Cartoonist

Democracies of course have their cause cartoonists and their underground artists. What distinguishes each is the freedom to draw when and what they please. As I leaf through a book such as Estren's on underground comics, I am struck with how much these drawings exude the atmosphere of a 10- to-12-year-old, all-boy, secret clubhouse in a middle-class neighborhood. Feverish discussion, such as on who we are going to beat up after school tomorrow, secret codes and signs, treatment of the "other sex" as humanoids (a suggestion found in R. Crumb's vision of utopia), dirty words that we write out that would shock mother if she ever found out, and sporadic production. Drawing such cartoons seems to be more of an interlude than a career.[7]

The kind of political cartoonist I wish to discuss here, rather is epitomized by the 150-or-so pros who make a living out of the game by publishing their work in the mass media. They live a little more conventionally all around. Almost all until recently have been men. Among the women are Etta Hulme of the Fort Worth *Star Telegram* and Kate Palmer of the Grenville (S.C.) *News*.

The working cartoonist in a democracy is, I believe, the most important of the cartoonists that I have thus far discussed. They lack the flamboyant style of life of the authoritarian critic, or the frisbeelike existence of the flower kids of the underground, and are less petted than the totalitarian cartoonist, but they have their rewards, and they serve this important function — of peddling realism and sanity about the humdrum world that we for the most part live in.

Facing Reality

What differentiates the democratic artists most from the other cartoonists is that they have to come to terms with their dreams. This means "being practical" — horrible words and thought. Some can't, because it seems like a sellout, and perhaps it is for them.

It is not a simple process. It is not only that drawing cartoons becomes a way of making a living that cannot be jeopardized, especially with the kids about to start college. It is also that the Quixotic impossible dream is pretty much irrelevant when something needs to be done now. It can be argued that such dreams are, in fact, a form of self-indulgence, like alcohol. The professional cartoonist needs to comment about the messy issues, rather than floating around pure and undefiled out in upper space. It is easy to build utopias, if you can assume that everybody will be altruistic and other-serving when they live in them. It is also relatively easy when you can assume that people can be made so by marching them along in lockstep and chopping down any deviants. The trick is to come to terms with a kinky human world in which self-serving men and women are common, and are accepted as such and still valued — at least enough to keep a reserved seat for them in the world you plan to create for tomorrow. The trick is to protect those one thinks should be protected.

The democratic cartoonist gets used to treating easy and beautiful visions with a bronx cheer of skepticism. But also they have once in a while to pirate in some hope for improvement, if it is only for elimination of evil. Even such visions do not come easy. Bronx cheers do not allow for emotional shadings. Some cartoonists have been luckier in this regard than others. They find a crusade that affects their preferred group in a way they can latch onto, without any self-doubts. Tenniel's defense of Victorian English gentlemen, at times approaches such intensity. His kind of belief is relatively rare today among cartoonists. Others, like Thomas Nast, have found instances of what they could regard as vile corruption — immigrant bosses that they could pursue to their lair without let-up. The battle against the wicked trusts at the turn of the century, and against the Vietnam warlords, provided such a diversion for some. Recently, the tracking down of a president until the last tape was heard provided a recreational activity and career. Others have found an outlet in holy warfare against a foreign monster such as the Kaiser, who was to be hung from a sour apple tree. But most cartoonists have had to settle for victory on a smaller scale — victory that comes through sniping at some of the enemy, and occasionally winging one. This is not so psychically satisfying as crusading. You may even have to face the ultimate pain, the discovery later that you were fighting for the wrong side, that you winged someone who deserved better.

In the chapters that follow this one, I shall review how a number of working democratic cartoonists faced the problem of creating constructive criticism in a democracy. In these I deal with American political cartoons, following a historical chronology but placing special emphasis on those who have created memorable work. In the remaining part of this chapter I wish to deal with the workaday world of the democratic cartoonist.

But first let me detour again, to discuss how hard it seems to be, even with freedom, to keep producing cartoons and trying at the same time to light fuses that will blow up the system. Revolutionary cartoonists have rough going in democratic systems. Perhaps this is an example of Herbert Marcuse's repressive tolerance. In a weakened democracy, such as Weimar was, a cartoonist who attacks the legitimacy of the system may, as I have suggested, be popular while at the same time being successfully destructive in his nihilism. But, in a relatively stable democracy, such artists seem to face the fate described so movingly by Bartholomew Vanzetti as his own expected role as social critic: "If it had not been for these things I might have lived out my life talking at street corners to scorning men. I might have died, unmarked, unknown, a failure."

The subsequent role of that brilliant set of cartoonists associated with the *Masses* before World War I is as instructive as that of the authoritarian cartoonist. Only Art Young continued into the twenties as a radical professional cartoonist who had an audience. Oscar Cesare found himself at the beginning of the war on the New York *Sun* as editorial cartoonist. His were vocal pro-allied and pro-war views. A goodly number, John Sloan, Adolf Dehn, Glen Coleman, and Stuart Davis, moved to pure art and illustration. Boardman Robinson took to an art school and teaching. Robert

Minor became a Communist party functionary and abandoned cartooning. Henry Glintenkamp moved to small radical publications, where he joined men like Fred Ellis. They were cartoonists of only average ability, but their work was perhaps known less than it should be. Other radical cartoonists have made the same switch into the mainstream for a variety of reasons. Jacob Burck, whose work the Communist Party eulogized and published in book form,[8] three years later joined the St. Louis *Post Dispatch* staff and later, on the Chicago *Sun Times*, won a Pulitzer Prize. A. Redfield (who drew in the style of Syd Huff) had work published by the Communist Party under that pseudonym. Huff, on the other hand, became a magazine comic cartoonist of some note, without much radical social comment in his cartoons.

The poor cartoonist cannot even depend on radical publications to always be radical and libertarian. Despite their proclaimed dedication to liberty and other goodies such as equality and fraternity, such journals are not always even so tolerant of dissent as the big bad capitalist press. Al Hirschfeld, who later became theatrical caricaturist for the Sunday *New York Times* and drove a generation of its readers to distraction searching for the tributes to his daughter Nina buried in those cartoons, reports his experience with the *New Masses* of the radical thirties. A cartoon he drew free attacking Father Coughlin, the radio preacher who might be regarded as having somewhat extreme rightist affiliations, caused an editorial crisis. The editorial board of the *New Masses* feared that the cartoon would alienate loyal trade unionists with a Catholic bent. The cartoonist and artists and editors of the magazine reasoned with him at length to withdraw the cartoon. Hirschfeld concludes:

> Insisting that sanity, reason, honesty, political truth were all incontestably on my side, I finally convinced them that I was not only stupid, willful, and irresponsible, but — this from the proletarian poet — that I also was acting like a lousy dictator. At any rate, the drawing was never used, and I have ever since been closer to Groucho Marx than to Karl.[9]

Even in a democratic system, the attacker of system legitimacy, it seems, needs unusual talents, persistence, and perhaps a thick hide to survive as a professional working cartoonist to whom anyone pays any attention.

Constraints by Publishers

The working professional since the turn of the century has been a newspaper editorial cartoonist, and it is his or her problems that I will discuss rather than those of the printmaker or magazine cartoonist of an earlier day.

The first point to note is that, as in other fields, it is a buyer's market for average or unestablished talent, and a seller's market only for those who have established reputations. This means that the young man or woman coming along finds it a tough field to break into. And that they are not, as a rule, in a position to make fancy demands. David Low, after he had arrived in London from Australia, took a big chance. He was so disheartened, as already noted, by the one or two column smudges in which his work was presented that he went to his publishers with this proposal: "Give me a chance and if at the end of three months I am not justified, we will tear up the contract. If not, I am willing to call the whole thing off right now." Despite what he describes as "consternation," Low got his way. The paper experimented with printing his work half-page size. But Low was already an established Australian product. He had been imported at some expense from halfway around the world. Most beginners have less leverage in their bargaining with publishers.[10]

To begin with, most have not even developed their own distinctive style. They can try to do this on high school and college publications or at apprentice occupations, such as in the art department of newspapers where they work on photos or do lettering or half a hundred other chores, or in the art department of some ad agency or company. Those who can develop style on the job as working cartoonists are the fortunate.

A still surprisingly large number of political cartoonists have followed the Rube Goldberg pattern of no art training. Hugh Haynie, one of the best artistically, is an example. Some still enroll in correspondence schools. A growing number, such as Bill Mauldin, Jules Feiffer, Fischetti, and Don Hesse had art-school training. A few like Paul Conrad and Art Poinier got art training in college. The general pattern is for apprenticeship in art departments or elsewhere. Even two such talented practitioners as Herblock and Fischetti spent years in editorial art for the syndicates. Their work became markedly more punchy after they moved on.

To summarize: the cartoonist begins at a disadvantage. Freedom to comment at all and special artistic privileges are things not thrust upon artists. Rightly or wrongly, these are treated by publishers as privileges they must earn.

The cartoonist, until syndication became common, held a peculiar role in relation to his or her paper that affected this freedom even more than it did with other commentators. Like the editorial writer, they presented opinions that generally appeared on the editorial page next to the newspaper masthead. Yet, unlike the editorial writer, but like the local or syndicated columnist, cartoonists signed their work. The assumption held by publishers was that the cartoon should be regarded as an extension, or restatement in a different form, of the official newspaper position, or even more specifically, of the meat of the lead editorial. Thus they have felt it their right to review what was to be published. Nast was censored by *Harpers*, and many publishers have felt it their right to order up from their artists pretty pictures on specific political subjects. More did so in the past than is the case now, but it is not unheard of still for cartoonists to be fired.

In 1902 Charles G. Bush of the New York *World*, described by his interviewer as the "dean of our cartoonists," rather coyly described his own position as follows: "Without letting you into the secret of my political feelings, I may tell you that very often it happens that a cartoonist who is a Republican has to earn his bread and butter by ridiculing his own party, and vice versa. You can draw your own conclusions from that statement, while I — excuse me — resume another sort of drawing."[11]

The practical nub of the matter for most editorial cartoonists today is whether the cartoonist meets with and is part of the editorial board conference, and so gets his or her cartoon themes handed out. John Tenniel received his instructions a century ago after Wednesday-evening dinner at the *Punch* mahogany table. Such conferences compromise independence, since the cartoonist is regarded as just another cog of an organized machine. Unless he or she can willingly be part of the unified team effort, which happens from time to time, there will be problems drawing the cartoons. At best, the artist is only one among many contributors to the cartoon. Everyone has ideas and suggestions. Any demurrer looks like willful sabotage. The cartoonist may of course be just naturally of an agreeable nature, in which case he or she is probably in the wrong profession.

Thus most cartoonists, if given a choice, prefer to spend the early morning figuring out what they think are the major current news stories, and what should be said about them, and then about 11 AM present the editor with from three to a dozen roughs of cartoon ideas from which to choose.

This method has two advantages. It permits cartoonists to be realistic about who is boss and, at the same time, to preserve some self-respect. It harmonizes with the common stance of "I am not obliged to draw anything over my own signature that I do not wish to." Also, cartoonists know that they are likely to come off better, on the average, in one-to-one bargaining with a single person than in attempting to convince a whole group, any one of whom may have a few of what he or she conceives of as excellent ideas — "just the way Herblock would do it."

Even this compromise causes some chafing and uneasiness among cartoonists themselves. In shoptalk at two in the morning with fellow political cartoonists, one young and first-rate artist in a group I was with complained to others that when he gave his editor a dozen roughs, his editor always seemed to take from the end of the scale that the cartoonist had himself ranked 10 - 11 - 12. A second countered that the cartoonist should definitely move to another paper, where he could decide for himself what should appear. A third argued that he himself welcomed and needed the advice and guidance given by a sympathetic editor, since he was not infallible. So it goes.

A related difficulty in the roughs-to-editor method, is that the artist, either from weariness or intimidation, may be tempted, or may unconsciously begin, to second-guess the editor. He or she can anticipate what kind of ideas will be greeted with enthusiasm and which not. Just as knowledgeable pitchers discovered that it was unproductive to serve up low and outside fast balls to Lou Gehrig, so cartoonists may learn to avoid certain offerings to editors, perhaps — and this is the ultimate horror to some — without even in time being consciously aware when they are falling into the habit of doing so.

Beyond the editor's personal constraints, the political cartoonist faces social taboos that editors will enforce, even when they do not wholly agree with them. This may especially operate against the syndicated cartoonist. These taboos come under the heading of "It's a family newspaper," even though the ads covered in what is generally titled the amusement page may headline something like "Lucy, the GAY Strangler, with His Motorcycle Gang." The constraints include prohibitions of too explicit sex, violence, sadism, or other breaches of the canons of good taste. They have been relaxed slightly in the editorial cartoon, but not so much as in Al Capp's "Lil Abner" strip, for example. Note how few really sexy females parade through editorial pages. But the taboo constraints may also be in part self-imposed, since working cartoonists in the mass media deal in laughing satire and this requires of them less diving down into libido and id than it does of, say, the revolutionary atrocity-monger.

Excluding for the moment those who voluntarily and wholeheartedly support their newspaper's editorial policy, a few political cartoonists do have as close to absolute freedom as they could hope for in an imperfect world. David Low takes the spotlight. This Socialist artist was permitted to caricature rather unkindly, but with delicious accuracy, his capitalist employer, Lord Beaverbrook. (Even at that, he voluntarily left the *Standard*, after almost twenty-five years, for the more ideologically congenial Socialist *Daily Herald* and, later, the *Guardian*.) I can think of no other publisher on the right or left who permitted or would welcome the attention that Beaverbrook tolerated. Colonel McCormick of the Chicago *Tribune* indicated his pain at the Col. McCosmic series by Jensen in the Chicago *Daily News*, and they were discontinued. Some publishers have allowed cartoons in opposition to their editorial policies, but since I can at the moment cite very few really good examples (Paul Conrad and the Los Angeles *Times* during the Goldwater campaign is the only one that comes readily to mind), I conclude that this has not occurred often or on very significant issues. A few cartoonists have held out in silence, and this kind of stalemate is the more common result of opinion clashes. John McCutcheon, on the politically hidebound Chicago *Tribune* of Colonel Robert McCormick, states in his autobiography that he did not draw an anti-Roosevelt cartoon until the president openly abandoned isolationism. Herblock took a vacation from the Washington *Post* in 1952 when it backed Eisenhower. Daniel Fitzpatrick in 1936 refused to draw pro-Landon cartoons, and when the election was over he posted in the editorial room of the St. Louis *Post Dispatch* (but not in an editorial cartoon) a sign that said :

Country: 523 Electoral Votes
Country Club: 8 Electoral Votes

So, to summarize: in a clash of opinions between boss and employee, as in other fields the boss's opinion generally prevails, through the sheer force of logic — economic logic, that is.

117.   David Low : "Situations Vacant." August 1925. London *Star*.

118.   Cecil Jensen : (Col. McCosmic). 1943. Chicago *Daily News.*

Constraints from Government

I am going to sketch in lightly only a few of the details of the legislative attempts to muzzle cartoonists, since they were almost universally welcomed by cartoonists for the crusades it permitted them to mount against such foolhardy lawgivers. The most famous American instance was the bill unsuccessfully urged by Governor Samuel Pennypacker in Pennsylvania in 1902-3. He is also the father of state police forces. His cartoon bill prohibited drawing a politician as a bird or other animal. Charles Nelan was daily presenting Pennypacker to Philadelphia citizens as a particularly obnoxious parrot. Walt McDougall of another Philadelphia paper responded by drawing the Governor as a series of vegetables.

Boss Platt of New York tried in 1897, to muzzle the Hearst artists just as Tweed had tried to stop Nast with an anti-cartoon bill. It only provided Homer Davenport with theme materials for a series of blockbusters linking Platt with the late and infamous

119.   Homer Davenport : A Misfit. 1896. New York *Evening Journal.*

Boss Tweed. Like other such attempts — in California (1899), Indiana (1913), and Alabama (1915) — it backfired. In the more recent seventies, cartoonists have been active against court decisions requiring newsmen to reveal sources of stories and what they feel has been intimidation of newsmen by the Nixon administration.[12]

Cartoonists have also been threatened with libel by politicians, but no one has made it stick yet.[13] A most amusing case was that of Tammany boss Charles Murphy, who threatened to sue W. G. Rogers if he continued to draw him in prison stripes. Rogers responded with a cartoon in which Murphy is walking down the street carrying a "libel suit case" saying "Last year's stripes will no longer be worn." All of the other half-dozen street gawkers in the cartoon have prison stripes across their everyday clothes. Earlier James Blaine, presidential aspirant of the 1880s, let it be known he was considering prosecuting *Puck* on an obscenity charge for its tattooed-man series on his candidacy, but he wisely reconsidered.[14] In the early teens the Associated Press objected to Art Young's portrayal of the Association in the *Masses* as part of his House of Prostitution cartoon (Fig. 32) The A. P. brought a libel suit against the journal, but after a decent interval the organization quietly dropped the suit. Young triumphantly noted the occasion with a cartoon of an overly fat matron labeled A.P., who was told from on high, "Madam, you dropped something." An innocent scroll labelled "Masses Libel Suit" was behind her. But then, those were more conventional times. Young would have known better how to label and draw such an item today.

Outright suppression by the government is rare and appears most likely in wartime. During World War I the *Masses* editor, Max Eastman, and others including the

189

120.   W. A. Rogers : Murphy says, "Last year's stripes will no longer be worn."
1904. New York *Herald*.

cartoonist Art Young, were brought to trial for sedition. Young fell asleep during the hearings. The *Masses* board was not convicted, but the trial did in effect destroy the journal. The *Liberator*, which took its place, was much tamer in tone. Young's subversive cartoon "Having Their Fling" is printed here for the edification of later generations. During the McCarthy period Jacob Burck, who had once drawn for the *Daily Worker*, was threatened with deportation, but the matter fizzled out.

During World War II Winston Churchill concluded that a cartoon by ZEC in the London *Mirror* attacked the government policy of bringing in oil through submarine-choked waters. It showed a torpedoed sailor hanging on a raft with the caption "The Price of Petrol has been increased by one penny — Official." The government threatened to ban the paper, but lost out in the subsequent Commons debate on the matter and backed down. But the flareup probably to some extent intimidated critics of how the Churchill government was waging the war.[15]

Politicians are more subtle as a rule than the above illustrations suggest. Jim Berryman of the Washington *Star*, in a biographical comment, proudly stated, "I could never get along with FDR and Truman. Both of them summoned me to the White House to give me hell. FDR even tried to get me fired." Other cartoonists have reported such pressure on their publishers from governors and senators. Sam Caufman, Jr., of the Wilmington *News*, says one governor stopped talking to his publisher for a week after a cartoon.[16] In reverse, pressure may take the form of subtle bribery, as in invitations to the governor's mansion for self and wife, or other

EDITOR CAPITALIST POLITICIAN MINISTER

121. Art Young : Having Their Fling. 1916. *The Masses.*

recognitions. Daniel Fitzpatrick, of the St. Louis *Post Dispatch*, to avoid such possible taint, refused to join the St. Louis Country Club, which he regarded as a devil's den, or to meet socially any of the prominent businessmen of the community. He was probably correct in his assessment of the subtle pressures, but his sacrifice was possibly not among the great ones of journalism.

Deadline Pressures

The artistic problem that plagues cartoonists is the pressure created by deadlines. Fischetti movingly describes those days in which he can't get an idea and his colleague in the same building on the Chicago *Sun Times*, Bill Mauldin, wanders in dying to tell him *his* idea, but won't until Fischetti gets his. Fischetti describes the scene, "He'll just walk off smugly saying 'I've got a lulu!' Then of course all I can think is 'He's got a lulu . . . he's got a lulu.' "[17]

The modern cartoonist has a tougher schedule than his predecessors. James Gillray produced prints when his acid stomach or his acid spirit moved him. John Tenniel had a week between cartoons, but only from Wednesday to Friday evening to mull out how he would draw them. He tried to extend his deadline by getting management to push back the roundtable meeting to Tuesdays, but this happened toward the end of his fifty-year career.

Today's cartoonists have to produce from four to seven cartoons a week. If they do fewer than three, their readers may forget they exist, and their employers may regard them as too expensive a luxury. A few do more than seven. When those who are syndicated have a daily cartoon that deals with a local or state issue, they must produce an additional one for syndicate subscribers. Vacation breaks require cartoons drawn in advance. It is perhaps significant that the annual meetings of the American Society of Editorial Cartoonists have frequently coincided with the Memorial Day weekend. Two such imperishable subjects as our fallen heroes and highway safety stand ready at hand.

122. Bill Mauldin : (Kennedy Assassination Cartoon). November 22, 1963. Chicago *Sun Times.* Copyright ©1963, The Chicago *Sun Times.* Reproduced by courtesy of Wil-Jo Associates Inc., and Bill Mauldin.

One may sympathize with the problem faced by cartoonists but also note that college teachers have to lecture whether they feel quite ready or not; clowns, we are told, occasionally have to laugh while their hearts are breaking; and all of us somehow have to get to work on Monday mornings.

Deadlines have at least three effects on political cartooning. The bad one is that they encourage mediocrity and triteness in ideas, since cartoonists occasionally run dry and get desperate. The so-so one is that it encourages simplicity in drawing. John Tenniel figured this one out. He became noticeably frigid about any idea that required more than two figures in the drawing. This may speed up comprehension for the viewer but it may also somewhat limit what is portrayed. One thinks of the detailed work of cartoonists such as the Canadian Aislin. A good part of his effect would be sacrificed if he simplified. The good effect of deadlines is that good ideas come to those who demand them regularly on schedule, as Anthony Trollope, with his ticking watch, demonstrated in the writing of his novels. This is also clear in the work of many first-rate cartoonists who have done superior cartoons under deadline conditions. Even a few of the most memorable cartoons have been dashed off as quick space fillers, such as John T. McCutcheon's "The Mysterious Stranger," J. N. "Ding" Darling's "The Long Long Trail," commemorating Theodore Roosevelt's death, and, more recently, Bill Mauldin's inspired comment on the Kennedy assassination. Deadlines keep the subconscious perking up good ideas.

Professional Peers

Equally important, too, are the subtle influences felt from other professional cartoonists. Political cartooning is an activity with set routines, and some public prestige. It has a national association and a prize, to be given annually and carrying prestige of the Pulitzer, with an initial screening committee of cartoonists. All of this professionalism means that cartoonists themselves begin to articulate some standards as to what *quality work* consists of. In the case of political cartooning, the clearest criteria are in artistic style. Fads or fashions develop. In Victorian times everyone drew like Tenniel. After World War II the Herblock cartoon was in; now, modifications of Oliphant and MacNelly.

Do these fashions affect content? To some degree. With the style often goes a mood — a kind of stance toward life that Tenniel expressed in imagery like the British lion and the noble figures of Britannia, Germania, and the rest of that forbidding women's culture club, and that Oliphant expresses through his old-fashioned flying Jennies, his penguin mascot Punk, and the gentle mocking style in which he draws furniture, houses, and other props. These too get absorbed into the work of his fellow craftsmen and subtly affect the way they package their messages and the messages themselves. A generation latches on to a mood that seems appropriate, given the position of the dominant groupings and life styles within the society. Herblock's style was developed for the defense of the working-class sons and daughters who were making it into the technical class. It was a style that expressed a liberal attack against the older *Saturday Evening Post* kind of life and especially against those privileged through inherited or unfairly earned commercial wealth. Oliphant speaks more for the second-generation suburbanite who has seen the dream get a little tarnished. The liberalism is expressed with more ambivalence. For the first time perhaps in its history, the American Civil Liberties Union is ridiculed by a popular cartoonist, as a meddling old lady, for some of its more esoteric stances on behalf of those who commit crimes that the average working stiff is given the opportunity to underwrite. That kind of mood shift is also transmitted; the ACLU, the Israelis, and other heretofore almost sacrosanct groups can expect lumps from others — not Neanderthal-fringe cartoonists, but other skeptics who may be encouraged by the kind of reception Oliphant's work seems regularly to receive.

123. Pat Oliphant : "She wants to know why you men over-react so nastily towards terrorists who use cyanide bullets and 50-caliber machine guns!" June 5, 1974. Denver *Post*.

Don't misunderstand me to say that what becomes admired by professionals locksteps all cartoonists along in artistry, mood, or content. It is just one of many influences, but it is a significant one. Because cartoonists are human, they like to be admired by fellow professionals, to win prizes they control, have their respect, and have this status recognized in other subtle ways by them. They also know when what they do is likely to be frowned upon or even will outrage their fellow professionals. It would, for example, perhaps take a cartoonist of a remarkably foolhardy temperament, or an isolate, to defend before his or her colleagues the Supreme Court's present stand on requiring journalists to reveal sources of news stories. It would not be a popular stance, with good reason, among fellow professionals whose livelihood depends upon the journalistic enterprise and whose sincere beliefs support the value and virtue of that body of critics and information-gatherers in a democracy. Even to work for a paper that takes that stand may be viewed as a handicap.

Other Parts of the Job

Cartoonists face other minor artistic and expressive hazards and problems. They feel to an unusual degree the necessity of keeping up to date. While John Tenniel could get away with drawing bicycles without seats and pedals on the wrong side, Herblock reports that the cartoonist had better be sensitive about how a Washington bus is put together, or he will get letters, letters, letters. Arthur Poinier of the Detroit *News* got a great flood of letters when he pictured a mousetrap with the spring going the wrong way. It was a mousean dream: it wouldn't snap. He suspects that viewers who disagree with him about politics may lie in wait to give him this kind of put-down.

Some minor irritations also go with the job. The cartoonist knows that his cartoons about local politics will get little national play unless he happens to be Thomas Nast. Who else cares what Herb Block says about Rock Creek park, or the Washington, D.C., subway? His editor, that's who; so a few get drawn on the subject. Cartoonists also get used to a certain number of nuisance letters attacking them and calling them Fascists or Communists. Fischetti finds it particularly irritating that such writers often mail in defaced copies of his work when expressing such sentiments. Very rarely, the cartoonist gets some veiled threats. They also get nuisance letters requesting originals. They used to be able to drop those originals into a nearby library and write it off on income taxes as a gift — but no longer. This it seems to me is short-sighted internal revenue policy (I suspect that perhaps ex-President Nixon would agree), since it deprives posterity of large-scale collections of original drawings at really very little cost to the public. So some citizens now get the originals, or they get lost or scattered. Cartoonists also get bugged to make appearances at professional meetings, and even in classes. Since I have been guilty of this, and successfully so, I say let's change the subject.

Let me turn now to the rewards the political cartoonist may receive in a democracy. Curiously enough, these also can be viewed as constraints on freedom, since they may be thinly disguised bribes. I begin by looking at the rewards of the job itself.

The editorial cartoonist is relatively well treated if he or she can get and hold a job. It is a nice living, though not a sensational one in monetary terms. Big Money is with the comics. Chase lists a dozen or so editorial cartoonists who tried to break into the comics but didn't quite make it.[7] Only Rube Goldberg seems to have moved the other way to editorial cartooning, and that at the close of his long career.

The cartoonist also gets dished lots of psychic rewards to make up for the monetary treatment. Deference is shown, important people occasionally request originals, and the cartoonist has an excuse to get close to all VIPs who come along. If he or she is especially successful, the political cartoonist will have some work syndicated, reprinted in national magazines such as *Time* and *Newsweek*, and perhaps published in book form by the newspaper or, even more prestigiously, by a commercial press. And most political cartoonists end with the satisfaction of having served long in the vineyard and of earning their passage out of the vale to perhaps a better one, which is probably more psychic satisfaction than a retiring underwear salesman feels after a hard career.

Honorary awards also beckon, and the cartoonist can be sure to get good local newspaper play on any he or she wins. Six British cartoonists have been knighted; Max Beerbohm, John Tenniel, Leslie Ward (Spy), F. Carruthers Gould, Bernard Partridge, and David Low. America since 1922 has the much-sought-after Pulitzer Prize for political cartoonists, and other democratic nations give recognition similar to Canada's National Newspaper Awards for political cartooning.

I shall discuss the Pulitzer Prize in a moment in more detail, but let me note a few other awards first. The National Cartoonists Society, which mainly includes comic strip and magazine cartoonists, gives an annual award for the best cartoonist in each of several categories, including editorial cartooning. It also gives an overall award called a Reuben, after Rube Goldberg. Herblock won it in 1956, Bill Mauldin in 1961, and Pat Oliphant in 1972.

The political cartoonist may also be elected to office in the National Cartoonists Society, or the much more specialized and smaller American Society of Editorial Cartoonists, may be picked, as Eugene Craig of the Brooklyn *Eagle* was, to design a postage stamp on the battle of Brooklyn, or, as Edward Kuekes of the Cleveland *Plain Dealer* was, picked by LBJ to design the cover of a Democratic booklet, or may even land the contract for Army-Navy football programs, as Gib Crockett of the Washington *Star* did.

A host of other awards abound. Almost every self-respecting organization has an award for cartoonists. From John Chase's book of biographies of 140 cartoonists, published in 1962, I have compiled a partial list (down through where names begin with L): George Washington medal, Freedoms Foundation, Sigma Delta Chi, Headliner, Eddie Cantor, New York Newspaper Guild Page One Award, Lincoln Foundation, the Christophers, George Polk memorial, University of Missouri citation for Distinguished Service to Journalism, Parents Magazine, the Silurians, American Cancer Society, Disabled American Veterans, Brotherhood Award of the National Conference of Christians and Jews, National Safety Council, Heywood Broun award, McQuade Memorial, U. S. Treasury Distinguished Service, and many, many others. Add to this honorary degrees from colleges: even crusty old Daniel Fitzpatrick accepted an honorary doctorate from Washington University of St. Louis, for example.

The most famous, or perhaps infamous award, with monetary prize, was that offered by the American Medical Association in 1950 for the best published cartoons against "socialized medicine." This approach lacked a certain amount of subtlety and has not been repeated in quite so bald a form since.

So much for the minor prizes and the potential for bribes and threats that they contain. Now on to the Pulitzer.

The Pulitzer Prize

Back in 1966 Pat Oliphant had been two years with the Denver *Post*. He was only 30, a migrant worker from Australia, and wanted very much to establish himself quickly as a first-rank editorial cartoonist in his adopted country. He in fact did so very quickly because of his new, imaginative style, but the way to make this status obvious to everyone was clear — he needed to win the Pulitzer Prize for the best cartoon of the year. The following story is perhaps apocryphal.

Oliphant set about the task methodically. He and his wife studied the winning cartoons of past years, and the rules of selection. Then he fashioned a cartoon strictly for the Pulitzer advisory board, which is generally composed of newspaper editors and publishers. As it turned out, this cartoon on Vietnam to be described later, was not much in his usual style, but it did win the prize. What, then, was the magic formula he found?

Before making a muckraking analysis of this and other Pulitzer cartoon winners, let me briefly review the terms of this Oscar-like contest. The Columbia University School of Journalism administers the program. The prizes were first awarded in 1917, with awards for editorial cartoons beginning in 1922. The prizes are designed to recognize *current* efforts rather than overall lifetime contributions. In cartooning, through 1967, they were given for what was deemed to be the best cartoon of the year, though as early as 1964 Paul Conrad had won for his work over the whole year. After 1967, and much more sensibly, the prize was awarded for the artist's general work throughout that year. A committee of four to six jurors who are professionals in the field sorts through six cartoons submitted by each formal entrant, usually receiving about 80 to 90 entries. After peering at these 500-plus cartoons, they make a recommendation of a name or names, or that no award be given. This goes to the advisory board, made up of fourteen dignitaries with a good seasoning of publishers, who consider the nomination or nominations and pass one along to the Columbia University Board of Trustees, which officially announces the award. Traditionally, the story appears on the first Tuesday in May.

The Pulitzer Prize is not just another award that editorial cartoonists may receive to convince themselves and their editors and publishers that they are among the leaders of the profession. It is the top award because it is prize currency that cuts across many fields of journalism and means excellence in each of them. An analogy is provided by the Academy Awards. The television viewers of the Oscar festivities do not really know much about what makes the best color cinematography in costume for a year, but they recognize that the elated men and women who are scurrying up to the podium to get that silver statue are ranked the same way in their fields as are the better-known winners whom they can judge, as Elizabeth Taylor and Richard Burton. Like the Oscar, the Pulitzer is an interchangeable good. The editorial artist who receives it has, at least for the moment, hit the peak of the profession, and there is no doubt about it for other journalists or the general public. The rest must be content with awards from Freedoms Foundation or the National Safety Council or a Sigma Delta Chi National Headliners Club Award, or even a National Cartoonists Society editorial award, but they are not going to be listed in the real record book, in this case the *World Almanac*.

Such a prize then will affect the quality of current editorial cartooning, just as Pulitzer hoped it would. It not only rewards the exceptional but also encourages emulation of their deeds — even such calculated emulation as that of Oliphant's. What, then, have been the norms that the award committee has sought to, or in fact did, foster? More important, have these norms changed to keep up with the times?

One is first struck by the fact that what later generations recognize as the best cartoonists of a previous day generally get on the list. Rollin Kirby won the prize three times, as did Edmund Duffy; two-time winners included Daniel Fitzpatrick, Vaughn Shoemaker, "Ding" Darling, Bill Mauldin, Paul Conrad, and Herblock. Single winners include Clarence Batchelor, Jacob Burck, and John T. McCutcheon, and many other younger men who may win again, such as Pat Oliphant, John Fischetti, Jeff MacNelly, Tom Darcy, and Don Wright.

But one also finds a great many others on the list. Mixed in with this distinguished group of what is the very cream of the profession are what one suspects are a few sentimental accolades for old timers, whose editorial cartoon work may not be long remembered after their retirement but who deserve recognition for long and honorable service if for nothing else. This includes such men as Nelson Harding (who somehow won twice), Charles Macauley, Rube Goldberg, and Lute Pease. Perhaps giving the award within six years to the father, Clifford, and then the son, Jim, of the Berrymans, also fits this category of sentimental awards, though both were competent craftsmen in a very central location on the Washington *Star*.

Is anyone significant left off the list? Among today's cartoonists who are as good as many on the list, Hugh Haynie, Bill Sanders, or Don Hesse, and — if his work fell within the classification guidelines — Jules Feiffer. For the past, it is hard to make much of an argument for anyone who was a newspaper editorial cartoonist. Men such as Herbert Johnson, Dorman Smith, or Fred Seibel could have won in place of some who did, without its being a great shock to Joseph Senior's memory, but it would be hard to mount a crusade for any of them. The only memorable name I can think of not on the list is that of Art Young, who was not a daily editorial cartoonist during the award period. One can regret that the prize did not come sooner, so that such first-rate men as Homer Davenport and Frederick Opper could have received the accolade, or such competent craftsmen as William A. Rogers, Oscar Cesare, Luther Bradley, and others, for their life's best work.

What comes through though is that the committee of working cartoonists who do the sifting have some appreciation of talent and insure that, at least once, the very best do gain recognition. If there is a bias here, it was probably a slight one toward the more conservative winning in the early years of the award and the more liberal in the last fifteen years, but with notable exceptions in each case. There was also a tendency for the liberal end of the continuum to bag multiple wins, but that is the end of the ideological spectrum in which perhaps more first-rate editorial cartoonists than not hang their hats.

What can be said about content? Let us begin by looking at winners before 1967, when awards were passed out for "the" cartoon.

One is struck by the fact that the awards did not go to the best cartoon of the year, despite what the big print used to say. If they did, in the last thirty years at least, judging by what did win, Herblock would have won almost every year rather than just twice, the way Ty Cobb or Babe Ruth used to dominate their specialized categories year after year.

Several commentators, notably Gerald Johnson, have directly or indirectly speared the insipidity of much of this cartoon output.[19] It is a shame, but only a few of the prize-winning cartoons are themselves first-rate and worth remembering. I would suggest that these are perhaps Rollin Kirby's "Tammany!", Daniel Fitzpatrick's prophetic statement in 1954 on Vietnam, "Would Another Mistake Help?"; Bill Mauldin's *Up Front* cartoon; and Clarence Batchelor's death's-head prostitute who, as War, invites any European youth of 1936: "Come on in, I'll treat you right, I used to know your daddy." A few others like Herblock's "British Plane", or Edmund Duffy's acid comment, "California Points with Pride" (to a lynching), Vaughn Shoemaker's New Wage Demands trying to catch up with his cost-of-living shadow, or Darling's moral sermon against the drugstore cowboy of 1924 (Fig. 27), would be quite acceptable in a bound collection of their life output. Some may wish to include other cartoons, whose appeal to the emotions seems to me to have all the ring of true sentiment of Al Jolson's singing "Mammy" in blackface. Most of the rest are often dull, pretentious, or just bad, and it is hard to imagine anyone, even of their day, paging through the early May New York *Times* for the illustration of the winner and, coming on it, shouting "Of course! I should have known it all along!"

All of the above sums up to the conclusion that the cartoon was only an excuse for rewarding a cartoonist whose work other cartoonists and journalists already admired. This is not unlike the Academy Awards, in which an actress wins the award a year or two after that of her finest role, or an old stager receives the silver statue and applause while the viewers wipe away a sentimental tear. And I should add that this is as it should be in a civilized society, since it does achieve the prize's purpose of rewarding and encouraging the better practitioners by giving them recognition. One passes over the heartbreak of the just-not-quite-good-enough, who also happened to be the just-not-quite-lucky-enough. For second- and third-level talents, life is often capricious.

The cartoon winner, one hopes, only encouraged others to draw cartoon entries,

124.   Rollin Kirby : "Tammany" (Pulitzer Prize, 1929). New York *World.*

and did not have a marked influence on their work or on the general run of cartoons from 1922 or 1968. Let us briefly review that content.

The winning cartoons are generally high-minded sermons against sin, with a thick icing of artificial religiosity. Take the example of Daniel Fitzpatrick's 1926 offering, "The Laws of Moses and the Laws of Man," which shows a poor, small, beaten down creature in manacles, with ball and chain, with bowed head before the big mound of today's laws and the simple tablets of Moses. Its message seems to be that all we really need to order the complicated modern world are those good old Ten Commandments, hammered out to guide a wandering Semitic tribe through desert and wilderness. This is pretentious foolishness that should have made the hardbitten Fitzpatrick blush in embarrassment. Other cartoon sermons have the same empty, ostentatious loftiness, and often their messages have become out-of-date and quaint.

Because the subject matter has to flow from a spiritual tone, this means that a great many subjects have to be left out, as if they had never happened. Politics, and especially political campaigns, are avoided like poison because, one assumes, of their dirtiness. Only Kirby, bless his memory, could get away with a really forceful partisan comment, his "Tammany!" In the world of the Pulitzer, there is silence on the 1932 election, and even Harry Truman's 1948 surprise party. No, petty politics is not a fit subject to win a Pulitzer with.

There is hardly even any oblique allusion to politicians other than the Kirby cartoon. It is as if cartoonists thought the government was administered by eunuchs or computers. Hoover gets a glancing reference (that gets his birthdate wrong) and so does Harding in Darling's 1924 winner, and Duffy in 1934 gives a plastering to an otherwise-forgotten governor, Sunny Jim Rolfe of California. A brief, henscratched imitation representing FDR in 1944 and a portrayal of the terrible-tempered Mr. Truman in 1952 are the only others. Foreign devils come off only slightly better, with only Hitler and Stalin so honored.

Equally bad is any form of social conflict. That's nasty-nasty. One looks in vain for a decent comment on the civil rights struggle any time from the Supreme Court decision in *Brown* vs. *Board of Education* (1954) to the present. Only the lynching of a white

125.   Clarence D. Batchelor : "Come on in, I'll treat you right. I used to know your Daddy" (Pulitzer Prize, 1937). Copyright 1936 New York News Inc., Reprinted by permission.

man, a heinous crime all deplore, is brought to notice. When other social conflict is touched on, it is in a high-minded "a plague on both your houses" tone. So Ross Lewis won in 1935 for "Sure I'll Work for Both Sides." It is a castrated statement on the intense labor conflict of the 1930s. It is regrettable that his Pulitzer winner, rather than some of his much better work of the period, is preserved for review. But the board's standards were as rigid as those of a prairie-town ladies' uplift club; the conflict of petty politics or among society's groupings is no subject matter for this distinguished award. (In 1949 a committee slipped in an award to Lute Pease for his comments on John L. Lewis and the coal strike, but then they were honoring an 80-year-old veteran, and exceptions must be made for age.)

What, then, is suitable subject matter? Events that may pass into oblivion are of course not fit subjects for comment, but sometimes their essence may be distilled into homily. Their more generalized subject matter must be ennobled and teased out as the cartoon is raised to the level of noncontroversial moral generalization. Only great events are to be so enshrined, and the greatest of these events is war, especially if the cartoonist can portray them while thumping his drum for peace in the best Salvation Army tradition of understatement. Comments that in one way or another make the point of war's waste abound.

The appropriate style is to load the cartoon with a symbolism that smacks of unctuousness: a dignified Uncle Sam, or War drawn as Mars, or Death, or abstract symbols like the burning treaty or the Cross. If these symbols are religious or can be given a Moses smell, so much the better. A recurrent holiness theme hangs over the whole collection, like cheap incense from the dime store. If high-minded sermons are what is wanted, then cartoonists can supply them, and what would please better than some ecumencial allusion to life's great religious truths?

This is the movable feast that the Pulitzer committee has treated us to. This is the disservice they perpetrated on cartoonists for forty-five years, making them parade around in costume for a prize. This minor humiliation is to be deplored, but it is more than made up for by the fact that most of the time prize-winners have been cartoonists who deserved to win. Oliphant had to humble himself to get the prize quickly, but he won it, and not for his Machiavellian enterprise in packaging just right his sentiments concerning war. The drawing showed a villainous Ho Chi Minh striding out of the smoke and ruin carrying a dead Vietnamese and saying "They won't get *us* to the conference table, will they?" The cartoon has not been reprinted in either of Oliphant's boks to date, though it earned the prize for the brightest light to appear on the cartoon scene since Mauldin and Herblock.

The long list of winners gives us the opportunity to see whether the awards have kept up with the times. Clear signs show that changes have occurred, and these have generally been for the better, including, as already noted, the dropping of the best-cartoon-of-the-year requirement. Let us look at what the statistics have to tell.

One peculiar indicator is "no award" years. I was told by a friend of his that Daniel Fitzpatrick was responsible for the 1936 "no award." He wanted to beef up standards and particularly to encourage a bit more daring and a little less sweetness and light. If so, he succeeded, judging by the 1937 prostitute winner penned by Batchelor.

No-award years also occurred in 1923, the second year of awards, and in 1960, 1965, and 1973. If these do in fact function as the kind of prod Fitzpatrick envisioned, one notes that in the last fifteen years they have jumped to one no-award year out of every five. Up to 1960 the average was one no-award year out of every nineteen. Obviously something has been stirring lately in the editorial-cartoon field.

Now next look at the cartoonist's age when he got the award. The age pattern shows this remarkable feature: in the two decades of domestic turmoil, the thirties, the sixties, and the early seventies, young men under forty received the big helpings. In quieter times the awards have gone to the more established artists in their middle forties and fifties, with more frequent accolates to old stagers in their sixties and seventies. The 1950s of Eisenhower got the prize for the decade of contentment. It seems reasonable to assume that these younger artists are likely to be little bit more iconoclastic in style and content than the more established, though not in every case. At any rate, the data suggest again that the field has been percolating more in recent years. I shall return to this in a moment, but first let us look at how other features of the award-giving have loosened up in recent years.

TABLE 7.1

AGE AT RECEIVING PULITZER PRIZE

Decade	No Award	21-30	31-40	41-50	51-60	61-70	71-80
1922-1931	1	—	2	5	2	—	—
1932-1941	—	1	6	2	—	—	—
1942-1951	—	1	1	4	—	—	—
1952-1961	1	—	1	3	2	2	1
1962-1971	1	—	5	3	1	—	—
1972-1976	1	3	1	—	—	—	—

The newspapers that have had winning cartoonists in recent years are different from those which won in the first twenty-five years. At the beginning, to put it bluntly, the backlands were largely out of it. The awards were monopolized by the New York, Baltimore-Washington axis, plus Chicago. The accompanying Table 7.2 shows a shift that came about during World War II and is reflected in the tabulations from 1950 on. For example, before 1950, 35% of the total awards went to newspapers in New York City (43% if you count the wire services as located there). This does not include two wins by "Ding" Darling, whom I counted as with the Des Moines *Register* but whom the awards committee listed both times as with New York *Herald Tribune*. That would boost it to 51% for New York City. After 1950 the New York City total drops to a skinny 5%, 10% if you count Trudeau's Doonesbury win as New York's. Before 1950 the Chicago-Washington-Baltimore group walked off with 34% of the prizes; after 1950, they reduced by more than half to 15%.

TABLE 7.2

PULITZER PRIZES

	1922-1949			1950-1976		
	Newspaper Winners	Cartoonist Winners	Total Awards*	Newspaper Winners	Cartoonist Winners	Total Awards
New York	5 (28%)	6 (32%)	9 (35%)	2 (10%)	2 (10%)	2 (5%)
Washington-Baltimore	3 (17)	3 (16)	5 (19)	2 (10)	2 (10)	2 (5)
Chicago	3 (17)	3 (16)	4 (15)	2 (10)	2 (10)	2 (5)
News Services	2 (11)	2 (11)	2 (8)	1 (2)	1 (2)	2 (5)
Other	5 (28)	5 (26)	6 (23)	15 (68)	15 (68)	18 (69)
Total	18 (101)	19 (101)	26 (100)	22 (100)	22 (100)	26 (99)

*Total number of different newspapers and different cartoonists awarded a prize (multiple wins counted only as once).

The big shift is, of course, to the "other" category, the outland papers, which jumps from about 25% to a whopping 69%. The number of newspapers honored is spread around too; it triples in the last period. Each recent decade has added about five new newspaper winners to the list of first-time winners, suggesting that the juries are now out searching the second-level papers for major-league talent. For example, of the winners in the decade 1962-1971, only the Chicago *Daily News* and Los Angeles *Times* had ever won before. Added to the first-time list of newspapers with Pulitzer prize cartoonists were the Hartford *Times*, Denver *Post*, Miami *News*, Charlotte *Observer*, and *Newsday* of Long Island. The awards of the next decade went to four more first-timers, the Richmond *News-Leader*, the Boston *Globe*, the Universal News Syndicate, and the Philadelphia *Inquirer*.

What explains this shift? Obviously, fewer of the winning artists work in the Big Three cities. Like money and other commodities in *Hello, Dolly*, the award is being spread around — among more artists as well as among more papers. Multiple winners are in sharp decline. No longer do groups like the psalm-singing Brooklyn *Eagle* clique or the Kirby-Duffy oligopolies score three times. Between 1950 and 1974 only Paul Conrad won twice. Between 1922 and 1950, four of the Big Three papers won more than once, plus "Ding" Darling (New York or Des Moines). There were other second winners between 1950 and 1974 and even these are instructive. Herblock, Bill Mauldin, and Daniel Fitzpatrick won a second time; their first wins were prior to 1950. It is hard to fault the committee for any of these. Perhaps coincidentally, only one of these two-time winners, Daniel Fitzpatrick, was working for the same newspaper or service at the time of his second win. Paul Conrad, who won twice after 1950, also shifted papers between wins.

Less shifting of winners up to the Big Three cities goes on, along with there being fewer winners there to begin with. Of the post-1950 winners, Mauldin made such a move, from the St. Louis *Post Dispatch* to the Chicago *Sun Times*, and later Pat Oliphant from the Denver *Post* to the Washington *Star*. Herblock and Fischetti were already there before the war and only shifted within the Big Three cities. Post-1950 winners have moved very little perhaps, because syndication gives them all the advantages the big city slot used to. Pat Oliphant, for example, once said that he preferred Denver because he did not get too close to the people he had to caricature. Maybe so, but later he moved to Washington, D.C. The Big Three city papers, through Mauldin, Herblock, and, secondarily, Fischetti and Darcy, still contribute a large share to the syndication market, but so do the other areas, through men such as Oliphant, Wright, MacNelly and Conrad, and such non-Pulitzer winners as Hugh Haynie and Don Hesse. The balance seems to have tipped to the boonies.

To summarize, the Pulitzer is no longer, or at least for the present is not, the possession of a select few, or a private club. It is being passed around to top-flight artists, wherever they draw and whatever their age.

It is hard to make a judgment on content. For one thing, the "cartoon of the year" misrepresents the quality of the earlier period, the cartoons which are presented are much more stodgy and high-minded and cliché-ridden than they really were. Nevertheless, the winners since Conrad's first in 1964 are of a different generation. The cartoons these artists produce seem to have two traits that distinguish them. They sting hard from time to time, and they are amusingly original, backing off about as far as possible from the hackneyed editorial-cartoon stereotype of grandiose symbolism. A goodly number show sprightliness in style by using a less-conventional, wider-than-high style of cartoon box, emphasizing caricature and humor in the art itself and putting in plenty of action. One cartoonist, the winner of 1975, is Garry Trudeau, who draws the syndicated comic strip "Doonesbury." A large number have adopted variations between Conrad's big shoes and bulb-nose, old-time movie style (his early style) and that more recently popularized by Oliphant. Their cartoons have life and sparkle and sophistication.

So I conclude that the Pulitzer Prizes have gotten much better. What might be done to improve the competition?

One drawback of the present system of having no cartoon-of-the-year award is that, in the process of eliminating an abomination, the committee threw away the

203

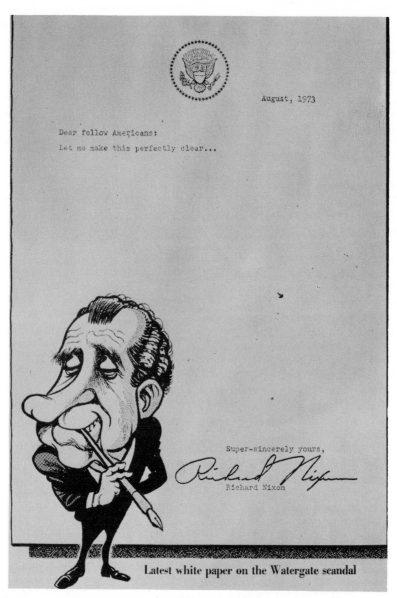

126. Hugh Haynie : Latest White Paper on the Watergate Scandal, August 17, 1973. Louisville *Courier Journal.*

opportunity to give the winner a lasting showcase. Such a showcase is perhaps less needed today than, say, during the Great Depression, but it would still be helpful. Twenty-three of the total of forty winners have up to 1976 at least some of their output published in paperback or hard covers. In some cases these collections predate the award by some years or are a very, very brief collection. Of winners since 1950, less than half, nine out of the nineteen, have ever been published in book form.

127. Paul Conrad : Match each of the above with the cause for which each is best known : A. Gun Controls, B. Election Campaign Reform, C. Indian Rights, D. Prohibition. 1973. Los Angeles *Times.*

The good editorial cartoon, the kind for which an artist should be remembered in later years, should probably involve caricature or great symbolism in a way that clicks at the time, and also does so later, because it so well sums up the event. Robert Minor's "The Perfect Recruit" and McCutcheon's peculiarly appealing TR "My Day" cartoons all have this unforgettable quality. Most of the men who won the prize, even the less-well known, have had some cartoons that have at least some of this. It is for these cartoons that they deserve to be remembered in hard-cover form. The Pulitzer committee has, I think, an obligation in this respect.

The award winner might be asked to make a selection of, say, half-a-dozen cartoons from the past year's work and perhaps another half-dozen from a longer period. The winner would derive the satisfaction of knowing that he or she would be remembered by the best work, and the selection, itself would be of some interest to other cartoonists as well as the general public. A collection of such cartoons, in the style of the Johnson or Spencer volumes, issued every five years or so, would be a treat to look at casually and would also be worth serious study. But most important, it would also be a fitting tribute to American editorial cartoonists. Barring this, the annual volume that at this writing has been issued since 1973 under the editorship of Charles Brooks, permits the Pultizer winner a display of current work in its pages.[20]

An additional improvement is to continue the policy of having as few two-time winners as possible. It would be nice to have the award given only once, as with a knighthood or election to the Royal Academy or Baseball's Hall of Fame, but the terms of the overall award make that impossible. The prize must single out the best work of the year — but to continue to have the one-time tradition breached only or unusual circumstances or unusual individuals seems desirable.

Finally, it seems a little sadistic to make no awards, as in 1973, when the group of nonwinners included talent as good as Haynie, Hesse, Sanders, or the 1974 winner, Szep. For the health of cartooning it probably does do some good to keep artists a little off balance and every so often throw in a no-award year. But not when so much first-rate talent is lying around, waiting to be picked up and recognized.

128.   Tony Auth : "Then it's unanimous! We reject the President, mercy and binding up the nation's wounds!" (1976 Pulitzer winner). August 25, 1975. Philiadelphia *Enquirer.*

A Closing Note

The role of political cartoonist demands artistic and personal freedom as much as humans need air. The conditions of publication set certain restrictions. Luckily, cartoonists can function in something less than mountaintop ozone, but if they continually feel a choking sensation around the Adam's apple, whether due to pressure by a publisher, private group, government, or even professional peers, the quality of their output nosedives.

Fiercely independent souls do not seem to advance to the stage of preparing cartoons in totalitarian societies — at least no totalitarian country has yet produced a cartoonist Solzhenitsyn. Only conformists seem fit recruits. They can then be daringly critical about the unpatriotic slackers at home and portray anyone abroad who disagrees with the party line as vermin in the full spirit of Socialist realism or Nazi orthodoxy. They may console themselves with the thought, if they wish, that they have the freedom to be "right," and Big Sister says no-no when it comes to the freedom to make "mistakes."

The authoritarian cartoonist lives a bolder and more adventurous life. When romanticized, it comes out like *The Vagabond King*, that operetta on François Villon, the beloved rogue and hero of the masses. When the cheering falters, however, being such a cartoonist can be a grinding experience. To be unofficial gadfly under such conditions means dodging many swats, and it is a life that few cartoonists seem to bear up under for long.

Democratic cartoonists are more prosaic and perhaps a little more frustrated from time to time. They have little trials and rewards, and they face pressures for conformity of one kind or another. They can't try for daily blockbusters, in part because they are rushed. But also because they have some sense of allegiance to his government and society. So they use their freedom for pricks and stings and occasionally just to amuse or approve, and they hope that, in the process, they have occasionally hit the bulls-eye, as well as earning a fair living under relatively pleasant circumstances. But then, most of us accomplish little more in this relatively brief life.

8

The Birth and Development of
Cartoon Symbols

Most commentaries on political cartoons are framed as reviews of history or, at the least, they present cartoons in chronological order. The reasons are good, since cartoons can be understood only in terms of their historical setting.[1] It also permits one to study some of the landmark cartoonists and place them in the parade of artists so that one may speculate on who influenced them and whom they in turn influenced. I bow politely to this convenient convention and follow it here.

But I have also a second purpose. It is to examine how workaday cartoonists function in a stable democracy. What kinds of ideological assumptions characterize their work and what mood do they broadcast in their imagery and artistic style? I shall concentrate on American cartoonists and ethnocentrically wall off the prominent artists from other stable democracies into a single chapter.

We begin with a review of the development of America's graphic symbols, followed by comment on their content. The way treatment of such symbols develops suggests how cartoonists and perhaps the public as well viewed the system. Relevant to this discussion is the question raised a decade ago by historian Allan Nevins: are our American symbols now outmoded in respect to the modern democracy that has evolved? And he asks, particularly in reference to the political symbol of Uncle Sam, are they "grotesque stereotypes?"[2] He also suggests an appropriate response — "Guilty! Guilty! Guilty!" I would like to submit a brief for the defense, Your Honor.

The Snake and Other Early Symbols

Early American symbols for the nation vary from images concocted by enemies and used derisively to self-consciously constructed symbols. Littering the symbolic landscape are false starts that caught on only for a generation or two and then faded out, as well as imagery that seemed appropriate to its inventors but never quite caught fire. For example, Roger Butterfield notes that the figure of a bucking horse, a beaver, a codfish, a deer, and a pine tree were all once used in colonial or revolutionary cartoons as emblems to symbolize the nation.[3]

The most important of the false starts tells us what traits are discarded, and also indicate that Americans and their governors have been somewhat sensitive about how they were portrayed, since they very properly considered these portrayals to be of some importance.

The first portrayal of America, a natural one for Europeans, was that of a Pocahontas-type Indian girl, or as E. McClung Fleming calls her, the Indian princess.[4] These Indian representations date back to the early 1700s and lasted through the Revolutionary War. By the time of Rousseau, the image of a noble savage seemed particularly romantic and attractive one to characterize the new American colonies. A British cartoon issued as late as 1782, concerning a hoped-for reconciliation between Britain and America, shows Britannia welcoming to her bosom an Indian maiden with feathers dancing on her head.

It is fairly easy to understand why this representation of Americans was very early devised by Europeans to symbolize the New World, and also why it was ultimately rejected by Americans. The first American political cartoon, in 1747 ("Hercules," chap. 1), thought to have been drawn by Benjamin Franklin for the cover of one of his pamphlets, hits hard on the subject of frontier battles with the Indians and the need for colonial self-defense. This was a recurring and rancorous theme in American colonial cartoons, since the French, and later the British, leagued themselves with these Indians in battles against the colonists. The colonial Americans did not adopt a sentimental view of the red man, nor did they seemingly wish to be represented by an image of the American Indian.

A different kind of image sprang up in the period of revolutionary boiling and fervor. Benjamin Franklin, in the first American newspaper cartoon in 1754, drew the familiar snake divided into eight pieces, labeled the parts with the names of colonies, and titled it "Join or Die." His cartoon, as noted earlier, was used in every conflict of the colonies up to and throughout the Revolutionary War. The rattlesnake at that point was adopted as a symbol by some of the more fiery revolutionary bodies, such as the Culpepper Minutemen. They used it with the accompanying phrase *Don't tread on me,* and featured it on their emblems on several flags.

Loyalist editors were quick to point out the negative symbolism of the rattlesnake. James Rivington in the New York *Gazateer* of 1774 published a poem that taunts: "Ye sons of sedition, how comes it to pass, that Americans [be] typed by a snake-in-the-grass."[5] He had a point, it appears. During a time of revolution and sedition, when citizens loathe their leaders and their government and hatred of both is at a fever pitch, they might wish to identify themselves and their cause with a venomous reptile. It is perhaps appropriate that the Peoples' Bicentennial Commission, an unofficial group highly critical of current American trends, resurrected the coiled snake for some of its literature. But in calmer times, after the Revolutionary War was won, the snake symbolism fell into quick disuse. By 1800 it was featured in a Federalist cartoon to represent the despised Jacobins ("the Providential Detection"). Almost a century after the Revolution, in 1861, during the Civil War, the snake was used rather aptly by C. G. and E. H. Leland to represent the Copperhead Southern Sympathizers. They gave it the face of the leader of that group, Congressman Clement Vallandigham of Ohio. It had completed a cycle from national symbol to symbol reserved for national enemies and traitors.

Even in recent times symbol-mongering has been attempted, but with mixed success. During World War II, to sell war bonds, the patriots at the advertising-agency front adapted the figure of the Minuteman from the statue at Lexington. While this symbol gave a certain nobility to the enterprise, the Minuteman never became animated enough to seem real and therefore has not quite entered the mainstream of symbolic figures. Similarly, such symbolism as the liberty tree and, from the Great Seal, the All-seeing Eye and the Great Pyramid, which were to represent strength, went nowhere — this despite the repetition of the seal on the back of the one-dollar bill.

Static Symbols

Some symbols have limited use because they don't move, but they do exude dignity. All those I know of are symbols invented and certainly nurtured by official sources rather than symbols invented by cartoonists. The Minuteman is an example of a contrived static symbol — an inanimate object, a statue in this case consciously adapted by an official body to function as a national symbol. The most important static symbol, also contrived, is of course the flag. Most other such symbols are located in or near Washington, D.C.; such major buildings and monuments as the Capitol, Mount Vernon, the White House, and the Washington, Lincoln, and Jefferson Memorials. Philadelphia provides Constitution Hall, and South Dakota, Mount Rushmore. Most of these have appeared on official documents, stamps, or currency. The map can also be so used. In cartoons of the early 1800s the busts of Washington or Franklin also served. The Liberty Bell, first cast in 1753 but gaining an enhanced attractiveness after it cracked while tolling at the funeral of Chief Justice John Marshall in the 1830s, falls into this static category, as do representations of such national documents as the Constitution, the Declaration of Independence, and the Bill of Rights.

The flag was among the symbols consciously planned by an official body. On June 14, 1777, a year after independence, Congress adopted the official description of our flag, which was then made by Betsy Ross. A flag of this design very possibly existed before this action, but if so, it has disappeared. The Congressional Act carefully symbolizes the nation by the well-known device of having each star represent a state and the stripes stand for the original thirteen colonies. The flag attracted the nickname of Old Glory and later became the subject and title of the nation's national anthem. The flag is, in a special sense, the universal symbol; it is used at official functions and in cartoons by itself, and it has also become a part of most of the animated graphic symbols, which from time to time have been dressed in flag bunting. It also is flown with or draped over many of the other inanimate symbols, as, for example, the Capitol or the Washington Monument. Its stars and stripes are also found as part of the Great Seal of the United States. Its advantage among the static symbols is that it can be given the semblance of life and motion as it waves.

The limitations of such static symbols for cartoonists flow directly from their strength. Their lack of animation can suggest solemn dignity and gravity, but they are always at rest and this limits somewhat the range of emotions they can express. To enhance their utility, cartoonists frequently use the static symbols as props or stage settings rather than as images that stand alone. Animated figures are often placed with them, giving the cartoon more life, even though this makes for some rather clumsy cartoons.

On certain occasions, however, the formal static symbol is indispensable. In the volume of cartoons that memorializes the assassination of President John F. Kennedy, almost every other cartoon uses one or another of these static representations.[6] In many of these the static symbols are used in a way that is trite and predictable, yet they still lend a sense of dignity and solemnity to this sad occasion. That weekend's cartoons would somehow have been unthinkable without these familiar static symbols to express the deep sense of grief most Americans felt.

An additional problem with the static kind of symbol is that doing something new or original with it is a severe challenge to the cartoonist. The Kennedy assassination provides one successful example. The most memorable of the cartoons, and one not included in the above collection, is Bill Mauldin's grief-stricken Lincoln of the Monument, with hands to eyes (fig. 122). A more difficult symbol to use with originality is the map of the United States. Few cartoons using it have been particularly striking or memorable. However, one is still reprinted — an imaginative cartoon of 1894 by Gillam in *Judge* showing President Grover Cleveland shaped from the United States map. He is represented bowing obsequiously to Britain and to its ideas of Free Trade. This kind of originality, similar to Mauldin's effort, in effect making a static symbol animated, is the exception. Most use of static symbols veers more in the direction of the trite because it is difficult to play it again Sam in a new way. Static symbols are useful enough to survive, but the democratic cartoonist requires symbols that have a greater flexibility and can express a variety of emotions, including something besides solemn adoration of the nation and its government.

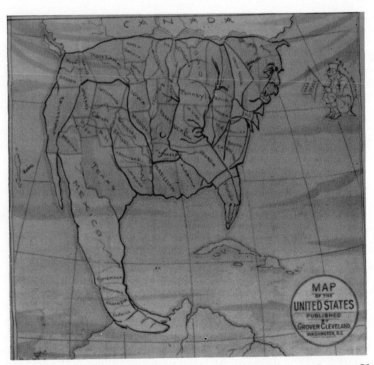

129.   Victor Gillam : All that there is of U.S., according to Grover Cleveland. "My Country 'tis of ME, Sweet Land of Liberty, of ME I Sing." January 6, 1894. *Judge*.

The Animated Symbols

I pause to note that animated symbols that are not representative of the whole nation, but merely a part, such as "Congress," will not be considered here. Nor will I deal very long with the use of current or past presidents to symbolize the nation. Use of the president as symbol creates a blurring of the distinction between the nation and its government or regime. Their use is most appropriate for American cartoonists when the president is a strong leader who is speaking on behalf of the nation in time of crisis, such as war. But a number of European cartoonists have reported that they no longer use Uncle Sam to represent America, but utilize instead the incumbent in the White House, or sometimes the Secretary of State. Such representations create problems because they are time-bound. As one writer in the discussion of Allan Nevins's article suggests, a Wilson is succeeded by a Harding or, I may add, a Nixon resigns under pressure, and the point is forcibly brought home again that the current president always represents the incumbent administration and hence only for a time, if at all, can symbolize the nation itself. For home consumption, at any rate, American artists use the president less frequently than foreigners do. A different kind of problem is presented by use of a past president. Lincoln, of course, is by all odds the favorite, useful especially for both civil rights and assassination occasions. But too many such guest appearances throw a certain blackish pall over the proceedings.

The Eagle

The first of the animated symbols that weathered the test was the American Eagle. It was an official symbol cemented into the national consciousness as part of the nation's Great Seal. On the same date that the Declaration of Independence was proclaimed, July 4, 1776, the Continental Congress also set up a committee of Thomas Jefferson, John Adams, and Benjamin Franklin to design a Great Seal. Several false starts were made over the next few years before a final design, by Will Barton, a Philadelphia specialist in heraldry, was adopted by the Congress in 1782. Parenthetically, it should be noted that Benjamin Franklin favored the turkey for the Seal, because of its peaceful image, while he rejected the eagle, because he saw it as a predator "who like those among men who live by sharping and robbing, is generally poor and often very lousy — besides he is a rank coward." Nevertheless, though he may have been correct about the eagle and even about the turkey, as William Murrell notes, the American Eagle has become the longest lasting in the history of American cartoon symbols.[7] Very early, clawing both warlike arrows and peaceful olive branches, it appeared in cartoons, on coins, and on bills and has since gone to feature status on stamps, military medals, and even on the insignia of such private organizations as the Boy and Girl Scouts.

The Eagle, like the British Lion, is especially useful on military occasions, but it can be adapted to other functions. The early Federalist cartoon of 1800 called "The Providential Detection" shows a hovering American Eagle discovering Jefferson secretly worshiping at the shrine of the Jacobins or, as it is put in the cartoon, at "the altar to Gallic despotism." Jefferson is properly put down.

130.   American cartoon : The Providential Detection. Ca. 1800.

Columbia and Liberty

A female American figure, however, actually predates the invention of the American Eagle, but her history is more checkered. A peculiar series of face- and body-lifts has occurred in respect to her. William Murrell notes that as revolutionary fervor grew hot, the Boston *Gazette* in 1770 withdrew the figure of Britannia from its masthead.[8] In its place the editor first substituted Minerva, the goddess of wisdom. From this point on the figure evolved into what Fleming called "The Plumed Goddess," but also, as Murrell notes, it appeared as the Goddess of Liberty, Dame Freedom, Justice, or Miss Columbia. As early as 1799 it appears as Columbia, with some of the apparatus of Dame Liberty, in a cartoon concerning the editor William Cobbett: "See Porcupine, in Colours Just Portrayed." During the Revolutionary War and after, the neoclassical symbol of Columbia appears to have become very popular, especially among the educated and possibly more conservative classes. Some patriots even argued that the new nation should be called Columbia (not Columbus), and there was, in fact, an organization formed in 1788 known as the Sons of Columbia and a song was composed during the period called "Hail Columbia." Kings College of New York was, of course, redesignated Columbia, and the capital of the nation, the District of Columbia.

131. William Charles : Columbia Teaching John Bull a Lesson. 1813.

But the symbol had difficulties because, I suggest, of its revolutionary connotations. The early female figure that Fleming calls "The American Liberty" is a beautiful young woman holding the traditional staff and Phrygian cap. This cap was the Roman symbol for freed slaves. It first appeared in Dutch cartoons against Spain in the late 1600s, but came into its own as a popular symbol of the French Revolution of 1789. Predictably, this led both to a negative reaction by American Federalists, and other conservatives since, against using the symbol of the French Revolution. It led to attempts to transform Dame Liberty into a more acceptable symbol such as Columbia. In the early cartoons, and even on American coins, the cap and pole appear with the draped female figure, but when she is identified as Columbia, "Liberty" is often stamped on the bonnet that forms part of her hairdress, in perhaps a kind of downgrading of the symbolic cap, and, to some degree, a de-emphasis on the moral value of liberty as well. This is true up through Civil War, when the symbol is muddied further. Shortly before the war Jefferson Davis had served as Secretary of War. In this capacity he had decided that the figure of Dame Freedom that would grace the top of the U.S. Capitol would have no anti-slavery liberty cap or staff. The statue as he approved it was put in place in 1863 and remains there as he planned it, with a crested helmet. Cartoonists began to follow this lead, and for a time the Victorian vogue shifted to a Columbia-like female who became more a representation of the nation than of the value *liberty*. In the next generation a further blurring of the image

214

occurred when in 1883 France presented America with the Statue of Liberty. On her head is a crown of spikes rather than a cap, and in her hands are a torch and tablet rather than a staff. She is neither Columbia nor the traditional Goddess of Liberty, but partakes somewhat of both and is also something of neither.

132.   **Charles Dana Gibson : Columbia's Greater Task. 1918.** *Red Cross Magazine.*

The competition then became one between a cold goddesslike figure, such as graces New York Harbor, and the Victorian idealization of womanhood, which might be fairly saccharine and uplifting, but sometimes looked human. In the late-nineteenth-century cartoons, the image of Columbia in a shift was still dominant. Thomas Nast attempted to spruce up the lofty Columbia by taking her out of her nightgown and dressing her in the current fashions of the day, but that did not catch on either. *Puck* artists made her very much the rounded woman. The popularity of the traditional Columbia as a national symbol was possibly further enhanced by her use by the 1893 Columbian Exposition in Chicago.

But in the twentieth century a shift in emphasis occurred. Possibly it was the result of selling the war bonds of 1918, and of Liberty Loans, and of the need to reemphasize that value during wartime, or perhaps it was just that Victorian womanhood went out of style as the Jazz Age came upon us. All of the Kennedy collection of cartoons, previously noted, that use the figure present her literally as a Statue of Liberty with torch and spiked headband. A collection of ten cartoons of the assassinations of Lincoln, Garfield, and McKinley, reprinted in the same volume as an appendix, shows nine with the symbol of America, in each the weeping Columbia of the old style — which suggests the kind of change that has continued to occur with respect to this symbol. For modern taste, Columbia appears to be regarded as a little embarrassing, someone on the level of a second-rate classical dancing teacher with her flowery movements and postures. The more austere, less humanized or female, and more statuesque Statue of Liberty is preferred.

The favorite posture of the female symbol of the nation, goddess or idealized woman, when she is not weeping, appears to be standing dignified, firm, and uncompromising, whether it be against a foreign enemy or a local politician. She epitomizes the schoolmarm stance of Carrie Nation and, in recent times, proclaims the virtue of liberty to petty tyrants at home and abroad.

Brother Jonathan

The history of the political symbol of Uncle Sam has a long development, beginning with the early British derision of the Yankees even while they were colonials and were just beginning to oppose the British Stamp Act. Albert Matthews traces "Yankee Doodle," the melody, to Andrew Barton's *The Disappointments, or the Force of Credulity: A New American Comic Opera* performed in America for the first time in 1767.[9] A year later, when the British troops arrived in Boston, they had words to the tune, which they called "Yankee Doodle." These familiar words make fun of the gullibility and coarseness of the Yankee country bumpkins. The verse describes a rawboned American farm boy who takes his horse off the plow and makes a trip to the big city. He puts a feather in his cap and imagines he is in style, like the fashionable Macaroni of Britain. The Macaroni were the young men of the time who traveled to Italy, hence the name, to study the works of culture on the European Continent, and particularly those of the old Roman Empire. They were stylish fops, which Yankee Doodles definitely were not.

By 1775 Americans had developed their own version of the song — a kind of official one, the traditional but less-remembered one about "Father and I went down to camp" to see the soldiers drilling to fight the British. The tune and these words cropped up in the training camps and on the battlefields of the Revolutionary War. This version was used in Royal Tayler's play *The Contrast*, which was first published in 1790, though performed earlier. It became a colonial anthem of sorts, and Yankee Doodle became an early version of what was to evolve into the figure Uncle Sam. But it is interesting to note that the derisive version of the song, not the official one, is the one we remember most easily because we were taught it as children.

The figure of Yankee Doodle, the clodhopper colonial, merged first into the figure of Brother Jonathan, a nickname also presumably invented by the British to use derisively against the colonists. It is reported by Matthews that, when the colonists recaptured positions at Bunker Hill, they found that the British had set up straw sentries to confuse them on the number of defenders, and had placed a big sign on one saying "Welcome Brother Jonathan."[10] Jonathan also appeared as a supporting character in Tyler's *The Contrast.* What was planned as a minor part became, as the play continued, a role considerably embellished. The British had labeled as defects the crudities and lack of sophistication of the colonists. The character Jonathan turns these defects into virtues to be proud of, and he becomes the stage Yankee, shrewd and down-to-earth, who continually demonstrates his natural common sense, Will Roger's style, at the expense of cultured snobs. This version of the Yankee American became very popular, according to Constance Rourke, in the early 1800s.[11] By 1825 an actor named George Handel Hill began giving soliloquies and short sketches with this figure, and over time began to dress himself up in the familiar star-spangled costume that we now associate with Uncle Sam: red, white, and blue, with a tall white hat and old fashioned bootstraps to help when riding a horse. Yankee Hill, as he called himself, was popular on the American stage, according to Miss Rourke, between 1820 and the early 1840s. The point of his skits was to contrast the honest, commonsense American Yankee with the kind of effete English travelers who began coming to America during this period and wrote it up as rough and uncultured. His act seems to have been similar to that of George M. Cohan, another self-proclaimed Yankee Doodle dandy, who in his early-twentieth-century plays repeatedly foiled the sophisticated European.

133. Amos Doolittle: Brother Jonathan Administering a Salutary Cordial to John Bull. 1813.

The first cartoon of Brother Jonathan shows him with the traditional Revolutionary War costume of top boots, great coat, and queue. The cartoon "A Salutary Cordial" by Amos Doolittle, drawn in 1813, shows Brother Jonathan administering a dose of Perry (a pun) to John Bull, a reference both to the American naval hero of the War of 1812 and to a well-known paregoric. Brother Jonathan began to put on parts of the patriotic costume in cartoons of the early 1830s, a direct influence from the stage Yankee. The first part of the costume to be widely used was the striped pants. But even as late as the beginning of the Civil War, the costume was not completely set.

All through this period Europeans continued to use the term *Brother Jonathan* derisively against the United States. *Punch*, in its first issue of 1841, had a column called Jonathanisms. A sample: "There's an old fellow in Nashville who snores so loud that he is obliged to sleep at a house in the next street to avoid waking himself." Former residents of Warsaw will recognize the formula. These mild witticisms, occasionally filled with "I reckons" and "I swan," continued to amuse Europeans by alleging that most Americans were uncultured and uneducated, and a little simple. As late as November 1915, Bernard Partridge, in a cartoon in *Punch*, still persisted, somewhat patronisingly I think, in calling the United States by the name of Brother Jonathan, even though the cartoon portrayed an Uncle Sam.[12] The symbol Brother Jonathan began to fall into disuse among Americans in the 1850s and it died out completely during the late 1860s and early 1870s. The change is a significant one because, as I shall note, something of the earlier figure was consciously eliminated.

Major Downing

One other image that is related to Uncle Sam emerged in the 1830s. Seba Smith, a Portland, Maine, newspaper editor, invented a character he called Major Downing. Downing also starts out as an uncultured Yankee farm boy, like Yankee Doodle, but somewhat early in the series he enlists in the militia, is made a Captain by President Andrew Jackson and later, as a result of action in the field, is promoted to Major. At this point he becomes a figure of slightly more stature, whose comments on national politics are presumably filled with conscious or unconscious humor, depending on the writer. Major Downing was widely appropriated by other writers, especially Charles Augustus Davis, a New York newspaperman. The Major Downing of Davis was anti-Jacksonian, using the technique of writing effusive and naive letters that appear friendly and supportive of Jackson. Henry Ladd Smith considers this Downing more full of witticisms and better written than the original created by Seba Smith.[13]

Major Downing appeared in a number of cartoons from the Jackson period onward, and some lithographs by E. W. Clay were issued and credited to a Zek Downing, the "neffew" of Major Jack, and that word in quotes gives a fair clue to their content and level of humor. They featured a young, wisecracking Major usually dressed up in striped pants but otherwise having no distinguishing features. Murrell and H. L. Smith both state that Downing almost became the symbol of the American people, one that might replace Brother Jonathan. However, with the death of Seba Smith, the Major Downing fad died out just as had the Yankee Doodle one before it, and by the time of the Civil War references to Major Downing in cartoons had largely disappeared.

Uncle Sam

The origin of Uncle Sam was in the War of 1812, and again it was a symbol used

134.   John Tenniel : A Family Quarrel. December 20, 1861. *Punch.*

derisively, this time against United States policy. It was said to have been fashioned by American Doves who were members of the 1812 Peace Party. Alton Ketchum's rather thorough research leads him to conclude that Sam Wilson of Troy, New York, a supplier to the U.S. Army, was indeed the original inspiration for the title *Uncle Sam*, a fact that Albert Matthew's earlier research had led him to conclude had not been fully established. (Congress, in 1961, passed a resolution backing the Wilson version and thus it becomes the official American one.) Whether Ketchum or Matthews is correct, Uncle Sam in this early period, it seems to me, is continuously associated in cartoons with such practical matters as money, taxes, banks, tax collectors, and custom houses. He smacks of both government and dollars right from the start and so is a social cut above the cracker-barrel clodhopper. The earliest cartoon of Uncle Sam dates from 1832 and concerns the national bank. It was called "Uncle Sam in Danger" and was followed in 1838 by another on money matters, titled "Uncle Sam with La Grippe." From then on, Uncle Sam seems to be firmly identified as representing the U.S. government in cartoons, but his pictorial image is far from consistent. In the early cartoons he has no whiskers and is often very young, say in his late thirties or early forties. In many he has parts of the traditional Uncle Sam uniform, especially the striped pants, but in some he is, so to say, dressed in street clothes of the day. As late as the Civil War an attempt was made in two Currier and Ives prints, "Stephen Finding His Mother" and "Uncle Sam Making New Arrangements," to portray the character as a kind of elderly Benjamin Franklin, dressed in revolutionary-style dress.

The final evolution of the cartoon figure appears again to have been the result of derision. The cartoonist of *Punch,* John Leech, drew a Brother Jonathan who was anything but flattering to Americans. He wore a kind of Panama hat, had straggly hair in back, had a cat-o'-nine-tails in his back pocket to symbolize that he was a slave master, puffed a stogie, and otherwise had a lean, ugly, and nasty look about him. (fig. 48). During the Civil War the famous *Punch* cartoonist, John Tenniel began to merge the figure of Leech's Jonathan with the rough frontiersman who was then president, Abraham Lincoln. In the process, chin whiskers were added to Leech's original, the cat-o'-nine-tails was removed from the back pocket, and the figure grew taller so that the clothes were tight and short in the arms and legs. The Tenniel Brother Jonathan continued to suggest a crude and unflattering character, one in line with *Punch's* opposition to the North and to Lincoln. When Lincoln was assassinated, Tenniel tried a few cartoons in which he merged President Andrew Johnson and Brother Jonathan in the same image, but gave up the matter as unsatisfactory and returned to drawing his Lincolnish Brother Jonathan to represent the United States. This image, from 1861-62 on, though unflattering, began to look somewhat more like the Uncle Sam of today than had any preceding image.

In June 1869 one of Tenniel's cartoons ridiculing America was answered by Thomas Nast in *Harpers Weekly*, and Nast in fashioning his reply stated to his biographer that he had carefully studied the Tenniel drawings. It appears that he began to borrow technique and imagery from them. In November of 1869 one of Nast's cartoons, "Uncle Sam's Thanksgiving Dinner," does in fact show an Uncle Sam complete with whiskers and traditional costume, but for some reason Nast shortly after abandoned this image. In any case, Frank Weitenkampf, after extensive research, states that the Nast drawing was not the first such American-drawn Uncle Sam dressed in the traditional costume and labeled Uncle Sam. The first appeared some months earlier, also in *Harpers Weekly*, that of February 6, 1869.[14] This drawing continues the tradition of a relatively young Uncle Sam, but with whiskers. Weitenkampf was unable

135.   Charles G. Bush : The Championship of the Atlantic. Uncle Sam : "Come, John, we're ready." John Bull : "Can't get my boy up to scratch, SAM." February 6, 1869. *Harpers Weekly.*

to determine who the cartoonist was, since the signature was only two letters superposed, C. G. or G. C. Other cartoons, unmistakably by the same hand, appear through July, signed either with these initials, one over the other, or by "Hunk E. Dore." My own surmise is that the C. G. stood for C. G. Bush, who as a young man of 27 appears to have just joined *Harpers Magazine* about January of 1869. In July 1869 his cartoon of the Boston Peace Conference is signed "C. G. Bush." The distinctive script *G* in both signatures varies from that generally used. Both C. G. and Hunk E. Dore stopped contributing as the signed cartoons of C. G. Bush began to appear regularly in the magazine. Since Bush later became one of the first practicing newspaper cartoonists and by 1900 was called the Dean of American editorial cartoonists, it seems fitting to accord him the honor of having drawn the first completely costumed Uncle Sam cartoon.

More important, actually, was the fact that Thomas Nast returned to the whiskered figure in *his* cartoons. In the late summer of 1872, during the election involving Grant and Horace Greeley, Nast turned out an Uncle Sam as the polished and homey figure that is now so familiar to us. He drew an Uncle Sam who threw aside the stogie that C. G. Bush had given him and became more mature, more serious, a little thinner, and a

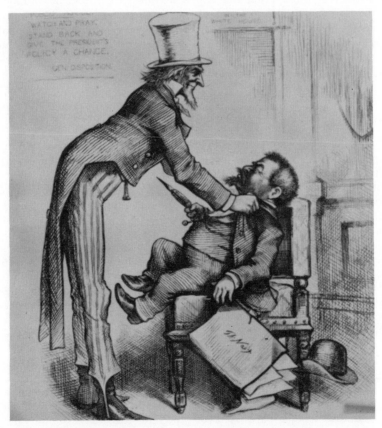

136. **Thomas Nast : "Nay, Patience, or We Break the Sinews" — Shakespeare. U.S. "Our artist (Nast) must keep cool, and sit down, and see how it works." May 5, 1877.** *Harpers Weekly.*

little less slouchy, with a greater air of dignity and, as Weitenkampf states, he was a good deal nattier. The popularity of Nast's drawings during this period helped stamp his version of Uncle Sam as the traditional one, and it has remained so to the present.

It does not follow that all the characteristics of his predecessors shone through in the post-Civil War Uncle Sam as presented by Nast. Major parts of Yankee Doodle, Brother Jonathan, and Major Downing were absent. Uncle Sam is a good deal more mature and successful in Nast's drawings. He is a man of proven merit and substance, not a callow youth. Uncle Sam is also no longer "the common man" of the lower-middle class, or a person just arrived from homesteading on the frontier. His grammar no longer is uneducated and back-woodsy, with all the funny spellings that make those pre-Civil War humorists so hard to plow through today. He has learned to join the ladies, his style has some grace, and his dress is no longer cast-offs. Uncle Sam is rural and still Yankee, but to me seems someone who has arrived — solid Establishment and middle class, a country town lawyer or even a county-seat banker. He is also something other than the wise-cracking cracker-barrel philosopher that is the staple of so many edited collections of American humor. This man has dignity and seriousness of purpose; in fact he rarely if ever smiles. All of these changes go in the same direction. They all suggest a boost in social and economic status for this representative American not too different than that experienced by John Bull earlier in England.

This figure is by far the most used of American national symbols. For example, in the Kennedy book one would expect cartoonists to maximise official symbols over political ones. There are 50 flags at half-mast or draped over the coffin, but also 35 Uncle Sams while it contains only 5 of Liberty and only 2 eagles. Uncle Sam is presently the all-purpose national symbol for cartoonists.

John Q. Public

One other symbol should be added to the animated category, though Alton Ketchum omits it from his otherwise thorough discussion. Since the morality plays of the fifteenth century, the figure of Everyman was in general currency. William Murrell argued that in the early part of the nineteenth century, Uncle Sam was used to represent the nation and Brother Jonathan to represent the common people of the nation, and there are a number of cartoons that bear him out. It is clear that after Nast, once the more-dignified Uncle Sam figure was adopted, cartoonists seemed to sense the need for a representation of the common man. Thomas Nast, as a number of cartoonists since have done, occasionally cast himself in this role. (Fig. 136). Joseph Keppler and other *Puck* artists reached for standard stereotypes, such as the exploited farmer or the downtrodden immigrant, as specialized representations for the common people, but they did not develop a general stereotype that could be repeated from cartoon to cartoon.

As far as I can determine, and I follow Hess and Kaplan here, the first figure of the common-man symbol used in American cartoons was that of Frederick A. Opper in about 1900. He drew a "common people" figure with tiny hat, crossed eyes, and short stature. In figure 137 we see his complete life cycle as a victim of the trusts. In such Opper cartoons he is continually being kicked around by the trusts, the small man lost in the big organization world, the Charlie Chaplin of *Modern Times*, without the ability to thumb his nose back. At about the same time, T. E. Powers developed a similar figure who was a member of his down-and-out club. Again these are essentially derisive figures. They are weaklings, not wisecracking common people. They proved to have too little spine and so later artists began to help the little man work his way up

222

137. Frederick Opper : Monopoly Lodge Entertainments, 1904. New York *American.*

the social-status scale just as Uncle Sam had before him.

The familiar, balding, father figure that we know as John Q. Public generally was short, had glasses, moustache, a felt hat and suit and tie, and sometimes a cigar. He looks like a small businessman. He appears in "Ding" Darling's and other artists' work during World War I, but was given his name and stamped into his characteristic costume by the Chicago *Daily News* cartoonist Vaughn Shoemaker at the beginning of the Depression. At the same time, in 1933, Will Johnstone of the New York *World Telegram* drew a figure that continued the older tradition: a thinner, naked figure that he labeled *Taxpayer*. His costume was a barrel with a hat for clothes, but he has the same kind of ragged moustache and glasses that John Q. Public has. Both figures bear a relationship to British representation developed by their cartoonists after World War I, the John Citizen of Poy (Percy Fearon) and the "Little Man" with derby and umbrella of Sidney Strube. All share the same characteristic of the early morality plays: exploited decency, but with courage and humor to survive trials. The common-man figure takes on dignity even as he is being tricked or cheated.

Herb Block has used two figures for the common man, suggesting a further evolution. Block began his cartoonist career on the Chicago *Daily News*, and his first figure, which he sometimes calls Mr. Public, is like that of many other cartoonists. It bears a striking resemblance to Shoemaker's John Q. Public, with moustache, hat, and fatherly image. But this figure disappears from the Block cartoons, or at any rate appears less frequently, beginning sometime during the late fifties. He is replaced by a

223

138.   Vaughn Shoemaker : Cloud 12. 1964. Chicago *American.*

modern version of common man, a younger, taller, white-collar professional, a character that looks somewhat like Herb Block himself. No female version of the common person has appeared.

Official Vs. Political Symbols

The symbols described above fall into two other classifications. Some are officially invented by the government, but others are unofficial symbols, invented and developed by persons outside of government for political purposes.

The development of American symbols demonstrates the role to be filled by official symbols: to affirm, without any compromise or shilly-shallying, the legal authenticity of the nation and its government. One can see how a revolutionary body with no legitimacy or legality would feel an immediate need to drop the imperial British Symbols and create new American ones that would inspire loyalty. The government of the new American nation began creating official symbols to signify its legitimacy on the same day that it declared its independence from Britain, July 4, 1776. The importance of the symbols was further underlined as the major members of the drafting committee of the Declaration of Independence were designated as a committee to create the first official symbol. On official documents, and in the popular journals of the day as well, a number of symbols began competing with each other for adoption as the official ones for the nation.

The degree to which these official symbols must, like Caesar's wife, be above reproach is also borne out by this history. The uncompromising nature of official symbols required that those having any negative connotations be rejected once the Revolution seemed assured of success. Symbols that pump emotional poisons into the system are useful to oppose a tyranny in a prerevolutionary stage or during wartime, but they can not be officially identified with what one cherishes and wants accepted as morally legitimate. For example, one such symbol that seemed to me should have survived is that of the Liberty Tree. The neat tree on the flag looks like a moving symbol for a nation with many magnificent forests. It was perhaps dropped because of its resemblance to a hanging tree. The Liberty Tree is shown as such in several early cartoons, an association that calls to mind the similar unappetizing image of Thomas Jefferson's "The tree of Liberty must be refreshed from time to time with the blood of patriots and tyrants. It is its natural manure." Even after the Phrygian cap and staff had appeared on coins and official documents as part of Liberty's costume, they were not accepted wholly, presumably because of their suggestion of freed slaves and of the French Revolution, and this meant difficulties for the symbol. The Columbia symbol was not fully accepted as a compromise either, perhaps because its identification with the moral value of Liberty was only partial. Only with the development of the Statue of Liberty into the official national symbol did acceptance become complete and unambiguous. Significantly, the most successful official symbol is the eagle, though it was used by the old Romans, and by many nations since, to symbolize majesty and military might. A trite cartoon setting even in recent times is that of the American eagle swooping down on an enemy; Bill Mauldin drew it with Castro as a rat with a missile in his paws; and Vaughn Shoemaker showed it so, scattering North Vietnamese and Vietcong. This symbol is, like Liberty, uncompromisingly moralistic. The static official symbols represent the same uncompromising aspirations, though less effectively because of their lack of animation. Their primary appeal is thus more emotional than moral. The cracked Liberty Bell provides emotional reinforcement by suggesting an instrument that destroyed itself in the noble cause of proclaiming liberty. So, also, do the memorials to our past presidents, or the flag, or the Capitol remind us of sacrifices for this ideal and for the nation, and thus appeal to us to live up to this noble heritage.

None of the these official symbols can be easily humanized, nor were they designed to be. When they are besmirched or purposely damaged, the patriotic citizen is expected to regard the act as an outrage and sacrilege — a reason why using the flag as a pants patch set off, and was meant by wearers to set off, intense negative feelings. Thus Thomas Nast struck a false note when he portrayed Columbia or Liberty, dressed realistically in modern clothes, as a shrew berating Uncle Sam. His imagery, if successful, would inevitably have damaged its official usefulness by sacrificing a large part of the idealistic and moral element of that symbol. What we officially aspire to must remain unsullied by life's compromises. The official symbols remain moral aspirations presented as already achieved.

The making of such official patriotic representations is the relatively easy part and is engaged in by every nation, especially, one supposes, those headed by governments that have reason to doubt that the consent of the governed is fully or freely given. Any animal that is not downright repulsive will do as a symbol to represent strength. And the lofty qualities can be symbolized by a pure woman dressed up in a flowing formal; always on hand is the imposing governmental building or public monument or shrine to a great leader of the past. But only rarely, and possibly only in developed and stable democracies, do citizens themselves fashion imperfect but sympathetic symbols to represent the nation. Such figures, given the American experience, take time to develop, though the need to create them in America appears to have been felt by some citizens almost as soon as the date of the creation of a democratic polity. With us, as with Britain in its creation of the John Bull figure, the need was not felt by the government itself but by its friendly and loyal critics. The democratic mood encourages the fashioning of such less-than-perfect symbols because only in democracies will citizens be permitted to create them, and only there can loyal citizens be permitted wryly to face up to having a less-than-perfect nation with a less-than-perfect government in a less-than-perfect world. These symbols pay a moral price by being human, but they are thereby more useful to fling at the public official in the day-by-day political sniping that goes on. My remaining comments will center on these unofficial political symbols and their present-day use, since they seem to me by far to outrank in importance the more sterile creation of official representations.

The political symbols are commonly used to project an attitude toward government and to the nation that is sharply at variance with the patriotic posture encouraged by official symbols. This kind of mood does not harmonize too well with the screaming Eagle, the majestic Statue of Liberty, or all those solemn static representations. The idealized official symbols are in fact too uncompromisingly self-righteous. The attitude projected by political symbols rather mixes regard for the nation with healthy skepticism, a mood that we have called laughing satire.[15] There is respect for the legal legitimacy of the nation and government, an implied acceptance of the distribution of social, political, and economic benefits as just enough to merit the support of citizens. But this is combined with a sense that conditions might be somewhat improved.

Margaret Sherwood, in an *Atlantic* article of fifty years ago, tried to analyze more precisely the attitude suggested by the Uncle Sam symbol at the close of World War I. She argued that it was a figure composed of two conflicting personalities, that of a shrewd Yankee and that of an idealistic Don Quixote.[16] I would amend her analysis and thereby suggest that the traits are complementary rather than in conflict. One aspect of the symbol is indeed the common sense and self-reliant Yankee who sees it as his duty to take care of himself and not be a burden to others. This character trait is found in all the symbol's predecessors: Yankee Doodle, Brother Jonathan, and Major Downing. In Uncle Sam the self-reliance theme is doubly emphasized because he is presented in the role of solid citizen and community builder, rather than as a wisecracking wise guy on the sidelines. But if the other aspect of this character were Don Quixote, critics of the symbol such as Allan Nevins might find the figure of Uncle Sam more attractive. It is precisely the suggestion of searching for the impossible dream that he says he misses in the Uncle Sam image. Uplift and inspiration are Dame Liberty's routine, not Uncle Sam's. The second part of the Uncle Sam figure, however, seems to me to be also typical Yankee and also typically American: hopeful and kindly rather than utopian, pragmatic rather than ideological, one whose idealism consists of taking the long over the short-sighted view. It is a cast of mind, like self-reliance, found likewise in such otherwise diverse Americans as Benjamin Franklin, Mark Twain, William Allan White, Franklin Roosevelt, Harry Truman, and Will Rogers, to name but a few.

The mingling of these traits results in a combination of common sense and good will, well suited to contrast with the stupidity or self-serving found in day-to-day democratic politics. Rather than symbolizing ideal virtue and purity, the figure of Uncle Sam suggests taking the next sensible step to improve things. The figure recommends strength of character and traditional virtues in an imperfect world rather than a striving for perfection. This is perhaps why the image of Uncle Sam is purposely portrayed by cartoonists as old-fashioned. It was an old-fashioned and out-of-date figure that Thomas Nast put the finishing touches on in 1872. The kind of striped pants with bootstraps and beaver hat that he drew had gone out of style at least a generation or more before. He latched onto this old-fashioned costume for perhaps the same reason that we turn to Currier and Ives and old-fashioned Christmas cards — they seem to represent a certain uprightness and character strength, without being unrealistically angelic.

Limitations of National Symbols

A symbol for a heterogeneous America can not be representative in the sense that all the variety of races and ethnic groups appear in the figure, any more than the president of the United States can be representative of all the nationalities that make up the union. The official symbols and those created by cartoonists such as Nast, who was an immigrant from Germany, are all WASPS to the core, including, I suppose, even the eagle. This is the heritage of the nation because WASPS were here before most of the rest of us, and thus put the first stamp on the nation. The WASPS have also, however, contributed their share of admirable presidents and national heroes, and so this heritage need not, I think, be viewed too negatively. If an alternative polyglot symbol can be created, so much the better, but in the meantime these WASPS serve.

Cartoonists have also been tempted to move the Uncle Sam image from the small town with its general store to the big city with its immense industrial plants. What seems to suggest itself is adding sixty to eighty pounds to the venerable Uncle's midsection. Frederick Opper did this in the nineties, rather irreverently; John McCutcheon attempted a more solid-citizen, fashionably stout kind of image. But none of these caught on, perhaps because artists were trying to refashion a familiar figure rather than create a new one. The change, when it comes, will be similar to Herb Block's reworking of Mr. Public from small businessman to white-collar organization man.

Degrading National Symbols

Symbols have only the content that artists put into them. A common practice of those who wish to attack the system is to reverse the traditionally accepted content of the symbol. Benjamin Franklin used on his stationery a cartoon showing Britannia with colonial arms and legs hacked off. (fig. 61), a suggestion of the lack of legitimacy of the British government in respect to the colonies. Conversely, the Victorian Age went to other extremes and John Tenniel presented Britannia in *Punch* as a goddess and such political leaders of the nation as Gladstone as knights fighting dragons and other invidious monsters (figs. 47-56). And as we have seen (fig. 75) a recent comment by the English cartoonist Ralph Steadman transforms Britannia into a hung over and haggard hag, with twisted trident and battered shield, a cigarette dangling from her lips and stubs on the floor around her. Some Americans have been pained at how

227

easily the Uncle Sam figure can be changed in content and thereby degraded. In the Soviet Union publications such as *Krokodil* the beard has been blackened, the hair grows a little longer over the ears, and spectacles have been added to give Uncle Sam a kind of meddling-busybody, tightwad look. Our own home-grown underground artists can do as well. Jan Faust, during the Vietnam War, drew a sly and forked-tongued Uncle Sam. De Mar at the turn of the century drew a figure made out of bullets and guns but the fact is that any symbol can easily be caricatured and denigrated. The noble British Lion has been drawn as flea-bitten, with knots in his tail and with false teeth, and even living persons such as Churchill and FDR were cruelly distorted by the Nazi cartoonists. No symbol, however noble in its conception, is proof against such treatment. And such treatment can also be very illuminating. Charles Bush parodies Homer Davenport's cartoon (fig. 36) "He's good enough for me" by replacing Uncle Sam with a figure made up of trusts.

139.　Charles Bush : "He's Good Enough for Us!" 1904. New York *World.*

Cartoonists today use the Uncle Sam figure not so frequently for patriotic posturing, as one would anticipate, as for criticizing what is happening in the nation. A bewildered, outraged, or chagrined Uncle Sam is portrayed reacting to an unpleasant political reality. The first cartoon in which the symbol appeared was appropriately titled "Uncle Sam in Danger." Since then, cartoonists have kept the figure continuously in boiling water heated up by our own foolish, or knavish, but still American, political leaders. In some instances the criticism is biting, in others only a means of laughing at ourselves and our leaders.

This human quality is also why cartoonists have found the Uncle Sam figure effective in dealing with national tragedies, more so in our sophisticated and shell-shocked times than would be some high-minded Victorian female. Like Abraham Lincoln, the Uncle Sam symbol contains little of the fanatic. He can be shown effectively expressing the human feelings we have all experienced in the face of political extremism gone wild, as in the Kennedy assassinations.

The same comments apply to the figure of the common man, the other side of the leader-public relationship that the cartoonist deals with. This figure has also moved up the social scale into the solid middle class, but he has not lost his humanity in the process. He started off a pitiful worm, being browbeaten on every side by the trusts and other forces too large for him to control, and he ends up today as a figure with basic bedrock strength and decency, though still being hassled by fools and knaves. But he is portrayed as continuing to have faith in the American system despite being often made painfully aware of its multiple defects.

A clue to the degree to which present-day cartoonists accept the traditional attitude projected by the Uncle Sam image is suggested by the frequency of the image's use. Cartoonists commonly use Uncle Sam more sparingly than in the past, perhaps only three or four times a month. This may be in part an attempt to avoid triteness. But some American cartoonists rarely or never use the Uncle Sam or John Q. Public symbols. Those who are largely uncritical of the political establishment tend to present the political scene as a form of humorous entertainment, with Uncle Sam seldom used. They prefer humorous presentations of politicians or ordinary people, with the impact on their lives of some political event shown, such as, for example, how national daylight saving time affects a jewelry-store owner. This is a kind of status-quo, politics-is-mild-fun school of comment. Absent is political bite. Alternatively, cartoonists who become deadly serious in their desire for radical change but still want change by democratic means also tend to shy away from the political symbols, perhaps because in their serious commitment and moral righteousness they can neither wholly accept nor wholly reject the symbols, and so feel uncomfortable using them. They do not care to denigrate them nor can they embrace them, because the political symbols appear to imply a measure of support along with a kind of nondestructive, accepting kind of criticism.

The way cartoonists use the Uncle Sam symbol to represent the nation in dealing with other nations makes this supportive element of the symbol most apparent. American cartoonists commonly portray the other nations by their leaders: for example, Thatcher for Britain and Brezhnev for the Soviet Union, a natural symbol for dictatorships and, as Herb Block notes, also for parliamentary systems. But in this crowd appears Uncle Sam to represent the U.S., a logical incongruity. The reason, I suggest, is that the Uncle Sam symbol gives cartoonists, as critics, the opportunity to present a realistic and unofficial figure, but one who can rise a little above current political maneuvering and express slightly longer-term interests than the figure of any current president might.

To some critics, however, the Uncle Sam symbol verges too far on the chauvinistic patriotic, though, of course, the American Eagle and some of the other official symbols as usually presented can more justly be criticized for this. Nevins, for example, argues that Uncle Sam "gives off the air of jingoistic Manifest Destiny.[17] The type of portrayal he is perhaps thinking of is James Montgomery Flagg's famous poster "Uncle Sam Needs You." But even here, at its most patriotic, the Uncle Sam figure does not seem to me to give off the aura of that virulent type of mindless patriotism. The figure in the poster suggests to me that a dirty job needs to be done in a nasty situation, rather than that we must all march off on the kind of high-minded crusade those females in flowing robes might call on us to undertake (fig. 104). Uncle Sam's appeal is to the practical job of protecting our own homes and families and common

140. Homer Davenport : Now that Congress's Candle Is Out, What Noxious Odors Rise." 1896. New York *Journal.*

decency rather than of saving the world for democracy or some other ism. The humanness of the symbol at least permits the artist using it to remind the viewers that the nation does not have a monopoly on wisdom, or virtue.

The political symbols of Uncle Sam and Public thus are capable of encouraging the kind of healthy sanity that democratic government is supposed to nurture in its citizens. Official symbols are too straitlaced and moralistic for this purpose. The political symbols suggest an understanding of human fallibility in the Niebuhr world of moral man in immoral society. These sometimes pathetic symbols for a great nation do not suggest that we seek perfection, but hold up a standard of less lofty traits: common sense and good will. They expect and ask less of us and of the politicians who govern us — just to use good sense and be kind. Note the human Uncle Sam holding his nose at the antics of Senator Mark Hanna and Speaker Reed, as portrayed by Homer Davenport.

A Closing Note

The description of the use of American graphic symbols by artists suggests a process of natural selection of national symbols whose survival, one suspects, is not accidental. Some symbols thus flourish a bit, then wither, and finally die, presumably because the environment proves uncongenial to the mood they project. Other symbols survive but are artistically wanting because they are static or are well adapted to only a few restricted purposes or occasions. Hence both official and unofficial sources strive to create animated representations. For this purpose, American artists within and outside the government have created and used, as described, four all-round, animated symbols — symbols for all (or at least most) seasons.

The argument I have presented is that America, like all nations, has through its governmental agencies struggled to find or develop animated and other symbols of an idealistic, uplifting sort. These official symbols present the moral aspirations of the nation as already achieved. But private citizens have created another type of symbol, unofficial and more human, that invites criticism of the government and nation. The process of developing such symbols, based on American experience, has been a slow but steady one. Hence they are found, one suspects, only where the free development of opinion has been valued over a relatively long period.

With these humanized political symbols, artists can as critics of the politics of their day demonstrate the conflicting tendencies within democracies. The political symbols as commonly used suggest as a standard neither Stephen Decatur patriotism nor selfless service to mankind. Rather, these political symbols as commonly presented suggest a practical human compromise that one may live with — a standard that calls for striving for the decent and the possible in the imperfect politics of an imperfect world.

9

Early Prints and Magazine Cartoons

My rather unpatriotic suggestion is that, until the Civil War, American political cartoons were on the whole bad. The cartoons of the colonial period were largely imitative of those of Britain, which is not astonishing. Benjamin Franklin, the author of what is thought to be the first American cartoon, was a friend of William Hogarth — in fact Hogarth received a letter from him on the morning of the day he died. Real disaster in cartooning struck after the break with the mother country, when the last of prerevolutionary war imitators died and the new nation built a tradition of its own.

Political Cartoons: The Pre-Civil War Period

Four types of cartoon can be distinguished: the emblematic allegorical, the imitations of the British cartoonists James Gillray and Thomas Rowlandson, the symbolic, and the Currier and Ives. The first three characterized the period before 1830; the Currier and Ives is what I shall call the new style.

Fewer than 100 pre-1830 cartoons have been found by scholars, though perhaps a dozen more have been alluded to in newspaper editorials or ads but not yet discovered. Most of these were prints, but a few were newspaper cartoons.

Why the emblematic allegory came so naturally to Americans is no puzzle. One suspects that it is especially attractive for the kind of moralists who mount revolutions, as was the case in medieval times when the style was developed. The kind of ideology that lends itself to such treatment is that of suspicion of a conspiracy against the people by the Establishment. It is made to order for those peddling any variety of devil theory of history, and one should add that only readers inflicted with a touch of paranoia are likely to have the patience to decode the worst examples. That it seemed an appropriate means of expression in the early revolutionary period is not astonishing. The symbolism and complicated tags and allusions are relished as one smites down the oppressive devils once and for all. It is also a style that permits the artists to extend

232

themselves, and to parade their stylistic abilities with a flourish. In more realistic or cynical times, this kind of outburst may be greeted with impolite derision. But there is an additional reason as well. Cartoons were few and far between in those days and were read rather than glanced at. One had to be sure the customers got their money's worth.

William Murrell presents a startling illustration from the pre-Revolutionary War period: a print produced in England in 1765 against the Stamp Act and the same print as redrawn for American consumption. The English original is a far from modest or self-effacing effort, with the king, Britannia, and American Indian, and four other figures in flowing robes in the foreground, eight more in the background, the north wind or God up high blowing away, and all tied together with nine comments in balloons. But this drawing has a neat and simple crispness compared to what an American engraver, Wilkinson, produced. This is the American artist's description of his interpretation as he presented it in the Pennsylvania *Gazette* of November 1765.

On the Fatal First of November, 1765, was published a caricature Print representing the deplorable state of America, and under what Influence her ruin is Attempted. At the Top is a Figure representing France holding in one hand a Purse of Money to a Comet, marked with a Jack-Boot, and out of her mouth a Label by which we found she actuates the Star to shed its baneful Influence on Britannia; who presents a box to America, telling her it is the Stamp Act; but on it is wrote: Pandora's Box (which according to the Poets was filled with all kinds of Calamities). America, who is in deep distress, calls out to Minerva to secure her, for she abhors it as death! Minerva (i.e. Wisdom) forbids her taking it, and points to Liberty who is expiring at the feet of America with a label proper to his extremity. Close by is a fair Tree inscribed to Liberty; at whose roots grows a Thistle, from under it creeps a viper, and infixes its sting in the side of Liberty. Mercury (who signifies Commerce) reluctantly leaves America, as is expressed by the Label. Boreas near the Comet, blows a violent Gust full upon the Tree of Liberty; against which Loyalty leans and expresses her fear of losing her support. Behind, a Number of Ships, hauled up, and to be sold; a Crowd of Sailors, dismissed, with Labels proper to them. On the other side, a Gallows with this Inscription: Fit Entertainment for Stamp Men. A Number of these Gentlemen, with labels expressing various Sentiments on the Occasion. At the Bottom is a Coat of Arms, proper for the Stamp Men.[1]

A number of these emblematic treatments survive. The earliest American cartoon (Fig. 14, a woodcut credited to Benjamin Franklin), showing Hercules urging on a farmer who represents the colonies, could be classed as such, though the treatment is a good deal simpler than most of the breed. One of the best (Fig. 130) showing Jefferson caught in the act of worshiping libertarian France, "the Altar of Gallic Despotism," by the American eagle, no doubt tipped off to what was happening by some properly suspicious Federalist. Burning on the altar are the works of Godwin, Paine, Rousseau, and Voltaire. As late as the Jackson nullification threat from South Carolina, such art was still being produced.

Also in the pre-1820 period, and in that which followed, are what are purported to be representations of actual scenes but are hoked up to peddle a propaganda line. The Paul Revere print of the Boston Massacre, already described (Fig. 62), is an illustration. Revere, not unaware of the moving qualities to be attained with tags, added the label "Butcher's Hall" to one of the buildings in his version. But there are too few of this kind of illustrated atrocities to merit a category.

141. Peter Pencil : Intercourse or Impartial Dealings. 1809.

The second school is that of the imitators of Gillray and Rowlandson. As Stephen Hess and Milton Kaplan demonstrate in *The Ungentlemanly Profession*, more than just style was appropriated. As with cartoonists everywhere, ideas also found their way from the prints of predecessors to the copper plates of their descendents. The American artist of this group the most generally revered is William Charles, who arrived in America from Scotland in 1806 at age 30, and whose death in 1820 scholars report as a great loss. (See Fig. 131). He was not the only one to borrow heavily. A Federalist attack on the Jacobin clubs, reproduced by William Murrell, looks very much like one of Gillray's devil drawings. But some, I think, borrowed legitimately — that is, learned from Gillray and Rowlandson how to draw simple and forthright political statements and added something of their own individuality to the presentation. One of the best of such was Amos Doolittle, who gave us one of the first drawings of Brother Jonathan (Fig. 133). Predating his work is that of an anonymous artist whose drawing of Jefferson with his pockets being relieved of cash by both George III and Napoleon is one of a few very fine prints to be produced. Only three prints by "Peter Pencil," as he signed his work, survive, but this kind of simple style did not take.

The ideological mood of these cartoons is close to the mocking style of Gillray, Rowlandson, and other British print makers, with its plague-on-all-your-houses quality. Politicians are caricatured into grotesque shapes and made to look ridiculous and act ludicrously. A difficulty was that the style caught on here just as it was going out in England. It is a form of levity suitable for those uncertain times when rulers are looked upon with universal suspicion. Despite all the roughness and crudity of the Jackson period, the Gillray technique did not quite ring the bell.

Also produced before 1830 are the few cartoons that by our day's standards would be classed as excellent. These I have called symbolic. Both of the best I know of are of animals. Both are simple and easy to understand and have the wallop of a baseball bat across the skull. The first is the still-famous Ben Franklin snake cut of "Join or Die," produced for the Albany convention in 1765 and hauled out for each succeeding crisis until the union became a reality. The second is that of the gerrymander, a combination of the map of the new Boston suburban legislative district, laid out with some partisan forethought by Massachusetts Governor Elbridge Gerry, and a mythical amphibian based on the salamander. The drawing immortalized Gerry after a fashion, since the word still survives to illustrate the practice of finagling district boundaries for partisan or personal advantage. For many years this drawing was credited to the painter Gilbert Stuart, but it was later found to be the work of another Yankee, Elkanah Tisdale, who unfortunately, so far as we know, was never inspired to similar work. Also eligible in this class is the simple print of columns rising for the constitutional edifice. As each state convention ratified the document, another pillar went up. It passes, but no one will be moved to ecstasy in viewing it.

Perhaps I have been too hard. A period of seventy-five-or-so years that produces two memorable cartoons should not be condemned completely out of hand. But with

142.   Elkanah Tisdale : The Gerry-mander. A new species of Monster which appeared in Essex South District in January last 1812. Massachusetts *Sentinel.*

regard to the period from about 1830 on, I make no apologies for my boorishness. These are cartoons drawn by people who not only misunderstood what a good cartoon might be, but ran out with cudgels to meet anything they suspected was of that species and beat it into insensibility just as one would treat a venomous snake.[2] This is a way of saying that a new and distinctive American style of cartoon was developed, one that I do not admire. I have called it the Currier and Ives style, though this firm printed only about eighty of such works, beginning in 1848, and a number of now-forgotten lithographers each printed as many or more — some earlier. Murrell estimates the total number of lithographs at 600. Most were social and humorous rather than political. He dates the first lithograph as 1828. Among the first with a political slant was one called "A New Prop of the United States." It showed the tail of the alligator of Jackson tied to the tail of the tortoise of Adams, with the appropriate politician seated on each and shouting insults in lariatlike balloons.

Before I review the Currier and Ives political print in detail, the question may arise as to why it became such a staple. One reasonable hypothesis is that there was no alternative offered. And it has some truth. A parade of comic-magazine imitations of *Punch* and of the *Illustrated London News* was stillborn or survived for only a few issues. The American formula just could not seem to be found. The public had to await Frank Leslie's *Illustrated Newspaper* (a weekly) begun in 1855 and, a little later, *Harpers Weekly* in 1857 and the short-lived but high-quality *Vanity Fair* in 1859. Meanwhile, the factory-produced lithograph became an institution, but with a marked difference from the Gillray-Rowlandson model. The manufacture of these works was a business proposition. Cartoons were produced on order, just like tarpaper and chicken wire, or any other commodity, to fit the buyer's specifications. Just as today the manufacturers of political campaign buttons mint them for any and all political parties or movements, so each print manufacturer mass-produced political lithographs for those on all sides of the current political issues.

The canny publishers naturally were reluctant to build up individual artists, and did so no more than Fisher Body advertises its individual designers. The same impetus to imaginative production may be observed in both industries. Currier began his firm in 1835 and added his bookkeeper Ives as a partner seventeen years later. Their most prominent artist was a German immigrant, Louis Maurer, perhaps the best known because he survived into the 1930s and so was around to tell his story when the antiquarians and historians from places like the Smithsonian and the WPA began to get interested in this sort of thing.

The artistic style developed for political prints may come as a surprise to nostalgia buffs. The Currier and Ives name conjures up brightly colored prints of steamboats, of railroads speeding across the prairies, or simple snowy rural scenes showing grandmother's home at Thanksgiving. But almost all of the Currier and Ives political lithographs were printed in black and white.[3] They were perishable throwaway items manufactured for specific campaigns, rather than stock prints upon which more than a weekend's attention might be lavished.

These political prints had several characteristic features. First, the scene looked like a posed tableau, even when it was supposed to represent action. The runner stuck his leg out as if he were awkwardly holding it and teetering while a camera was snapped or a sketch made. This introduced a wooden quality to the drawing that makes John Tenniel's work in *Punch* look like that of a writhing belly dancer. Second, the print was representative art, so much so that one had the feeling that the drawings of the bodies were kept in stock and cut-out heads of the current politicians were pasted in place on their necks. Very little caricature went into this effort. The goal was to produce a likeness, but the result tended to make those portrayed resemble a convention of solemn undertakers or rather, perhaps, their clientele.

143. Currier and Ives : The National Game. Three Outs and One Run. Abraham Winning the Ball. 1860.

Because these drawings were produced on demand, and mainly for campaigns, little thought was given to original settings. Since presidential elections were and still are called races, they suggested sporting events to these inspired designers. Someone then concluded that sporting events were the obvious way in which politics must be presented. Occasionally a more daring illustrator would stumble onto a more original conception, such as the horse and buggy on the train track. Note that this is a particularly inventive treatment because there are two horses pulling the democratic buggy in two opposite directions; but then, 1860 was a four-party election, which would certainly challenge artistic ingenuity, since no sport with four teams on the field at once comes readily to mind. Even representation of John Bell of the Constitutional Union Party was accomplished in the coal tender. But this was an exceptional election. For the run of the mill like that of 1844, the Great Presidential Steeplechase idea would do.

An additional characteristic of the political lithography was the detailed allusion. These drawings carried on the emblematic tradition and were a good deal like William Hogarth's in inspiration, though not in quality; they were designed to be studied for all their little knickknacks and sly comment. Little tags were attached to the individuals, or papers were drawn sticking out of their pockets to represent semi-secret practices of one sort or another.

But the great sources of such allusions were in the statements of the political actors. In the balloons the designers extended themselves, because the litho firms claimed that the product would not sell without them. The balloons are as wordy as the ones found in the Mary Worth strip today when she is setting some temporarily misguided young female on the path of virtue. They go on and on, and they contain whatever is the real

144. Currier and Ives : Progressive Democracy — Prospect of a Smash Up. 1860.

life and attraction to be found in these drawings. There are first of all puns: all the changes, for example, that an ingenious hack can ring on quinsy, as in John Quincy Adams. Second, there are witticisms or, more often, what passes as such. Particularly favored is the put-down or heavy-handed insult, with the receiver, instead of yelling "Yi!" as in Little Orphan Annie, commenting that he guesses he will take off as fast as he can on a trip up Salt River.

The balloons are a major reason that these are bad cartoons. They cause the best and least pedestrian of these works to be not cartoons at all but only picture vehicles for witty comments. Artistry and imagery conveyed through the drawing are secondary. Not all of the cracker-barrel witticisms are outdated either, but one must have the patience to study the fine print with a magnifying glass. In the accompanying lithograph, Lincoln is shown about to enter an insane asylum while riding a rail. He is announcing that as soon as he does, the millenium will arrive. Around him and cheering him on are a bunch of Victorian weirdos chanting their "demands." The women's rights biddy is flanked by an advocate of "the free love element." Along with them are an assortment of cranks and knaves who want the right to pick people's pockets, to free rum and food at a governmental hotel, Mormonism, and the inevitable redistribution of wealth. The drawing is aptly titled "The Republican Party Going to the Right House."

Equally funny but artistically uninspiring is a print of the Clay — Frelinghuysen ticket of 1844. The background is that the vice-presidential candidate is something of a puritan prig who is questioning the mellower Clay about the pictures of cockfights, duels, cards, horseracing, and so on that he finds hanging on the wall. He gets such evasive answers as that the rooster represents the cock that crowed while Peter denied his Lord, and the like. The drawing is abominable, but the comment is full of fun of a rather high quality.

No doubt our forefathers enjoyed these works. But by political cartoon standards

45. Currier and Ives : The Republican Party Going to the Right House. 1860.

they are monstrosities. They are stilted and cluttered, wooden and pedestrian. Most of all, the drawings smack of insincerity and so give off the smell of embalming fluid. As far as the artistry is concerned, they are manufactured products as individualized as the worst of calendar art.

This period also had a few good political cartoons, but not of such high quality as survived from the earlier period. Of those I have picked out, only a few, surprisingly enough, are commercial lithographs. From the shaky magazines survive only a few genuine caricatures that give the glimmer of new horizons. One is of a flickering candle with the head of President Buchanan, a charitable view of an incompetent published in Frank Leslie's *Illustrated Newspaper*. The often-reproduced Eagle plucked by Michael Angelo Woolf was originally a cartoon from *Yankee Doodle*, showing the Mexican Eagle. Woolf's lithograph applies it to 1860. A commercial lithograph of Santa Anna, sitting on a horse and looking out at Americans, is genuine satiric caricature worthy of any age. Its artists are Sarony and Major. One wonders if only enemies could be accorded this broad caricature treatment.

A number of Jackson items also show some life. One poster on hanging comes immediately to the point. A favorite item is of King Andrew the First; the artist, while giving in somewhat to the temptation to elaboration and gingerbread, still presents an acceptable work. Variations on the cartoon of cabinet members as rats deserting Jackson by E. W. Clay seem to have made a hit. David Claypoole Johnston, who billed himself as the American Cruickshank, exaggerated his skills. From time to time he produced series of drawings that he called *Scraps* and at least one memorable cartoon, "Symptoms of Lockjaw," showing Henry Clay, author of a gag rule, sewing up Andrew Jackson's mouth with needle and thread. But even such as these are few and far between.

239

146. Michael Angelo Woolf : Our National Bird. 1861.

147. Sarony and Major. Santa Anna. Ca. 1844.

148.   David C. Johnston : Symptoms of Locked Jaw. 1834.

Finally, shortly before the Civil War, *Vanity Fair* began publishing drawings by
Henry L. Stephens that are very much in the mold of the *Punch* cartoon of the week,
with few figures, some caricature, and an obvious point. But he was an exception, and
he lacks impact because he was merely a competent craftsman imitating an established
line. The drawings somehow show it.

The period really ends with a famous cartoon, "Compromise with the South" by
Thomas Nast from *Harpers Weekly*. This drawing was used by Lincoln Republicans
to beat back the McClellan challenge of 1864. It is full of allusion, allegory, and
flowery sentiment. While the drawing has some power, it does not even come close to
suggesting what fine work Thomas Nast would produce within a few short years. That
he did not rest on his laurels as Lincoln's "best recruiting sergeant" and continue to
turn out these elaborate tableaux suggests a great deal of the quality of his genius. But
to that in a moment.

To return to the questions: was the pre-Civil War political cartoon bad? and if so,
why? To the first, I say the answer has to be yes, or at best a qualified "most of these so-
called cartoons should not be classed as such." Still, the cartoons were foisted off on

241

149.   Henry L. Stephens : Seward's Grand Starring Tour. King Richard III —
Up with my wigwam! Here will I LIE tonight.

150.   Thomas Nast : Compromise with the South. September 3, 1864. Harpers
Weekly.

the public and up till now few besides me seem to have complained. So, perhaps I am wrong.

But granting my point, the question then is, why were they so bad? Part of the reason is that they were produced for relatively trite occasions to make a little money for the lithographers. Only occasionally does a subject such as Andrew Jackson jolt the artists into producing something special. The freeing of the cartoon also awaited great events, the election of Lincoln and the Civil War. It is not so much that the cartoonists were inspired. It was rather that the trite clichés about footraces could not be used and something better was needed.

This touches on the main reason why so much of this work was bad. It is, I think, because these cartoons artistically have all the spontaneous joy of life of a bunch of Uriah Heeps traipsing around preparing for a mortgage foreclosure. Everything else about these cartoons is more imaginative than the artist's contribution. They are bad because the artists, at least from 1830 on, were for the most part mere hirelings. The people who thought up the funny patter lines were not, or at least they were given a little artistic freedom by Nathaniel Currier and James Merrit Ives and their counterparts in the commercial lithograph business. But the artists were given a take-it-or-leave-it commission with the scene set for them by someone else. Like buck privates in yesterday's army, they were not supposed to think. Their work showed it.

Their release came when their talents were genuinely needed. This was when magazine publishers out to build circulation and dress up pages of dead type scrambled for their services.

In what follows, note how much of the impetus for originality and individuality came from artists who were foreign born. William Charles, at an early date, was such and, while an imitator of others, he at any rate knew that there were models to emulate. The new immigrants had similarly been exposed to better cartoons than what passed as such in America. Some, like William Newman, a *Punch* artist, and Thomas Nast temporarily backslid to make a buck. But the urge to improve was there.

The Civil War: The Beginnings of Life

The weekly magazine, as noted, began to stimulate cartoon art that freed itself from Currier and Ives. In 1850 Frank Bellew arrived from England and soon became a magazine staple. His cartoons continued into postwar period, and seem to me to have consistently pointed the way to what a really talented cartoonist might accomplish.

What distinguished his work was imagination. The caricature had snap and crackle even if the drawing had no great political pop. The best known of these is the elongated drawing of Abraham Lincoln after his 1864 reelection to illustrate the pun "Long Abraham a little longer."

Bellew fell short of starting a renaissance in political cartoons, despite his artistic skills, because he had nothing in particular that he felt very excited about. Even after Nast had established the editorial cartoon format in the 1870s, Bellew's work continues to display the same artistic originality without saying very much politically.

I have already written about Adalbert Volck of Baltimore, who was the genius of the Lincoln period. The vividness of his conceptions outstrips the work of his contemporaries, but in time one of these, Thomas Nast, clearly topped him.

151. Frank Bellew : Long Abraham a Little Longer. November 26, 1864.
Harpers *Weekly*.

Thomas Nast

The man whom most other cartoonists who reflect at all about it consider America's
greatest began drawing in the emblematic style of the old-fashioned allegory. But even
here there was some difference. Some of his art reminds one of Jacques Callot on war.
His symbolic drawings were accompanied by many active vignettes of what war means

152. Thomas Nast : The Border States. 1863. Harpers *Weekly.*

to a reporter who commented on what he saw. In these scenes are the drama of emotions: horror, anger, pity, and fear, but also sentimentality. "The War in the Border States" was typical of Nast's Civil War output for *Harpers.* It was interpretive reporting at its best. In the center are Union troops giving some of their limited food to hungry women and children as they march by through the cold and snow. A facing scene shows a wife kneeling by her husband who has just been killed by a Southern sniper. Her children are crying and afraid and her home is in ruins as the ever-present marauding soldiers ride by on horses. Around these two large scenes are six smaller scenes of soldiers firing into a village, burning down a bridge, driving off a farmer's cattle, and rushing a home while its residents hide in the brush. Above is a man peering out of prison and below carrion birds hover over a skeleton off in the deserted woods. Nast was telling Northern women back home not only what kinds of things were happening to their husbands, sons, and sweethearts, but what they should think about it — that it was desolation and horror. But with this came a recurring theme: that what their men risked was not an unnecessary sacrifice, but one for a great cause. When the Emancipation Proclamation was issued, it became *the* theme to justify the heartbreak and misery.

These cartoons made Nast famous while still in his early twenties, but it is not on these that his fame with later generations depends. To modern eyes these drawings have a quaintness and often naiveté that are the quintessence of Dickensian Victorianism. Like the great novelist's works, Nast cartoons are full of angelic women, strong brave men, innocent children, grateful retainers, with a few villains and their dark deeds thrown in to add taste, like raisins in a cake. Comic figures, however, are

245

rarer. Nast favored the melodramatic presentation of great human emotion.

From the beginning Nast showed an inclination to use cartoon comment in the aid of a great moral crusade. He was preachy. He had not, as yet, perfected the artistic technique or imagery to best present his sermons. Nast's mood of moral fervor, however, was set in concrete.

At the end of the war, Nast had a tremendous advantage as a cartoonist. It was one that William Murrell feels might have made either E. W. Clay or David Claypoole Johnston more successful. He had a weekly forum and a regular salary, rather than having to free-lance among fly-by-night magazines or lithograph companies. To Nast's credit, he did not rest but set about exploiting this advantage.

Something began to happen to the Nast style. Already hints of what was to come were suggested in a few of the earlier vignettes. Through 1867 to 1869, as he participated in the Johnson impeachment and Grant election campaigns, his style alternated between the more murky and involved grand scenes done with brush and simple posterlike statements done with pencil. It was in 1869, while drawing an answer to a Tenniel cartoon, that he studied Tenniel's style closely and realized how well it could be adapted to his own purposes.[4] By 1870 the simple line drawing in bold pencil strokes replaced the shadowy half-tone efforts and became his regular style. It suited magazine production on poor paper. It also emphasized that Nast was more than an illustrator of scenes with an occasional opinion; he was a commentator with a moral message that he meant to get through sharply and unambiguously. His drawing began to serve better the purpose of the message and would not always be so decorative a presentation that it detracted from what was being said. Nast began to draw the way some less-than-subtle but still compelling women dress, in order to rivet attention onto themselves and send through a message loud and clear.

To this change in style he added experiments in imagery. He moved from allegorical figures to real people but began to present them with a caricature twist, sometimes as animals, seeking for ways to show that how persons looked also symbolized the policies they were championing.

By 1870 he was ready, and at hand was Tammany Hall's Boss Tweed. Nast's attack in one year effectively destroyed the Boss's machine and raised the circulation of *Harpers* from 100,000 to 300,000 per issue. Behind this and his previous work was Nast's moral commitment.

A careful and scholarly examination of Nast as political ideologue was made by the historian Morton Keller.[5] He argues that Nast's moral fervor and beliefs were those of radical Republicanism: liberal and commercial as opposed to the slaveholding Southern aristocracy, secular Protestant as opposed to the Catholic church, and patriotic American as opposed to the national and ethnic ties of the Old World of Europe. To supplement Keller, I suggest that it is all summed up in those sentimental Civil War vignettes, such as the one of the brave Northern Officer and his pious wife and children back home on Christmas Eve. These people were for Nast the salt of the earth, and seemingly always would be.

Keller argues that Nast spoke for the small-town Protestant who, through the capitalistic ethic of hard work and sobriety (Nast assumed), was transforming America into the New Jerusalem. The admirable part of this creed is expressed in Nast's profound sympathy for the plight of Negroes and his demands that they be given greater opportunities and be brought to full citizenship. This spilled over into sympathetic cartoons for frontier Indians and the Chinese as well. The seamier side of the creed was a virulent anti-Catholic and anti-Irish no-nothingism (by one who was himself raised as a Catholic). Nast feared what these groups might do to the heavenly city of Protestant America. Also part of the creed was a blindness to the chicanery

246

53. Thomas Nast : Christmas Eve. 1863. Harpers *Weekly*.

of business operations of the Gilded Age. This led Nast to an obsession about anarchists and a coldness toward the grievances of Labor. Nast was, in my opinion and not to hedge it, a dedicated and sincere, unreconstructed, economic conservative and a secular bigot, with an enthusiasm for civil rights and civil liberties of some but not all of the oppressed. His loyal support of Grant was based on more than personal ties — he really convinced himself that political leadership by the General and the common ruck around him would purify the American Protestant democracy; perhaps because the alternative seemed too horrible.

Keller traces in Nast's cartoons the unfolding of this ideology during and after the war to its gradual frustration and decline by the 1880s. The fight against Tweed and the Catholic and Irish-dominated Tammany Hall is placed within this context of assumptions. So too is Nast's attitude to Andrew Johnson's plans to bring the Southerner back to the Union at what Nast saw as at the expense of the Negro. The bitter criticism of the Liberal Republican-Democratic movement of Horace Greeley in a campaign in which Matt Morgan was imported from England by Frank Leslie's *Illustrated Weekly* to counter Nast, brought Nast to a white ideological heat. Other issues show black and white lenses in his spectacles, his attitude to the Tilden and Hayes election and to the subsequent treatment of Negroes, and to America's posture in respect to Europe's wars — all reflecting this ideology. All are seen through the eyes of a man convinced that America's destiny would be achieved through liberal and secular Protestantism.

Little by little the contradictions of circumstance knocked this ideological dream

154. Thomas Nast : Who Stole the People's Money? August 19, 1871. *Harpers Weekly*

structure into a shambles, the way rising water shakes foundations and pushes them off base. The Republicans led by Grant were less high-minded than even a Warren G. Harding might have approved of. Nast had continually to avert his gaze from the politically and economically ambitious among this crowd who saw public office not as a public trust but as a public trough. High-minded allies of old times were of no help. Some switched sides and allied themselves with the Democrats. Particularly maddening was that abolitionist New England crew whose supercilious Brahmin liberalism had given such initial force to the radical abolitionist ideology. These men now saw civil service as the overriding issue. Nast found himself fighting former friends with disquieting associates at his side. He began to taste the ultimate of disillusion, which is not succumbing to a victory by one's enemies, but being faced with what looks more and more like a sellout of the cause by one's friends.

By 1880 Nast was disengaging himself from passionate politicking and looking on as a relatively disinterested observer. By 1884 Nast and also *Harpers Weekly* no longer supported the Republican nominee. Bitterly, Nast too ended up in the camp of those he had fought so long. His pencil was to aid Grover Cleveland, not the first Democratic presidential nominee to be elected by popular vote after the Civil War, but the first Democrat actually to assume the office. Ironically, some have claimed that the Protestant battle cry that Nast as much as any one else had previously hammered on, "rum, romanism, and rebellion," cost the Republican Blaine the election. Whether it did so or not, Nast no longer found the phrase relevant in making his own political choices. The campaign cost him old friends without making him new ones.

By 1886 the quarrels and conflicts Nast had had with his *Harpers Weekly* editor and publisher came to a head and he resigned. At age 46 he was a has-been. His last years before his death in 1902 are a disgrace to the nation. The man who would now be awarded a Medal of Freedom was allowed to rust and drop into such shabby gentility that his grandson reports that to pay for a New York outing in 1902 for both, Nast had to cadge money from his children for the day of fun.[6] Nast lost his artistic punch as his ideological underpinnings became rickety. His willingness to make enemies made people shy from him as controversial. Walt McDougall, a cartoonist, found him a "vain egotist" after Nast, perhaps quite correctly, opened up the conversation when they met for the first time with "I know you! You're the first man who ever swiped one of my ideas!"[7] Nast lost his fortune in a series of unfortunate enterprises: first and ironically in the Grant brokerage venture, then in a mine, and finally in a magazine he founded and edited. His drawings had gotten more out of tune with the mood of the times. In his prime in the late sixties he had tried great art in the classic style. He now returned to it between projects. Of 33 large paintings (8′ x 12′ each) that he painted, five were recently recovered, just like the work of the late Christopher Bean, in an old chicken coop in New Jersey. No one seems to have bothered to save the rest.[8] Nast continued in late life to experiment with painting to his last years, doing a portrait of Grant at Appomatox for Kohlstatt, publisher of the Chicago *Daily News* and an old friend, and a Shakespearean scene for Henry Irving. Thus he drifted from one short-run project to another. At 62 he wangled a minor consular post in Guayaquil, Ecuador, from the Theodore Roosevelt administration. After six months there, apart from old friends and family, he contracted yellow fever and died. Among his effects was found a cartoon suggesting that he might not survive in the southern climate.

When one looks through the pages of hack drawings turned out since the Civil War, in the present and any other period of American journalism, or observes the professors and other public servants who have in effect retired for their last 15 or 20 years in a tenure system, it seems strange that someone did not provide Nast with a job or at least a sinecure. They did not because he would not, or could not, compromise his views. He died relatively young and so avoided the tragedy of living to be a senile old man, unless one considers him prematurely old in his fifties.

From this period of fits and starts, he left one bittersweet artistic legacy, produced in 1889 as *Thomas Nast's Christmas Drawings for the Human Race*. In 1886 *Harpers* attempted to keep him on retainer and, when this failed, suggested that he publish in book form a selection of his Christmas pictures of the last 30 years, with some new additions. This he did, and in these drawings the modern image of Santa Claus is stamped into the American consciousness, to the everlasting gratitude of Norman Rockwell and the Coca Cola company.

Nast was successful in projecting a lasting Santa Claus for the same reason that he was a masterful political artist: he gave an imaginative presentation on a subject about which he had something to say. His Santa Claus personified all that one would wish were the official Clausian policy on Christmas joys, and with that policy Nast was in full agreement. He captured and put down on paper the pleasure of Christmas in a single figure.

Let us reexamine why Thomas Nast was so great and remains so as a political cartoonist. Was it because of his political message? Perhaps for a short time, for his contemporaries, but it was a bitter and self-righteous morality that must have grated on many even then. Now much of its illiberalism is even more obvious. Were those he admired, for example, really so admirable? President Grant? To be even more heretical, were the people he attacked so vigorously really guilty of unpardonable sins, as the vigor of his attack implied? Historians might now conclude that Horace Greeley was often a political fool and a crank, but not the traitor to righteousness that Nast painted him. Greeley now seems to be understating when he commented that during the "campaign of caricature" he sometimes did not know whether he was running for the presidency or the penitentiary. Andrew Johnson's views on Reconstruction are not so patently villainous now as they appeared to the early Nast. They were, in fact, swallowed by the later Nast when they became the policy of President Hayes. One may even risk the ultimate in moral censure by daring to ask, "Were even Tweed and company fully deserving of the treatment they got from Nast?" The answer is that to an extent they were, but what treatment then does one reserve for the real monsters — the Hitler who marches six million off to gas ovens? The morality of "The Battle Hymn of the Republic," with the inner belief that Jehovah as always is right there at one's side, does not, when one looks at how it was applied in specific situations, excite unmixed admiration. It is not the message of the cartoons that continues to make Nast great. Another artist presenting the same stirring themes might well be filed away in the drawer with *Uncle Tom's Cabin*.

155.   Thomas Nast : Baltimore 1861-1872. "Lets us Clasp Hands over the Bloody Chasm." August 3, 1872. Harpers *Weekly*.

The Nast cartoon is great because of the emotional impact of its presentation. It continuously goes beyond the bounds of good taste and conventional manners. Nast is like the man who rings your bell and, when you open the door, runs in shouting insults at you and throwing rocks and mud at you and your wife and on your front-hall walls. Your reaction is that what excites him must be a grievous wrong you somehow unwittingly committed, because it would be so if you yourself were ever moved to act in this way to a stranger, or even a friend. This is the first element of Nast's impact, a low boiling point, and such a boiling pont requires at least a target who can be believed to have committed heinous crimes.

156.   Thomas Nast : The Only Thing They Respect or Fear. October 21, 1871. Harpers *Weekly.*

Nast's moral fervor required a stark and simple style, and with this he always struggled. He was too fond of embellishments; he wanted to be sure no one missed the message; he put posters on the wall; plastered his marble columns with long, involved statements; had newspapers or other materials sticking out of people's pockets; and also cherished using little vignettes to make a group of pictures. In his prime years he largely curbed these tendencies or made them artistically serve his themes, as with the running gag on Greeley, a paper in the pocket in every cartoon titled "What I know about —." But this simplicity is only a negative virtue that many other artists could have matched and perhaps achieved even better, because Nast, in truth, was no great draftsman.

The major element is an unforgettable vividness. The happenings that Nast chose to illustrate were symbolic of the true meaning of the event as he saw it, and one continues to see it the way he did even when disagreeing with him. Greeley continues to shake hands with the South over the bloody chasm of Andersonville, and the Tweed Ring in the circle in "Who's to blame?" could well serve as a model for every city boss's crew down to Daley. Frequently Nast appropriated a comment in the news of the day, such as Oakley Hall's ill-considered remark "The Storm Will Blow Over," which Nast made the theme of a series of bone-crusher cartoons. The phrase helped provide the kicker that would sear it into the viewer's memory and signify forever Nast's disdain.

Nast's greatness thus seems to me to rest on his command of vivid imagery. He painted unforgettable character types, just as Charles Dickens had, and these in a

157.   Thomas Nast : "What Are You Laughing At? To the Victor Belong the Spoils." November 25, 1871. Harpers *Weekly*.

flash personified policy just as Santa Claus personified Christmas. He used every trick and developed new ones to get the drawing itself to send out this message of ridicule. He mastered the art of caricature so that he was presenting more than a photographic likeness but was also revealing the character of the person. Tweed was well enough done that the cartoon was used to identify and capture him in Spain. But in Tweed's greedy eyes the character of the man emerges. To these facial expressions Nast added props that shouted character qualities — the ring of dollar signs that wreathe his brow, the glazed glasses of Mayor Oakley Hall, the flapping coat of Greeley, the boots of the unreconstructed Southerner — all told a story that exactly fitted the person and his character.[9]

Nast went beyond this to turn persons into animals, or even inanimate objects such as the Senator Matthews steel trap. He is of course best known for symbolizing organizations through animals such as the Democratic donkey, Republican elephant, and Tammany tiger. All but the last are too hackneyed by now for us to make even a reasonable guess at their early impact. But just as chilling today as when drawn is the

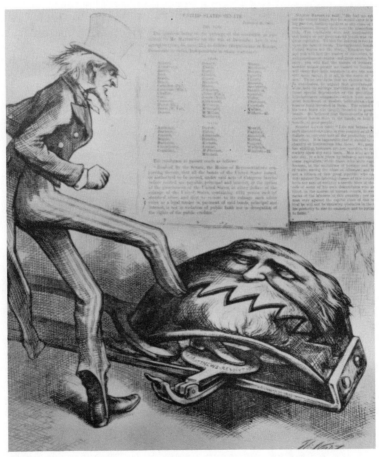

158.   Thomas Nast : The First Step Toward National Bankruptcy. February 16, 1878. Harpers *Weekly*.

Southern snake that, almost like something out of a Freudian dream, attacks a metal file that represents the Republican party.

All of this imagery was reenforced by repetition. Viewers got in the habit of looking for the "And Gratz" tag on Greeley's coat (note how artfully the vice-presidential candidate's name was often nearly totally hidden) and the "What I know about —" in his pocket to see what Greeley was making a fool of himself about this time. They expected to find dollar signs associated with Tweed and they expected to see the two-headed tiger or the inflation rag baby (*rag* was the term for greenback paper money) pop in and out of the campaign's drawings.

How can anyone help looking at such drawings, as long as they can convince themselves that the artist is sincere and has something genuine to be excited about? They raise political comment to the realm of art.

It was the problem of having something to be excited about that stifled Nast's creative ability. He began to have doubts, and so did his viewers. One begins to wonder about the mudslinging neighbor after the second or third shouting match. Perhaps one suspects that he even begins to wonder about himself, or that he should. Nast did.

Nast's trouble was he had created a magnificent machine for great crusades. He could not pace himself to operate at twenty miles an hour in *Go Slow Quiet* zones. He always had to push the throttle all the way down and use the cutout, or why take it out of the garage? This in part explains his neglect after 1885. Who could afford to hire him, and who wanted to listen to what seemed more and more a stuck shrill whistle? But it is also his glory. He was willing to sacrifice all he loved to what he regarded as his calling. He had resisted money bribes from Tweed at a hundred times what he was paid annually. He would not bend in his later years to what he regarded correctly as intimidation. He could not compromise his basic views and do good work. And perhaps the most amazing fact of all — even in the end he did not succumb to bitterness or self-pity. He accepted his fate with a certain simple sweetness of nature.

Joseph Keppler: Puck *and* Judge

The failure of Nast to continue to find an audience and the success of Joseph Keppler and Co. is in harmony with the notion that being a media critic in the mass market is being part of an interaction process. Nast, the moralist, wanted all the messages to go in one direction, outward from himself. With *Puck* and *Judge* we have artists who become more a part of the process of give and take, from and to politicians and from and to their publics.

Puck was begun in the German language in St. Louis as another humor magazine. It began English publication a few years later in New York in 1877. But this copy of *Punch* succeeded magnificently. *Judge* promptly followed in 1881 and *Life* joined the crowd in 1883.

Puck's founder was Joseph Keppler, a German immigrant who, after experience with Frank Leslie's *Illustrated Weekly*, struck out on his own. *Judge* was an offshoot of *Puck*, founded by one of its artists, James Wales. *Life* was begun by John Ames Mitchell, a cartoonist, and Edward S. Martin.

Within a few years *Puck* and *Judge* dominated the magazine market of political comment. *Life* was more refined and artistic and favored social comment with a good dash of social snobbery thrown in. Until photoengraving made daily newspaper

59.   Joseph Keppler : The Contest of Beauty. 1884. *Puck.*

cartoons practical around 1900, these three journals dominated the market of cartoon comment and, like Nast before them, *Puck* and *Judge* produced work that set the themes of national presidential campaigns. *Life* got into this type of direct political comment with any force only in 1898, when its artists took potshots at the Spanish American War.

How, then, did *Puck* and *Judge* differ from Nast? The first striking point is in style. It is not that the artists could not draw like Nast. A cut by Bernard Gillam, himself an English immigrant well acquainted with Tenniel's work (November 9, 1881, *Puck*) shows a clear resemblance to the old bold woodcut style. It is rather that *Puck*'s artists chose deliberately not to draw like Nast. Keppler and those who followed him first used wood engravings, then moved to the fuzzier shadings of the lithograph, and then added color. It was color that ran riot in yellow vests and green pants. Where Nast's crisp black-and-white cartoons suggested his stark, puritan morality, Keppler's rainbow prints suggested a Mardi Gras. The second striking feature is that only one artist in this school, Frederick Opper, displayed real individuality. The work of Joseph Keppler, Jr. and Sr., Wales, Zimmerman (Zim), Hamilton, Dalrymple, Bernard and Victor Gillam, Pughe, and Taylor merged into a common style with minor variations, whether they were drawing for *Puck* or *Judge*. It was Joseph Keppler, Sr., who set that style of art at the beginning in both artistic technique and imagery. Also, at the editorial conference (what he called a weekly idea session) from 1883 on, he decided on the editorial subject for the week's cartoons and how it would be treated.

The Keppler style was that of the three-ring circus. His journal had illustrations on the covers and centerfold, with other smaller illustrations throughout. The pictures were crowded with recognizable politicians. The politicians were gently caricatured or

255

given a straight representational likeness. The trick was to make every individual in the crowded drawing count and make him or her contribute some little bit to the general theme. The humor or impact of the drawing was not in the portraiture or even in exaggerated activity of the politician, but in the staged scene.

The typical *Puck* drawing was one that placed a group of politicians in a ridiculous and, if possible, an embarrassing pose. The cliché was to present them as children. The pièce de résistance was dressing men up in women's clothing, a thigh-slapper whose assumptions would not be lost on a modern women's libber. The next most common device was to put the actors in some kind of Shakespearean or historical garb with a slightly ridiculous twist. Roman togas were favored. Frequently classical paintings or statues were reinvigorated. If the beauty contest or the pseudo-historical setting failed to inspire, then the scene was likely to be one of everyday life, with the kicker provided by dignified politicians dressed up in unfamiliar costumes of farmers milking a cow or of street sweepers. Boat and train scenes were particularly favored for the double-page centerfold. Extremely tempting, of course, was to put the politicians in a slightly off-color situation. The big bed of Brigham Young filled with twelve weeping wives in their nighties, drawn at his death in 1877, no doubt caused some titillation. The Garfield wedding, with the stranger with the baby interrupting just as the preacher is intoning, "If any man knows . . .," no doubt caused more ("Forbidding the Banns"). There were other such cartoons. Those who attacked *Puck* for obscenity and vulgarity missed the point. *Puck* was in the business of cutting down stuffed shirts, and the off-color joke or situation was too tempting a way to do it to pass it by when it fitted.

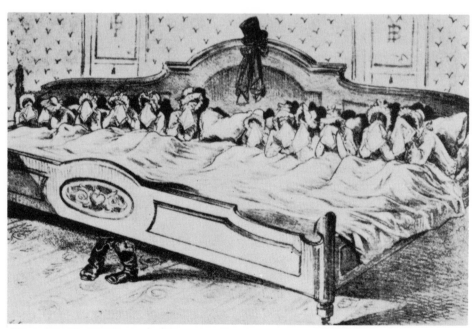

160. Joseph Keppler: In Memoriam Brigham Young. "And the place which knew him once shall know him no more." 1877. *Puck.*

As in the stage melodrama, the humorous stereotype was widely used. The mood of fun, fun, fun was kept up by the costumes. Uncle Sam had a rural jauntiness, while the maidens representing nationalities stepped down from the pedestals and let a little of the nobility John Tenniel had endowed them with drop away as they played straight men for the comics just as in old-time burlesque. All were drawn with a good-humored gusto, including even the stereotyped Jews or plutocrats. But there were few pratfalls and no talky balloons.

Keppler and Co. also demonstrated that Nast was not the only one who could dig up themes for a series of cartoons. The first great success was Gillam's presentation of Blaine, the Plumed Knight to his followers, as the tattooed man in a freak show. The tattooes were deals he had made with corporations. Later, Benjamin Harrison appeared in the large hat that his grandfather had worn. But the paucity of invention of this sort suggested that such themes were not the forte of this school, any more than was deeply revealing caricature that blazoned out character, political and personal. As Draper Hill, Keppler's biographer notes, the *Puck* artists in 1884 were frequently apologizing in print to Nast for borrowing his symbolism.[10]

The cartoon presentation rather fairly closely mirrored *Puck*'s motto, "What Fools We Mortals Be." Where Nast had searched the news for stark morality plays in the tradition of John Bunyan, Keppler found Vanity Fair. It was not that politics was seen as all fun or that reform disappeared from cartoon art. But where Nast found sins he could not forgive, *Puck* found weakness and venality that they understood even while they censured. *Puck* wrote off a very small part of the human race. It accepted all of the rest, particularly the broad, middling mass where political questions were a matter of middling preferences of one path and one value over another. *Puck* particularly favored preserving what was good in the status quo.

In ideology *Puck* favored policy that would expand opportunity for the common man, and for Keppler that was the hardworking immigrant. He never lost his view that America was the land of opportunity for the downtrodden, and he fought to keep it so. He hoped that others could repeat his own success. *Puck* was thus critical of industrial monopoly and high tariffs as well as of labor union shops and inflation of the currency. It remained suspicious of the Catholic Church and of prohibitionists. It was worried about importation of cheap labor, particularly of the Chinese. It was no friend of Europe's monarchs. It championed civil service reform and jobs on merit over party preferment for jobs.

All of this adds up to a policy of keeping opportunity open for the second-generation immigrant by prohibiting practices that lead to special privilege for a few. The assumption is that if society can prevent what is the social equivalent of cheating, such as conspiratorial combinations against the individual, favoritism, and forms of regimentation, everything will work out well in that the deserving will succeed, the undeserving will not. Note the absence of any helpful policy in respect to Negroes. They were, like the Chinese, regarded as outside the pale, a different racial culture not to be melted down in the common pot.

Nominally these opinions led *Puck* to support the Democrats, but this was a fitful backing without much enthusiasm most of the time. On at least one occasion Keppler called for a new party. Keppler finally found his hero and ideological mate in Grover Cleveland. But when faced with what it regarded as the lunacies of William Jennings Bryan, *Puck* found itself for McKinley. Keppler would probably have approved of the domestic Woodrow Wilson but, in between Grover and Woodrow, would have chosen on the basis of that revered strategy, the least bad.

Opposing the mild reformism of *Puck* was *Judge*. Its ideological leanings were

161. Joseph Keppler : The Biggest Joke of the Season. Mr. Blaine's Candidate for 1892 — According to the New York *Tribune.* April 1, 1891. *Puck.*

toward the Republicans, since the magazine had been bought out lock, stock and barrel by that political organization. It too claimed to speak for the common man, but it placed greater emphasis on the young man, a generation or two from the gangplank — one who would build for the benefit of himself and the rest of the nation. Whenever the chips were down, it plunked for the GOP and the rugged individualists.

These magazines lasted as long as the production processes permitted them to. They were enough in tune with current opinion to stay afloat. Their style was laughing satire that patiently pushed and tugged the nation away from pitfalls and toward a better

162.   Frederick Attwood : December 1898. *Life*.

world. Their artists lacked power, but they wore well. Week after week readers, as *Puck*'s editor H. C. Bunner said, looked at front and back covers and centerfold "and somewhere along the way got a guffaw."

Life *and Politics*

The big crusades in the early *Life* cartoons were against two great evils: young American ladies who threw themselves away on titled Europeans, and gaffes committed by the nouveau riche. Could anything speak louder as to their allegiances? The style and snobbish mood were similar to those of George du Maurier in *Punch*, but the art work in at least one case was far better. Charles Dana Gibson was a breathtaking craftsman who deserves all the praise that has been or can be heaped on him. He changed the way women dressed and even walked and set the upper-middle-class mood for a generation. But because he drew few political cartoons outside of World War I recruiting posters, I shall pass him by. (See Fig. 132 for his wartime Columbia.) Henry (Hy) Mayer was an occasional contributor.

We should also note that gentle but often incisive political comment of Francis G. Attwood, who each month from 1887 until his death at 44 in 1900 drew a one-page review of the political events of the month for *Life*. These vignettes, tolerantly and in a well-bred way, viewed the world from the Harvard background from which he had emerged. Attwood's work shows the gentlemanly contempt for bullies, braggarts, frauds, and hypocrites that those who have a guaranteed annual income can indulge in most easily. He delighted in caricaturing the crude and shrewd swashbuckler Ben Butler. At the same time Attwood had a broad sympathy for the exploited.

His comment tends to be like William Makepeace Thackeray's in tone and mood. His artistic style and imagery are full of subtleties, sly digs, and private jollies, with an occasionally brutal but camouflaged assault. Typical of his work was a double-page spread on Queen Victoria's Jubilee procession, which led off with bobbies, followed by horse guards bearing copies of her unsold literary work for free distribution among the populace, the choir boys of Westminster Abbey led by Lord Tennyson, pensioned relatives 24 abreast, the Queen and Prince and retinue, and concluded with nine pompously presented floats illustrating "Glories of the Reign," with tableaux of such typical scenes as an Irish eviction for nonpayment of rent, the British alliance with Southern slavery, and the like. The drawing had 150 figures and was the early example par excellence of what would later be called the ant-hill drawing.[11]

From the decade of the middle eighties to the nineties, Michael Angelo Woolf, who had earlier drawn the plucked eagle, found his métier in depicting slum waifs with a pathos and humor similar to those of Phil May of *Punch*. I mention him because some of this work, when he didn't go over the boundary line into sentimentality, is still haunting almost a century later.

163.   Michael Angelo Woolf : "Agnes, does your father drink, too ?" Ca. 1895.
Life.

Also contributing to *Life* and other journals was Henry (Hy) Mayer, whose comment on the aging Edward fits the tone of the magazine.

164.   Henry (Hy) Mayer : Prophecy for 1947. 1897. *Life*.

Life also contributed the most scathing of anti-Spanish-American War cartoons, in harmony with its upper-middle-class tradition of sneering at grubby politicians. These were the work of E. W. Kemble, William H. Walker, and Frederick Thompson Richards. *Life* soon tired of political criticism, but the result of their effort was several striking cartoons. Perhaps more important, the short-lived *Life* crusade presaged the work of another group of middle- and upper-middle-class artists and writers, that appeared during World War I in the *Masses*. By that time technology had clearly doomed the mass magazine of current political comment. What was left was the smaller-circulation magazine of specialized politics, usually radical left, and to the *Masses* was drawn an outstanding group of young liberal and radical artists, a number of whom moved there directly from college. But this was a group outside the mainstream in which the mass media paddled, and since I have already discussed them, I leave off here.

A Closing Note

The period of the print and weekly magazine highlights several characteristics of the democratic cartoon as it unfolded in America.

The role of cartoonist as institutionalized critic became established. A first indicator of this position was that the artist came to be recognized by the public. Early prints through the Currier and Ives lithographs were for the most part anonymous. Only a few artists, such as David Claypoole Johnston, were able to build up a following of their own. With the coming of the weekly magazine this number swelled. After Thomas Nast, almost all artists put their name or "bug" on their work. A top-rank artist could not only make a good living but could markedly increase the circulation of the journal in which his or her cartoons appeared.

The second effect of the weekly magazine with signed drawings is that it set up deadlines for comment. Readers expected to turn over the pages of *Harpers Weekly* each week and get one or more comments about current events from Thomas Nast. Cartoonists were steadily moving from the carefree role of free-lancer to professional on retainer or salary. They could no longer comment just as the spirit moved but were expected to comment on schedule.

An added characteristic is less clear. I refer to the tendency of professional cartoonists in America to stay within the bounds of light laughing satire rather than pursuing their enemies with hot hellfire and tongs. This period contains some notable exceptions to this generalization in the truncated careers of Volck and Nast. One notes that these two artists, whose mood was fashioned in a civil war, were probably the two best cartoonists of the whole hundred-year period. At the same time, their experience suggests that the doctrinaire, messianic messages they broadcast wore on their democratic viewers more than did the mood projected by less-talented and even mediocre colleagues. Theirs was perhaps a mood too disruptive of civility to flourish long in a stable democracy such as ours. Wearing better, even in the hands of artists of lesser skill, was the spirit of good-natured, pragmatic skepticism. Amelioration of problems, or even a grin-and-bear it toleration of them, seems more in harmony with the democratic method of reaching consensus than bitter condemnations of evil by very talented cartoonist critics.

Those who see the misery in the world often have reason to be unhappy with this fact. They see the pragmatic, laughing-satire kind of comment as buttressing the system as much as attacking it, as mildly reforming to conserve rather than champing to replace. They are, I think, right about this, but wrong in preferring blockbusters to needling. But wrong or right, laughing satire is the style that, as I shall argue in the chapters to follow, characterizes American political cartooning through most of its history.

10

The American Editorial Cartoon:
The First Fifty Years or So

For Thursday, October 30, 1884, Walt McDougall, with the help of a Russian portraitist new to the United States, Valerian Gribayedoff, drew a mammoth cartoon called "The Royal Feast of Belshazzar, Blaine and the Money Kings." Joseph Pulitzer plastered it across all eight columns of the New York *World*'s front page. Its imagery was borrowed from one of those Bible-story illustrations where a poor Lazarus with his wife and waif plead for crusts from a table full of plutocrats. At a bountiful feast at Delmonico's Restaurant were such recognizable worthies as Jay Gould, William H. Vanderbilt, Andrew Carnegie, Russell Sage, and John Jacob Astor. The dishes were such tasty viands as Lobby Pudding, Navy Contracts, Monopoly Soup and other rich foods that the tattered poor would probably not have liked or appreciated anyway.

McDougall's cartoons had been appearing in the *World* for four to five months, but this one was special for election week. It was large-sized and it featured the likenesses of a bevy of the powerful. This "rogues' gallery of millionaires" was a blockbuster that caused a newspaper sensation. Today it looks rather stiff and traditional. Pulitzer was delighted. He had discovered an additional way to shock readers and build up circulation. Walt McDougall, in his extremely amusing autobiography, modestly and briefly describes his delight at the reader reception. It also was a major breakthrough for the newspaper cartoon. What this cartoon did more than any other was to make every self-respecting newspaper editor think about getting his very own political cartoonist for regular work.

How It Started

There are of course always a variety of claimants to the title of innovator — in this case a claimant to the honor of following up on Ben Franklin's occasional cuts and of being the first with a series of political cartoons in a newspaper. The first such series of daily editorial cartoons was actually said to have appeared in the souvenir programs of the World's Peace Jubilee in Boston, from June 17 to July 4, 1872, an early experiment with photoengraving. But others also have claims. In 1873 the New York *Daily Graphic*, begun by Canadians, began using photoengravings from time to time, and in the early 1880s the New York *Truth* published some very poor daily illustrations. But in early 1884 Walt McDougall sold a series of cartoons to the short-lived New York *Extra*, and these are probably the very first daily newspaper cartoons on political subjects, as far as anybody knows, and I suppose I should add, cares.[1]

Walt McDougall's version of how daily newspaper cartooning really got started is that later in 1884, in June, he was over in New York City from Newark and had an anti-Blaine cartoon that *Puck* had rejected and returned to him. McDougall was reluctant to throw the drawing away and was musing on which magazine to send it to when he passed the ramshackle old *World* newspaper office, just purchased by Joseph Pulitzer. He impulsively went in, shoved the cartoon into the elevator boy's hands and told him to give it to the editor to print if he wanted it, free. Then he rushed off to take in a baseball game. Pulitzer printed it in five columns, unaware that he could have reduced its size, or perhaps disinclined to do so, and then promptly telegraphed McDougall to come in from New Jersey. He offered him a steady job. As McDougall later remembered it in his autobiography, Pulitzer said, "in a hearty and enthusiastic tone: 'We have found the fellow who can make pictures for newspapers! Young man, we printed the entire edition of thirty thousand copies of the *World* without stopping the press to clean the cut, and that has never happened in this country before!'" McDougall adds: "I did not tell him that the cartoon looked like the crab's eyebrow without the proper reduction in size to refine its coarse lines."[2]

And so McDougall at 26 had a job at the handsome figure of $50 a week, and daily editorial cartooning as a profession was born. McDougall stayed on for 16 years. When a fellow worker complained that he couldn't draw, Pulitzer, always with an eye to the main point, answered, "He draws circulation; that's enough!" Within a couple of years, most other New York papers had political cartoonists and, as with other fads, the rest of the nation gradually followed suit.

The Birth of Quality

It was not really until the 1896 political campaign that newspaper political cartoons caught on. A major reason for the delay seems to be that the cartoonists themselves did not immediately take to the retooling required. Most of the cartoonists of *Puck* and the other magazines were too refined for a newspaper world that was aiming its product at those who moved their lips as they read along. While McDougall admits that the new cartoonist recruits to newspapers were often better artists than he was, he adds: "But [they] were too artistic and high hat for the class to which newspapers appeal, and they rarely made news pictures. They produced clever, well-drawn sketches of life at the race track or the sea beach, but they were geared too low for the fast-moving stuff that hopped circulations up."[3]

The daily deadline also brought about a shift in focus that cartoonists had to get used to. Where the weekly cartoon would comment on general trends and political principles, the daily addressed itself to events almost as they occurred. Daily cartoons had to demonstrate timeliness. Some aspect of an event had to be dealt with briefly before the artist turned to a variety of other topics. The new cartoonist had to be knowledgeable about what was currently happening and did not have time to philosophize on what was the major message for the week or month. There were also, as McDougall notes above, other distractions. It was still the day in which photographs had to be redrawn for printing, and there were such exciting events to be recorded as Grant's funeral, the electrocution of Gibbs, the blowing up of Hells Gate, and "dozens of like happenings" that McDougall reels off like Dr. John Watson dropping hints of Sherlock Holmes's more intriguing unrecorded cases. McDougall had a $60 camera that Pulitzer bought for him, and he was thrown out daily, hot on the trail of fresh news pictures.

Improvements in photoengraving by the turn of the century eliminated the need for such "assignment artists," who rushed from fires to courtroom to other disasters. They also spelled death for illustrations whose main point was a photographic realism. Belshazzar's feast, for example, is really one of those Keppler-like political extravaganzas, full of many figures and portrait likenesses. For the moment the masses would be astonished, but the camera, plus half-tone photoengraving, killed the impact of this kind of precise reproduction. No longer would a mere likeness of a plutocrat be treated with the awe that innocent savages feel toward someone who has their picture and thus has an evil power over them. The job of assignment artist died, and with this reduction of chores the role of the editorial cartoonist became more clearly defined as opinion monger.[4]

Artists began to concentrate on what putting out a daily cartoon of political comment would require besides timeliness. One effect of daily deadlines, as well as of the reduced size of newspaper cartoons as compared to the double-page spreads of *Puck* or *Judge*, was to put a premium on simplicity. It began to dawn on some cartoonists that a drawing with a few bold figures sharply and crisply presented had advantages. Also, caricature of faces and action would attract attention. Some went back to restudy Nast for the secret of punchiness. It became clear also that readers expected drawings about current events. Cartoonists who attempted to philosophize too often, or to draw ahead for a day's vacation, would find that the railroad strike had been settled or a new story had broken that made the prearranged cartoon obsolete or irrelevant.

This deadline rush also was thought to have a deadening effect on artistic quality. Most observers believed that quality declined, and so it probably did at first for artists making the switch from magazines. It did so permanently, for some perfectionists who could not adapt to deadlines. An interesting study is the work of Fred Opper, whose drawings became more and more simplistic as the years went on, presumably on the assumption that fancy art work detracted from, rather than added to, the impact of the idea. Nevertheless, a good many of the run-of-the-mill editorial cartoons of the day were certainly as well done as most pre-Civil War drawings. And if Nast's artistic quality alone is held up as the model, many editorial cartoons of the turn of the century approach or surpass it.

What critics refer to as artistically deplorable is probably the birth of correspondence-school art, which blossomed on the third- and fourth-level newspapers. Its essence is artistic cliché. Every shoe is drawn like every other shoe. Only one funny way exists for a man's hat or a lady's knee. Every head is big on a small body. Once you learn all the formulas, one or two a week by mail, you can put them together into cartoons. Art does not follow nature but is put together like a tinker toy. But the very best artists, even in the early 1900s, did not draw that way and some who started with these clichés evolved their own distinctive styles. Correspondence-school art continued, however, and in later years lent itself to parody, as in R. Crumb's "Keep on Trucking."

Where quality dropped most precipitously, however, was in the idea department.

What had popped up in Tenniel or Keppler's stable as an occasional tired metaphor now became rampant, and only another cliché such as *rampant* is appropriate to describe what happened. Daily demands encouraged allegorical shortcuts. The cartoons of Tenniel and others were combed for images that common humanity could appreciate. Most allusions from the classics had to be thrown overboard, but many others lived on. Over and over again the ghost of Napoleon or Bismarck imparted messages to the Kaiser or Theodore Roosevelt or anyone else who came along. The political game was presented as sports, and presidential candidates struck out, or trained for the boxing match, or put on track pants, and so on. (And sometimes they still do so today.)

The old symbols and Nast's political menagerie were gratefully latched onto, particularly if they could be presented humorously. The Republican elephant lent itself to this better than the Democratic donkey. And Uncle Sam was always ready in the wings to be trotted on for a turn or two.

165. Frederick Opper : "Make Way For Republican Prosperity." 1903. New York *American.*

But this was the day-to-day ruck. What is to be remembered is not the forgettable output of the unoriginal, or even the average offerings of the gifted. What can be emphasized is that in this mound of corn kernels were some genuine gold nuggets. Some cartoonists met the deadline requirements, and yet, through the unpredictability of such matters, were able to produce some first-rate work.

And as the decades rolled on, so did technology. In time the comic pages of the newspapers themselves, then radio, and finally television, drew the mass audiences away from the editorial cartoon. It was left with the more politically sophisticated audience and the occasional reader who lost his way between the front page and the funnies. This further professionalized the trade, for editors sought out quality products. It took more than a correspondence-school dropout with a talent for drawing funny noses to do the daily political cartoon. Cartoonsts more and more needed a little political sophistication.

The number of editorial cartoonists and their quality have been in accord with the audience-demand cycle. At the turn of the century, when every daily paper needed its own artist and before mergers had killed off many weak sisters of the newspaper tribe, there were as many as 500 political cartoonists. Almost immediately, beginning with Fred Opper and T. A. Dorgan (TAD), some of the very best cartoonists were attracted to the more lucrative field of the syndicated comic strip. By the end of World War I, many of the young talented cartoonists moved directly to the comics, without any layover at all in the editorial department.

The number of editorial cartoonists was also reduced, as noted already, by the growing movement to syndication. But for one reason or another, a few of the most talented remained with the editorial cartoon. Some who were ideologically inclined, such as Daniel Fitzpatrick, would only with difficulty have adapted their views and style to the daily comic. But men like John McCutcheon, "Ding" Darling, or Herblock would almost surely have made the grade with comic strips had they wished to.

It is my intention to concentrate on some of these artists, generally at the expense of the run-of-the-mill draftsman. The latter's work is important and significant for its effect on opinion in the mass market, but it is often derivative. In every generation a number of artists are the pacesetters, and other artists, consciously and unconsciously, imitate their artistic style and imagery, and even their politics. The very talented were artists who created their own world by presenting images worth looking at, even when the specific political events that inspired them are half forgotten. They speared and put on a pin certain political events, personalities or beliefs in a way that everyone else since cannot think of them without seeing them as the cartoonists portrayed them. To such artists we turn.

The Gold-Dust Twins — Davenport and Opper

During his early Citizen Kane days as a radical Socialist, William Randolph Hearst had corralled with his cash the two best political cartoonists in America for his New York *Journal*. Homer Davenport he found out in California in 1894, when he used some of his cartoons in the San Francisco *Examiner* in a fight over the election of a U.S. Senator by the California legislature. Davenport did so well that Hearst brought him, at age 27, to the Big City to work on the New York *Journal*. He paid him the magnificent sum of $10,000 a year. Frederick Burr Opper was enticed over from *Puck* in 1900, and stayed with Hearst for 32 years until his eyesight failed him. If the circulation wars depended on the political cartoons department, Pulitzer knew that he and his New York *World* had a fight on their hands.

In a strange way, Davenport and Opper are repeats of Nast and Keppler, transferred to the newspaper world. Both were able to simplify, just as Nast had done. Both had individual styles. Both had the most important ingredient — imaginative ideas. Both created memorable symbols, and each had his own distinctive ways of applying them. Davenport and Opper offset and complemented each other. Their complementary drawings of Mark Hanna and trusts form an interesting contrast that tells a great deal about their differing approach to the editorial cartoon.

Homer Davenport was born in Silverton, a village east of Salem, Oregon. As he was growing up, his family filled him full of good-old-New-England high-minded idealism. For a middle name they chose Calvin, and, one assumes, not by chance. Both mother and father Davenport encouraged young Homer to find his role and moral purpose in his cartoons. His father, writing him in 1903 when Homer was 36

166. Homer Davenport : "Gentlemen, let me introduce my friend." 1896. New York *Evening Journal*.

167.   Homer Davenport : How Long Can He Stand It? 1896. New York *Evening Journal.*

years old and was planning some chalk-talk lectures, could still ring the changes as follows:

My Dear Son Homer:
I wrote a letter yesterday, but last night my fancy started again upon the proposition or fact of your being a platform speaker, and thought of the kind of speeches you will make and of the preparation for them. Of course I had to think of them in comparison with those of Phillips, Beecher, Webster, Everett and others, all of them learned and great orators who could plead a *cause* with hardly less effort than Demosthenes.[5]

All this is to say that Davenport emerged from his small-town background as a Puritan prophet right out of the Old Testament, ready to cut down evils around him like so many weeds to be cast in the blazing flames. B. O. Flower describes his early cartoons as "colossal, brutal and somber." Mark Hanna, who was a target of many of them, broke into tears when showing a fellow Senator one of Davenport's 1896 campaign efforts. "That hurts" he blubbered, "to be held up to the gaze of the world as a murderer of women and children, I tell you it hurts."[6]

The dollar-sign suits, the uncouth, paunchy, boss figure and the boot kicking labor's skull about on a string, were cruel, and they maligned Mark Hanna. Davenport meant them to hurt. He viewed events with all the high-minded, narrow idealism of a village moralist. Davenport probably came to regret these Hanna drawings.

Davenport's other great effort was an Assyrian-like monster with whip in hand to represent the trusts. The big muscular body had a pea-pod head. It was the

269

reincarnation of the genie out of the bottle, or the Frankenstein monster ready to do the master's bidding. He claimed that he got the idea from a statue of Samson. It left liberals like Flower wondering if the symbol did not suggest that the trusts were too powerful to tame or ever overthrow. Perhaps it did. I do not find it a particularly compelling symbol and so am not a good judge. At any rate Davenport published his work with a fine puritan title that juxtaposed the materialistic and the spiritual: *The Dollar or the Man?* Homer, the highest-paid political cartoonist in America, thought of himself as on the side of the latter.

Davenport's artistic style showed competence but little flair. It lacked Nast's bold blacks, but had some of his genius of imagery without the laughter. It did, however, have more comic caricature. And his cartoons have for me a kind of scruffy tone. But like Nast's, they too were made to order for crusading.

But the puritan Davenport did not go the way of Nast. Rather, he found his way to the less strenuous life. He left Hearst and took a job in 1904 with the New York *Mail and Express*. In 1905 B. O. Flower would moan: "It is a subject of deep regret to thousands of Mr. Davenport's friends that his present work does not give him freedom and scope to make pictures anything like so powerful in their influence over the mind or so effective as teachers of great truths, as was his work while he was in the employ of Mr. Hearst. He has drawn some good cartoons for the *Mail and Express*, but they are for the most part disappointing, and some of them grievously disappointing to the friends of democratic progress." In fact, at the time, Davenport was beginning to enjoy life. He visited Europe and sketched some of its great political and cultural leaders. As a transplanted rural boy in the East, he bought a New Jersey farm and became fascinated with expensive horses. Not one to go half way, he traveled to the Middle East and brought back twenty-seven Arabian steeds, the first to be imported by an American.[7] Horsebreeders, I am told, still revere him, and named the Davenport breed in his honor.

His work showed a mellowing process. His art became more representational and more staid. In 1904 Davenport drew the famous "Uncle Sam: 'He's Good Enough for Me'" for TR and his Republicans, (Fig. 36) and in 1908, "Well Begun and Well Done" with the same cast of characters plus good old Bill Taft puttering around in the background. He also wrote a book about the Arabian horse, and another, in a nostalgic vein, about his boyhood. In 1912 he returned to Hearst, but died tragically of pneumonia shortly after — a better man perhaps, and most certainly a more tolerant one than when he grabbed his suitcase and left Silverton humming the Battle Hymn of the Republic.

Had Homer Davenport lived through to 1920 he might have recaptured the old moral fervor and fire in cartoons on World War I, just as some of his contemporaries did. But from an artistic rather than a personal view, perhaps it was just as well that Providence worked out things as it did.

Frederick Burr Opper, I think, was the greatest humorist of American editorial cartoons, except only, perhaps, Herblock. He was one of the few who made the switch from magazine to newspaper with ease. In fact, after eighteen years of crowded *Puck* drawings, the simplicity required in newspaper cartoons acted on him like sunlight on one of Beethoven's prisoners in *Fidelio* freed from an underground dungeon. In his newfound freedom he at first lost none of the good and gained in power.

Opper drew political cartoons steadily for Hearst only from 1900 to 1903, at which time he switched to the more lucrative funny papers, churning out over the years "Happy Hooligan," "Alphonse and Gaston," "Maud the Mule," "Mr. Dubb and Mr. Dough," and "Our Anteluvian Ancestors." But he always drew a few political cartoons, even as late as the 1920s. As I noted earlier, his artistry became steadily more primitive, to the everlasting loss to cartooning, I think.

Opper's political cartoons were essentially comic strips. His greatest works were "Willie and His Poppa," featuring President McKinley, Nurse Hanna, Poppa Trust, and Willie's rambunctious new little friend, T. ROOSEVELT!!! Proper Willie, in his Lord Fauntleroys, was frequently on the verge of tears, with TR kicking up a storm but Poppa Trust always quietly smiling since he knew he had everything under control with the help of Nurse Hanna. Opper's second really great series, the "Alphabet of Joyous Trusts," dedicated a letter of the alphabet each day to represent one of the trusts bamboozling the little man who represented "the common people." The Democrats published it as a campaign document.

168. Frederick Opper : "Goodness me, Willie, what ails you this time?" "We're playing Republican Campaign Trip, and Teddy's making all the speeches from the rear platform and he says I'm merely a brakeman." 1900. New York *Evening Journal.*

Opper's technique was aimed at the cynical and cosmopolitan urbanites who knew that pull, politics, and power plays were all a part of everyday life on the streets, where many cultures clashed. His work immediately attracts the eye. His outrageous drawings prepare you to laugh before you know what they are all about. The hooker comes a second later when you get the message: "You're being taken for a sucker,

169. Frederick Opper : "The Candidate and the Committee were then Photographed" — News Dispatch. 1904. New York *American.*

chum, and by a not-too-bright bunch of slobs either." One almost waits to hear Nast's thundering question "What Are You Going to Do About It?," except that Opper did not feel the need to ask it. He felt that you could find the way to salvation on your own if you wanted, without his having to provide the road signs. As Frank Weitenkampf has observed, he favored the sly dig over the stinging lash.[9]

Opper is the most neglected of the really great American political cartoonists. He is the first really urban cartoonist. His political art should be republished. He also deserves a full-scale biography. His technique and caricatures are masterful. His drawings leave behind a taste in the mouth that most people find good. His sympathies lay with the underdog, but the world Opper pictures was neither highly moralistic nor one of ism versus ism. Rather, it was composed of everyday backsliders like you and me, plus people absentmindedly dropping pianos on each other. If he pictured it that way often enough, perhaps he thought it would probably stop or be changed some way. But then again, maybe not, or maybe, instead, new troubles and miseries would be invented for his little man, to take the place of the old ones.

Small Town Crosshatch Nostalgia

The urbanization of America presented a great opportunity to political cartoonists — to think back fondly on a youth of rural joys — while living in and enjoying all the comforts and amenities of the big city. A school of such cartoonists sprang up who would emphasize humor over satire. Some of the very best, such as Clare Briggs, Fontaine Fox, H. T. Webster, and Gaar Williams, started as editorial cartoonists but drifted over into the more lucrative funny paper market with such truly imperishable series as "The Thrill that Comes Once in a Lifetime," "Among the Folks in History," "Toonerville Trolley," "How to Keep from Growing Old," "Life's Darkest Moment,"

272

"The Boy Who Made Good," "The Days of Real Sport," "The Powerful Katrinka," "Ain't it a Grand and Glorious Feeling?" and "When a Feller Needs a Friend." These deserve to survive as more than just as a slogan on the side of a tin of tobacco.

A majority of editorial cartoonists before the Great Depression fit into the genre. The most notable of the crew, John T. McCutcheon, seems to have started the whole thing by drawing these nostalgia panels for his Saturday offering. They could be turned out ahead of time to insure a long weekend. Others, who introduced them as variation from political comment, include "Ding" Darling, J. P. Alley,[10] Carey Orr, and hosts of even lesser knowns whom I'll mention in a moment. All expressed the McCutcheon mood of rural nostalgia in their drawing techniques, all used the similes and metaphors borrowed from a rural childhood to illustrate complex political problems, most put in friendly or comic animals and boys and, most of all, all expressed a similar philosophy — one associated with the names of Edgar Guest and perhaps James Whitcomb Riley — that the world was a pretty darned good old place with just a few of the ornery and misguided occasionally making it dog gone tough for the rest of us.

170. John McCutcheon : Campaigning with Bathhouse John. The Poet candidate gives an author's reading before literary circles in the Lodging-House District. 1903. Chicago *Tribune.* **Reprinted, Courtesy of the Chicago** *Tribune.*

171. John McCutcheon : Entertaining Prince Henry : Boston. 1901. Chicago *Record Herald.* Reprinted, courtesy of the Chicago *Tribune.*

The cartoon formula was well stated by McCutcheon in his autobiography: preaching and scolding day after day made one a bore and someone not apt to be paid attention to. It was far better to emphasize the sunnier side of life on most days and occasionally introduce what McCutcheon called "pictorial breakfast food." Then, when one had to criticize, the cartoon's impact had double effect.[11]

The artistic style was loose, often featuring many figures in busy activity and occasionally long conversations in balloons. A particular criticism leveled at this type of cartoon when it had a political theme was the propensity to draw in everything that moved. As Rollin Kirby in his *Encyclopedia Britannica* article notes, "The sudden impact of the idea is diffused through the multiplicity of incident."

McCutcheon lived by an honorable political code that was essentially the same as his code of personal morality. Most of his artistic life was spent with Colonel Robert McCormick's Chicago *Tribune*. They let him wax enthusiastic about Theodore Roosevelt and his sorting out of good and bad trusts. Admiration for FDR was harder to express in Tribuneland. But McCutcheon writes that he never drew a cartoon against the New Deal, nor against Roosevelt until FDR abandoned isolationism, and

172. John McCutcheon : The Presidential Holiday, "Hurry up boys! I've got 'em treed." 1909. Chicago *Tribune*. Reprinted, courtesy of the Chicago *Tribune*.

never against prohibition. Most of his political attacks were reserved for those who strayed in political life from the eternal virtues and whose actions made life more miserable for others. He tended to treat social problems in terms of individual moralities as, for example, in a biting commentary on greedy coal dealers, which would, of course, not be applicable to "good" coal dealers.

But the rest of the time McCutcheon filled his gently crosshatched boxes with sentimental nostalgia for life in Bird Center, with an ever-present dog with wagging tail, a barefoot boy who had to mind his little sister during baseball season, and humorous presentations of the harmless and ridiculous antics of political figures. So far as I know, he invented and certainly excelled in drawing the ant-hill cartoon with figures swarming around, each going about his own business. The series of the German Prince Henry's visit to the United States in 1902 set the pattern that he was to use frequently.[12] Another gem was his series of drawings of TR: treeing a bear cub, on a point-to-point hike, or going through a day's work and play before breakfast. Few other pictures can as quickly capture the effervescent mood created by that occupant of the presidential office. Only Mr. Dooley catches the same thing in words.

The political cartoon for which McCutcheon is perhaps best remembered, "The Mysterious Stranger" (Fig. 10), catches the tone of his day-to-day political comment. Its message is that the old wounds of the Civil War are silly and are healed over. A sheepish but determined Missouri leaves the rest of the South in 1904 to take a place in the long Republican line-up, to the astonishment and delight of such figures as Maine, Michigan, and Co. Like Opper's work, the appeal is light-hearted, but McCutcheon's is also sunny. But McCutcheon also re-creates a scene that is somehow hauntingly familiar, as if it happened just that way to ourselves once. The message is simple — life is a pleasant and somewhat humorous experience. The important thing is to be kind.

Not all of the members of the bucolic fraternity were so good-humored as John McCutcheon, but all had a touch of this good will in their nature. A certain sourness occasionally cropped out as this village morality faced big-city callousness and sophistication. When the favored way of life was attacked, the bucolic could be as reformist as the best of them. One cartoonist of this inspiration was Jay "Ding" Darling of the Des Moines *Register and Tribune*. He too was capable of nostalgia for the old swimming hole and could turn it to incisive and even bitter comment, as his Depression farm-sale cartoon illustrates (Fig. 37). But he could also be practical about the old days. For years he pressured Iowans to preserve natural beauty spots and protect wild animals and birds. ("Birds can't lay eggs on a picket fence. There should be a puddle for every duck.") He became a park commissioner in Des Moines and a member of the state Fish and Game Commission, and in the thirties became for a time U.S. Chief of the Biological Survey. He was also President of the Iowa Conservation Association and later of the National Wild Life Association.

Perhaps a greater degree of boisterousness was in his makeup than in McCutcheon's, and a little more acid surfaced when he faced up to New Deal intellectual professors and planners (spooning out brains). He also felt the same ties to TR, and in his case he imbibed a very practical dose of the Roosevelt conservation doctrine. Over the years, before it became fashionable to be whole earth and ecological, he produced a steady flow of cartoons on what was then called by the informative tag of *conservation*. In foreign policy, Darling followed the good guys and bad guys model, seeing problems as stemming from deficiencies of personal morality. A pre-World War I cartoon predicted the holocaust with a homely metaphor: a hunter labeled Austria aims at a rabbit labeled Serbia in front of a building labeled dynamite storehouse. But Darling was more inclined than the Chicago *Tribune* school to welcome the policeman as a

173. Jay N. "Ding" Darling : Standing Room Only. 1935. Des Moines *Register.*

cure, rather than hoping for self-reform, and so he embraced both the League of Nations and U.N.

Darling was hired away from Des Moines by the New York *Herald* in 1911, but after two years he elected to return to Iowa. In 1917 the *Herald* decided to use him once more as their cartoonist while he stayed in Iowa. During World War I he was syndicated by them and became nationally known, being the first cartoonist, it is said, to earn a million dollars drawing political cartoons.

Like McCutcheon's, his cartoon characters reflect the rural nostalgia. One series was of Alonzo Applegate, a farm boy who goes off to college and joins a fraternity, much as Darling himself went off to Beloit College in Wisconsin.

His most famous cartoon, fittingly, was "The Long Trail" drawn at Theodore Roosevelt's death. Among his best remembered was "Halloween," which portrays Farley, Hopkins, and Roosevelt as little village boys running off with a "private rights" privy with John Q. Public peeking out of the door.[13]

174. Jay N. "Ding" Darling : Evening Up the Brains. 1935. Des Moines *Register.*

Others that fit into this school are, of course, McCutcheon's colleagues on the Chicago *Tribune*, Joseph Parrish and Carey Orr. When one looks at some of Orr's vitriolic anti-New Deal comment at the end of his career, it is hard to recall that in the beginning he may have been a good deal less a scold. The *Literary Digest*, in the happier days of 1925, quotes him as saying "There is really nothing finer than a good cartoon that makes people smile. If the American citizen begins the morning smiling, the American cartoonist has done a big thing."[14]

If one reviews the files of *Cartoons* Magazine in the World War I period, the widespread popularity of this type of cartoon is readily apparent. Less known today but worth resurrecting are E. A. Bushnell of the Cincinnati *Times Star*, R. M. Brinkerhoff of the New York *Mail*, and Will Chapin of the St. Louis *Republic*. McCutcheon influenced a generation of cartoonists. Luther Bradley of the Chicago *Daily News* and later the Chicago *American*, James H. Donahey of the Cleveland *Plain Dealer*, Reg Manning of the Arizona *Gazette*, Clifford Berryman of the Washington

175. Will Chapin : T'was Ever Thus! 1916. St. Louis *Republican.*

Star, and Billy (William A.) Ireland of the Columbus *Dispatch* were all to some degree influenced by McCutcheon.[15] A host of other cartoonists borrowed from him stylistically and sometimes borrowed the mood of these drawings, including such latter-day urbanities as Vaughn Shoemaker, Dorman Smith, and Arthur Poinier.

But as Hess and Kaplan say truthfully, the Chicago *Tribune* became the last outpost, "a kind of Yellowstone Park for the disappearing herd of cartoonists."[16] The audience who understood rural allusions or could relive the old Fourth of July celebrations in the village square began to dwindle and thin out. So too did the prewar mood of simplicity, innocence, and confidence about the goodness of life and one's neighbors, the assumption that problems stemmed only from lack of personal virtue. Some of the mood has remained in the work of cartoonists even to the present, but these are for the most part older men who started their careers in an earlier day. The

176.   Lowery : His Favorite Author. Ca. 1906. Chicago *Chronicle.*

177.   James H. Donahey : The Golden Chariot. 1899. Cleveland *Plain Dealer.*

sun has pretty much set on the times of the Rough Rider. The Great Depression, Hitler and Stalin, and the Op-Ed page of the New York *Times* have pushed on stage to set a new mood. America is quite possibly the poorer for it.

Indignation in Dripping Mud

The sunny philosophers of the Midwest did not have it all their way, even in the happy days preceding the First World War. A competing style, which paralleled the growth of realism and urbanism and the Ashcan school in art, hit the cartoon world. Its chief exponent was Boardman Robinson, who, in prewar years from 1904 to 1914, was cartoonist for the New York *Tribune.*

Robinson stated his creed early: "The best political cartoons often grow out of a sense of indignation. They express one's reaction from the meannesses and futilities of life, one's feelings of resentment at social wrong and oppression." Most of those who have drawn in the style he popularized also shared his skepticism about the direction in which America was headed under a corporation-dominated capitalism, but fewer have shared his strain of anti-war pacifism. One has the feeling that these artists tended to speak for and sympathize with the drifter and the loner against the whole world — the kind of Humphrey Bogart out of Casablanca, but without the romantic trimmings. The community builder, particularly in the form of booster, was their natural enemy and target. They were the outsiders who sympathized with all the other outsiders looking in.

Robinson was to hammer home his political creed in a style of cartoon that differed sharply from that of the bucolic school. His cartoons stressed the idea, and tried to cut out any nonessentials that detracted from its presentation. Rather than being busy pictures that projected a mood of hilarious activity, his drawings were focused as much as possible on the essentials. Daumier, Steinlen, Forain and the French school of political art were the masters he turned to.

Robinson saw the potential of the grease pencil for this kind of cartoon, following along once more the road already being pioneered in France by his contemporary Forain. With photoengraving a new effect could be achieved by using the grease pencil or carbon pencil on heavily grained paper with tooth. This technique breaks up the smooth greasy line into a kind of staccatolike effect of grayish dots. The result, in the hands of a master such as Fitzpatrick, is a drawing of considerable artistic merit (see Fig. 111).

The shaded drawings that resulted lent themselves to a certain somberness, solemnity, and austerity, though *Editor and Publisher* in 1915 rather irreverently described the work of this school as "dripping mud." Artistically, the Robinsonites provided a vigor and freedom that particularly spotlighted the quaintness of the old crosshatch style of cartoon art. The new style of drawing also helped move the editorial cartoon in the direction of the stark statement of the poster. One of their number, Robert Minor, who in 1912 drew for the St. Louis *Post Dispatch,* as noted argued that the blunt grease pencil was especially useful for simplifying drawings, since detail had to be omitted.

Robinson discovered that the grease-pencil technique was particularly suited to the heroic kind of personal symbolism. In the beginning he and others caricatured politicians to represent policies, in the style of Nast. But such drawings always came out with a certain amount of shadowy grubbiness about them. They were okay when

178.   Boardman Robinson : Labor. Ca. 1904. New York *Tribune.*

179.   Robert Minor : Discarding the Ace (Negro Policy). Ca. 1904. St. Louis *Post Dispatch.*

one drew tramps or crooks, but were not for presidents. The style conflicted with the passionate, high-minded statement that the grease pencil was capable of. It was like watching John Barrymore in his last years lurching about the stage in insipid comedies. Far more appropriate for this style of presentation were the human types about whom one could express a sense of indignity; as in the personification of the capitalist or the militarist, one could even return to Daumier, Tenniel's amazon symbolizing "Peace", the spirit of liberty, or some such. All such presentations, it should be noted, are cliches of the left, useful to those who question the legitimacy of their society's rulers: social, economic, and political.

The style also lent itself to abstract symbolism. Robinson had drawn Germany as the New Goth, but Daniel Fitzpatrick of the St. Louis *Post Dispatch* drew Hitler's army as rolling swastikas. Others developed other mechanized symbols, which in contrast portrayed humanity in all its weakness.

The technique became a school for sure when Boardman Robinson drifted out of newspaper cartooning during World War I and became a teacher at the Art Students League after it was over.[17] His contribution was to set the main outlines of the style and train a generation of artists in it. Clive Weed drew such cartoons for the New York *Evening Sun*, but his work never reached the quality of the others in the school. He contributed later in his career to the Communist *Daily Worker* and finally ended up on humor magazines such as *Judge*. Robert Minor, Jr., was called from the *Post Dispatch* to the New York *World* and then moved to the New York *Call*, a Socialist newspaper, and the *Masses*. From there he drifted to the small radical press in San Francisco, drawing cartoons for *The Blast*. After the war he became more deeply involved in Communist Party politics, and, regrettably, gave up cartooning altogether. In 1951, when Earl Browder went to jail, he served as secretary of the Party. Daniel Fitzpatrick of the St. Louis *Post Dispatch* developed the style most fully and beautifully.

Other artists of the *Masses* or its successors, *The Liberator* and *New Masses*, Henry Glintenkamp, William Gropper, Jacob Burck, Fred Ellis, and Adolf Dehn, all imbibed the style. Sloan's drawings of the Colorado coal strike particularly catch the heroic possibilities. Many of these artists left cartooning and drifted into studio art. After a stint with the *Daily Worker*, Jacob Burck moved to the St. Louis *Post Dispatch* and then the Chicago *Sun Times*.[18] Glintenkamp joined Fred Ellis on the *Daily Worker*, where they ground out grease-pencil posters par excellence. As Mike Gold says in his introduction to the 1926 collection of *Daily Worker* cartoons, "Art, the Bolsheviks say, is useful or it is nothing. The cartoon is a strong weapon, the most direct and powerful one can find."[19] What he neglected to say is that it perhaps helps if the artist has at least a five-by-five-by-five area of breathing space to say what he wants to. Too many of the cartoons in these collections breathe the words *formula art*.

A few artists remained on the fringes of the style. Art Young shared its radical sympathies and turned out some grease-pencil cartoons that precisely mirrored the Robinson mood as well as its style. One such drawing shows a bum and dog sharing the same garbage pail. Others, particularly those of trees, remind one of Daumier. The most memorable, though, states his creed about those who conform: "The World of Creepers." But mostly he preferred to draw with the heavy blacks and crosshatches of pen and ink, in a kind of variation of the bucolic school gone bad and turned radical. Ross Lewis of the Milwaukee *Journal*, Jerry Doyle of the Philadelphia *Record*, and Tom Little of the Nashville *Tennessean* used the style but reflected less naturalistic indignation toward life.[20] In this they were in mood more like Rollin Kirby, Oscar Cesare and, somewhat later, Bill Mauldin. These all used the grease pencil, but for a different artistic effect. They drew back from the heavy shadowing that gave such pretentiousness to much of the work of this school, and emphasized instead its lightness and fuzzy line to suggest the rapierlike sting of their satire. Their goal was to downbeat the artistry and highlight the idea instead.

180.   Art Young : The World of Creepers. 1910. *Life.*

Let us briefly review some of the output of the major artists of the grease pencil.

Robinson's own work is limited to a relatively few drawings that are reprinted over and over. One might almost say that his working years as a cartoonist were spent developing the style and that, by the time he had perfected it, he quit. Only a few of his anti-war cartoons catch the full potential of his technique.

If Robinson is known for few cartoons, Minor is best known for only one, but it is a memorable one. "At Last, a Perfect Soldier," from the *Masses* of 1916 (Fig. 11), does everything Minor was trying for. From the same period on the *Masses* is his attack on the prudish Anthony Comstock, showing him dragging a bewildered woman in nightie into court because she gave birth to a naked baby. An earlier and more conventional attempt to symbolize suggests an exploration period of false starts. On Sunday, July 12, 1912, the *Post Dispatch* proudly reprinted cartoons from the Jersey *Journal,* Philadelphia *Inquirer,* Tacoma *Daily Ledger,* and others, showing that Minor's symbolic nut and bolt to represent TR's bolt from the GOP in 1912 had become part of the arsenal of other cartoonists. The problem is that the big bolt with a nut on it is a meaningless cliché that Minor tried to substitute for the former Big Stick associated with Roosevelt. But it tells nothing about the man or his policies (I think), and so was soon assigned to the cartoonist ash heap. Minor could be better remembered for other works which, while not reaching the level of the *Masses* cartoon, are still competent workmanship. One other cartoon, on intolerance, generally unknown, shows his potential. One, from later *Daily Worker* days, on child labor jumps out from the usual dreariness of the radical output.

181.   Robert Minor : Intolerance. January 1, 1917. *The Blast.*

182.   Robert Minor : The Sandwich Man. December 12, 1925. *The Daily Worker.*

183.   Robert Minor : Child Labor. December 22, 1924. *The Daily Worker.*

184.   Daniel Fitzpatrick : Piece by Piece. July 30, 1937. St. Louis *Post Dispatch.*

The dramatic development of the school's potential comes in the work of Daniel Fitzpatrick, a native of Superior, Wisconsin. His jaundiced stoicism is particularly suited to the style. One gets the feel of the Duluth-Superior waterfront in his drawings, with its toughness and potential brutality rather than of the middle-class homes farther back from the lakefront. Men are made to look like pygmies, and institutions are symbolized as machines about to crush them. He especially favors presenting his scenes about the way a bird flying by two miles to the right might view them.[21]

His cartoons frequently leave the feeling of impending Drang and doom, as if the floor is held up with rotten timbers, unbeknownst to those who are doing the conga above. Seldom does the specific politician appear, unless he is clearly a crook — only dead statesmen like Lincoln, who can look down sadly on the human comedy of present-day opportunists and chisellers in Rat Alley or down at the small loan-shark office on the corner. For Fitzpatrick the most common emotion is indignation, at the hands dealt from the deck of life. The attitude does have the advantage of drawing back from conventional radicalism. Joe Stalin and his crowd also come in for their share of undiluted scorn. The Nazi Pact of 1939 only confirmed Fitzpatrick's dark suspicions about that part of the human race.

185.   Daniel Fitzpatrick : One Person Out of Every Ten. January 16, 1938. St. Louis *Post Dispatch*.

186. Daniel Fitzpatrick : "Down to Bottomless Perdition." May 7, 1945. St. Louis *Post Dispatch.*

The bleakness of this view may cause one to overlook its attractions for the cartoonist. It is very comforting to keep proclaiming to the world every day that it is going to Hell in a breadbasket. The time for others to say "He told us so" comes around regularly and inevitably, and one in the meantime gets a reputation for purity and righteousness. Fitzpatrick had such a reputation. Sometimes he was merely self-righteous and a little pretentious. At such times he carped unfairly, as in his unending vendetta against businessmen or Harry Truman, or, if the story is true, in his ungenerous act to his colleagues in the field when he argued against awarding the Pulitzer Prize the year he was a judge, since no work was good enough. But he could also be right on target, and as such, he was a valuable citizen to have around in a democracy. It was not only what he said, but that often he said it so well, in a way that is difficult to forget ("My Country 'Tis of Me").

Fitzpatrick's is a strain of bleak skepticism that has, for the moment, at least, largely disappeared from cartoons in an affluent society. And, as with the disappearance of the rural sentimentalists, the nation is somewhat the poorer for the lack of Fitzpatricks.

187. Daniel Fitzpatrick : New National Anthem. December 20, 1943. St. Louis *Post Dispatch.*

Bittersweet Satire

More than any other cartoonist, Rollin Kirby represents the voice of sweet liberalism against narrowness. He is the first to speak out for those who populate the modern society we Americans live in. One sees in his cartoons not the drifter but the well-meaning, white-collar, college graduate who is sure that heaven can be brought a little closer if the old inherited prejudices are first laid to rest. For the type, see William Allen White's description of the 1912 Bull Moose convention. It is from this vantage that Kirby criticizes and takes his stand for reform.

His cartoons have a message with a bittersweet, satiric bite or, as Walter Lippmann described them, "They are never embittered to the point, which is so often reached in other great political cartoons, where the cartoonist deprives his victim of human standing. *They are civilized cartoons.*"[22]

The twenties was made to order for such work, if a cartoonist such as Kirby was could find a publisher, and he did so in Ralph Pulitzer's New York *World.*

Kirby had left Hastings, Nebraska, for an artistic career in New York. From the Art Students League he had drifted on to Paris but was back in New York by 1900. For the next eleven years he drew magazine illustrations and continued to exhibit "serious" art, but fortunately — or unfortunately from his view — he never made a sale. In 1911 he landed a job on the New York *Mail* as a news illustrator, but very shortly after a fight with the editor he left to join the *World.* In the next few years he taught himself how to be a political cartoonist just as he was approaching age 40. He very quickly established his mastery of the field, as the files of *Cartoons Magazine* of the period illustrate. Appropriately for a Pulitzer-paper cartoonist, he went on to win the first Pulitzer Prize for cartooning in 1922. He stayed with the *World* as it became the *World Telegram* and then quit and later joined the more liberal New York *Post*.

Kirby's style was grease pencil, but without the deep-bass sound effects. He cultivated the light touch. His audience didn't need to be singed with a blowtorch to feel the warmth of emotion.

Kirby's best work dwells on the underlying theme of tolerance. He attempts to sell his line by making intolerance look ridiculous because it was out of date, rather than by painting it as merely sinister. The Klansman who can't even use grammar correctly pays off Senator Tom Heflin, the stupid William Jennings Bryan studies the monkeys, the belligerent Teddy Roosevelt sells his World War I jingoism, the insipid Boston librarian goes into ecstacies over *The Six Little Peppers*, the Republican Fat Boy wants to make one's flesh creep with Red scares, narrow-minded Calvin Coolidge types out his newspaper column with the ever-present inspiration of Old Glory, the buffoonish Big Bill Thompson pastes George V on the snoot, and in Kirby's crowning symbolic achievement, prohibition turns out to be a seedy-looking, ignorant hick, rather than a high-minded idealist. Even at his biting best, Kirby never approaches being the intolerant bigot that Fitzpatrick is capable of being. Kirby's target is not the human race but the cultural lags. Precisely the people whom the bucolic cartoonists romanticize, he shows as out of date.

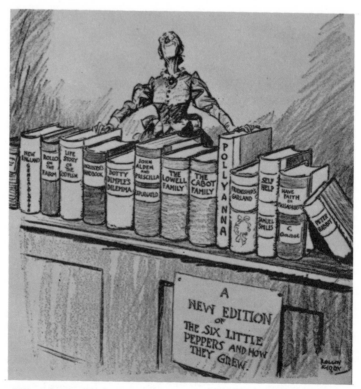

188. Rollin Kirby : Boston. September 19, 1929. New York *World*.

189. Rollin Kirby : "I wants to make their flesh creep." October 16, 1924. New York *World*.

190.   Rollin Kirby : "Buck up, you're a noble fellow." February 23, 1928. New York *World*.

Kirby's work also reflects a strain of quiet integrity. Just as he quit the *Mail* over editorial disagreements, so later in life he left the Scripps-Howard New York *World Telegram* and, after a period of rest and restlessness, began doing cartoons for the liberal New York *Post*. Kirby was one who spoke out for tolerance of modern views, and he was capable of quietly insisting upon it for himself as well as for others.

Another artist of this period and style deserves mention — for his reputation, rather than because people remember his cartoons: Edmund Duffy of the Baltimore *Sun*. He won three Pulitzer Prizes and was generously acclaimed by colleagues. What is available of his cartoons shows the same strong commitment as Kirby's, but with more bite. But neither the Baltimore *Sun* nor Duffy himself ever bothered to collect or issue any of his work, and so it rests in newspaper files in the Baltimore Public Library just as, from 1949 on, it slept for a few years in the *Saturday Evening Post* archives. His cartoons are there for anyone who thinks it worthwhile to do the digging. If no one does, we must be content with the assurance of the day's commentators.

The Passed-Over and Largely Forgotten : Pre-Pulitzer Days

From the 1920s on, the Pulitzer Prize at least served the function of securing recognition of some of those who had not published books of cartoons and were not among the very, very best cartoonists. I should like to observe briefly, using the sources noted, some of the second-level cartoonists of an earlier period who had an individual style and some talent for imagery.

For the muckraking period of Davenport and Opper up to 1910, we are at the mercy of those who write magazine articles and the author of one book for information about the second rank of artists. Most work has been lavished on the best-known worthies already dealt with, but some exceptions exist.

A Socialist eccentric with the improbable name of B. O. Flower gained control of *Arena* magazine for a while between 1900 and 1906, and ran it with articles full of the social gospel. He also was an enthusiast of political cartoons wrote a series of articles about prominent liberal cartoonists. I have already cited his work on Homer Davenport. He also did one, predictably, on Nast and on Opper. From the other articles I cull some brief comments and surmises.[23]

A second source is a 1904 book by Grant Wright on how to draw cartoons, with a concluding chapter on "Modern Masters of Comic Art." His comments are painfully brief and he produces no cartoons in this section, but he does talk of the cartoonists as if they were friends and fellow professionals. He also follows the maddening practice of showing pictures of some cartoonists without a word about them in the text.[24]

One artist of particular interest at the turn of the century is Dan Carter Beard, some of whose work shows imagination and vigor in his attack on the trusts. The cartoon produced here is in his most radical phase. He is of particular interest to me as a former tenderfoot and avid reader, since he ended his life as the grand old man in shorts attending national Boy Scout camporees and writing articles for *Boys Life*. He lived a strenuous life into his nineties. It is a pity the BSA never made a collection of his work, but perhaps it's just as well.

I have previously mentioned the cartoons of Charles Nelan, whose work in the Philadelphia *North American* against Governor Pennypacker inspired the following outburst from His Honor to accompany the legislative introduction of a press libel

191.   Daniel Beard : As It Is Today in America. 1905. *Arena.*

law : "An ugly dwarf, representing the commonwealth, stands on a crude stool; the stool is subordinate to and placed alongside of a huge printing press with wheels as large as those of an ox team, and all are so arranged as to give the idea that when the press starts the stool and the occupant will be thrown to the ground. Put into words, the cartoon asserts to the world that the press is above the law, and greater in strength than the government. In England a century ago, the offender would have been drawn and quartered and his head stuck on a pole without the gates." Nelan's work is also seen in a collection of Spanish-American War cartoons.[25]

Men of this type developed for newspapers the "standard editorial cartoon" as it appeared in the *Punch* of Tenniel or the *Vanity Fair* of Stephens. Here are others. W. A. Rogers left *Harpers* for the New York *Herald;* and Charles Bush, who drew the early Uncle Sam cartoon (Fig. 135, also Fig. 139) was the standby for the New York *World* and L.C. Gregg of the Atlanta *Constitution.*

293

192.   Charles Nelan: Be Careful. 1898. New York *Herald*.

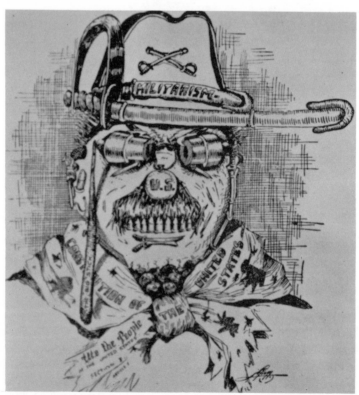

193.   L. C. Gregg : For President! (T.R.). 1904. Atlanta *Constitution*.

What characterizes their work is competence. They are like reading C.P. Snow or watching a good documentary. They avoid the grotesque, but are never completely representational. They are not consistently funny, but occasionally have their moments. Their drawings are easy to understand and occasionally are very good. They tend to take a mildly liberal line in politics. They are good, and even occasionally memorable. But you rarely take off your hat and cheer.

Almost all that period from 1910 to 1920 has to show for itself, outside of a few books and the news and comment magazines that reprinted cartoons regularly, is that most notable effort of H. H. Windsor, *Cartoons Magazine*. This journal was published monthly from 1912 through 1924.

194. Robert Carter : The Trumpet that Shall Never Call Retreat. Philadelphia *Press. 1917.*

Among the more popular cartoonists during World War I, but now in obscurity, was Robert Carter of the New York *Evening Sun*. He died during the war. More than any other cartoonist except Rollin Kirby, his work dominates the files of *Cartoons Magazine*. His style was in the mood of the English *Punch* artist Bernard Partridge or Howard Pyle with its "Robin Hood" realism : a kind of theatrical dress-up done a little too much to perfection to be lifelike. He was among the artists who early took a pro-Allies stance and drew some of the most impassioned anti-German cartoons. Not surprisingly, *Outlook* Magazine, with which Theodore Roosevelt was associated, stated that every month they looked over the crop of cartoons and ended up reprinting his work more than that of any other. Carter's statements are certainly the equal of those of W. A. Rogers, Oscar Cesare, or Luther Bradley, but he alone among them was a nonpublisher in hard covers.

Since I perhaps dealt harshly with Pulitzer Prize winner Nelson Harding earlier (chap. 8), I include here his comment on Henry Ford's Peace Ship.

Also particularly attractive to me is an artist I know nothing about other than his work : Fred Morgan of the Philadelphia *Inquirer*. He has a distinctive crosshatch that gives his drawings a neat but antiquarian look that I find appealing in a homespun, Yankee, Uncle Sam way, and so I throw him in.

195.   Nelson Harding : "Here they come." 1915. Brooklyn *Eagle*.

196.   Fred Morgan : Pleasant Reading for Carranza . Uncle Sam : "Gol darn it, what are you laughing at?" 1916. Philadelphia *Inquirer*.

Brinkerhoff, Donahey, and Bushnell, all already mentioned, do boyhood nostalgia almost as well as Clare Briggs, Gaar Williams, and H. T. Webster, who were also, during the World War I period, editorial cartoonists reprinted often in *Cartoons Magazine*. Cory's drawing of William Howard Taft deserves to be preserved if only because it so closely fits our image.[25]

Other men I have dealt with extensively in discussing wartime cartoons : Luther Bradley of the Chicago *Daily News;* Oscar Cesare of the New York *Evening Post,* a Swedish artist who incidentally married O. Henry's daughter; and W. A. Rogers of the New York *Herald.* A few others who are often reprinted have appeal for others, and so I mention them in passing: Charles S. Sykes of the Philadelphia *Evening Ledger,* Cassel and G. W. Rehse of the New York *World,* and W. K. Starret of the New York *Tribune.* They contributed a good deal to the hubbub of the day but, as with the efforts of most of us, their work faded into relative oblivion as time moved on and they stopped production.

Finally, I put in one cartoon by Herbert Johnson from this period. He was later to become a *Saturday Evening Post* staple.

198.   J. Campbell Cory : Big Ball. Little Club. 1912. *The Cartoonist's Art*

197.   R. M. Brinkerhoff : The Sirens, Uncle Sam : "No sir, you don't get me!"
1916 New York *Evening Mail*.

199. Herbert Johnson : The Faith of the Common People. "Now that Roosevelt is home again, everything will be all right." 1910. Philadelphia *North American.*

A Closing Note

What the first fifty years or so of editorial cartooning suggest is a few major approaches that develop further the artistic and content themes of Nast and Keppler. The significant fact is that they are reshaped for different kinds of citizens as America begins to feel the full impact of urbanization.

The mass media cartoonists begin by being divided into either good-humored commentators or reformers. Appropriately, the humorists favor light caricature with a certain awkward, good-humored, artistic style, while the reformers go in for heavy blacks and grays.

Those who romanticize the drifter at the expense of the community builders tend to raise questions about the legitimacy of the American social, political, and economic system, and move off to the general oblivion of the radical journals. And some of the nostalgic turn increasingly sourer as the composition of America changes. What is left in the mainstream of the daily papers are mainly those who trade in laughing satire, with a few sentimentalists and skeptics thrown in. This I have argued, is the style of cartooning typical of and possibly most appropriate to a stable civilized democracy. Day-to-day production results in a merging of entertainment and mild reform into the

299

standard kind of editorial cartoon. The healing balm of irreverence is always present, even among cartoonist sycophants, who revere the system, but so too is an understanding of human limitations.

Such cartoonists also, it appears, are curiously hemmed in by the national mood. When issues or fads stir mass opinion, cartoonists are in the middle of the mess. In the early 1900s the work of all cartoonists even those of the McCutcheon school, attacked the trusts, some with as much gusto as did the authors of muckraking articles and, in many cases, a good deal more effectively. But while they agreed in criticism, some attacked all trusts and the whole trust system while others personalized and separated good and bad trusts, a subtle way of saying that the system itself was sound. But none could sidestep the fact that they agreed that trusts were the problem of their age.

That mood also, it appears, is a consensus, expressed with some moderation. Only in the World War cartoons against the "frightfulness" of the Kaiser's Kultur, or later of Hitler's Nazism, did the mass media cartoonists let themselves go to paint untouchables who are outside the pale. The kind of moralistic bitterness that destroys, fashioned by Nast, or the nihilism projected by Gillray, is again short-lived in domestic affairs and becomes tempered and watered down with humor in the period under consideration.

Agnostic or good-humored skepticism, which has a mildly self-correcting effect, is the recurring mood of this fifty years. The cartoonists seem to suggest that democracies are not in the business of building the City of God by tomorrow after lunch, but only in making life a little more decent, humane, and tolerable. F. A. Opper had it all right at the start.

Other newspaper cartoonists seem to me, more or less, to have been groping their way to his formula.

11

Since World War II

The modern political cartoon lives in a different environment from its immediate predecessors. Most important as already noted, it caters to a more select audience.

The decline of newspaper influence is an old story. The final coup de grace came shortly after World War II as television made its way out of the bar rooms into living rooms. In the next ten years television news was refined as an entertainment art form. For the masses, the newspaper, and especially its editorial pages, had had it.[1]

In the twenties and thirties, newspaper publishers, already pushed to the wall by radio, spiced up the editorial page with syndicated columns, at considerable variation from their own dull and predictable editorial offerings. But the syndicated cartoons remained politicized versions of the Bobbsey Twins, only without the sense of high drama or the deep wells of humor found in the work of Laura Lee Hope.

In the postwar world, newspaper editorial pages further sharpened their appeal to what was left — the politically knowledgeable. And whether knowingly or not, the editorial cartoonists found that the techniques and message developed by Rollin Kirby on that intellectual outpost of the twenties, the New York *World,* exactly fit the bill. .

Controversy was not only tolerated in syndicated cartoons, but finally became chic, and one man, Herblock, exploited these opportunities to the hilt and up the arm. In the fifties he became the most influential American political cartoonist since Thomas Nast. To my mind he is one of that small circle of the really great American cartoonists. I reserve negative comments for the moment. His strength was the half nelson he got on a generation of the politically active. More than of any other cartoonist or, for that matter political columnist, it can be said of him that a

301

generation of the politically interested sized up political events and used, without too much second thought, the stereotypes he created. I think that that generation, which is my own, has since had some of its assumptions knocked kitty-corner, and Herblock has increasingly lost appeal with new publics of the late sixties and seventies. It is partly a matter of style, but it is also one of content. In this chapter we examine this change, using the cartoons of the three current greats : Block, Mauldin, and Oliphant. Then, I take swipes at other editorial cartoonists. In the chapter to follow I shall take a side glance at how politics has slopped over into the funny papers, including therein the editorial box and even such a great as Jules Feiffer.

Herblock

Before we examine the images of political reality that Block beamed out, let us note a few facts about their author.[2] Herbert Block was born in 1910. He began regular cartooning after high school at age 19. From 1929 to 1933 while others of his age group were in college, he worked as cartoonist for the Chicago *Daily News*. For the ten years from 1933 to 1943 he did daily political cartoons for the Newspaper Enterprise Association (NEA), a Scripps-Howard syndicate. In this period cartoons for the NEA and other syndicates were expected to pull punches so as not to offend any of the variety of newspaper subscribers. Nevertheless, one of these drawn by Block in 1941, attacking a target all could agree on, the Nazis, won a Pulitzer Prize, suggesting that what Herblock drew was favourably viewed by his peers as the work of a competent craftsman and as above the ordinary wishy-washiness.

About this time William Murrell, one of the most perceptive students of American cartoons, reprinted one of Block's cartoons to illustrate that "out of disciplined modern technique, a new cartoon tendency emerges. In the rigorous simplicity of semi-abstract and mechaniized symbols," he wrote, "artists seek to get to grips with issues instead of ridiculing persons. They represent a promising new development."[3] The cartoon this caption described represents a tendency toward abstract symbolism, but what Murrell saw as a new trend seems to have been only Herblock trying out some of the style of Fitzpatrick. This experimenting increased but it veered off in a new direction when Block went into the army. There, he says, three factors influenced his style. He was, first of all, pulled out of a rut and forced to innovate and experiment with new ways of drawing to fit himself to more primitive conditions of reproduction, including even, he says, drawing on mimeograph stencils. This led to a second pressure, to simplify not only his line but his content as well. Finally to get the hold the attention of his army audience, he turned on the humor.

When he got out of the army, Herblock was a well-trained craftsman of 35, able to caricature faces in a recognizable way, with a vigorous style and a vein of rich humor that he had discovered led to pay dirt. His captions became wisecracking one-liners that hammered home both the mood of the drawing and the message.

What Block had developed par excellence was the ability to telegraph the ridiculous cue as no cartoonist had done so well since Thomas Nast put "What I think about — " notes in Horace Greeley's pockets and the "and Gratz" note on his coat tail. Take any Herblock drawing of almost anyone and look carefully at the details. It is like looking carefully at a slice of fruitcake. His drawings are full of little jokes that make them uproariously funny. Take the one reproduced here, which is not one of his most memorable. The battling Nixon in the poster has a mean, lean look behind his big gloves. The bottles have their special labels. Note the pun in Long Weekend Club.

Every little movement has its meaning, but there is no unnecessary clutter. Every detail is a cue that counts toward the message. When he lets himself go like this, as he now proceeded regularly to do, Block's imagination supplies a steady flow of such ideas and gimmicks.

200. Herblock: "Man, if you want to stay in this game, you'd better get in shape." February 1973. Washington *Post*. Copyright 1973 by Herblock in the Washington *Post*.

Those gimmicks are great because they are not just little jokes, but actually telegraph cues about the political character of those he draws. A favorite technique is to use such gimmicks to demonstrate that those portrayed are exactly the reverse of what they tell others they are, in fact the reverse of what they think themselves to be. And Block makes his the image that sticks, as former President Richard Nixon observed when he announced to his team in 1968, "we've got to erase the Herblock

303

image of me." Block repeats the attack over and over, from different angles but with the same message.

Perhaps other cartoonists were doing these things too, but not so well or so often. Block is one of those artists whose work seems so inventive that it inspires imitation even by those who are not consciously trying to ape him. He provided the clichés for a decade of artists to follow, just as Nast or Tenniel had.

Politically, Herblock is a second-generation New Deal liberal, and one of what I have already, I think accurately, described as of the true-blue, ever-loyal sort. So far as his salt of the earth is concerned, he picks up where Rollin Kirby left off. He speaks for the emerging educated, urban, middle-class citizen. But his hero is a trained specialist from the lower-middle and working class, the ones who got where they are after the Depression through the New Deal and the G.I. Bill. One gets the feeling that Block's Organization Man is not from the farm but is city bred. He is also only first-generation immigrant to white-collar country. His kind of family had previously visited Harvard only to haul out the ashes, though they probably drove the truck. Block's cartoons, like Nast's, have a message on behalf of these nouveaux, middle-class citizens. They seem to shout out, "Are you going to stand for this nonsense?" As he said about himself, "Whenever the occasion calls for it, raise bloody hell." And he raised hell on behalf of the new white-collar types who were beneficiaries of the early New Deal. Block found an increasingly congenial home on the Washington *Post* staff as the paper began to get with it and became more liberal. His newspaper home and the additional advantage of putting him right at the center of national politics, and he has been there ever since.

A number of themes crop up over and over again in 30 years of Herblock cartoons. Unlike Kirby, his initial attack is much sharper on the traditional upper classes. These are the Old Establishment, discredited and brushed aside by the New Deal. But like Kirby, he presents these ideological conservatives for the most part as silly, inept, or somewhat bewildered, rather than as innately vicious. He cues them so that no one will miss his point. His unforgettable Daughters of the American Revolution in flowered print dresses, and their Napoleon-hatted military friends with wooden sword and small cannons, are drawn as fugitives from reality, the kind of people you could meet in an upper-class *Arsenic and Old Lace.* His AMA doctor, with pointed French moustache and dapper, well-manicured hands and well-padded appearance, has the artificiality of an upper-class toady and the same lack of contact with the real world. His cartoons of Senator Robert Taft, leading Republican in Congress, gave off hints of a kind of John Bircher kinkiness to a man who liked to think of himself as the solid-oak representative of dignified and responsible conservatism. And President Eisenhower, the all-American boy and military hero, was drawn with a distinct resemblance to Carl Anderson's speechless and bald "Henry" of the comics, with a vaguely foolish look on his face.

The rest of the cast of these foolish characters of the fifties and early sixties fit into a mixed gallery of those who have imperfections but whose defects still mark them as human. The dignified and stiff DeGaulle was presented as a vain little boy in a sailor suit clamoring for attention as the parade for Kennedy passed. Khruschchev was a boastful golfer pointing at sputnik. Even the more sinister figures in this crew, because of the jovial humor they exude, do not have the jolt of really vicious types : the merry Russian soldier of 1956 slaughtering Hungarians, the unshaved atomic bomb putting his measuring tape around the world, and even Stalin trotting off with death are not quite beyond the pale. Their affableness keeps them out of the group of the permanently damned, despite their crimes, as if with education and firmness, they might still be tamed into civility. Even the MIRV rocket, with its many snake heads and apelike arms, is presented as something out of a Woody Woodpecker cartoon. It

201.   Herblock : The Shot Heard Round the Immediate Vicinity. April 1949.
Washington *Post* — from *The Herblock Book* (**Beacon Press, 1952**).

too seems to mean well, and errs through stupidity rather than viciousness. It just
needs to be tamed and brought under control and then it too can make a useful rather
than a harmful contribution.

A favored ridiculous image is of the hustlers of politics and business, those whose
average intelligence is overwhelmed by a kind of jolly greediness, sloth, and gluttony.
The typical fat and bald congressman, like something out of the first row at an old-
time burlesque house, is drawn sawing legs off chairs or putting buckets of water over
doors, or floating blissfully downstream through chaos. The fat legionnaire in World
War I tin hat creeping up on Girl Scouts toasting marshmallows fits into this gallery.
Slightly more sinister, but still exhibiting the good-humoured, shallow fellowship of a
Sinclair Lewis Rotarian, is the lobbyist, greedily but with a big smile, grabbing all he
can get. These, it should be noted, are middle- and working-class types who got
seduced by business values. Presumably they can be educated back into useful citizens.

Somewhat farther down the social scale are the dim-witted, who project an
ignorance that is unaware of its viciousness. This includes the hillbilly louts with
handy rocks or clubs who oppose integration and most of the rest of civilized virtues.
These come close to Kirby's ignoramuses who are culture lags.

305

202. Herblock : "Stand fast, men — they're armed with marshmallows." August 11, 1954. *Washington Post.* — from *Herblock's Here and Now* (Simon and Schuster, 1955).

Over time Block has varied the costumes and the expressions to fit the politician or a group he was ridiculing, but his basic message has been fairly consistent: this crew of conservatives and others opposing the good common sense of New Deal reforms are just ignorant or a little stupid and are blinded by misguided selfishness. Hopefully they can be educated out of it.

Block regards only a relatively tiny category of humans as really vicious and depraved. While they are few in number, they have never been absent from his cartoons over almost thirty years of mass production. The prime recruits to this group are those whom Block views as undermining the right to free expression especially of those of whom he approves that is, those who express commonsense, liberal views such as his own.

When Herblock plays the civil liberties theme, he is most moved and most clearly shows his deepest loyalties. Perhaps more than at any other time, he demonstrates

306

whom he considers as part of the way of life he identifies with, and who is on his own enemies list. Leaders of congressional investigating committees were, until Watergate, his favorite targets. They in turn were self-proclaimed defenders of America against subversives (defined as Communists and sometimes Socialists), and the old, small-town traditions against the new liberal, urban and secular notions of progress. Block was as much a missionary for the new as they were for the old. The symbolic tip-off by which Block identifies the bad apples of this crew of congressional sleuths has a curiously lower-middle-class twist : they are bums with tattered clothes and in need of a shave. Senator Pat McCarran, who was hot after foreign-born subversives, got drawn as a rum-soaked and possibly diseased hobo. Richard Nixon, from the Hiss days on, but especially after his 1954 campaigning, became a permanent Block property to be wheeled on to scare little children. In 1954 he was drawn crawling out of a sewer to meet his welcoming committee, a cartoon Nixon never forgot and whose image he sought to erase forever after. But the drawings without even a single glint of human sympathy were those reserved for Senator Joseph McCarthy of Wisconsin. Against him Herb Block crusaded in deadly earnest in what was an admirable display of sheer courage. If these cartoons had a message, it was that people like McCarthy were akin to psychopaths. The malady that the Senator suffered from was not slothful stupidity or ignorance, cultural lag, or even from political opportunism gone wild; it was that he had a serious character disorder. McCarthy was Satan trying to turn back the clock and take it all away.

203. Herblock : "It's sure hard to get help these days." October 1947. Washington *Post.* — from *The Herblock Book* (Beacon Press, 1952).

204. Herblock : "I have here in my hand —" May 7, 1954. Washington *Post.* —
from *Herblock's Here and Now* (Simon and Schuster, 1955).

Block's stable of heroes gives more cues to his preferred citizens. All are those who are finding salvation through education; one can almost call it the urban, third-generation-immigrant's dream of paradise. They are portayed as society's nonpartisans out to right the world's evils through knowledge. A dubious hero, for my taste, is occasionally shown only in the robe and feet and dignified stance of the judge, who symbolically rises above the muck and moil of day-to-day democratic poltics and social conflict and provides Americans with solemn and reliable guidance. One is tempted, given the past and probable future history of the American Supreme Court, to make rude noises and remind Block that American judges are not of the same cut of cloth as the prophet Samuel, nor are they likely to be. In a democratic society, it is not, thank God a Superman in robes who will probably save us, if we get saved at all, but someone more on the order of Herblock's average muddling-through Senator or Congressman.

The Judicial image is similar to Block's deferential treatment of pure scientists and such usually maligned types as social science professors and other assorted social planners. These are the technicians of our society, the educated elite that came out of nowhere when given a chance. These are the people that he, and many of his fellow citizens, feel will save us in the end.

An especially revered image is that of the educable black. The black drawn by Herblock is the serious young student who, if just given half a chance, will advance into the professional classes. His is, of course, a reverse image of the shuffling and shiftless Negro whose ignorance sentences him to the sharecropper farm or to mugging anyone who wanders into the ghetto. Block's assumption is that all the black needs is opportunity, and then the problems will drop away like raindrops on a Burberry.

Perhaps as revealing as any other image is his idealization of the common man. Block had two figures for him. His middle-aged, moustached one with old-style hat, glasses, and comfortable pipe is a hangover from NEA days and looks like the John Q. Public of many other cartoonists, including especially that of Vaughn Shoemaker. He comes in to add a sense of middle-class stability and decency, and is in fact a kind of figure of the previous Depression generation — such as one's father was. This is the kind of decent person the New Deal was meant to help out of a degrading depression. But as time goes on this figure fades pretty much out of Block cartoons. The good, decent small clerk or businessman with only a high school education is no more, or at least is no more as an ideal in the modern postwar world.

The figure Herblock increasingly identifies with looks pretty much like himself, and is the same kind of middlebrow intellectual and decent citizen that he himself is. He is clearly an urbanite raised on big city streets, with none of the nostalgic hokum for small towns. He is also a white-collar organization man, some kind of professional or technician. But like the figures of cracker-barrel wisdom, he also possesses common or uncommon sense. He knows a rip-off when he sees it. Most important, however, he is decent, well meaning, and sincere, and therefore continually astonished by the blatant stupidity and crass selfishness of Block's gallery of culture lags from the worlds of politics, business, and the sheltered upper-middle classes. In the role of priest or scientist he has a bewildered Little Orphan Annie look about his eyes as he views with some wonder the greed or stupidity of the human comedy in business and politics. Sometimes Block also presents a feminine form, usually as a helpmate or, if alone, in some educated white-collar role such as librarian.

These characters pretty well illustrate the political line Block has peddled to a generation of Americans : educated expertise must replace selfish partisanship. The response he got suggests that he hit pay dirt. Partly this is because his cartoons lack the sophistication and cynicism of those in *The New Yorker*. They come a good deal closer to the traditional vein of American social-gospel liberalism and goodwill. He tells his public that the system is not hopelessly corrupt, except for a few psychopaths. Rather, humans are weak and selfishly stupid because they are so often ignorant about their true interests. For their own good they need to be prevented from doing certain things that deprive others of their opportunities. The school house will save us. What America needs is a series of commonsense structural reforms that will be devised by nonpartisan experts to stymie the power and greed of politicians and businessmen and encourage the innate goodness in all men. This is to be achieved by bringing in expertise and by democratizing the process further with — such reforms as integration of schools, jobs, and housing, reapportionment, civil service, abandonment of congressional seniority, lobby and campaign regulation, and abandonment of the electoral college system and others championed by good- government advocates. Give the average man a chance, and things will change for the better.

This vision falters as soon as one begins to get skeptical and ask questions or when one faces such events as a combined inflation-depression with rising taxes that the experts can't seem to figure out either. Since the middle sixties that has begun to happen in America. The expert no longer seems so expert. The New Deal begins to look a little harried and it too seems to need a shave and a new suit. Despite all our well-meaning efforts, things seem to keep on going wrong. One problem may be that most of us humans may be a good deal more like what Block characterizes as the greedy and stupid congressmen and even the slothful lobbyists than like the experts of his dreams. Then too, our representatives may not be the deviants, but at times, in their good as well as bad qualities, like many of the rest of us in the public whom they are paid to represent. Perhaps these politicians deserve more respect for trying to handle difficult jobs in a fishbowl rather than being treated as if they were a collection of potential inmates who are one jump ahead of the man with the net, Block seems to me to be measuring them against some impossible standard of rectitude. After all, those professional experts who have ideas about how society's institutions should be refashioned, also somehow get mixed up in the messy conflicts and power plays.

It is also hard for Block and the rest of us to face the fact that education may not be able to eliminate all this selfishness, sloth, or other weaknesses of character in our public and private servants, or in ourselves. Herblock's simple-hearted faith in the goodness of man is a little more difficult to take than was formerly the case. Perhaps it is the efficiency of the media that has made us more aware of human potentiality for evil. As I write this, in the news is the story of six men who met a woman going back to her car with a gas can. They made her pour the gas over herself, but you can guess the rest; not for some great cause but for a moment's diversion of punks, she lost her opportunity to live out her life.

Also a little harder to believe is the notion that expertise is that good; that it will solve all the problems pronto, just the way those expert (with the emphasis always on the last syllable) rug cleaners say on the radio they will scientifically clean your carpets. Block assumes that, once we get the facts, it is clear what the solution must be, and only the selfishness of the privileged few keeps us from putting it into effect. In some cases, he is precisely right. But other problems are a little tougher. Some of the foreign policy tangles, or our welfare system, may have to be outgrown rather than solved. What our New Dealer generation has constructed sometimes seems to have us boxed in in a way that makes going in any direction — up, sideways, down, north, south, east, or west — a potential catastrophe for clients, administrators, do-gooders, and the rest of us. These who know the most and are the best educated in a field seem sometimes to be the most confused and at times the most disheartened.

Absent from Herblock is the notion that government may just have to contrive to stumble along and muddle through. No machine or organism yet devised operates without waste products that are harmful to itself and to others. One may expect that an institution as imperfect as government might follow the same pattern for some time to come.

So like Thomas Nast before him, Block has become a little dated and his shots occasionally glance off target. The privileged in wealth, like the Margaret Dumonts of the Marx Brothers' movies, are no longer so stuffy but are prancing around in pant suits with long cigarette holders, spouting what they just read about in *Newsweek*. It is in fact their present, more sophisticated life style that provides some of the more controversial issues of present times. They and their bewildering offspring have sometimes joined hands with the outcasts of society to give the rest of us a whole new line of social issues that muddy the old, simple New Deal dividing line between the privileged and the working masses; issues such as abortion, drug abuse, amnesty, women's lib, the death of God, the Gay life as a normal alternative, and a host of upper-middle-class fads that would make the old-fashioned Methodist, as well as the working-class Fathers in *Going My Way,* blanch and perhaps, more important, make labor hardhats of the New Deal coalition, for the moment at least, see red white and blue.

Block, to his credit, goes all the way with Kirby in attacking the culture laggers who want to preserve racial segregation or re-create a Babbitt kind of businessman's conformity. But he and his technician friends find it a little harder to get a hold in a swinging society. That techician is a decent family man who still kind of hankers for the decent middle-class suburban home with kids and Sarah Lee apple strudel in the microwave oven.

But I have carped enough, or probably too much. What I wish to say is that Herblock is one of the really great cartoonists of the world and he should get a Citizen's Medal if any cartoonist should. He devised a political cartoon that was most unlike the work of anyone else before, but so good that its tricks were borrowed by others almost on sight. At the same time he has projected the traditional liberal faith of the optimistic and cheerful American. Few men or women in their own fields have had the impact that he has on his colleagues or on the political actives of his generation.

Bill Mauldin

Herblock's faith in traditional liberalism that education would overcome all, while dominant, was not the only kind of cartoon after World War II. A more skeptical message, one equally indigenous, appears in the world of Bill Mauldin. Mauldin predated Block in widespread popularity because of the attention paid to his war cartoons. In these "Up Front" blockbusters,which won him a Pulitzer, none of the easy optimism of Herblock seeps through. Rather his heroes, if such they are, maintain an inner sweetness in the face of frightfulness, some of which they realize they helped create. They have no easy solutions to problems. They do their duty, they bridle at clear-cut injustice, and they automatically embrace the simple notion of being kind to the victimized, when one can be. Their humor is wry and often bitter.

Following the war, Mauldin made an abortive attempt to establish himself as a syndicated cartoonist of social and political comment. He then lapsed into semi-retirement until beginning his day-to-day job as editorial cartoonist on the St. Louis *Post Dispatch* about a decade later, in 1958. A few years after this, in 1962, he moved to the Chicago *Sun Times,* where he won his second Pulitzer Prize. He carved out the role of roving cartoonist for this paper, and has stayed there since, spending a good part of his time in Arizona. Throughout the sixties he hit his stride.

Bill Mauldin has written at some length about his early postwar syndicated work in *Back Home,* a book that reproduces some of these cartoons. His artistic style in them was similar to the heavy black brush work of his "Up Front" output, but somehow grubbier looking. These cartoons, he said, leaned to the use of a sledgehammer rather than a needle. He became, he says, a bore, shrill and off target.

This self-criticism is only partly just. Some of the work, too strong for the early post-war years, would have been acceptable and applauded in the late sixties when standards of subtlety were noticeably lower. A number of the cartoons still look good and right on target — as many, I think, as are found in the yearly output of many regularly featured cartoonists today, or at that time.

205. **Bill Mauldin : The battle-scarred ghost of Ezra Mulligan (Thompson's Pennsylvania Rifle Battalion) pays a visit to his great-great-great-great-granddaughter's D.A.R. meeting. 1946. Copyright © 1947** *Back Home;* **reproduced by courtesy of Bill Mauldin.**

What jarred most about the cartoons, I think, is that, as someone perceptively told him, they seemed to be designed for radical workers' publications — journals printed with red covers and lots of arms with hammers — the IWW handout of 1907, published on yellow wood-pulp newsprint. What gives the drawings this flavor is that they were drawn from the point of view of a romanticized underdog radical, and of this type America hardly had any in the early 1950s. In part this may be because Mauldin was transferring his sympathy from dogface to the working stiff. It may also have been the result of adolescent romanticizing of radical types by someone who had at best a marginal, lower-middle-class upbringing. His romanticism would have been better understood in an age where one can buy ready-made jeans already worn to tatters and with sewn-on patches to give the aura of radical underdog sympathies.

This view was romantic because it was phony Mauldin. Despite the depression hardships of growing up described in *A Sort of Saga* and *The Brass Ring*, Mauldin came out of the experience with straight middle-class motivations; he somehow found a way to leave New Mexico and his truck-driver, motor-cycle-type friends, to go all the way to the Chicago Academy of Fine Arts and try to work his way through, Horatio Alger style. Nor did he stop running until he had made it to the top at least twice. He could sympathize with the really victimized, such as Europe's war refugees or the blacks in the South but not really with the self-exploited, the deadbeats and wasters. Trying to pretend that the latter were like the former was a strain, and it rang false. In

312

actual fact Mauldin was pretty much the same sort of post-depression beneficiary of New Deal policies as Herblock. He was going to end up living in nicer suburban homes than he had ever dreamed possible. (And so were a good many of his ex-dogfaces.)

The romanticized working stiffs presented in the early postwar drawings also put off the middle-class readers of the fifties, and probably, if the truth were admitted, even the white-collar progressives who patronized the liberal-radical journals. It was not that the sentiments expressed were unacceptable, or even that which was being criticized was so radical (Bilbo, realtors, doctors, etc.). Block and many other successful cartoonists had the same targets. It was that the mood that seeped through was all wrong. These salt-of-the-earth people and scenes they stumbled through were run-down and shabby. The heavy, swirling black lines emphasized this rattiness. The message was pretty much that of all bitter drifters and failures, that the world was out to screw the best people, namely, themselves. Instead of also portraying the minor joys of such people, as John Steinbeck did in *Cannery Row,* Mauldin pushed the view of his characters as somehow cheated and unfairly victimized. Eulogized were the failures who couldn't make it, the washed-out, those who didn't really try, and all the other crowd of the self-exploited. Those trying to better themselves were all wrong. Mauldin was painting a booming America, which with all its faults looked pretty good to those who survived a world war and depression, as if it were a dismal wasteland. The people who bought newspapers did not like it, even when they could not say why. Even the CIO wasn't that way anymore, nor did it want to be. It too was working into the middle class with a lust for suburbia.

By 1958 Mauldin had had several careers and inevitably he had changed. He now seemed to know who he was and one could take it or leave it. The change is reflected in his cartoons. His first drawings continued the black brushwork with swirling skylines that suggested the view out of a dirty train window entering the tunnel. But this style dropped away in about three months and Mauldin began experimenting with a grease pencil, in a way reminiscent of Rollin Kirby. The main artistic innovation was in introducing light into the drawings. Instead of the picture looking like the moment when the smoke itself was not sure it was going to clear, the picture now looked as it were made in the sunlight, with the figures neatly posted. The openness is emphasized by the abandonment of borders around the drawing. There was, as well, a move to light outlines and from unrelieved blacks to grays.

Some of the other innovations in technique were less laudable. Caricature went out the window. Mauldin confessed that in the beginning it was embarrassing having to label well-known politicians because he couldn't draw their faces, so he avoided such caricature when possible. But even humanized caricatures of cartoon stereotypes such as the AMA physician were tossed out, so that the idea would be everything. Only the Coon Creek boy type of Southerners got the vitriolic caricature treatment. The whole setting and props of the cartoon were also radically simplified. Mauldin began to play around with the old-style symbolism of cartoons, and some of the worst clichés from the card game among national leaders to you name it. He also tried a few abstract symbols, like dripping faucets, but seemed to decide that abstraction wasn't his bag.

The imagery also came out middle-class, or perhaps white-collar liberal would be more descriptive. A Vietnam soldier looks as if he had stepped out of the parade of the wooden soldiers. Gone were the moth-eaten threadbare sad sacks, and in their place was a pretty mild set of mannequins that Mauldin pushed around to illustrate his points. The idea was the important part, not the drawing or the presentation in fancy imagery.

The cartoon formula was to feature a deadpan comment which, with a sting said

313

206. Bill Mauldin : "Let that one go. He says he don't wanna be mah equal."
March 2, 1960. Copyright © 1960 St. Louis *Post Dispatch;* reproduced by courtesy
of Bill Mauldin.

something like "this it the way they say it is, but isn't it really this way?" The humor
stayed pretty tight-lipped. The mood he beamed out could create sparks, but there
was also enough inventiveness in his work so that an occasional cartoon came close to
summing up the national sentiment at the moment. And in the sixties there was the
civil rights movement, which provided an issue that bought out all the best of
Mauldin's talent for biting comment without ever getting too shrill.

The big change, then, was in the mood. The sledgehammer approach was out, and
the Kirby light-touch-with-a-little-bittersweet was cultivated. As Mauldin put it, [it
has] "to be thrust gently, so that the victim doesn't know he's stabbed until he has six
inches of steel in his innards."

The guts of the message was of the suburban middle class that can not forget the
Depression or the army. It was pretty simple — "Don't trust anyone who's in charge;

they can always be expected to screw it up in some way." The cure was likewise simple. No longer was it a good guys-bad guys drama of the radical left or of the liberal Herblock, but a stance of skepticism more natural for the New Mexico kid who fought his way up to Oklahoma and then the world. The only way to make life tolerable, he seems to say, is to have gadflies who will sting leaders into doing what they knew was the right thing to do in the first place. But critics have to do it adroitly so they won't be so hated as to be hounded out of existence. His creed was, as he said, "if it's big, hit it," "circle and stab, circle and stab." At another point he spoke of cultivating, through not mixing with his victims, "the proper state of objective malevolence."

The cartoonist's job also, as he saw it, was to get on the public agenda issues that might otherwise be overlooked, by accident or design. Specifically, this means issues that might cut back on special privileges for those who have more than their share of wealth, status, and power. It means checking for ignorant and callous self-indulgence

207. Bill Mauldin : "Are you sure he's stopped swearing?" January 29, 1960. Copyright © 1960 St. Louis *Post Dispatch;* reproduced by courtesy of Bill Mauldin.

at the expense of others. Segregation and ill-treatment of blacks are the most outrageous examples of such acts, but the world provides plenty more every day and, when we correct these, another set will spring up among the underdogs who have become overdogs. For the most part, this does not seem to many a too unrealistic approach to the urban world of today.

But it too had its problems. The thing didn't quite hang together when the good guys with the white hats got elected in 1960 and really began to throw power around. Mauldin faced a real and continued ambivalence: what to do when those he admired got power and issued lofty sentiments, or about those dictators abroad who really did attack entrenched privilege and claimed to be acting for the common people. It was not that he looked the other way. Rather he was a little schizoid. Sometimes he followed his skeptical inclinations and ripped into them when they needed it, but other times he just modestly genuflected. Mauldin never quite got around to pouring on all the acid for the Kennedys. The bile doesn't flow up so naturally as it does for the Nixons or even Rockefellers. The New Left liberal busybody does not often enough get his full deserts from Mauldin, even when rich, fat, and sassy. The Communists abroad provide enough events, from the Hitler pact through Hungary and Czechoslovakia, to come in for some rough treatment, but it is off again on again. Mauldin keeps getting divided. This posture is most clear in a *New Republic* article, in which he confessed his sin and apologizes for his split personality on the Vietnam war. In 1973 he excuses the patriotic outbursts of earlier cartoons as the result of visiting Vietnam and getting personally involved with the dogfaces.[4] The plea stinks of a Salvation Army kind of confession session for a hot meal, and it is a disservice to his best work, which is built on the stance of the independent and critical spirit rather than the person who follows someone else's line about the good guys and the bad guys. The line he notes that he was following in this case, though he presents it as one bringing him the light, was words of wisdom from his offspring.

What Mauldin's work boils down to is the very useful message of *do not expect too much in this world* or probably from the next. But that does not mean that you should give up trying to make things more tolerable for yourself and the other poor slobs who don't have your advantages.

One may well ask why this cartoonist who was given one chance in the mass market and blew it, was able to come back so strong — and was able to do this without the clear artistic and imaginative skills of Herblock: humor, caricature, imaginative cues. What made him any better than thirty or forty other pros? One answer is that often enough he followed his own bent. Artistically, it has not always led to happy results, since it sometimes seemed to turn editorial cartooning into a branch of mechanical art. But in terms of defending the interests of the post-FDR generation, his own generation, he is like a tough big sister to a little brother. The second answer is that, in acting as if the idea is everything and whatever detracts from it isn't worth the bother, he doesn't muddy the message. You get it. Mauldin's ideas zing onto target, and when they are his own ideas and not someone else's clichés, they have a realistic kind of saneness and they ping deep. But most important of all as an answer, I think, is that Mauldin draws for grown-ups. He has come up from under and absorbed enough to know that on occasion the American Dream can go sour now and then and he doesn't try to hide the fact with a cartoon vaudeville act, nor does he give up.

When Mauldin draws it like he sees it, his cartoons turn out to be of a pretty high order. His Lincoln on the death of Kennedy is moving as were few others that day. His Gene McCarthy throwing his halo ring in the hat in 1968 caught it on the first bounce. One could do worse than to have a Mauldin cartoon staring out of the newspaper at one every day.

Pat Oliphant was brought to the Denver *Post* from Australia in 1964 when he was only 31. He had already had a good ten-year apprenticeship down under. Within a few years he had won a Pulitzer Prize and established himself as the leader of a new style of cartooning in America.

Oliphant has a different approach and style from what was typical in American art previous to his arrival. His first impact on other cartoonists was through artistry. Like many English artists and like Fischetti here, he favored the rectangle wider than it was high. Second, like Giles and other Englishmen, his artistry suggested a comic satirical mood. In his case the mood was projected in mocking imagery somewhat reminiscent of the cartoons of the British cartoonist Ronald Searle. The flowing lines themselves gave off the aura of a full-blown lampoon of the comic-operetta establishment of Graustark. Mixed in was the Charles Addams humor and imagery about weird monsters . All of this was presented with filigree and Victorian gingerbread.

208.   Pat Oliphant : "Wheee.e.e..." September 19, 1967. Denver *Post*.

More than anyone else, Oliphant seems to be striving in his caricature to lay bare the personality of a politician. David Low desired to have the caricature of the politician reflect his policy. Perhaps this is what Oliphant sometimes does. But more frequently he seems to be arguing that the personality of leaders, their foibles and strengths, are what determine the style of their policy and politics. A *Time* comment said it rather well: Oliphant's political characters are "the hopeless victims of their own personalities." Oliphant boils down to a psychological analysis of political character and events.

In all this fanciful political world, Oliphant's hero is the unassuming, law-abiding citizen, not too well educated, probably not a college graduate, a little bewildered, but no dope. Probably he is blue collar or a white-collar worker such as a barber. He is sometimes portrayed as the victim and sometimes as the onlooker or innocent bystander. He looks pretty much like the fellow you see walking along the curb toward the pavilion window at a Big League baseball stadium. You expect that he'll buy a program, maybe some peanuts and a bottle of beer as he watches the fine points of the game. He is not — repeat not — much of an intellectual.

With this citizen as a focus, Oliphant can take zigzagging stands as far as the usual liberal-conservative drawn battle lines are concerned. In foreign policy it's pretty much a plague on both your houses and a plumping for compromise and reconciliation. His average guy isn't enthusiastic about wars, whether they're called police action or something else. On civil-liberty kind of issues, it is saying whoa to the weakening of the criminal code. As noted, Oliphant has even had the guts to portray the American Civil Liberties Union as a meddling old lady do-gooder and, I may add, it's about time someone did. On other freedoms, such as of the press or speech, he is more liberal. What keeps him on keel is his little penguin, Punk, off in a corner mouthing off. These comments help draw attention to whose going to get helped or hurt, especially when the fellow playing end man in a crack-the-whip line is Oliphant's law-abiding citizen and wife.

The message Oliphant sends out is pretty simple and helpful. He says that it is a spooky world full of old-fashioned knaves and the gullible, muscle-bound idiots they lead around. At the heart of the process are the ambitious — ambitious for themselves

209. Pat Oliphant : (Tapes). April 1974. Denver *Post.*

above all, no matter what they tell you about crusades. Underneath the humor is, I think, a note of tragedy.

His role, as he sees it, is to ridicule idiocy whenever he sees it. But he doesn't have a solution as Herblock did, nor does he often have the urge to punish that Mauldin has. It more often takes the form of revealing true character, as the partially deleted expletive he puts into the mouth of the sanctimonious Nixon. Implicit in his approach is the assumption that the poor in spirit will be always with us. Oliphant thus has a good deal more cheerful cynicism than either Mauldin or Herblock, and thereby escapes the torture of deciding whether or not to attack liberals or the left when they seem to be up to idiocy. Everybody is fair game for him. He expects to find idiots outside as well as within the Establishment. He finds them in the Israeli kibbutz and in the Arab tents. A pleasant skepticism tempers his enthusiasms.

But if Oliphant in general is mocking and a little cynical, his deadly serious side crops out occasionally uncamouflaged. Artistically, these cartoons crawl out of the woodwork like hidden-away Dorian Grays. The cartoons take on a darkness, and are peopled with emaciated types with large heads and blank stares. These are cartoons about such ultimate horrors as overpopulation and destruction of the earth. Oliphant is aware that this is a world of limited resources and not one with a tacked-on label, "Guaranteed Safe for Humans."

To summarize, the usual style of an Oliphant is light, flippant, and sophisticated. But it is not empty-headed. Oliphant seems to me to be saying that the world is often absurdly tragic because of man's nature but is also peopled by a great number of decent and hard-working types. It is only reasonable that whenever possible, the cards should be reshuffled and dealt out to benefit the latter.

210. Pat Oliphant : "First Golda and now Willy Brandt — that's two world leaders who have gracefully resigned recently..." 1974. Denver *Post*.

Each of the three cartoonists discussed so far has or is having an impact on the way Americans view politics. Herblock, through sheer inventiveness and technique, is the all-time leader — for my own money surpassing even Thomas Nast or anyone else who was supposed to be a genius of the editorial cartoon. Only Opper, during the short stretch when drawing political cartoons for Hearst, could over time have approached his quality. Block has an additional advantage; Americans would certainly like to believe that the world is the way he sees it.

Mauldin is the staple. His standard output is like the union label. One can expect high quality but little to reach the thin air of the *Up Front* drawings. This is damning with faint praise, but I don't know what else to say about .285 outfielders except that it's useful to have them in the lineup. In his recent work he has returned to ink drawings more in the mood of the *Up Front* days. I think it's an improvement.

To Oliphant, it seems to me, the future belongs. Other cartoonists have begun to imitate his artistic style. Fewer can bring themselves to adopt his more cynical, humorous viewpoint on politics. Some use the style for crusading, and dump in a bit more bitterness. Others use the style for mainly nonpolitical fluff that just happens to feature politicians. But all this catches little of the Oliphant mood. It is that viewpoint, however, which I suspect will dominate American cartoon comment and the public opinion of the immediate future.

And the Rest

The other popular cartoonists fit under several major headings. One group is the college-daily crowd, those popular with perhaps the least-discriminating section of the voting public. Just as the taste for campus speakers in the sixties ran to people with a prison record or people who are defending themselves from charges by law-enforcement officials, so the student taste in cartoonists has been, until recently, for running dogs whose mouths drip red paint from their slashing attacks on the Establishment. This group as noted, applauds Paul Conrad of the Los Angeles *Times* first and formost, with such as Tom Darcy of *Newsday* a three-lengths-behind second-placer. Often first-rate talent is there, but subtlety is a rarer commodity. The cartoons of Don Wright of the Miami *News* and of Paul Szep of the Boston *Globe* fall within the loose fringes of this group. Of this group Conrad seems to me often great; at other times he has produced cartoons flawed by their bitterness. Wright is like someone in a tobacco-spitting contest who keeps getting progressively better and better as he learns control.

A second category of the syndicated includes the competent liberals with originality in style and content. Hugh Haynie of the Louisville *Courier-Journal* has worked out his own single figure, backgrounded by a box form of cartoon. Next to Mauldin, be comes closest, in my mind, to providing a staple daily cartoon. It is hard-hitting and current, and an incisive comment about what one is reading about on the front page. Also of this group of above-average quality is Fischetti of the Chicago *Daily News*. His needle was in Nixon-Agnew up to his elbow, but his talent comes through, though not consistently at the level of the heavyweights. Coming up on the outside and to my taste among the most promising, are Bill Sanders of the Milwaukee *Journal* and Tony Auth of the Philadelphia *Inquirer*.

211. John Fischetti: "You'd *better* be tough. The world you'll live in will be *filled* with Chinese and Kennedys." 1963. New York *Herald Tribune*.

212. Jeff MacNelly: "Higher." 1972. Richmond *News Leader*.

Then there are the conservatives. Don Hesse of the St. Louis *Globe Democrat* most clearly fills the bill, being a rightist equivalent of Fischetti. Different in style but also conservative are Karl Hubenthal of the Los Angeles *Herald-Examiner*, Charles Werner of the Indianapolis *Star*, and Tom Curtis of the Milwaukee *Sentinel*. Wayne Stayskal of the collapsing Chicago *Tribune* presents more frequently than not a humorous side of the news but when comment is present, say about once in four, it is tilted right. His style is loosely modernistic in the direction of childish scrawl. There aren't many attempts at earth-shakers, but there isn't any pretentious moralizing either Jeff MacNelly of the Richmond *Times Dispatch* is more clearly in the Oliphant mold, but with a conservative learning. He won a Pulitzer early and since his cartoons keep improving so that they are now among the most incisively funny of the profession. He also has a comic strip "Shoes."

Besides these are the older style cartoonists who are approaching retirement. Art Poinier of the Detroit *News* has a standard comment, with occasional outstanding work. The same can be said for a number of others such as Gib Crockett of the Washington *Star*, Roy Justus of the Minneapolis *Star*, Scott Long of the Minneapolis *Tribune*, Lou Grant of the Oakland *Tribune*, Bill Crawford of NEA, and Ed Valtman of the Hartford *Times*.

213. Wayne Stayskal: "Where's it all going to end, O'Brien?" 1972. Chicago *Tribune*

214. Tom Curtis: "Can I have some Rhodesia with my Angola?" 1976. Milwaukee *Sentinel*.

215. Art Poinier: "Don't confuse me with facts." 1960. Detroit *News*.

The most scholarly of political cartoonists in relation to his profession is Draper Hill of the Detroit *News*. He knows more about the history of political cartoons than anyone I have ever met, as I have found to my embarrassment on occasion. His works on James Gillray are standard. His Harvard undergraduate thesis on Keppler is a basic source and, as I noted earlier, really should be published. He has also experimented in his own work with new forms of cartoon style and presentation. The words *scholar* and *gentleman,* though perhaps with a dash of pepper, describe him reasonably well. He has been a friend to me just as he has to the many others interested in the political cartoon who have bugged him with questions over the years.

Why there are not so many first-rate conservative political cartoonists as there are liberal political cartoonists remains a question. Maybe it is because liberalism has been "in" with newspapers and few papers have more than one cartoonist. On the other hand, a paper can hire a stable of columnists. The Washington *Post* presently runs, from right to left, columns of the Washington editor of the conservative *National Review,* George Will, the more middle-of-the-road liberal David Broder, to the out-and-out liberal Nicholas Van Hoffman; but it has only one political cartoonist, Herblock, who now closely reflects their editorial position.

But styles change and in the long run conservative institutions tend to be dominated by conservatives, so probably present trends should not be regarded as permanent or unchanging, any more than the turn-of-century muckraking style dominated comment of the twenties.

216. Draper Hill : (Nixon). May 3, 1974. Permission to reprint granted by *The Commercial Appeal,* Memphis.

217. Jim Palmer : "Ha! Ha! Ha!" October 3, 1972. Springfield (Mo.) *Leader Press.*

Two other astonishing facts I note in the editions of the *Best Editorial Cartoons* edited by Charles Brooks.[5] Each contains the work of 140 or so cartoonists with several of the best-known not included. What is striking are the number of smaller papers now having political cartoonists. Many of these have never before, or not for some time, had them. Most are in growing cities with in larger metropolitan areas rather than in small towns. Second, most of these new recruits follow a similar style, one I haven't precisely described as yet but one that could be called political one-liner. It's a style closer to Herblock in the verbal joke and closer to Oliphant in artistic mood, but without tragic overtones or penetrating bite. But the new kind of editorial art is in a real sense unlike either. It is more inclined to making jokes out of politics than in sugar-coating serious political messages with humor or fanciful imagery.

218. Charles Brooks : "You blasted idiot! I keep telling you I'm feeling fine!"
1972. Birmingham (Ala.) *News.*

A Closing Note

   As much as before, modern editorial cartoon comment is laughing satire. The
destructiveness and vulgarity of the Gillray type seem to cause its own recoil.
Democracies require civilized comment for their public discussion, and America,
despite what one might expect, appears to be no exception. Its modern political

cartoons show signs of having grown up somewhat. By this I mean, I suppose, that the old clichés are no longer appropriate since their falsity is readily apparent. This includes all of the high-blown sentiment and simple-minded ultranationalism more common in the past, as well as the trite liberal opinion that sees us every day in every way getting better and better. Unfortunately it doesn't yet include tossing out all of the new clichés too.

What this trend reflects is a growing-up, not only of cartoonists but of America as well. Public discussion has a new seriousness; perhaps sometimes regrettably. Problems no longer seem so simple, nor are the solutions so inevitable. Psychology, with its knowledge of the kinkiness within humans, seems especially relevant to some for providing insights into why things go haywire. Every generation probably feels that its predecessors lived in a state of blissful innocence, so why should we be an exception?

Most important, when faced with sometimes tragic events, the cartoonist has had humor come riding in from the wings. We no longer can settle for a steady diet of high-minded pretentiousness to dodge the issue. In the American editorial cartoon it is humor that gives us the courage to look at reality and face up to it. It also, in its way, provides a faith that in the end humans may somehow win out.

12

Politics in the Comics

The comics have always been more than pure fun drawings. From the beginning they have been full of social comment and occasionally have drifted off into political comment. The first sequence of a comic, Richard Outcault's yellow kid in February 16, 1896, was titled "The Great Dog Show in M'Googan Avenue." It was a Hogan's Alley tenement takeoff on the fancier Madison Square Garden dog shows of high society. As Steve Harvey of the Los Angeles *Times* correctly observes, the yellow kid was "guttersnipe impudence towards the Establishment."[1] This kind of Huck Finn thumbing of the nose at social sacred cows has never been completely eliminated from the comics, even in its action and soap-opera phase in the thirties. What it has earned them is a big bushel basket of criticism from school teachers for their violence, bad grammar, and questionable morality — criticisms, I should add, that seem just, though not particularly upsetting.

This frowning on the funnies by the better elements because of the possible effect of comics on the young, became especially focused as syndication became big business at about the time of World War I. At one time King Features had a written list of 35 major "don'ts", and many more that were just taken for granted. Mort Walker, the artist who draws Beetle Bailey, as late as 1973 was carrying on a running feud with his syndicate because they carefully airbrushed out the belly buttons he drew on females.

Despite these occasional clashes between artist and syndicate, many of the previous barriers to social comment are now down, and those involving politics are being more loosely applied. I want to review briefly some of the major landmarks in respect to political comment in the syndicated comics. But I want to emphasize that these cartoons are the exception. — Most comics try only to entertain, a few others champion social causes from time to time, but very, very few openly show their political biases, even today.

The Comics in Politics

In the 1920s Andy Gump ran for president. Predictably, and who is to say such citizens were any more misguided than their fellows, he got some write-in votes in the actual election against Calvin Coolidge, John W. Davies, and Robert LaFollette, Sr. But the satire, if one can call it that, was pretty mild, and all in what was widely advertised as "in good fun."

The years immediately following President Roosevelt's election in 1932 seem to have been a turning point for serious political comment in the comics with differing results for two artists. The earliest clash I can find is between Percy Crosby and the Hearst organization, which syndicated his strip "Skippy."

As a doughboy, Captain Percy Crosby drew a World War I comic private. After the war he began publishing in *Life*, where he developed the appealing and mischievous small boy cartoon "Skippy." In the late twenties this was picked up by the newspaper syndicates. At the same time he began showing paintings in prominent art museums. Meanwhile, he was also off on a private crusade against prohibition. As our story opens, Crosby's strip was at the height of its national popularity and he was in his prime. In 1931 a movie had been made of it, featuring the child star Jackie Cooper. A sequel, "Sooky," was in preparation. At this point Crosby veered to a new hobby horse. Crosby writes :

> In 1933, when the nation seemed to be overpowered with Communist propaganda, I decided to attack such condition, and, at the same time to attempt to awaken the patriotism of the nation on Memorial Day. I sent a strip where Skippy prayed for a return to American standards.[3]

In the strip Crosby had Skippy praying to stop the reduction of the army and navy and included such sentiments as "Lot of the girls laugh at a feller now if he stands up for his country. It just seems out of date 'cause the girls all listen to the fellers who boast that they won't fight for this nation" and "I couldn't salute the red flag, God, I just can't!"

The syndicate gulped (!*!) (gasp!), and suggested to Crosby that the cartoon be sent out as an extra strip, compliments of Percy Crosby. Crosby bridled and insisted the strip be released through regular channels. And so it was, printed, he says, by every subscriber except the Des Moines *Register and Tribune*.

In the months that followed Crosby had a running battle with the syndicate head, which he began to interpret as a conspiracy to silence him; perhaps even a New Deal or Communist inspired plot to keep him quiet through censorship and harassment. He vowed, however, not to be throttled in his crusades against "Communism, pacifism, prohibition, and gangsterism." (One character, "Spumoni" was used to attack Al Capone). He ran ads in The New York *Times* attacking Franklin Rooservelt and his other political enemies including on occasion among them the Hearst syndicate. He wrote books and pamphlets that he published himself, gave lectures, and kept introducing his patriotic sentiments from time to time in his Skippy comics. The Hearst organisation went along but with a little foot-dragging and questioning. From then on Crosby was in continual conflict and turmoil. The next crisis came when cartoon sizes were reduced, a clear blow to an artist who favoured long philosophical conversations among his small-boy protagonists. Crosby again took out national ads, and continued to publish books about the New Deal as a probable Communist plot in what today we would call the radical right style. Finally, in ill health at age 51, and now into his third marriage, Crosby in 1942 abandoned the Skippy cartoon to devote full time to his crusades. In 1948 he had a mental breakdown. He died in a mental institution in December 1964. His daughter claims his copyright was violated freely.

It is an interesting story that deserves a biographer. What it tells is that, at this point at any rate, King Features didn't welcome even patriotic politicking in the comics. Taking political stands in the comics entailed high risk.

A more notorious crusader against the New Deal was Harold Gray, whose strip "Little Orphan Annie" was syndicated through the Chicago *Tribune* — New York *News* Service. Begun in 1924, it did not take on the big political battles until the thirties. It differed from "Skippy" in that the politics was an integral part of the story line, and that story line, while melodramatic, hooked readers. In 1934 Richard Neuberger, later Democratic senator from Oregon called the attention of liberals to the propaganda line in the strip, and in the following decades there were frequent

219. Percy Crosby : How did Uncle Sam get the B.T.'s anyway? 1933. *Three Cheers for the Red, Red and Red.* **Reprinted with permission of Joan Crosby Tibbetts.**

articles or allusions especially in journals of the left, to Daddy Warbucks and his fascistic allies.[4] The line taken in the strip was not too different from Crosby's : Straight-out verbal attack, with occasional violence mixed in on what its author called Reds, welfare chiselers, pinko professors, etc. with strong, ultra-nationalist, America-first flag-waving. In comparison, the political cartoons on the *Tribune* editorial page by McCutcheon peek out wan and weak.

When Gray died the *Tribune* tried a new artist, who changed the cartoons style and announced he was dropping the political line. But evidently it wasn't the same. The *Tribune* is now, several artists later, taking to reprinting the old Gray epics on Sundays. The one I saw recently had the little chatterbox eulogizing Teddy Roosevelt, with arf! arf! from Sandy.

By 1938 Ham Fisher had President Franklin Roosevelt himself in a panel of Joe Palooka. World champion Palooka had joined the French Foreign Legion and Fisher claimed he was stuck in getting him out. He hit on using a request by FDR to the President of France to get his champion prizefighter released from his five year hitch. The two-day appearance by FDR was not a political endorsement, but then, it didn't exactly help FDR's political opponents either.[5]

With the entrance of America into World War II, patriotism in the comics became the vogue, with a number of heroes enlisting in the armed forces in one way or another. "Terry and the Pirates" by George Wunder, had already been mixed up in the China-Japanese conflict. Steve Canyon, by Milt Caniff, adopted the Air Force for his own and, during the war and later, frequently became a mouthpiece for its point of view. Buzz Sawyer did it for the Navy. Other services found lesser champions. Comic heroes chased Nazi spies and foiled the wily Jap, or, like Skeezix, enlisted and had an honorable service career at the front.[6]

With the end of the war and the beginning of the cold war, a few cartoon characters continued to foil plots against the nation. The Chicago *Tribune* — New York *News* Service encouraged Smiling Jack in his Red hunting, and permitted Dick Tracy to become more outspoken about the effect of Supreme Court decisions on criminal activity; and Little Orphan Annie went merrily on. By the sixties Buzz Sawyer was in Vietnam, someone called Thorn McBride was attacking "fuzzy-minded" pacifists, and Winnie Winkle took a fashion show to Russia, where the Kremlin sabotaged it. Clearly, a little politics could be used to prop up a sagging plot line.[7]

But even most of these few cartoonists who let politics enter in did it as a quick flash to titillate reader interest, much as Ham Fisher had done earlier with Palooka and FDR. In the early 1950s *The Nation* approvingly was calling the attention of its readers to a sequence in a strip called "Napoleon and Uncle Elby," in which Uncle Elby defends his dog Napoleon against a neighbor, Bessie Bigotry, who was for restricting the neighborhood to keep out mongrel dogs. I personally would not have been pleased as Punch, or even as the *Nation,* to be so patronized if I were a black, green, or yellow, but the pickings were slimmer then.[8]

Somewhere in this period Al Capp's "Lil Abner," which had long specialized in biting social comment, drifted over occasionally into political satire. Capp found that he had struck a gold lode and proceeded to belabor conservatives of various stripes. When *The World of Lil Abner* was published in 1952, it had an introduction by John Steinbeck, who described Capp as "the best writer in America today," and "very possibly the best satirist since Laurence Sterne," and added : "It is one thing to criticise and quite another to make the criticized not only admit but accept and enjoy criticism. I can think only of Cervantes and Rabelais who have succeeded in doing this before Capp," and "if the Nobel Prize committee is at all alert, they should seriously consider him." Also thrown in was a complimentary foreword by Charles Chaplin.[9]

The traditional Capp formula was to do stereotypes of the money-hungry millionaire, like J. Roaringham Fatback and General Bullmoose, or the society matron and her son Dumpington VanLump, or Rockwell P. Squeezeblood of the Squeezeblood Comic Strip Syndicate, and any other of dozens of exploiters of the common man. He then hit on parodies of living persons, giving them new names, such as Orson Wagon for a young genius of a movie director. By the 1960s he had moved directly into politics with these parodies, but the politics of Capp had changed. Whereas in the introduction to his 1952 book he spoke disparagingly of comics about "Little orphan girls with no daddy but the NAM to guide them," in 1970 he did an introduction to *Arf! The Life and Hard Times of Little Orphan Annie 1935-1945*, in which he wrote : "Harold Gray was a sharper observer of American trends, a truer prophet of America's future than Walter Lippmann. He created characters that have endured longer than Upton Sinclair's. He drew better pictures, in his seventies, than Picasso did."[10] I am not familiar enough with introductions to comic books to know whether such high-flown rhetoric is typical of them, or just of books Al Capp is associated with.

One of Capp's later-day crusades was against Joanie Phoanie, who sang peace songs on campuses. Another opposed S.W.I.N.E., Students Wildly Indignant About Nearly Everything. The sequence running in the Sunday papers as I write this begins "Poor people can't afford to live in Hyidealsport but they're perfectly welcome there — as stable hands, cleaning women, and dog walkers." The sequence features a chubby playboy type, talking high ideals with liberal rich friends by the side of what is unidentified, but looks suspiciously like a Massachusetts-type swimming pool.

Steinbeck's introduction to the 1952 book contains true prophecy. He wrote: "Being a writer I have found one thing that is pretty general. As soon as you get readers first to read and then to like your stuff, you find they want to write it for you. If you write anything that startles them or changes their opinion of what they expected you to write, they get pretty mad. A writer is somewhat in the same position as a baseball player. In either art it is very easy to go from a hero to a bum."

Capp has followed such a trajectory in the opinion of many in the critical media. Professor Roy Paul Nelson notes : "If Capp is no longer admired by the critics (one recent history of the comic strips labeled his work "tasteless"), it is because he made the mistake of directing his barbs at the extreme left with the same gusto he directed them at the ultraright."[11]

Capp himself says : "When I aimed at the right, I was on the cover of *Life,* I was on TV shows. I was the darling of the media. When I took on the left, I became a leper — except for the people. I must say it's been a hard road. I feel like the last rabbi left in Berlin."[12]

The next significant political breakthrough in the comics was Walt Kelly's "Pogo," begun in syndication in 1949. Kelly was art editor and editorial cartoonist on the New York *Star,* the short-lived survivor from Marshall Field's liberally oriented and adless *PM,* and he developed the feature there in 1948. Before that he had worked for five years with Walt Disney and during the war, for the U.S. Army.

Pogo's cartoon political takeoffs are many, but best remembered seems to be Simple J. Malarkey, a nasty-looking bobcat, who appeared at the time when Senator Joseph McCarthy claimed to be Communist hunting. Other animals resembling Khrushchev and Castro have appeared, and the John Birch society has also come in for its lumps. Pogo, the hero of the strip, was described by Kelly as being "the reasonable, patient, softhearted, naive, friendly little person we all think we are."[13]

The problem with the Pogo strip is that its humor and asides are somewhat subtle and even esoteric, so that it is widely regarded as a comic drawn for a highbrow elite

332

rather than the masses. It seems to make some of the latter feel left out. When I was a kid the average reader felt the same way about George Herriman's "Krazy Kat," and if the truth be known, I thought they were right then, as I still do now.

More recently, "Doonesbury," by Garry Trudeau, has joined Capp in zeroing in on politics for a wide audience. For his effort he won a Pulitzer prize for editorial cartooning in 1975. The strip's approach is that of the liberal, college-educated left, and Trudeau raises issues and deals with political events that concern that group. It features, for a sampling, a John Birch-type football hero, his Viet Cong friend Phred, a Marxist rich Jew out to convert blue-collar construction workers, an anti-lib female named Boopsy, a liberated middle-aged woman who has become the strip's most popular character, a Rolling Stone named Duke, his freaked-out nephew named Zonker, and many more. Who is this favored group? One notes that he treads lightly on the old upper middle class—his targets seem to be similar to those of the old *Life* of Charles Dana Gibson and of the college-bred intellectuals of the old *Masses*.

220.   Garry Trudeau : (Nixon and Lincoln strip.) May 1974.

What the strip does is make the far-out counter-culture types a little more believable and likable for the rest of us philistines, which means that from time to time we find, to our astonishment, ... we feel real sympathy for them. It puts the issues these types think important, and their points of view, on the agenda. Thus, I think it is without question the best political strip going at present. To boot, it is the most imaginative comic strip to hit the papers since the early "Lil Abner."

What a brief survey like this also suggests is that politics in the comics has been a risky business. Almost all of the artists who have introduced serious political comment have had strips dropped by individual papers subscribing to the syndicate output. A number have also been recipients of some fairly ponderous editorial criticism from the right and the left. The Catholic journal *America* in "No Go Pogo" slapped Kelly's wrist for satirizing Castro and Khrushchev, while *Commonweal*, also Catholic, defended him.[14] The battle over "Little Orphan Annie" raged in the liberal journals until Gray's death, when the strip's new continuity writer as noted stipulated, in taking over Annie and Sandy, that there "be no more John Birch stuff."[15]

A second fact is that to get away with serious political comment rather than titillation means building it into the guts of the strip itself. "Little Orphan Annie" did this with blood and thunder; "Lil Abner" did it with outrageous satirical fairy tales. "Doonesbury" makes it an integral part of each character, so that politics is as much a part of each personality as, say, his or her love life. One can hardly think of any of the characters without thinking at the same time of their political personalities.

A third fact is that only a small handful of comics dare to or care to treat any political subjects seriously. Most just use a little safe politics for show or minor shock value to snatch back lagging interest. Most are entertainers pure and simple. "The Wizard of Id" by Johnny Hart is a little closer to politics. It deals with the problems of monarchy and ruling just as O. Soglow's "Little King" of the thirties did. But this, like the content of Charles Schultz's "Peanuts," is usually closer to social than to political satire. The political satirists are Kelly, Capp, and Trudeau; the first two of whom are no more. They are joined by the creators of a few flag-waving adventure strips still slogging along to the tune of the spirit of '76.

Garry Trudeau says that a major characteristic of his kind of political comment is that politics in the comics always has to take second place, just as in most good political novels. He writes : "I am not an editorial cartoonist. My first aim is to entertain. Satire is my method, but it's not an end in itself." That being the case, the number of syndicated cartoons with genuine political comment is likely to remain limited, since, for most artists, to have to throw in a political theme only makes it a little harder to be entertaining.

I have omitted mention thus far of the underground political comics by Robert Crumb and others. The drawing of many of these is a parody of the old-time correspondence school cartooning art. The content is anti-Establishment politics, with wild humor tossed in. There's a no-holds-barred atmosphere that leaves me out. One sequence of Fritz the Cat features jamming coke bottles up females' rear ends for fun. I class this as sadism reminiscent of the Nazi's medical experiments and gas ovens.[16]

One first-rate underground cartoonist has surfaced, however: Ron Cobb of the Los Angeles *Free Press,* who published two paperback collections. His drawings are heavy black and white, and stark, with heavy black outlines in a kind of pseudo-representational style. They are in a square, black-bordered box and give off the mood of black humor.[17]

In an introduction, Cobb states his purpose as letting his viewers be "humbled by reality." The kind of reality he presents is the picture of reality seen underground by the intelligent and disillusioned draft dodger of the Vietnam War. His attack is on the big-mouthed, white middle-class, middle-aged, who, he concludes, made all the mess he sees around him. He expects,or assumes has already arrived, a police state of T-shirted yahoos.

If this were all, he would be ho hum. But he packages this message in a way that gives it tremendous visual impact. The scenes are drawn from every day life, or at least seem to be so at first. Occasionally they look like children at innocent play. But always a major injustice is neatly put on a pin to be destroyed. You get this in his best work only in a delayed reaction, because the message is coming through the drawing itself as your eye travels along. You take in the essentials of the picture at a glance and it seems all placid and sedate, until your eye is drawn along to the point where the incongruous wallop lies, partially hidden but there all along : the Indian skeletons under the pious family eating Thanksgiving dinner, the boys at the military academy practicing an execution off in a corner, the two pigs that are pontificating about the straying young piglets with a sign in the background that reads "Sausage City." The effect is shock, and a visual driving home of the point in a way to make it unforgettable.

A friend of his has told me that Cobb has pretty much given up cartooning and is driving a cab. If so, it is a loss. He would find it difficult to function as part of a mass media organization with its regular deadlines, but it would be worth trying all round.

Political-type fantasies also blossom in some comic books, using what may roughly be described as the old shazzam!! One that I have acquired features Prez, first "teen President" of the USA, versus the Boss of Slum City. Despite the posturing, the IQ level and sophistication of Prez are about what you would expect : not too far above that of the rah-rah Tom Swift series, despite the very hard trying to be cool.

The best magazine comics are those of *MAD* magazine, whose primary target is the business and especially advertising, world, rather than politics. Also on the newsstands is *The National Lampoon*.

The Editorial Page Box

Many editors feel that a good way to dress up all the unrelieved type of editorial pages, which are, of course, too sacrosanct and solemn for advertisments, is to balance the "serious" editorial cartoon with a boxed cartoon that features a little light political humor. A number of artists have made a good thing of this.

The formula takes about three routes. One is the Giles concoction of having a set of ordinary characters comment on or become involved in the days news. Norris does this with special effectiveness in the Vancouver *Sun,* and most editorial cartoonists try to throw in a cartoon like this from time to time . A second formula is to create political

221.   Frank Interlandi : "Take me to America, Comrade Angela Davis — I want to be oppressed like you are!" 1972. Editorial Cartoon by Frank Interlandi, Copyright, Los Angeles *Times.* Reprinted with permission.

stereotypes, the old Senator, etcetera, and have them go tumbling through the traditional hoops. In Britain, Osbert Lancaster has for perhaps thirty years or more been drawing a one-column feature he called a pocket cartoon. One of his standard characters is Maudie Littlehampton, who is described on the jacket of a collection of these as "that most baleful of characters...caustic, irrefutable and 'dead on.'" She is similar in many respects to the heroine of the American TV show, also called "Maude," the mod liberal. A similar American or Canadian feature is by Wick, a transplanted cockney. Brickman in "The Small Society" presents a beaten-down middle-aged American in a modern swinging world. Up in Boston in the *Herald* for many years, Francis Dahl did a daily strip gently chiding the Watch and Ward Society and commented lightly on various local events; most were nonpolitical.

The straight humor type of cartoon in America is best done, for my taste, by George Lichty, whose "Grin and Bear It" frequently features Senator Snort — staunch, fearless, atomic. A more biting version of this group is by Interlandi. Lancaster and Interlandi play a different game from that of the regular editorial cartoonist — their characteristic is entertainment and the inside joke, with pithy political comments thrown in.

A third formula is to use actual politicians, such as the President, chatting over events with wives or associates. The most successful at this gambit is Jim Berry's "World." He specializes in home scenes with the great, such as having Jimmy commenting to Rosalynn while he shaves and she combs her hair. The humor is light and with little of the sting of Lancaster or Interlandi, but with touches of humanzing, gentle humor as the great are reduced to scale.

Since David Levine reinvigorated caricature for the New York *Review of Books,* the field has revived. Levine caricatures are superb. Syndicated nationally are the caricatures of Renan Lurie. A particularly effective artist is Randy Jones of the New York *Times.*

The feature that I believe best blends entertainment with incisive editorial comment is the Jules Feiffer weekly offering. It doesn't quite fit any of the categories outlined so far, or perhaps fits all of them. Feiffer came out of comic-book art, did a movie cartoon, "Munro," before, in 1956, beginning publication in *The Village Voice.*

Feiffer's kind of entertainment holds us with a horrible fascination because we have all been there. In a kind of sloppy, meandering, high-middle-brow interview conducted by *Mademoiselle,* which announced a little daringly that they were now going to talk from time to time with those "whom we think of as Disturbers of the Peace,"[18] Feiffer states his creed as a cartoonist and is honest and serious enough to risk being thought somewhat brash. He says' "I think I'm a cartoonist who's commenting in stronger terms on urban times, on industrial man and woman in small and large terms than anybody has ever done in this form. I mean cartoons and commentators really. I don't mean to be modest, because I feel very proud and almost arrogant about it. Arrogant almost in an angry sense. I feel as if there is no competition and there should be. And goddamn it, there should be other people doing what I'm doing, because this is the road. This is what is really happening."

Feiffer is still waiting for competition. He lacks it because, unlike others, he is more willing than most to call the shots as he sees them, and this means more than dishing out the liberal line. He doesn't buy other people's formulas if he can help it. He tries to be, as he has said about himself, a nonpartisan radical, and the adjective has been harder to achieve these days than the noun. He is willing to take off the blinders when he can see enough to know they are there, and look at and report what he sees. He is seemingly not even afraid of being blacklisted by other intellectuals, which is the ultimate risk.

The Team

222.   David Levine : The Team. 1967. *No Known Survivors.* — **from** *No Known Survivors* **(New York Gambit, 1970). Reprinted with permission.**

The cartoons he draws are stylistically a recipe of what every cartoonist has been told not to do: unpolished drawing, little or no action, and much talk, talk, talk. But the formula is explosive. The characters are psychological types who are refugees from case histories. They try to explain what they experience to their own moral satisfaction and in the process the reader can only conclude that they are their own worst enemies. At the core of their rationalizing is what Feiffer's bartender defending the system of corruption states as the central problem : people publicly damn what they privately make their living out of. Feiffer's métier is spearing such hypocrisy — individual, social and political.

Much of Feiffer deals with the pseudo-Freudian, pseudo-intellectual, urban types who want to get with it and really swing, but who are, as he described himself, sore losers and guilty winners. It is in applying the formula in his strictly political cartoons that Feiffer tears off the mask most brutally. The white liberal and his token Negro are daring conceptions because of whom he attacks. While such cartoons have a nice bite, they are not his best. Rather the ones in which political actors explain why they do what they do, or at any rate try to do so, are the horrifyingly memorable. Few drawings have more deeply zinged to the heart of the subject of LBJ on Vietnam than "Death of Good Society." It is not only that it is devastating against LBJ in its pure vitriol; it is comment that goes beyond this and touches on tragedy. and leaves me, at any rate, with a sense of pity mixed with some loathing for LBJ as well as for the rest of us who lived through the period.

223. Jules Feiffer : (Great Society). Ca. 1967. *The Village Voice.* **Reprinted by permission of Jules Feiffer.**

Feiffer reports how he did a particularly strong cartoon on LBJ after the Detriot and Newark riots, "Let Us Reason Together," and then was disconcerted to have the White House request the original. Perhaps for that one, but not for "Good Society."[19]

I suppose I should take some note of the kind of avant-garde art that the New York *Times* has adopted for its Op Ed pages. If the purpose is to reproduce in pictorial form the shape and composition of the opinions expressed therein, I suppose it succeeds reasonably well and should be commended for its faithfulness to the truth-in-packaging concept. But as memorable political cartoons they are something else again.[20]

I do, however, recommend some of its more traditional art. The Senator weather vane used as frontispiece of this book and on the jacket is by Mischa Richter. It appeared on the New York *Times* Op-Ed page on August 4, 1974.

There are two other outlets for political cartoons that I shall mention only briefly : the book and the poster.

The book, especially the cheap paperback, has so far generally been used by cartoonists to reprint their already-published work for a wider audience, as in the "The Collected Cartoons of...," subtitled "A Cartoon History of Our Times." But some artists have drawn directly for the book form. This usually requires cartoons on a broad political theme, since it is difficult to build in current events and get into print on time. Of those already done, the theme of the threat of war is particularly popular. (Note the similarity to the old Pulitzer Prize themes.) In Britain a few such examples have occurred, which I list here in a footnote.[21] An American example was an anti-war book titled *John Brown's Body,* produced as Hitler got more hot and peppery, and which went nowhere. Osborn and James Thurber have both produced interesting anti-war books; the one by Thurber, *The Last Flower* is among his most moving works and is as close as we have to an American classic in this art form. The possibility always exists for a political cartoonist who is a newcomer to find his public through drawing such a political picture story book. Good luck!

The poster and broadsheet have been captured mainly by the cause groups as well they should be. A few are put out by ideologues of the right, but most are produced for the left, for college students and people who read carefully over the Marlboro book ads. A very few of these may be reprints of cartoons produced in other media. Some are originals and are quite good, but few have reached the popularity of James Montgomery Flagg's "Uncle Sam Needs You and You and You." The trouble is that the demand for posters is erratic. Few political cartoonists have found a way to make a steady living out of the poster market.[22]

A Closing Note

The political comic is an anomaly. First of all, we don't want or need too many of them in the funnies. We look at the comics for escape, and a steady diet of propagandizing, particularly by the less skillful, would get to be a painful bore, or so I would argue, if Blondie and the rest of the crew all set up soap boxes for the next election.

Second, the political comics that are just gentle spoofing — the Andy Gump-for-President type — are little more than a passing gesture. Like McCutcheon's nostalgia, they are nice to have around to dress up a dull page of type or even the funny page, and that is perhaps justification enough. They have had their sting removed and so hardly count as political.

But the truly political comic skillfully done, could become the most destructive of graphic weapons. The underground cartoonists show this potential, most closely approached in the mass media by an occasional Jules Feiffer or Trudeau, or particularly unsubtle Lil Abner or Little Orphan Annie episodes. These slice deep — deeper than a good many of the ordinary run of editorial cartoons, including, I would add, much of the seriously lugubrious satire of the straight underground editorial cartoon. The style permits a little skin diving into the political psyche in a way the straight box does not.

But the style can also be adapted to laughing satire, as Feiffer and Trudeau also illustrate. That so few editorial artists have used comic-strip continuity for an occasional series of cartoons suggests how difficult it is compared to creating the stereotyped series of the Great Powers playing cribbage or the visual political joke Marx Brothers-style.

Oliphant's penguin, Punk, in part provides this kind of comic-continuity line. The familiar characters that keep reappearing in Herblock and other cartoons do so too. Nevertheless, I have the feeling that a potential is still there to exploit, one that would attract and hold attention in a way that few regular editorial cartoonists can.

13

Other Democracies and Their Cartoons

When David Low arrived in England from Australia in 1920, he was determined to make the big splash. In his autobiography later, he proclaimed that he had pioneered a new, modern kind of cartooning — a tearing away from the stodginess and gentility of the Victorian cartoon. Back to Gillray for Low, back to the alley-cat artist who tried irreverently to portray his opinions of government policy in the pictures he drew of the politicians who made those policies. This is what Low aspired to.

It is appropriate to begin this brief review of cartoons in other stable democracies by looking at the cartoons of Britain before, after, and during Low. I re-ask the question: Does the style of pragmatic trimmer always characterize the mass cartoon output of stable democracies, or is something else possible and even desirable?

British Cartoons From Tenniel to Low

Earlier I covered cartoon development in Britain from the moralistic realism of Hogarth to the shock-nihilism style of Gillray. The last gasp of the Georgian irreverence was found in the work of Paul Pry (William Heath) in 1829-1830. Following this is an astonishing period of politer work, beginning with HB (John Doyle), eight years before the accession of Victoria and three years before the Reform Bill was passed. John Leech built upon this new trend and it was brought to full fruition in the cartoon of John Tenniel.[1] It should be noted that these Victorians, while polite and gentlemanly, nevertheless faithfully fulfilled David Low's criteria of a good cartoonist — as well, one is tempted to say, as he did himself. They embodied in their caricatures of the leading policy-makers of their day a clear and unambiguous statement of their opinion of the policies they made. Where they varied from Low is that they approved mightily of those policies.

Some time in the seventies or eighties however, we can detect the beginning of an artistic parting of the ways. One stream continues in the Tenniel tradition — carries on in fact, as already noted, all the way up to the end of World War II. The other stream begins in what seems now like fairly tame comment on some of the limitations of the Victorian system. This type of cartoon comes into its own when World War I smashed the Victorian system, The Tenniel cartoon-line from that point dips sharply and gradually dies out. Let us first examine the Tenniel type of cartoon, which continued to dominate the mass media through World War I and which David Low was reacting to so negatively.

Tenniel's colleague, drawing *Punch's* second cartoon from the middle eighties on, was Linley Sambourne. Most of his contemporaries rated him as high, or higher as an artist, as the master. His best work is imaginative with an ethereal, poetic quality, but somehow it does not stick in the mind as Tenniel's often more awkward tableaus do.

But other successors of Tenniel were less skillful in their art. The kind of full-bloom stuffiness that Low complained of does indeed characterize the cartoons of the latter-

224.   Linley Sambourne : The Stationary Crusader. President Roosevelt : Follow me (or 35,000 words to that effect). December 11, 1907. *Punch.*

day *Punch* crew, most especially the cartoons of Sir Bernard Partridge, whom I will use as a horrible example. Partridge continued to draw *Punch* cartoons every week through 1945. Sir Bernard lacked many things, but especially the humor of Sir John Tenniel, and so missed one important self-corrective to moral pontificating or coming to believe too much in one's own rhetoric. He also did not possess the soaring imagination of Linley Sambourne. Finally, his art stylistically rang as true as a quarter made out of plastic. Partridge's cartoons are full of the swank and false sentiment of World War I recruiting posters. He portrays political actions on a broad stage and seems to aspire to the nobility that Tenniel's art actually projected. But he missed it. The actors always look as if they had just got dressed up for a masquerade ball or a stage play in the provinces What saves them and makes them still worth looking at for

225.   Bernard Partridge : Unconquerable. The Kaiser : "So you see — you've lost everything." The King of the Belgians : "Not my soul." 1915. *Punch*.

a little while is that Partridge believed in this kind of old-fashioned flummery. It may be a world long gone and one, it should be noted, that Partridge hardly experienced for very long himself, but it is nevertheless a world that Partridge seems to have genuinely admired. In leafing through his work one sometimes wishes for a flashing moment that the modern world might be that way, if any world in fact ever was so.

Leonard Raven-Hill, Partridge's colleague on *Punch*, drew cartoons that certainly reached the level of workmanlike quality found in the average daily newspaper cartoon of today, but his work did not send viewers, then or now, into ecstasies of admiration. The same may be said of the political work of his colleagues F.H. Townshend and Frank Reynolds.

A little more favorable comment may be made on the work of England's first regular newspaper cartoonist, F. Carruthers Gould. He lacked artistic style and technique, but he caricatured faces well and he was at least on the attack rather than shamming a charge. His series of drawings on Joe Chamberlain, circa 1902-1904, fit Low's specifications very well; at least, from viewing Gould's output on Chamberlain I for one conclude that I would not care to have Joe Chamberlain taking care of the details of a will in which I was mentioned as a major heir. Also in the papers were W. K. Haselden, who adapted a comic-strip format to light comment on politics and Illingsworth, who drew in the old style up into the 1970s.

226. Frederick C. Gould : Spectacular Deception. Joe : Now then, gents you may think this loaf is a little un, but you just look at it through these patent Imperial Protection double magnifying spectacles, and you'll see the Loaf as large as you like. The Working Man : That's all very well, mister, but we want to *eat* the loaf, not look at it. June 27, 1903. Westminster *Gazette*.

227. Matt Morgan : Britannia's New Year Gift. January 1864.

Punch had another deleterious effect on British political cartoonists. It encouraged the lighthearted-nonsense type of humor cartoon, especially in the forced funny period of Francis Burnand's editorship (1880-1906) and the bland gentility era under Owen Seaman (1906-1932). While few of its artists applied the *Punch* comic, cute mood to political subjects, it slopped over into the work of others. For example, Poy (Percy Fearon), in newspaper cartoons, created such cut-out correspondence school characters as Government Gus, Dilly and Dally, and the rest of a crew that reminds one of Dorothy Parker's review of A.A. Milne, "Tonstant Weader Twowed Up." Score more points for Low. The political cartoon had degenerated so far that even humor didn't prick for much political purpose.

So, on balance, Low was right about the situation. Political heirs of Tenniel were getting more and more out of touch with reality in content and style and are a decline from the great Victorians. Cartoonists were peddling stale bread — and fake stale bread at that — rather than baking up their own concoctions with ingredients from the real world, as, incidentally, the Victorians had done.

But what of the other stream, the artists who may be playing second fiddle to the dominant theme, but who in a very real sense prepared the way for David Low. I believe that the high tide of Victorian dominance comes in the 1870 and at that point the changes begin to surface. Contrast two cartoons by Matt Morgan. The first, published in January 1864, shows Britannia offering peace to the world as traditional and Victorian as Tenniel. The second dates from five years later when Morgan started a magazine called *Tomahawk*. For us its title overstates its content, but not for fellow Victorians. It collapsed under severe criticism after a few years and Morgan shipped off to the New World to compete with Thomas Nast. The second Morgan cartoon from *Tomahawk* was thought to be extremely daring because it showed royalty in a very unfavourable light. The wayward young Edward VII is shown following the ghost of the self-indulgent George IV. The message of course urges the young prince to embrace truth and beauty and other Victorian virtues, as his faithful retainers clearly wish him to, but it also pushes into the foreground the question, After the Good Queen Victoria — what? Troubling.[2]

228.   Matt Morgan : The P****e of W***s to K**g G****e IV *(loq.)* "I'll follow thee!" 1867. *Tomahawk*.

In the eighties we get further occasional crossing of the line that Tenniel drew between respectable and unrespectable political art. A series of anonymous pamphlets that the British Museum now credits to George Stonach handles Gladstone roughly.[3] The cartoon reprinted here shows him as a common highwayman who has just committed murder. Not all go this far, but none appear to give "proper deference". In 1884, Tom Merry in St. Stephen's *Review* for a few issues left behind the usual staid style to portray William Gladstone as the hero of a parody of Hogarth's "The Rakes Progress" — Pretty gamey stuff.

Interestingly enough another jarring note comes from the *Punch* staff itself when Harry Furniss joined the table in 1880. Furniss had a real talent for catching a likeness quickly and accurately. But the late Victorians began to notice there was frequently a kind of nastiness about his art that one could not quite put one's finger on. It was a little like the person who imagines he is being clever and funny when he is perhaps only

229. George Stonach : The New Policy. "The uncrowned King" has changed his note, to quell the Irish row; And William G. has turned his coat, and goes Moonlighting now." Ca. 1884.

230. Tom Merry : The Rake's Progress. 1884. St. Stephen's *Review.*

being cruel. Not quite right, you know. Furniss left the journal in the nineties to start one of this own. He later drifted into movie making both in Britain and the United States and ended his days in writing and lecturing on how to be a cartoonist. He is such a jarring note because he was clearly talented and because he worked for that haven of Victorian respectability. *Punch.*

231.   Harry Furniss : Gladstone, Ca. 1890. *Punch.*

A farther loosing of Victorian inhibitions in the 1890s occurred notably in the mainly nonpolitical drawings of Aubrey Beardsley and Max Beerbohm. Beardsley developed his art style in an astonishingly short period of about seven years before his early death (1872-1898). His work was indirectly political, in that in straining to break down the constraints surrounding sex, he also encouraged a questioning of the other orthodoxies of Victorianism.

Max Beerbohm's political impact was a little more direct. As one of his biographers says, he was a "royalty-baiter" all his life. Beerbohm drew some rather wickedly penetrating caricatures of Britain's rulers, but his work appeared in limited editions for the high brows rather than in the mass market. It is hard to fault "The Rare and Rather Awful Visits of Albert Edward, Prince of Wales to Windsor Castle." Standing in the corner, being punished is a fat, bloated slothful Prince of some 60 years. An enraged and tearfully angry mother, Queen Victoria, fills up front stage.

232. Max Beerbohm : The Rare, The Rather Awful Visits of Albert Edward, Prince of Wales, to Windsor Castle. Ca. 1892.

Beerbohm's delightful series of eleven prints on William Gladstone's adventures in Heaven is also penetratingly funny (Fig. 3). Beerbohm also produced a work that had a small printing. It contained fifteen prints that contrasted the traditional John Bull image with the way Beerbohm claimed it was in the real world of post Boer War times, the latter of which was clearly less self assured or quick on the uptake.

Beerbohm's inspiration for his caricatures was pure Victorian. In the 1870s the British journal *Vanity Fair* had for a few years produced a weekly caricature by

Pelligrini, an Italian who signed himself Ape. Some of those works had as much bite as Beerbohm's did later. In time Ape was succeeded by Sir Leslie Ward, who signed himself Spy. Ward's early work was also sometimes stinging, but more and more his work became less caricature and more representational and flattering. As he approached retirement in 1915, he was knighted.

Beerbohm admired Ape and as an exercise copied his works as a means of encouraging inspiration in his own. His unique contribution was to sharpen Ape's irreverence. It was precisely this quality that Gould and Raven-Hill lacked, in an age when royalty and all other traditional institutions were coming under challenge to again justify themselves.

Also appearing in the nineties were the privately printed drawings of Cynicus (J. Martin Anderson), whose message was anti-capitalist and skeptical about the goodness of man. Cynicus mixed a Thackeray type of worldliness with an awareness of the exploitation of the lower orders. For a short time his drawings were faddish, but like those of Beerbohm and Beardsley, they remained out of the mainstream of opinion.

233. Cynicus (J. Martin Anderson) : With wealth, it matters not how vile you be; The world forgives all sin but poverty. Ca. 1895.

The only really savage comments in British newspaper cartoons before World War I were again out of the mainstream. These were the exceptional drawings of Will Dyson, a native Australian who drew for smaller-circulation Socialist publications and eventually the Socialist *Daily Herald*. His prewar cartoons attacked Victorian humbuggery in such wonderful cartoons as "Art Holding the Mirror up to Nature," in which a frumpy Britannia views herself as a svelte princess in a mirror held up to her by a flattering boy, the Royal Academy painter. His stance of contempt for what he regarded as illegitimate authority was released even more fully during World War I.

234. **Will Dyson : The Death Certificate (Women's Suffrage).** First Baby Farmer to Second Ditto (in mutual congratulations upon having succeeded in obtaining a Death Certificate) : "Of course ol'dear, you mus' hexpec' these parients to be onreasonable and plejudiced about these things, but wot I ses is — What right indeed 'as any child to be allowed to live when a hexpert ses it can't, and him the first Commoner in Hingland — I knows me place better." 1913. London *Daily Herald*.

He let loose his fury in an attack on German Kultur portraying the Kaiser as the devil's colleague in plotting evil. After the war he lost his fire and eventually drifted into attacks on bankers while embracing Canada's funny-money Social Credit party. Thus the dominant cartooning did conform to Low's strictures. Yet there were certain straws blowing about in a way to suggest that the wind had shifted in his direction.

David Low and His Successors

So Low came on the scene with great rumbling, playing to the hilt the character of the brash young colonial iconoclast. What Low did was a great deal; he brought to fruition a cartooning suited to modern conditions. He insured that after others saw his work their drawings would change in the direction of a more irreverent mood and a zippier artistic style. His bold, black- and- white brushwork, in oblong boxes wider than high, literally jumps out of a page of the old-style crosshatchers. There is a white spaciousness about them that demands attention. Besides having served a thorough artistic apprenticeship under the old system, Low had other advantages. He had some notion of the kind of snap a modern cartoon might have. He also shared the modern mood of reform. To this he added the talents that make a great cartoonist — humor, biting sarcasm, knowledge of politics, imagination and skepticism — and the ability to put it all across in his drawings. But Gillray he was not.

Whereas the eighteenth century printmakers, whom Low so much admired, were uninhibited primitives, Low was always to some extent chained to the system by his sense of decency and by social constraint. In 1936, when he visited America at the height of the Wallis Simpson-Edward row, he lamented that there was a gentleman's agreement that the royal family could not be caricatured in Britain except with the greatest dignity. "No one has done so in England," he said, "since the beginning of Victoria's reign"[6] Low could poke and jab other parts of the system forcefully, as in his Col. Blimp drawings, but these did not inspire hatred in reaction. One critic, rather, summed up the Colonel as "a pathetic, pompous, old walrus", and a movie made about him even makes him into a wonderful old hero.

Churchill, in his *Thoughts and Adventures*, characterized Low as "a green-eyed young Antipodean radical... particularly mischievous.... Low's pencil is not only not servile. It is essentially mutinous." But this was the restless, out-of-power Churchill. He

235. **Will Dyson : St. George, Defender of the Dragon.** *The Anti-Suffrage Knight* : Back, thou vote-snatching hussy, or I shall carve thee to the chine in defense of my exclusive right to defend thee from all maid-devouring dragons. *Suffrage "Hammerzon"* : But, old fraud, you know you are only defending a dragon from me. *Anti-Suffrage Knight* : Madam, don't descend to vulgar personalities. You know perfectly well there is a perpetual close season for dragons nowadays. 1913. London *Daily Herald*.

was wrong. Low might nag and nag, and even take some nasty swipes at the British system, but divorce was wholly out of the question. He would paint his victims mostly as stupid rather than as depraved and evil. Only in his anti-Hitler drawings, just preceding and during the war, was the artistic lid ever close to off, as it almost always was for Gillray. Here he could portray the depths of evil without feeling that he was losing his audience or making himself ridiculous.

If ever a man wanted to cross the line of respectability and restraint to become a force for radical reform, Low, as I read him, was that man. But as a prisoner of democratic civility, the libel laws, his sense of humor, and his own sense of fairness, such as it was, he was held back in his lashing out. He was essentially the middle-class reformer cleaning out the weeds and rubbish and laying out the stakes where a better world, hopefully was to be built. He epitomizes, I think, the best that may be expected of a democratic cartoonist. He well characterized himself as "a nuisance dedicated to sanity." Low was described elsewhere as someone who taught the common man to recognize who his enemies were, and that is a judgment that any democrat should be proud to have stamped on his or her work. I personally regard it as a higher honor than any James Gillray can be said to have attained.

Low, then, becomes a suitable anchor point at one end of the democratic continuum. Like the modern American cartoonists, he was domesticated to a degree

236.   David Low : The Man Who Took the Lid Off. October 4, 1935. London *Evening Standard.* **By permission of the trustees of the Low estate and the London** *Evening Standard.*

237. David Low : Stepping Stones to Glory. July 8, 1936. London *Evening Standard.* **By permission of the Low estate and the London** *Evening Standard.*

that Thomas Nast or Homer Davenport were not. While he demonstrated that domesticated cartoonists are not the same as puerile or stuffed-shirt cartoonists, he did not run completely free. The stings he let loose were deep enough to cause pain and were presumably to bring about some change, but he held a little back. The next question is whether all modern British cartoonists share this reserve.

Low's best-known competitor, Sidney Strube, hardly survives, except that his publishers, out to boom circulation for *The Daily Express,* had the foresight to put his work between covers — in up to around eight or nine paperback annuals. These cartoon collections shout out "the old pro." The drawing is modern and somewhat like Low's, but the imagery and mood are less so. Strube perhaps reinvented and certainly gave a big push to the situation-comedy kind of cartoon — the politicians in funny situations in cartoons like that of the lowly taxpayer on his way to the scaffold. Out were the old, solemn, pageants; in was a new liveliness. Strube kept the best of Poy's kind of figure, as "the rest of us," to stand for John Citizen. He presented a good deal of good-humored political caricatures of Britain's leaders in the kind of ridiculous poses that a man enjoys getting hold of and having framed for his office, to show that he also enjoys a good bit of joshing and can take a good joke about himself. What they lack is that, as a form of political entertainment, the critical comment when it's there tends to get lost in all the hilarity. They are almost completely innocent of political bite.

The cartoonists in the decades to follow develop these two streams. Low's spiritual and, some time later, actual successor on the *Evening Standard* was Vicky, Victor

238.   Sidney Strube : The Aristocrat. "Well, at any rate, it does make a fellow feel important." 1932. London *Daily Express.* Beaverbrook Newspapers, Ltd.

Weiss, a Hungarian Jewish refugee and dedicated Socialist. His style developed into a looser, jerkier, and purposely less-polished drawing than Low's but his content was similar. His Super-Mac cartoons of Conservative Prime Minister Harold Macmillan are his easiest to remember, but some of his other work has a little more venomous bite. But Vicky also saw the system as capable of peaceful reform. When he lost faith, he chose suicide over cynicism or revolution. He took his life, in despair, his biographer reports, at the Labour Government's actions after being returned to office in the sixties.[8]

A second artist, Michael Cummings, of the *Daily Express,* is also of the Low tradition, and in fact comes closer in many ways to the quality of Low than does Vicky. But he is unlike Low and Vicky in holding a moderately conservative view of politics. His caricatures are full of humor and some bite and, as a running commentary on the politics of a period, are much easier to take than the usual collection labeled "A Cartoon History of Our Times." I recommend him, especially for his handling of the Labour Party in power.[9]

Also with more comic art and considerable liveliness is Wally Fawkes, who signs himself Trog. Half of his charm is the grotesqueness of his large-head-small-body caricatures.

239. Vicky (Victor Weiss) : "The Prime Minister and I are always in agreement" — (Mr. Butler). June 17, 1964. London *Evening Standard*. Beaverbrook Newspapers , Ltd.

Perhaps you wish Attlee had the glamour of —

—Disraeli and his waistcoats

—Gladstone and his collars

—Lord Salisbury and his beard

—Lloyd George and his hair and cloak

—Baldwin and his pipe

—Chamberlain and his umbrella

—Churchill and his hats—

BUT nothing can ever ruffle him: —'Er, I have to . . . ahem . . . inform this House that the world will end tomorrow.'

7

240. Michael Cummings : Perhaps you wish Attlee had the glamour of — December 15, 1950. Reproduced by permission of London *Express*.

241.   Michael Cummings : If the Bevantes had run the Coronation. ... June 1, 1953. Reproduced by permission of London *Express*.

242.   Michael Cummings : Peace Blitz. "Marshall Zhukov, if those ferocious pen knives are to be part of our new uniforms, we shall hardly convince the West of our peaceful intentions. " 1951. Reproduced by permission of London *Express*.

The Strube-Poy political-comedy type of British cartooning, politics as a form of entertainment, was honed to a fine edge by a master: Giles — also, like Strube, of the *Daily Express*. His drawings developed the formula further: drop the politicians cartoon and portray the way their actions form the stimuli for a weird bunch of extraordinary-ordinary people and so get a *New Yorker* kind of social-cartoon comment on the daily political happenings. His "most unforgettable character I have known" is a terror of a grandmother. The third generation of her bewildering offspring do not look like a picnic either. Others of his characters are a cross section of those who get enmeshed, as part of their day-to-day routine as policemen, cabbies, housewives, or whatever, when the Irish cause their distinctive form of troubles, or the

243. Carl Giles : (Mother's Day). "Damn Flowers — never a bottle of scotch."
March 1971. London *Express*.

Common Market drives up the price of a little kidney. The political message, unlike in Strube, comes through. A nice, healthy, democratic skepticism emerges in "don't expect too much to come out of politics as long as human beings run it." If the optimistic vision of Vicky and Low are brushed aside, so too are the nihilism and despair of the Gillrays.

The England of the sixties saw the outcropping of a new kind of cartoon — one really reminiscent of Gillray rather than of David Low. By then even the straight media cartoons could get away with kidding royalty. But others went farther. The message of these cartoons was not reform, but a call to help destroy, or perhaps give a slight push toward the edge, a sick British society. This is not surprising, since Britain had been through two debilitating wars, had experienced a Socialist government with its moderate successes but also with the inevitable disillusion this might bring, and, most of all, had experienced a decline in real status and wealth. The Empire had been dismantled and by the late 1960s even the British Isles itself was under threat, with lively nationalist movements in Northern Ireland, Wales, and Scotland. Just over the horizon was the European Economic Community, a somewhat dreary prospect for a once-great imperial power.

Ralph Steadman and Gerald Scarfe, along with Timothy Birdsall and William Rushton in *Private Eye,* reflect this mood.[10] Their style soon spilled out into some of the mass-newspaper market as well. Their work has all of the characteristics of those who attempt to outrage and shock and, if possible, destroy. The drawing is of a studied slovenliness. The content and imagery are of the times of the Profumos, with their self-indulgence and disloyalties to friends, family, and nation. The fix, hypocrisy, decadence, and muscle fill this kind of Mickey Spillane world. Steadman's hung-over Britannia epitomizes this view of politics (Fig. 75).

That such cartoons were produced for the mass audience suggests that the cartoon of the mass market is not too bad a barometer of the health of a society's opinion. Not all in Britain shared the *Private Eye* view, but enough did to give it some hold on the public. It seems to have been especially welcomed by those who, it is supposed, held or would soon hold social, political, and economic power.

The popularity of the *Private Eye* school of art suggests that social constraints in a democracy can be brushed aside when the elite of that society loses confidence in itself and in the distribution of power, status, and wealth over which it presides. A healthy democracy produces skeptical, pragmatic, and reformist cartoonists, but not real enemies of the system. A sick democracy produces something else. No guarantee exists that democracy may not fall upon evil times and have its artists turn upon it and cry out for radical change.

About one other English artist at least a word must be said. Ronald Searle drew some political cartoons in his early days, but what I have seen of these drawings does not distinguish him artistically so much as imaginatively. His coiled-up black in the map of Africa is an example. But the mocking style for which he is known seems to have been developed fully at a later point in comic art for magazines. It has, as I noted earlier, now in turn influenced political cartooning, especially in America. It is a pity that Searle is not now, with his talents fully developed, drawn to politics.

Canadian Cartoonists

Early Canadian art was dominated by John Bengough, who started the magazine *Grip* in 1879 as an outlet for his own cartoons.[11] He is very much part of the genteel but not quite so dignified Victorian school of F.C. Gould. He was a Liberal, and anti-liquor and anti-smoking. His cartoons give off the aroma of the well-intentioned gentlemen helping to create a new and better Canada. His style was wooden and the faces representational; the conception tended to obvious imagery, using situations familiar to the middle class.

A little more of Frederick Opper's sense of the comic is found in the cartoons of Racey in the Montreal *Daily Star* in the first quarter of the twentieth century. His drawings had particular relevance for Americans during the early years of World War I, since they were widely reprinted to present forcefully and incessantly the pro-allied viewpoint. A modern equivalent is the work of John Collins on the Montreal *Star*.

Quebec, however, gave Canadian cartooning its real push forward in the familiar pattern of the outsider initially getting the ball rolling. In the 1920s, in *La Presse* of Montreal, Bourgeois developed a simple and forceful style of presentation but with a good deal of the old-fashioned style of cartooning still emerging in his drawings. The breakthrough came a decade later in the work of Robert LaPalme of Montreal. LaPalme's art was starkly modern, with heavy blacks and simple lines. His best cartoons are caricature portraits of leading politicians, which reveal character while giving off the aura of polished skepticism. Others of his cartoons were outlined brush drawings of traditional situations. LaPalme's drawings are as unlike the work of his contemporaries as are the contrasting types of female portrayed in the advertisements for Virginia Slim cigarettes. LaPalme freed Canadian cartooning from the corsets of correspondence-school art by demonstrating that a better and freer world existed.

Shortly after World War II, the Giles type of cartoon took root in Canada in the output of Len Norris of the Vancouver *Sun*. Norris used the same humorous survey of political actions as they had impact on the lives of ordinary people. His common ruck of humanity have some of the same faults and virtues of the Giles stable of characters, but the world of Norris is the happier one of the urbanized, but still West Canada, frontier.

But a development took place in Canada that somehow was missed in the Mother Country. The Giles mood and style were developed one step further by what can be viewed as a distinctive school of Canadian editorial cartooning. The school included the late Ed McNally of the Montreal *Star*, Blaine MacDonald of the Hamilton *Spectator*, Yardley Jones of the Toronto *Telegram*, Kuch of the Winnipeg *Free Press*, Chambers of the Halifax *Chronicle-Herald*, Ulashak of the Edmonton *Journal*, and, most important of all, Duncan Macpherson of the Toronto *Star*. All of these have the gay and comic mood of Giles's drawings and occasionally follow his standard pattern of showing how ordinary people feel about public policy. But more frequently they portray scenes in the traditional manner of David Low and Cummings, that is, politicians enmeshed with each other in working through policy. The big addition the Canadian School makes is exaggerated caricature of a comic sort with a sharp sting to it.

The man most responsible for developing this style of cartooning, and the man who rates among the top cartoonists drawing anywhere today, is Duncan Macpherson of the Toronto *Star*. His cartoons have everything a cartoon should have: they have humor with a real sting; they present political caricature that reveals the psychological character of politicians in a sometimes chilling fashion; they judge critically the

244.   Duncan Macpherson : (LBJ and the Generals). 1964. Toronto *Star*.

quality of the leaders' political efforts; and they package the whole thing together in a readily understandable way for a maximum wallop. If ever a man deserved to be regarded as an extremely valuable citizen of his nation and his time, it is Duncan Macpherson.

Macpherson's international fame has been limited by his staunch parochial Canadianism: he draws about national Canadian politics first and foremost and next adds a good sprinkling of provincial and local subjects, lathered and shaved clean. If he had taken the David Low route to London or hit the Oliphant or Szep trail to the United States, he would, I think, be recognised, as I believe he should be, as one of the two or three top cartoonists in the world. But Canadian politics does not get much international attention and their cartoonists get only an occasional fly-by in the New York or London *Times*. Despite Canadian political personalities, such as the Dirkson-like Dieffenbacher or flower-childlike Premier Pierre Trudeau, little attention is paid elsewhere.

Fortunately, Macpherson's work is available in annual paperback editions published by the Toronto *Star*. Give yourself a treat. Buy them.

A few of the younger Canadian cartoonists reflect the stance of Scarfe and Steadman. Anslin of the Montreal *Star* is a leader of this group. His caricatures of leaders are drawn in such loving detail as to suggest that each cartoon is a two- or three-day project. But while he may suggest toads coming out of the woodwork, his work falls far short of preaching the total rejection of the system as in British models, if for no other reason perhaps than his art suggests that he considers his subject matter worth taking infinite pains to portray exactly right.

245.   **Duncan Macpherson : National Election. 1964. Toronto** *Star.*

Australia has had the misfortune of having a number of its best-known political cartoonists pirated off elsewhere: for example, Will Dyson, David Low, and Pat Oliphant. In honesty, however, it should be admitted that it had, in turn, enticed David Low away from his native New Zealand. Aside from this crew, Norman Lindsay is also well known, but more for his artistic drawings in art-nouveau style.[12] He also did political drawings during World War I that have a certain overblown pretentiousness for my taste (Fig. 93).

246.   Livingston Hopkins : The Divine Right to Bleed. Britannia : "It's rather a pleasant sensation when you get used to it. Won't you come and share in the Glory of the Empire?" 1885. Sydney *Bulletin.*

When one reviews a collection of Australian cartoons such as *The Inked-In Image*, one can not help being struck with the similarity the collection has to the production of cartoons in other English-speaking democracies, such as Canada, Britain, or the U.S. The only difference is a more striking artistry in the early period of Australian cartooning.[13]

The late-Victorian Age features mostly Gould-like drawings by Livington Hopkins, an American transplanted in 1883 to the Sydney *Bulletin*. His drawings project a cracker-barrel style of humor characteristic of frontier societies, combined with a similarly characteristic moral earnestness. But some like the ones produced here, have real teeth. A livelier type of cartoon was produced by Phil May, an Englishman who in

247. Phil May: The Statue and the Queen. Mr. Boehm's Statue of Queen Victoria will be unveiled by Lady Carrington on Anniversary Day. Victoria: "Ah! What a beautifully accurate delineation! How truthful in every detail! Ain't it, Albert Edward?" Ca. 1887. Sydney *Bulletin*.

1885 migrated to Australia and, after a few years on the *Bulletin,* returned to England to draw humorous cartoons for *Punch.* He developed in Australia his type of simple line drawing, trying to leave lines out, and in the process he left behind a tradition in black-and-white drawing that put Australian cartoonists a decade or two ahead of the competition. For example, David Low's work for the Sydney *Bulletin* clearly shows the May influence, a debt that Low gracefully acknowledges in his autobiography.

The between-wars Australian cartoon production is competent but not memorable. In the 1930s some above-average political caricature was produced by George Finey in *Smith's Weekly.* Other drawings in the same journal, by Norman Lindsay, are political art described accurately in *The Current Affairs Bulletin* as the "giant forces at play" view of politics, "brooding and sombre." In the fifties Paul Rigby produced the Giles type of cartoon for the Perth *Daily News,* – so well, in fact, that he too was lured off to England, to work for the London *Sun.* Pioneering this kind of cartoon in Australia was Emile Mercer of the Sydney *Sun,* whose artistic style in time wanders away from Giles to a more comic-strip style, with an indigenous Australian slant.

An important original influence in the fifties onward, according to the anonymous article previously cited, was George Molnar of the Sydney *Morning Herald.* His early style is reminiscent of Steinberg mixed with Gluyas Williams, – filigree outline from Steinberg with heavy blacks and outlines from Williams. The style as it develops becomes more like Williams. I can only get some notion of his iconoclastic impact from his mild, black-humor, nonpolitical cartoons, published in America under the title *Statues.* What seems a little offbeat *New Yorker*ish to American eyes must have hit the Australian scene as the height of modern cynical comment when applied to the high tone of Australian politics. At any rate, Molnar's drawings appear to have released Australian political comment from a walled-in kind of restraint.

Modern political art has, it seems, been more influenced by the underground style of Scarfe and Steadman in Australia than in Canada or the U.S.[14] A series of political cartoon collections published by the Melbourne *Sun* and edited by Richard Walsh shows this influence most clearly in the style of Bruce Petty of the *Australian.* His cartoons are characterized by a slapdash thumbing of the nose at everyone and everything of importance. But more than irreverence, Charlie Chaplin-style is involved. The invisible line is crossed. The collection is a cross section. It reveals a curious mixture of this type of cartoon combined with a biting but mildly drawn Molnar and Down Under imitators of Giles. Of the newer artists, one who seems to me particularly worthy of attention is Les Tanner of *The Age.* This is probably because he seems to deal with political issues without the frenzy of the cynical new left striving for utopia in the bush, and without the cute hilarity of the Waltzing Matilda disciples of Giles.

The Other English Speakers

About the remaining former commonwealth or colonies or their artists, I can say very little. Back in 1932 H. R. Westwood wrote of Wyndham Robinson of the Cape *Times.* Samples of his cartoons suggest that as a Londoner born and bred Robinson imbibed a good deal of David Low in both style and content. The same influence is present in the work of J.H. Jackson, of the Cape *Argus,* who published a collection in 1961. But there is a considerable loosening of style à la Vicky, and less acid perhaps in the political comment. The general tone seems to suggest some constraint, but perhaps I am reading in what is not really there.[15]

In Northern Ireland the work of Rowel Friers of the Belfast *Telegraph* seems to me to have a desperateness — **an attempt to maintain a world of civility, tolerance, and humor in the face of ghastliness** — that gives it high marks for gallantry. His times and place are made to order for the cartoon of revolutionary hatred; moderation seems somehow ineffectual. His work shows considerable technical skill and imagination, but for me, despite its brave front, strikes a sad, false note, much as I wish it did not.

Israel also has produced a number of political cartoonists, but little out of the ordinary. The work of Aba, for instance, while not in English, is interchangeable with much that I have already described as watered-down Low.

The French

The strongest tradition of political caricature outside the British is that of France.[16] The French early had one great asset. Having a Daumier is a national treasure; it pays returns in interest for generations to come.

The earliest cartoons of France of the 1789 Revolution were similar to other totalitarian cartoons, a tame parroting of a laid-down political line. What is notable is the clear influence of Gillray and the lesser English printmakers. The Revolutionaries felt the sting and tried to return it but, like imitators generally, what they gave back was warmed-overs.

It is with Daumier and the group of artists around Philipon that French political caricature takes a distinct turn for the better and one on its own away from English copy work. It is not only that Daumier adopted the free-flowing grease pencil and lithography. The awakening is also reflected in the quality of his independent criticism. Others such as Grandville, Travies, Garvani, and Henri Monnier each go their own way out of political cartooning, but share this streak of free comment and individual artistry.

By 1870 a second generation had developed and the Third Republic had a first-rate crop of artists in André Gill and Cham, and in the next decade in Steinlen, Caran d'Ache, Willette, and Forain.

The best of these for my money is Forain, who was really a magnificent artist. He was, as I noted, the forerunner of the Boardman Robinson school in America. His drawings of the working-class types enmeshed in troubles are superb. He expressed the bitterness of their plight in simple lines. His wartime cartoons are among the great ones, since they catch the weary boredom of it all.

But all this art was built on a shaky democratic foundation. In 1897 the social instability that had found root in the Paris Commune of 1871 and its harsh repressions once more came to a boil with the Dreyfus case. The split was one between humanistic secularists and those loyal to the traditional values of church and state. The anticlerical outburst was often simplistic and bigoted, but no match for the narrow bitterness of its opposition. Tragically, the greatest of French caricaturists chose up sides. Forain, Léandre, and Caran d'Ache stood with traditional France, sometimes embracing an unlovely anti-semitism in their work in a way that is horrifyingly hard to believe possible today. The bitterness of this feud poisoned France right on through de Gaulle. In political cartoons it meant that the most effective cartoon statements were frequently from extreme positions rather than the middle, or were frilly, humorous, but politically irrelevant comment. In the twenties, Sem was the big gun. Modern cartoonists include Tim, Sempé, Siné, and Jean Effée.

The French experience suggests a third pattern that democracies may face, that of

248. Jean Louis Forain : (Urgently) Mother has said nothing since yesterday??
1898. *Pssst.*

an irreconcilably divided opinion. The tragedy of such a division is that each side is tempted to veer off to its extremist pole. Two public opinions are formed defending two kinds of community. The kind of skeptical, pragmatic comment that is characteristic of a stable working democracy is lost in the standoff.

The Rest of Western Europe

Other democracies of Western Europe have their pet cartoonists, but they are even less well known to us than the French. The barrier of language either makes their political cartoons a picture puzzle or they come out as simplistic pantomimes. We tend to forget that everyone else in the Charlie Chaplin movies talked. That's what made them intelligible.

Pre-World War I Germany had a group of cartoonists who were both outstanding and had their own original style — posterlike pictures full of humorous, long-faced lanky types. Among the best at this were G. Brandt, Bruno Paul, and T.H. Heine, the founder of *Simplicissimus.* The star portrait man was the Swede Olaf Gulbransson, whose caricatures of Ibsen and others are still reproduced. They have a fine-line weaving of a face and figure that combines simplicity with a kind of cold complexity.

249. G. Brandt : The Italian Deputation to Wilson. Count of Undine : "You Mr.
President, bear the shining light of humanity. You guarantee the victory of right
and freedom." Morgan (whispering in Wilson's ear) : "We can't lend anything
under 15 per cent." 1915. *Kladderadatsch.*

Holland's cartoons always seem to have somehow slipped through the language
barrier. The early Grand Old Man was John Braakensiek, whose work is reminiscent of
F. C. Gould's though perhaps a little fancier. He reigned from the 1880s all through
the middle twenties. The man whose cartoons had the greatest American effect was
Louis Raemaekers, who created a religious art in World War I against the German
Hun. It is almost unbelievable today, for it makes the Germans black-humored
monsters delighting in sinking ships full of women and children. Billed in America
during the war as the World's Greatest Cartoonist, he had sunk to near-oblivion by the
pacifist-isolationist thirties. Seemingly, his former admirers wanted to forget all about

him (Fig. 99) A more recent Dutch artist, Behrendt, gets reprinted fairly often here. He favors simple, stark political figures, drawn to stress angularity and a gray stillness.

The Danes provide Bo Bojesen, whose art looks a good deal like a Carl Rose drawing in the New York *Times Magazine:* Solid blacks with careful outline of detail and considerable humor. An earlier Danish artist, Robert Storm Petersen, has more of a comic-strip style. In content, judged by what is published in collected form, both offer mild redicule of officialdom and sympathy with the frustrations of the middle-class John Q. Public.[17]

A Closing Note

A few facts, most of which have already been met elsewhere, pop up again in this brief review of the political cartoon in democracies outside of America.

Styles in artistry are quickly borrowed and adapted from democracy to democracy. In earlier days this fertilization process depended upon the migration of cartoonists. Today it is the cartoons that migrate. Anyone can look at the world market of political comment, study the work of others, and swipe whenever and wherever he or she thinks it appropriate or useful.

What is borrowed most often is artistic style. The styles that migrate are those that tend to harmonize with current fashions of content. Style is the easiest way to telegraph the artist's attitude to the system. In politically stable times, even when there is percolation of ideas but not much real questioning of the system, the favoured styles are either straight-out representational and realistic or mildly comic exageration. In wartime there may be a veering off to the romantic realism of thunder and great events, or to painting adversaries as devils.

When the times become spiritually troubled, so too does the style. The style zig zags to the blatantly irreverent and slapdash. The dramatic and odd are sought out, along with any technique that suggests decadence, decline in society, and revulsion of it by the artist. The artist gleefully rolls in the mud like a dog who has just come out of a bath.

The choice of imagery follows fairly closely. The statuesque but unapproachable maidens that traipsed through their roles in flowing gowns as the representatives of the Great Powers are seen no more, or rarely, in our more irreverent age. Since the turn of the century the political cartoon has been inhabited by ordinary men and women, and often they are portrayed as caught in a kind of Charlie Chaplin *Modern Times* trap. Only recently, and not only in one democracy but in almost every one, has the imagery turned sour and rancid for a small group of cartoonists whose work gets mass circulation. Replacing the ordinary man in the gray flannel suit and the imagery suitable to him are up-to-date versions of the sharpers and floozies who inhabited the world of *Tom Jones* or James Gillray.

The same comments apply to content. With all their variations, the message comes through with a monotonous sameness. The democratic cartoonists are reacting to similar symptoms. Victorian England with all its cracks and patching over, was a rare period of stability for a democratic government. Its system of democratic empire seemed to be accepted by its cartoonists as the last best hope for the world. They seemed to believe in the inevitable and legitimate triumph of progress up and up through this glorious system. The main rumbles of irreverence came from out in the commonwealth provinces.

A healthier viewpoint, given the lessons of history and those of such dismal disciplines as economics and political science, is the more restrained reassessment of democracies that is reflected in the cartoons since World War I. It is as if cartoonists accepted Winston Churchill's view of the potential for democracy as the least harmful of all governments. A cheerful scepticism increasingly characterises cartoon comment in the English-speaking democracies from about 1880 through 1960. Pragmatism generally triumphs over abstract principle, and the desire for some peace over mounting the barricades for pure justice.

An alternative view, as I noted, is also being expressed more recently by what is still a minority. It is that democracy can no longer paper over the problems with which moderns are faced. The problems are variously seen as racial, religious, economic, of war and peace, and what have you. A preferred solution or just a resolution of any kind becomes more important than the sloppy democratic process.

The other conclusion that emerges from this review of the cartoons of democracies outside America is that political comment through cartoons seems to remain in touch with current opinion in democracies. The democratic cartoonist plays a role of critic and corrector, but he or she is shaped as well by the current trends of public opinion. The cartoonist is neither a passive reflector, as some suggest, nor the independent actor that some envisage. He or she is swimming in the same sea of molasses along with the rest of us.

Epilogue

What should artists put into their final efforts? John Tenniel's last cartoon, was a high-minded allegory on "Peace" that breathed reverence and inspiration for those running the system; George Grosz's last could well be exemplified by his painting of the empty hole that projected his loathing of the world and his despair. From the revolutionary and the totalitarian we would expect some apocalyptic vision of final perfection, destruction, or dissolution.

"Ding" Darling drew his last published cartoon some years before it appeared, and then had it set aside to be published at his death. As much as anything I can think of, "Bye Now — It's been Wonderful Knowing You" sums up what I've been trying to say about the democratic political cartoonist and critic.

But what do we get from Darling? What does this mess of turned-over ink bottles, unanswered mail, and mishmash of half-finished elephant and donkey drawings mean? One thing they say is that an artist who can cheerfully accept such lack of perfection in himself can also perhaps accept it in others. Few humans are to be written off as monsters; almost all can be accorded some measure of humorous tolerance. But that is only half the message. The ducks and other conservation art, and the TR farewell prominently displayed on the wall, remind one that reform and hope of improvement, even for ducks, is also part of the democratic experiment. Recognition of human fallibility need not end in complacency. The cartoon thus seems to me to be designed to express all the love that Darling felt for America and its democracy, combined with a healthy irreverence toward, and skepticism about its government, and about politics as it occasionally performs in practice.

Many other solidly competent craftsmen only rarely draw editorial page cartoons approaching Darling's. I want to emphasize, even at the risk of seeming condescending, that the second-level democratic cartoonist usually get fewer kudos than they deserve and I have not done as much as I hoped to when I started out in redressing that balance. We are better served by them than by those talented ones who use their talent only in destructive criticism. Better that they should bury it in a

369

250. Jay N. "Ding" Darling : "Bye now — It's been wonderful knowing you."
February 1962. Des Moines *Register*.

handkerchief, despite the biblical admonition. All of us need the occasional political slap across the mouth with a wet fish, but few of us require machine-gun bullets tearing through our jaw to remind us of the shortcomings and imperfections of ourselves or of our democratic system.

Let us, then, now praise the political cartoonists of our democracies. We may even praise as we swat at them when they do what Bill Mauldin said was their calling in life: to "circle and stab, circle and stab." By their continual buzzing and pricking they seem to me to suggest that we can still somehow suffer this sloppy democratic process for a little longer and yet not give up hope of getting occasional reform. So to them — Cheers.

Notes

1 THE POLITICAL CARTOON

1. Alan Dunn, *A Portfolio of Social Cartoons, 1957-68* (New York: Simon & Schuster, 1968).
2. Reproductions of these two cartoons may be found in that excellent early collection, Thomas Craven, ed., *Cartoon Cavalcade* (New York: Simon and Schuster, 1943), pp. 249, 401.
3. Eveline Cruikshank, ed., *Hogarth's England* (London: The Folio Society, 1957), pp. 31-36.
4. *See* Herbert Bittner, *Käthe Kollwitz Drawings* (New York: Thomas Yoseloff, 1959).
5. Ralph E. Shikes, *The Indignant Eye, The Artist as Social Critic in Prints and Drawings from the Fifteenth Century to Picasso* (Boston: Beacon Press, 1969).
6. Clare Briggs, *How to Draw Cartoons* (New York: Harper and Brothers, 1926), p. 8.
7. *Editor and Publisher,* January 28, p. 15.
8. William Murrell, "Cartooning in Wartime America," *Art News* 42 (April 1, 14, 1943): 21.
9. John Fischetti, *Zinga Zinga Za!* (Chicago: Follett, 1973), p. 96.
10. Draper Hill, *Mr. Gillray the Caricaturist* (London: Phaidon, 1965), p. 45.
11. Herblock, *The Herblock Book* (Boston: The Beacon Press, 1952), p. 168.
12. Thomas Wright, *Historical and Descriptive Account of the Caricatures of James Gillray* (New York: Benjamin Blom reissue of 1851 ed., 1968), p. 582.
13. British Museum, *Catalog of Prints and Drawings of the British Museum, Division I: Political and Personal Satire,* 11 vols. Vols. 1-4 ed. F. G. Stephens; vols. 5-11 ed. M. Dorothy George (London, volumes issued periodically between 1870 and 1954).
14. Draper Hill, *Mr. Gillray, The Caricaturist,* pp. 126-27.
15. Charles Brooks, ed., *Best Cartoons of 1973* (Gretna, La.: Pelican Publishing Co., 1973).
16. Sig Rosenblum and Charles Atin, eds., *LBJ Lampooned, Cartoon Criticism of Lyndon B. Johnson* (New York: Cobblehill Press, 1968).

2 TECHNOLOGY AND THE POLITICAL CARTOON

1. For a discussion see John Geipel, *The Cartoon, A Short History of Graphic Comedy and Satire* (London: David and Charles, 1972), chap. 2, "The Prehistory of Cartoon," and the excellent survey articles in various editions of *The Encyclopedia Britannica* s.v. Caricatures and Comic art.
2. Actually, both woodcuts and engravings in metal predate the invention of type by a few years. Students assume that the methods of print reproduction were, however, relatively primitive, though perhaps some artists began experiments with presses.
3. For a distinction similar to the one I use, but based on the division between reproduction for artistic values versus reproduction to provide accurate information, see William M. Ivins, Jr., *Prints and Visual Communication* (London: Routledge and Kegan Paul, Ltd., 1953. Reprinted Cambridge, Mass., The M.I.T. Press, in paperback).
4. J. Chal Vinson, *Thomas Nast, Political Cartoonist* (Athens: University of Georgia Press, 1967), p. 35.
5. For an excellent discussion see William A. Coupe, *The German Illustrated Broadsheet in the Seventeenth Century,* 2 vols. (Baden-Baden: Verlag Librare Heitz, 1966, 1967).

6. See especially the following Huntington Library (San Marino, Calif.), publications by Robert R. Wark: *Rowlandson's Drawings for a Tour in a Post Chase* (1964) and *Rowlandson's Drawings for the English Dance of Death* (1966). The standard work is Joseph Grego, *Rowlandson the Caricaturist* (London: Chatto and Windus, 1880; reissued New York: Collectors Editions, n.d., 1972).

7. Charles Press, "The Georgian Political Cartoon and Democratic Government," *Comparative Studies in Society and History* 19 (1977) pp. 216-38.

8. For a technical discussion see Draper Hill, *Fashionable Contrasts, 100 Caricatures by James Gillray* (London: Phaedon Press, 1966), pp. 20-24.

9. Draper Hill, *Mr. Gillray, The Caricaturist*, p. 45.

3 ANALYSIS OF CARTOONS

1. Michael. Milenkovitch, *The View from Red Square, A Critique of Cartoons from Pravda and Izvestia, 1947-1964* (New York: Hobbs, Dorman and Co., 1966).

2. A collection of this milder humor is found in Peter Tempest, ed., *Soviet Humor, Stories and Cartoons from Crocodile* (London: The Society for Cultural Relations with the U.S.S.R., n.d.).

3. E. H. Gombrich, *Meditations on a Hobby Horse* (New York, Phaidon, 1963), p. 111-14.

4. M. Dorothy George, *English Political Caricature, to 1792* (Oxford University Press, 1954), p. 18; R. T. Haines Halsey, "Impolitical Prints. An Exhibition of Contemporary English Cartoons Relating to the American Revolution." New York Public Library Bulletin, 1939; and Victor Alba, "The Mexican Revolution and the Cartoon," *Comparative Studies in Society and History* 9 (January 1967): 121-36.

5. David Low, *Ye Madde Designer* (London: The Studio, 1935), pp. 35-65.

6. Petr Sadecky, *Octobriana and the Russian Underground* (New York: Harper and Row, 1971).

7. W. A. Coupe, "Observations on a Theory of Political Caricature," *Comparative Studies in Society and History* (1969): 79-95..

8. Sig Rosenblum and Charles Antin, eds., *LBJ Lampooned*, (New York: Cobblehill Press, 1968).

9. David Low, *Ye Madde Designer* (London: The Studio, 1935), pp. 9-34.

4 DEFENDERS OF THE ESTABLISHMENT

1. G. M. Trevelyan, *The Seven Years of William IV, A Reign Cartooned by John Doyle,* 62 drawings with explanatory notes (London: Avalon Press and William Heinemann, 1952).

2. M. H. Spielmann, "Introduction, the Cartoons of Punch," in *Cartoons from Punch* (London: Bradbury and Agnew, 1906), 1:v.

3. Susan and Asa Briggs, eds., *Cap and Bell, Punch's Chronicle of English History in the Making, 1841-1861* (London: Macdonald, 1972), p. xxix.

4. The cartoons mentioned are found in these published collections: Matt Morgan, *The American War Cartoons* (London: Chatto and Windus, 1874); Judy, *The Right Hon. Benjamin Disraeli, Earl of Beaconsfield,* K. G. *From Judy's Point of View* (London: The Judy Office, 1880); *The Right Hon. W. E. Gladstone from Judy's Point of View* (London: The Judy Office, 1880 reissue) and *The Rake's Progress and Other Political Cartoons Reprinted from St. Stephen's Review* (London: the Conservative Press Co. Ltd., 1884).

5. Walter Crane, *Cartoons for the Cause, 1886-1896* (London: the Twentieth Century Press, 1896).

5. L. Percy Curtis, Jr., *Apes and Angels, The Irishman in Victorian Caricature* (Washington, D.C.: Smithsonian Institution Press, 1971).

6. William S. Walsh, *Abraham Lincoln and the London Punch* (New York: Moffat, Yard and Co., 1909).

7. W. G. Knop, ed., *Beware of the English! German Propaganda Exposes England* (London: Hamish Hamilton, 1939), foreword by Stephen King-Hall.

8. E. H. Gombrich, *Meditations on a Hobby Horse* (London: Phaidon, 1963; reprint ed. 1965), appendix plates 112-115; Bill Kinser and Neil Kleinman, *The Dream That Was No More a Dream* (New York: Harper Colophon Books, Harper & Row, 1969), cartoons pp. 83-88.

9. Michael M. Milenkovitch, *The View from Red Square, A Critique of Cartoons from Pravda and Izvestia, 1947-1964* (New York: Hobbs, Dorman & Co., 1966). Three collections of humor cartoons from Krokadil are also in print: Peter Tempest, *Soviet Humor, Stories and Cartoons from Crocodile* (London: Society for Cultural Relations with the USSR, [n.d. 1950?]; William Nelson, *Out of the Crocodile's Mouth* (Washington, D.C.: Public Affairs Press, 1949); and Rodger Swearington, *What's So Funny Comrade?* - (New York: Praeger, 1961).

10. Gino Nebiolo and Endymion Wilkinson, eds., *The People's Comic Book: Red Women's Detachment, Hot on the Trail and Other Chinese Comics* (New York: Anchor, Doubleday and Company, 1973).

5 ATTACKERS OF THE ESTABLISHMENT

1. William Murrell, *A History of American Graphic Humor*, 2 vols. (New York: Whitney Museum, 1933, 1938. Reissued New York: Cooper Square Publishers, 1967). Vol. 1, chap. 1 discusses colonial prints.
2. Oliver W. Larkin, *Daumier, Man of His Time* (New York: McGraw Hill, 1966) and Howard P. Vincent, *Daumier and His World* (Evanston, III.: Northwestern University Press, 1968). A good selection of the cartoons is found in Bruce and Seena Harris, eds. *Honoré Daumier, Selected Works* (New York: Bounty Books, 1969).
3. Jean Adhemar, *Doctors and Medicine in the Works of Daumier* (Boston: Boston Book and Art Publishers, 1970), p. 9.
4. Victor Alba, "The Mexican Revolution and the Cartoon," *Comparative Studies in Society and History* 9 (January 1967): 121-30.
5. See Dankwart A. Rustow, *A World of Nations* (Washington, D.C.: The Brookings Institution, 1967), pp. 290-91. But Robert Dahl and associates give no place to Mexico in their list of "Fully Inclusive Polyarchies," "Near Polyarchies," or even "Special Cases." Robert Dahl, *Polyarchy: Participation and Opposition* (New Haven, Conn.: Yale University Press, 1971), pp. 1-17 and 231 ff.
6. Ralph E. Shikes in *The Indignant Eye*, "Protest Art in Mexico," (Boston: Beacon Press, 1969), pp. 374-86.
7. Roberto Berdicio and Stanley Appelbaum, eds. *Posada's Popular Prints* (New York: Dover, 1972), p. 136.
8. **Bill Kinser and Neil Kleinman, *The Dream that Was No More a Dream, A Search for Aesthetic Reality in Germany, 1890-1945* (New York: Harper Colophon Books, 1969).**
9. Beth Irwin Lewis, *George Grosz, Art and Politics in the Weimar Republic* (Madison: University of Wisconsin Press, 1971). See also his autobiography, *George Grosz, A Little Yes and a Big No* (New York: Dial Press, 1946).

6 WARTIME CARTOONS: DEMOCRACY'S DARK SIDE

1. For a discussion with illustrations of the prints of Callot, Goya, Kollwitz, and Dix, see Frank and Dorothy Getlein, *The Bite of the Print* (New York: Bramhall House, 1963). See also Herbert Bittner, *Käthe Kollwitz Drawings* (New York: Thomas Yoseloff, 1959) and Carl Zigrosser, *Prints and Drawings of Käthe Kollwitz* (New York: Dover Publications, 1951).
2. "Russian Cartoons of Nazis are Savage," *Life*, March 29, 1943, p. 4 ff.
3. Michael M. Milenkovitch, *The View from Red Square, A Critique of Cartoons from Pravda and Izvestia, 1947-1964* (New York: Hobbs Dorman and Company, 1966), and William Nelson, *Out of the Crocodile's Mouth* (Washington, D.C.: Public Affairs Press, 1949).
4. See "Bismarck in German Caricature," translated from the German of K. Walther, *Cartoons Magazine* (June-July 1915), pp. 879-88, 117-24.
5. See prints in James de Haswell, *Napoleon III from the Popular Caricatures of the Last Thirty Years* (London: John Camden, n.d., circa 1874), p. 313. For an excellent collection see Susan Lambert, *The Commune in Caricature, 1870-71* (London: Victoria and Albert Museum, 1971), 119 pp.
6. "The Short-Lived War Cartoons," *The Literary Digest* 53 (December 2, 1916): 1464-65.
7. Hanny, *Looking Backward '16* (St. Joseph, Missouri, *News Press*, 1916); Luther Bradley, *Cartoons by Bradley* (Chicago: Rand McNally, 1917); W. A. Rogers, *America's Black and White Book, One Hundred Pictured Reasons Why We Are at War* (New York: Cupples and Leon, 1917); and Oscar Cesare, *One Hundred Cartoons* (Boston: Small, Maynard & Company, 1916). A collection of cartoons encouraged by the Cartoon Bureau was collected after the war, George Hecht, ed., *The War in Cartoons* (New York: Dutton, 1919).
8. Jay N. ("Ding") Darling, *Ding's Half Century* (New York: Duell, Sloan and Pearce, 1962), and *It Seems Like Only Yesterday* (Des Moines, Iowa, Ding Darling, n.d.).
9. Ernst Hanfstaengl, *Hitler in der Karikatur der Welt* (Berlin: Carl Rentsch, 1933) and *Tat Gegen Tinte, Hitler in der Karikatur der Welt, Neue Folge* (Berlin: Carl Rentsch, 1934). See also the excellent article by William Murrell, "Cartooning in Wartime America," *Art News* 42 (April 1-14, 1943): 8-15.

7 THE WORKING POLITICAL CARTOONIST

1. Art Young, *The Best of Art Young* (New York: Vanguard, 1936), p. xviii.
2. Herbert Johnson, *Cartoons* (Philadelphia: Lippincott, 1936), Foreword.
3. "Saying it Safely," *Time*, October 20, 1958, p. 56.
4. Dorman H. Smith, *One Hundred and One Cartoons* (Chicago: Ring, 1936).
5. "Soviet Freedom for Caricaturists," *Literary Digest*, January 28, 1933, p. 17.
6. "Russian Cartoons of Nazis Are Savage," *Life*, March 29, 1943, pp. 45-47.

7. Mark James Estren, *A History of Underground Comics* (San Francisco: Straight Arrow Books, 1974).

8. Jacob Burck, *Hunger and Revolt*, 2d ed. (New York: The Daily Worker, 1935).

9. Al Hirschfeld, *The World of Hirschfeld* (New York: Harry N. Abrams, n.d. [1970?]), p. 15.

10. David Low, *Autobiography* (London: Michael Joseph, 1956), pp. 86-87.

11. LaTouche Hancock, "American Caricature and Comic Art," *The Bookman* (October 1902), pp. 120-21.

12. For further details, see W. G. Rogers, *Mightier Than the Sword* (New York: Harcourt, Brace and World, 1969), pp. 198-204, and Stephen Hess and Milton Kaplan, *The Ungentlemanly Art* (New York: Macmillan, 1968), pp. 47-48 and 142-43.

13. In 1915 the Los Angeles *Times Mirror* sued the Los Angeles *Tribune* for libel and $125,000 damages for a cartoon "The Brute," which showed a hog wallowing in filth. The complainants said the cartoon was "understood by the readers to imply that the complainant was a brute, and, like the hog that wallows in filth and indecency, that he is an assassinator of character, and that salacious matter and unverified rumor are his stock in trade." All this was intended "to injure their business." When tempers cooled, the suit seemingly was dropped. *Cartoons Magazine* 7 (1915): 960.

14. Roy Paul Nelson, *Fell's Guide to the Art of Cartooning* (New York: Frederick Fell, 1962), p. 6.

15. Hugh Cudlipp, *Publish and Be Damned!* (London: Andrew Dakers, 1953), pp. 142-200, and Maurice Edelman *The Mirror, a Political History* (London: Hamish Hamilton, 1966), pp. 100-130.

16. See biographies in John Chase, ed., *Today's Cartoon* (New Orleans, La.: The Hauser Press, 1962).

17. Fischetti, *Zinga, Zinga Za!* (Chicago: Follett, 1973), p. 100.

18. See biographies in John Chase, ed., *Today's Cartoon* (New Orleans, La.: The Hauser Press, 1962).

19. Gerald W. Johnson, *The Lines Are Drawn* (Philadelphia: J. B. Lippincott, 1958). For a more deferential treatment, see Dick Spencer III, *Pulitzer Prize Cartoons* (Ames, Iowa: Iowa State College Press, 1951). Both books reprint winning cartoons through date of publication.

20. Charles Brooks, ed., *Best Editorial Cartoons of 1972* (Gretna, La.: Pelican Publishing Co., 1973). A second volume was dated the year of issue, 1974. Volumes are also available for subsequent years.

8 THE BIRTH AND DEVELOPMENT OF CARTOON SYMBOLS

1. These commentaries include some of the best, such as those by William Murrell, Stephen Hess, Milton Kaplan, Ralph Shikes, Thomas Craven, The American Foreign Policy Association, M. Dorothy George, David Low, and older works by James Parton, Frederic Taber Cooper and Arthur Bartlett Maurice, Graham Everitt, and Thomas Wright (see bibliography).

2. The criticism of the Uncle Sam symbol is found in Allan Nevins, "Let's Disown Uncle Sam," *New York Times Magazine*, (April 12, 1959), pp. 12 f. Six prominent historians comment on the article and Nevins responds.

3. The best compilations I know of dealing with the development of American symbols are Alton Ketchum, *Uncle Sam, the Man in the Legend* (New York: Hill and Wang, 1959), and E. McClung Fleming, "Symbols of the United States from Indian Queen to Uncle Sam," in Ray Brown et al., ed., *Frontiers of American Culture* (West Lafayette, Ind.: Purdue University Press, 1968), pp. 1-24. Other major sources include Roger Butterfield, "Introduction," in Ernest Lehner, *American Symbols of Pictorial History* (New York: William Penn Publishing Company, 1957); Henry Ladd Smith, "The Two Major Downings: Rivalry in Political Satire," *Journalism Quarterly* 41 (Winter 1964): 74-78 and 127; Sylvia G. L. Dannett, *A Treasury of Civil War Humor* (New York: Thomas Yoseloff, 1963); Constance Rourke, *American Humor, A Study of National Character* (New York: Harcourt Brace and Company, 1931; reissued by Anchor Books, Doubleday n.d.); William Murrell, "Rise and Fall of Cartoon Symbols," *The American Scholar* (Summer 1935), pp. 206-13; Albert Matthews, "Brother Jonathan," *Transactions 1900-1902, The Colonial Society of Massachusetts* (Boston: C.S.M., 1950) 7: 94-126); Albert Matthews, "Uncle Sam," *Proceedings of the American Antiquarian Society* m.s. 19 (April 15, 1907-April 21, 1909) (Worcester, Mass. 1909): 21-25; Frank Weitenkampf, "Uncle Sam Through the Years, A Cartoon Record, Annotated List and Introduction," unpublished manuscript, New York Public Library, 1949, 24 pp.; and "The Growth of Uncle Sam," *Life Magazine*, 41 (July 2, 1956): 22-24. For related discussions on British symbolism, see A. M. Broadley, "The Evolution of John Bull." *Pearson's Magazine* (1909) pp. 543-51 and Herbert M. Atherton, *Political Prints in the Age of Hogarth* (Oxford: The Clarendon Press, 1974). chaps. 4 and 5. For a study of monographic American symbolism, see Richard L. Merritt, *Symbols of American Community* (New Haven, Conn.: Yale University Press, 1966). This study tests alternative theories of political integration using the American experience between 1745 and 1775. The indicators used to define the growing sense of American community and separateness are references in colonial newspapers to American place names and to the American people as symbols of British authority and colonial-British unity.

4. Fleming argues that Americans accepted the Indian Princess theme but notes that the earliest such print is Paul Revere's "The Obelisk" of 1766. Revere used the figure in three other prints and it also appears on American congressional and presidential medals designed under American supervision by the French Royal Academy of Inscriptions and Belle Lettres. Fleming also notes its use in a wallpaper

pattern. But it does not seem to me to have been a figure generally popular, for the reasons I have stated.

5. Quoted in William Murrell. *A History of American Graphic Humor* (New York: The Whitney Museum, 1933; reprint ed. New York: Cooper Square Publishers, 1967), 1: 29.

6. Captain Raymond B. Rajski, ed., *A Nation Grieved, The Kennedy Assassination in Editorial Cartoons* (Rutland, Vt.: Charles E. Tuttle Co., 1967).

7. William A. Murrell, *A History of American Graphic Humor* (New York: Whitney Museum, 1933), 1: 308.

8. Ibid., p. 12.

9. Matthews, "Uncle Sam," p. 61.

10. Matthews, "Brother Jonathan," p. 125.

11. Rourke, *American Humor*, pp. 22-29.

12. *Cartoons Magazine* (1915), p. 680.

13. Henry Ladd Smith, "The Two Major Downings."

14. Weitenkampf, "Uncle Sam Through the Years," p. 7.

15. See William A. Coupe, "Observations on a Theory of Political Caricature," *Comparative Studies in Society and History* 12 (1969): 79-95.

16. Margaret Sherwood, "Uncle Sam," *The Atlantic* (March 1918), pp. 330-33.

17. Nevins, "Let's Disown Uncle Sam," p. 12.

9 EARLY PRINTS AND MAGAZINE CARTOONS

1. William A. Murrell, *A History of American Graphic Humor*, 2 vols. (New York: Whitney Museum of American Art, 1933, 1938), 1: 22-25. The other good sources for this period, listed in the bibliography, are the two Abraham Lincoln volumes by Albert Shaw and that by Rufus Rockwell Wilson; Alan Nevins and Frank Weitenkampf; and the annotated list of political prints by Frank Weitenkampf.

2. Since the above was written, I have found some confirmation of my view in an article by the founding editor of *Life*, whose pungent comment on pre-Civil War caricature was as follows: "The artistic side was ignored. Illustrations were considered good enough unless they were so aggressively bad as to startle the beholder." Speaking of the post-Civil War caricature viewer, he adds: "He had arrived at that state in which the contemplation of an ugly object was not in itself a delight. In this he differed from his ancestors." John A. Mitchell, "Contemporary American Caricature," *Scribner's Magazine* 6 (1889): 729.

3. I have found one colored political print, however, that somehow slipped through, in the Eli Lilly collection of the Indiana University Library. It is entitled "The Great Exhibition of 1860."

4. See J. Chal Vinson, *Thomas Nast, Political Cartoonist* (Athens: University of Georgia Press, 1969). Vinson's comments on Nast's style are especially helpful and indicative of the careful and informed study he made of the original sources.

5. Morton Keller, *The Art and Politics of Thomas Nast* (New York: Oxford University Press, 1968). This, like Vinson's, is an excellent book, with illustrations republished on good paper stock for maximum artistic impact. The basic source on Nast's life is Albert Bigelow Paine, *Th. Nast, His Period and His Pictures* (New York: Pearson Publishing Co., 1904; reissued Gloucester, Mass.: Peter Smith, 1967). For a collection of Nast cartoons with an introductory essay, see Thomas Nast St. Hill, *Thomas Nast, Cartoons and Illustrations* (New York: Dover, 1974).

6. Thomas Nast St. Hill, *Thomas Nast's Christmas Drawings for the Human Race* (London: Harper & Row, 1971), p. 104.

7. Walt McDougall, *This Is the Life* (New York: Knopf, 1926), p. 118.

8. Lloyd Goodrich, *Five Paintings from Thomas Nast's Grand Caricaturama* (New York: The Swann Collection of Caricature and Cartoon, 1970).

9. For a discussion of such cues, see Arthur B. Maurice, "Thomas Nast and His Cartoons," *Bookman* (March 1902), pp. 19-25.

10. Draper Hill, *What Fools We Mortals Be!, A Study of the Work of Joseph Keppler, Founder of Puck*, bachelor thesis, Harvard College, 1957. I say in print what I have said to the author: "This work should be published!" For an excellent collection of *Puck* and *Judge* cartoons, many in color, see Mary and Gordon Campbell, *The Pen, Not the Sword, A Collection of Great Political Cartoons from 1879 to 1898* (Nashville, Tenn.: Aurora Publishers, 1970).

11. Francis G. Attwood, *Attwood's Pictures, An Artist's History of the Last Ten Years of the Nineteenth Century* (New York: Life Publishing Co., 1900), 140 pp. See also Lloyd McK. Garrison, "The Work of a Great Cartoonist" *Cosmopolitan* 29 (September 1900): 550-60.

1. See, for more complete details, Valerian Gribayedoff, "Pictorial Journalism," *Cosmopolitan* 11 (August 1891): 473-81.

2. Walt McDougall, *This Is the Life!* (New York: Knopf, 1926), pp. 96-97. Note that in Valerian Gribayedoff's version the emphasis is different. He is more concerned with political illustration in representational style than with the political cartoon. The breakthrough came for him in a drawing he did all by himself called "Wall Street Nobility" and published in the Sunday *World*, February 3, 1884. He admits that the reproduction was crude but calls it "the starting point of the *great boom in newspaper illustration.*" Perhaps it was Gribayedoff's drawings that Pulitzer was thinking of when he talked to McDougall about ink clogging in the designs, or perhaps Pulitzer came to appreciate McDougall's view of large-size cuts. At any rate, about 1884, on the *World*, daily newspaper cartoons and illustration were both born.

3. McDougall, *This Is the Life!*, p. 99.

4. H. T. Webster, the creator of "The Timid Soul" and other comic characters, describes his boyhood admiration of the assignment artist Frank Holme of the Chicago *Daily News*, who, having no paper, drew on his cuffs in the courtroom and had these rushed off to the *Daily News* office. Webster went off to the big city at 17, determined to become an assignment artist, but by the time he was trained, the trade had pretty much disappeared. He became an editorial cartoonist and later one of the most successful of comic artists. John Monk Saunders, "This Cartoonist Gives Us a Look at Ourselves," *American Magazine* 98 (September 1924): 50 ff.

5. B. O. Flower, "Homer Davenport: A Cartoonist Dominated by Moral Ideals," *Arena* 34 (July 1905): 58-69.

6. Stephen Hess and Milton Kaplan, *The Ungentlemanly Art* (New York: Macmillan, 1968), pp. 127.

7. Flower, "Homer Davenport," p. 66.

9. Frank Weitenkampf, "American Cartoonists of Today," *Century* (February 1913): 540-52.

10. Alley was a Southern variant about whom Draper Hill has written a short, illustrated monograph, *The Lively Art of J. P. Alley, 1885-1934* (Memphis, Tenn.: Brooks Memorial Art Gallery, 1973).

11. John T. McCutcheon, *Drawn From Memory* (Indianapolis, Ind.: Bobbs-Merrill, 1950).

12. John T. McCutcheon, *The Cartoons That Made Prince Henry Famous* (Chicago: Chicago *Record Herald*, 1903).

13. Jay N. "Ding" Darling published at least six collections of cartoons plus travel books illustrated with his work. The cartoons mentioned are in Jay N. Darling, *Ding's Half Century*, ed. John M. Henry (New York: Duell, Sloan and Pearce, 1962). See also William J. Peterson, ed., "A Treasury of Ding," *The Palimpsest* (monthly journal of the State Historical Society of Iowa) (March 1972), pp. 81-177.

14. "Orr — Cartoonist," *The Literary Digest* 85 (May 30, 1925): 36. See also John T. McCutcheon et al., *War Cartoons Reproduced from the Chicago Tribune (December 8, 1941-September 28, 1942)* (Chicago: Chicago Tribune, n.d. ca. 1943), 171 pp.

15. For Luther Bradley see *Cartoons by Bradley* (Chicago: Rand McNally, 1917), Introduction by John T. McCutcheon. The Chicago *Daily News* published a series of Vaughn Shoemaker's cartoons as follows: *1938 A.D., 1939 A.D., 1940 A.D., '41 and '42 A.D., '43 and '44 A.D.,* and *'45 and '46 A.D.* An overview is given in *Shoemaker* (Chicago: Chicago American, 1966). For the work of James H. Donahey, *Cartoons by Donahey* (Cleveland, Ohio: Vinson and Korner, 1900), and a second volume of nostalgia cartoons with the same title (Cleveland, Ohio: The Korner and Wood Co., n.d.). I have seen reference to William Ireland collections but have neither seen one nor seen a complete citation.

16. Hess and Kaplan, *The Ungentlemanly Art*, p. 126.

17. Albert Christ-Janer, *Boardman Robinson* (Chicago: University of Chicago Press, 1946), and Boardman Robinson, *Cartoons on the War* (New York: Dutton, 1915). Some cartoons are also found in Boardman Robinson, *93 Drawings* (Colorado Springs, Colo.: Colorado Springs Fine Arts Center, 1937). See also "The Cartoon as a Means of Artistic Expression," *Current Literature* 53 (October 1912): 461-64. The anonymous author describes the new school of cartooning as "primarily a criticism of life" inspired by indignation. Most of the article is about Boardman Robinson; the last page is on Robert Minor.

18. See especially Jacob Burck's drawings in *Hunger and Revolt*, 2d ed. (New York: The Daily Worker, 1935).

19. See Walt Carmon, ed., *Red Cartoons from the Daily Worker* (Chicago: The *Daily Worker* and *Worker's Monthly;* 1927); Walt Carmon, ed., *Red Cartoons from the Daily Worker* (New York: The *Daily Worker*, 1928), and Sender Garlin, ed., *1929, Red Cartoons Reprinted from the Daily Worker* (New York: Comprodaily Publishing Co., 1929). See also Walt Carmon, ed., *The Case of Sacco and Venzetti in Cartoon from the Daily Worker* (New York: Daily Worker Publishing Co., 1927).

20. See Ross Lewis, *Cartoons of R. A. Lewis* (Milwaukee: The Milwaukee *Journal*, 1968), and Jerry Doyle, *According to Doyle, A Cartoon History of World War II* (New York: G. P. Putnam's Sons, 1943).

21. Daniel Fitzpatrick, *As I Saw It* (New York: Simon and Schuster, 1953).

22. Rollin Kirby, *Highlights, A Cartoon History of the Nineteen Twenties*, Foreword by Walter Lippmann (New York: William Farquhar Payson, 1931). p. xv.

23. The series by Flower, running mainly in 1905 and 1906, also included articles on Daniel Beard, Charles Bartholomew, Garnet Warren, Ryan Walker (the Socialist), J. Campbell Cory, J. W. Bengough (the Canadian editor and artist of *Grip*), Ray D. Handy, J. Sidney Craiger, W. A. Rogers, John L. DeMar, W. Gordon Nye, and G. P. Spencer.

24. Grant Wright, *The Art of Caricature* (New York: The Baker Taylor Co., 1904).

25. Charles Nelan, *Cartoons of Our War with Spain* (New York: Stokes, 1898).

26. J. Campbell Cory, *The Cartoonist's Art* (Chicago: The Tumbo Co., 1912).

11 SINCE WORLD WAR II

1. For an example of how the mighty have fallen, the humorist-columnist Art Buchwald indignantly noted in July 1973, when John Dean's White House enemies list was published, that he wasn't on it and neither were America's four leading editorial cartoonists. He reported that the five of them were starting a class action suit against President Nixon for being publicly humiliated and suffering grievous professional injury. "Buchwald Fights Back," Detroit *Free Press*, July 8, 1973.

2. Biographical material may be found in Peter Lyon, "The World of Herblock," *Holiday Magazine* 31 (April 1962): 118 ff.

3. William Murrell, "Cartooning in Wartime America," *Art News* 42 (April 1-14, 1943): (8-15 ff.).

4. Bill Mauldin, "Evolution of a Dove, Ain't Gonna Cover Wars No More," *The New Republic*, February 10, 1973. 18-20.

5. Charles Brooks, ed., *Best Editorial Cartoons of 1974* (Gretna: La.: Pelican Press, 1974).

12 POLITICS IN THE COMICS

1. Steve Harvey, "Kid-Granddaddy of Comics and Yellow Journalism," Los Angeles *Times*, Sunday, March 18, 1973, pt. VI, p. 5.

2. Roy Paul Nelson, "What th- ?!! What's Happening to the Comics? Biff! Pow! 2 KO's Show Trend," Los Angeles *Times*, Sunday, March 18, 1973, pt. VI, p. 4.

3. Percy L. Crosby, *Three Cheers for the Red, Red, and Red* (McLean, Va.: Freedom Press, 1936), chap. 2 "Skippy Meets with Censorship," pp. 4-16. I also wish to thank Joan Crosby Tibbetts for permission to reprint the cartoon and for further information about her father, Percy L. Crosby.

4. Richard Neuberger, "Hoover Is in the Funnies," *The New Republic*, July 11, 1934, pp. 234-35. *The Readers Guide* lists 13 other articles through July 1969 that follow this one. All take the same tack. They appear in such journals as *The Nation, Time, Newsweek, Social Problems in America*, and *The Saturday Review*.

5. "Reprieve," *Times*, July 18, 1938, p. 27.

6. J. C. Mathmore and H. Coons, "Fighting Funnies, Our Comic Strips Have Marched Off to War," *Colliers* 113 (January 29, 1944): 24 ff.

7. Ben H. Bagdikian, "Stop Laughing: It's the Funnies," *New Republic*, January 8, 1962, pp. 13-15.

8. "Comment," *The Nation* 1641 (May 14, 1947): 531-32.

9. Al Capp, *The World of Lil Abner* (New York: Ballantine Books, 1952). For favorable discussions of the early Capp see "Lil Abner's Capp," *Life* 20 (June 24, 1946): 58-66); E. J. Kahn, "Ooff! (Sob) eep! (gulp) Zowie!" *New Yorker* 23 (November 29, 1947): 45-50 and (December 6, 1947): 46-50; for a view of the changed Capp see W. Farlong, "Recap on Al Capp," *Saturday Evening Post* 243 (Winter 1971): 40-45.

10. Harold Gray, *Arf! The Life and Hard Times of Little Orphan Annie 1935-1945* (New Rochelle, N.Y.: Arlington House, 1970).

11. Nelson, "What th- ?!!", Los Angeles *Times*, March 18, 1973, p. 4.

12. Quoted by Donald Bremmer, "The Artists Speak: Humor Is a Must, 'Message' Is Secondary," Los Angeles *Times*, March 18, 1973, pt. VI, p. 5.

13. Anon., "Walt Kelly," New York *Times*, October 19, 1973, p. 42.

14. "No Go Pogo," *America*, June 2, 1962, p. 337, and "The Pogo Problem," *The Commonweal*, June 8, 1962, pp. 267-68.

15. Donald Bremmer, "The Artists Speak," Los Angeles *Times*, March 18, 1973, p. 5.

16. For a more favorable view, see T. Maremaa, "Who Is This Crumb? Underground Cartoons of the Late Sixties," New York *Times Magazine*, October 1, 1972, pp. 12-13.

17. Ron Cobb, *My Fellow Americans* and *Raw Sewage*, both published by Price, Stern, Sloan of Los Angeles, n.d. The cartoons were drawn in the late 1960s.

18. Even Auchencloss and Nancy Lynch, "An Interview with Jules Feiffer," *Mademoiselle*, January 1961, pp. 64 ff. Feiffer was suddenly in. See also Julius Novick, "Jules Feiffer and the Almost-In Group," *Harpers* (September 1961), pp. 58-62 and David Segal, "Feiffer, Steinberg and Others," *Commentary*, November 1961, pp. 431-35.

19. Sig Rosenblum and Charles Antin, eds., *LBJ Lampooned* (New York: Cobblehill Press, 1968).

20. For a sample, see Jean Claude Suares, ed., *Art of the Times* (New York: Avon, paperbound, 1973), 126 pp.

21, See Kem, *Toy Titans, Political Cartoons and Socio-Caricatures* (London: Arthur Barker, 1937), 96 pp.; Oistros, *Truffle-Eater, Pretty Stories and Funny Pictures* (London: Arthur Barker, n.d. [ca. 1933], n.p. Ben Martin, *John Brown's Body* (New York: Vanguard, 1939), n.p.; James Thurber, *The Last Flower, A Parable in Pictures* (New York: Harper, 1939); and R. Osborn, *War is No Damn Good* (Garden City, N.Y.: Doubleday, 1946). On a similar theme see Alan Dunn, *Is There Intelligent Life on Earth?* (New York: Simon & Schuster, 1960), and Edward Sorel, *Moon Missing* (New York: Simon & Schuster, 1961).

22. An ambitious study of political posters is Gary Yonker, *Prop Art* (New York: Darrien House, 1972).

13   OTHER DEMOCRACIES AND THEIR CARTOONS

1. For an excellent review of British cartoons from Hogarth to the present, with many illustrations, see Michael Wynn Jones, ed., *The Cartoon History of Britain* (London: Tom Stacey, 1971). For a commentary replete with *all* the names tumbled together, see John Geipel, *The Cartoon, A Short History of Graphic Comedy and Satire* (London: David and Charles, 1972).

2. Matt Morgan and others, *The American War Cartoons* (London: Chatto and Windus, 1874).

3. George Stonach, *The Gladstone Almanack, 1885* (London: William Blackwood and sons, 1885). This was part of a series of pamphlets with a cartoon on each facing page. They were issued between 1880-85. Other titles include *Diary of the Gladstone Government, The Gladstone A.B.C., The Liberal Mis-Leaders, The Egyptian Red Book, New Gleanings from Gladstone, More Gleanings from Gladstone,* and *the Irish Green Book.*

4. Max Beerbohm, *The Second Childhood of John Bull* London: Stephen Swift & Co., 1901). The Gladstone series is included in Max Beerbohm, *Max's Nineties* (London: Rupert Hart-Davis, 1958).

5. See Roy Matthews, "Spy" (Sir Leslie Ward), *British History Illustrated* 3 (June-July 1976): 50-57.

6. *The Literary Digest*, November 21, 1936, pp. 31-32.

7. As noted earlier, Low was exceedingly prolific between covers. A good introduction to his best work may be found in *Years of Wrath, A Cartoon History: 1931-1945* (New York: Simon and Schuster, 1946). But don't overlook the best book on political cartooning by a practitioner: David Low, *Autobiography* (London: Michael Joseph, 1956).

8. James Cameron, ed., *Vicky, A Memorial Volume* (London: Allen Lane, The Penguin Press, 1967).

9. Michael Cummings, *The Uproarious Years, A Pictorial Post War History* (London: MacGibbon & Kee, 1954).

10. See Richard Ingrams, ed., *The Life and Times of Private Eye 1961-1971* (London: Allen Lane, Penguin Books, 1971).

11. For an excellent discussion with many illustrations, see William C. Werthman and W. Stewart McNutt, *Canada in Cartoons* (New Brunswick: Brunswick Press, 1967).

12. A survey of political, social, and humorous cartoons is provided by Vane Lindsay, *The Inked-In Image, A Survey of Australian Comic Art* (Melbourne: Heineman, 1970).

13. I am indebted to an anonymous Australian cartoonist for his observations in "Black and White Art in Australia," *Current Affairs Bulletin*, December 23, 1963. His brief but incisive comments pack in a great deal of knowledge, coupled with opinion based on careful reflection. This is a way of saying that I came across his or her article after forming my own conclusions, and found to my satisfaction that mine are very similar to those he or she presents, except that he or she knows a good deal more about what he or she is talking about.

14. Richard Walsh, ed., *No Holts Barred,* (Melbourne: Sun Books, 1966). The same editor and publisher issued *Gough Syrup* (1967) and *Gortn the Act* (1968).

15. H. R. Westwood, "Wyndham Robinson of the Cape *Times*," *Modern Caricaturists* (London: Lovat Dickson, 1932), pp. 157-66, and J. H. Jackson, *Through Jackson's Eyes* (Cape Town and Pretoria: Citadel Press, 1961).

16. For a review of French cartoons with many illustrations see Jean Duche Deux, *Siècles d'histoire de France par la caricature.* (Paris: Editions du Pont Royal, 1961).

17. See Robert Storm Petersen, *Storm P.* (Copenhagen: Carit Andersen's Forlag, 1942); Bo Bojesen, *Parade* (Copenhagen: Hans Reitzel, 1958); and Bent Grasten, *Dansk Humor i Streg, Fratil Idag* (Copenhagen: Hans Reitzel, 1962).

Bibliography

Adhemar, Jean, ed. *Doctors and Medicine in the Works of Daumier.* Boston : Boston Book and Art Publishers, 1970.

Alba, Victor. "The Mexican Revolution and the Cartoon," *Comparative Studies in Society and History* 9 (January 1967): pp. 121-36.

Allen, Edison. *Of Time and Chase* (John Chase). New Orleans, La.: The Habersham Corp., 1969.

Anderson, J. Martin (Cynicus). *The Humours of Cynicus.* London: Cynicus Studio, 1891.

—— . *The Satires of Cynicus.* London : Cynicus Studio, 1892.

Anon. "Black and White Art in Australia," *Current Affairs Bulletin,* December 23, 1963

—— . "The Cartoon as a Means of Artistic Expression" (Boardman, Robinson and Robert Minor). *Current Literature* 53 (October 1912) : 461-64.

____ (Cliché Cartoons). *Editor and Publisher,* January 28, 1967, p. 15.

—— . "Comment," *The Nation* (Napoleon and Bessie Bigotry) (May 14, 1947) : pp. 531-32.

—— . (David Low comments). *Literary Digest,* November 12, 1936, pp. 31-32.

—— . "The Growth of Uncle Sam." *Life,* July 2, 1956 pp. 22-24.

—— . "Lil Abner's Capp," *Life,* June 24, 1946, pp. 58-66.

—— . "No Go Pogo," *America,* June 2, 1962, p. 337.

—— ."The Pogo Problem," *The Commonweal,* June 8, 1962, pp. 267.68.

—— . "Reprieve" (Ham Fisher's Joe Polooka). *Time,* July 18, 1938, p. 27.

—— . "Russian Cartoons of Nazis are Savage." *Life,* March 29, 1943, pp. 4 ff.

—— . "Saying it Safely." *Time,* October 20, 1958, p. 56.

—— . "Soviet Freedom for Caricaturists." *Literary Digest,* January 28, 1933, p.17

—— . "Walt Kelly." New York *Times,* October 19, 1973, p. 42.

Appel, John, and Appel, Selma. "The Grand Old Sport of Hating Catholics." *The Critic*, November-December 1971, pp. 50-58.

Atherton, Herbert M. *Political Prints in the Age of Hogarth*. Oxford : The Clarendon Press, 1974.

Attwood, Francis G. *Attwood's Pictures : An Artist's History of the Last Ten Years of the Nineteenth Century*. New York : Life Publishing Co., 1900.

Auchencloss, Even, and Lynch, Nancy. "An Interview with Jules Feiffer," *Mademoiselle*, January 1961, pp. 64 ff.

Bagdikian, Ben H. "Stop Laughing : It's the Funnies," *New Republic*, January 1962, pp. 13-15.

Barton, Stuart, and Curtis, R.A. *The Genius of William Hogarth*. Worthing, Sussex : Lyle Publications, 1972.

Batchelor, Clarence. *Truman Scrapbook : The Washington Story in Cartoons and Text*. Deep River, Conn.: Kelsey Hill Publishing Co., 1951.

Becker, Stephen. *Comic Art in America*. New York : Simon and Schuster, 1959.

Beerbohm, Max. *Max's Nineties, Drawings 1892-1899*, London : Rupert Hart-Davis, 1958.

Berdicio, Roberto, and Applebaum, Stanley, eds. *Posada's Popular Prints*. New York : Dover, 1972.

Berger, Arthur Asa. *Li'l Abner, A Study in American Satire*. New York : Twayne Publishers, 1970.

Bittner, Herbert. *Käthe Kollwitz Drawings*. New York : Thomas Yoseloff, 1959.

Blaisdell, Thomas C.; Selz, Peter; and Seminar. *The American Presidency in Political Cartoons : 1776-1976*. Salt Lake City, Utah : Peregrine Smith, Inc., 1976.

Block, Herbert. *The Herblock Book*. Boston : The Beacon Press, 1952.
—— . *Herblock's Here and Now*. 1955.
—— . *Herblocks Special for Today*. 1958.
—— . *Straight Herblock*. 1964.
—— . *The Herblock Gallery*. 1968.
—— . *Herblock's State of the Union*. 1972.
—— . *Herblock's Special Report*. New York : W. W. Norton, 1974.

Bojesen, Bo. *Parade*. Copenhagen : Hans Reitzel, 1958.

Boyd, Malcolm and Conrad, Paul. *When in the Course of Human Events*. New York : Sheed and Ward, 1973.

Bradley, Luther. *Cartoons by Bradley*. Chicago : Rand McNally, 1917.

Bremmer, Donald. "The "Artists Speak : Humor is a Must, 'Message'Is Secondary," Los Angeles *Times*, March 18, 1973, pt. VI, p. 5.

Briggs, Clare. *How to Draw Cartoons*, New York : Harper and Brothers, 1926.

Briggs, Susan, and Briggs, Asa, eds. *Cap and Bell, Punch's Chronicle of English History in the Making, 1841-1861*. London : Macdonald, 1972.

British Museums. *Catalog of Print and Drawings of the British Museum, Division I : Political and Personal Satire*, 11 vols. Vols. 1-4 ed. F.G. Stephens; vols. 5-11 ed. M. Dorothy George. London, issued periodically between 1870 and 1954. See especially the introductory essays by the editors.

Broadley, A.M. "The Evolution of John Bull." *Pearson's Magazine* (1909), pp. 543-51.

Brooks, Charles, ed. *Best Editorial Cartoons of 1972*. Gretna, La : Pelican Publishing Co., 1973, and subsequent annual editions.

Burck, Jacob. *Hunger and Revolt.* 2nd ed. New York : The Daily Worker, 1935.

Butterfield, Roger. *The American Past, A History of the United States from Concord to the Great Society.* New York : Simon and Schuster, 1947.

Cameron, James, ed. *Vicky, A Memorial Volume.* London : Allen Lane, The Penguin Press, 1968.

Campbell, Mary, and Campbell, Gordon. *The Pen, Not the Sword, A Collection of Great Political Cartoons from 1879 to 1898.* Nashville : Tenn. Aurora Publishers, 1970.

Capp, Al. *The World of Lil Abner.* New York : Ballantine Books, 1952.

Carmon, Walt, ed. *The Case of Sacco and Vanzetti in Cartoon(s) from the Daily Worker.* New York : Daily Worker Publishing Co., 1927.

———, ed. *Red Cartoons from the Daily Worker.* Chicago : The Daily Worker and Workers Monthly, 1927.

———, ed. *Red Cartoons from the Daily Worker.* Chicago : The Daily Worker, 1928.

Cesare, Oscar. *One Hundred Cartoons,* Boston : Small, Maynard & Co., 1916.

Chase, John, ed. *Today's Cartoon.* New Orleans, La : The Hauser Press, 1962

Christ-Janer, Albert. *Boardman Robinson.* Chicago : University of Chicago Press, 1946.

Clark, Kinnaird. *Rube Goldberg in the Machine Age.* New York : Hastings House, 1968.

Cobb, Ron. *My Fellow Americans.* Los Angeles, Calif.: Price, Stern, Sloan, n.d. ca. 1970).

———. *Raw Sewage* (Los Angeles, Calif. : Price, Stern, Sloan, n.d. ca. 1970).

Conrad, Paul. *The King and Us, Editorial Cartoons by Conrad.* Los Angeles, Calif.: Clymer Publications, 1974.

Cooper, Frederick Taylor, and Maurice, Arthur Bartlett. *The History of the Nineteenth Century in Caricature.* New York : Dodd Mead and Co., 1904, reissued Detroit, Mich.: Tower Books, 1971.

Cory, J. Campbell. *The Cartoonist's Art.* Chicago : The Tumbo Co., 1912.

Coupe, William A. *The German Illustrated Broadsheet in the Seventeenth Century,* 2 vols. Baden-Baden : Verlag Librare Heitz, 1966. 1967.

Crane, Walter. *Cartoons for the Cause, 1886-1896.* London : The Twentieth Century Press, 1896.

Craven, Thomas, ed. *Cartoon Cavalcade.* New York : Simon and Schuster, 1943.

Crawford, Charles, ed. *Cal Alley.* Mephis, Tenn.: Memphis State Press, 1973.

Crosby, Percy L. *Three Cheers for the Red, Red, and Red.* McLean, Va.: Freedom Press, 1936.

Cruikshanks, Eveline. *Hogarth's England, A Selection of the Engravings with Descriptive Text.* London: Folio Society, 1957.

Cummings, Michael. *The Uproarious Years, a Pictorial Post War History.* London: MacGibbon & Kee, 1954.

Curtis, L. Percy, Jr. *Apes and Angels, The Irishman in Victorian Caricatures.* Washington, D.C.: Smithsonian Institution Press, 1971.

Dannett, Sylvia, G.L. *A Treasury of Civil War Humor.* New York: Thomas Yoseloff, 1963.

Darcy, Tom. *The Good Life.* New York: Avon, 1970.

Darling, Jay N. (Ding). *Ding's Half Century,* ed. John M. Henry. New York: Duell, Darling, n.d. (ca. 1950).

—— . *It seems Like Only Yesterday.* (Des Moines, Iowa: Ding Darling, n.d. (ca. 1950).

Davenport, Homer. *Cartoons.* New York: DeWitt, 1898.

—— . *The Dollar or the Man? The Issue of Today.* Boston: Small, Maynard, 1900.

Dobbins, Jim. *Dobbins History of the New Frontier.* Boston: Humphries, 1964.

Donahey, James H. *Cartoons by Donahey.* Cleveland, Ohio: Vinson and Korner, 1900.

Doyle, Jerry. *According to Doyle, A Cartoon History of World War II.* New York : G. P. Putnam's Sons, 1943.

Duche, Deux, Jean. *Siècles d'histoire de France par la caricature.* Paris: Editions du Pont Royal, 1961.

Dunn, Alan. *Is There Intelligent Life On Earth?* New York: Simon and Schuster, 1960.

—— . *A Portfolio of Social Cartoons, 1957-1968.* New York: Simon and Schuster, 1968).

Dyson, Will, *Cartoons.* (London : Daily Herald, 1913).

Encyclopedia Britannica, s.v. "Caricatures and Comic Art." (all editions.)

Estren, Mark James. *A History of Underground Comics.* San Francisco: Straight Arrow Books, 1974.

Everitt, Graham. *English Caricaturists and Graphic Humourists of the Nineteenth Century.* London: 1885, reissued Freeport, N.Y.: Books for Libraries Press, 1972

Farlong, W. "Recap on Al Capp," *Saturday Evening Post* 243 (Winter 1971): pp. 40-45.

Feiffer, Jules. *Feiffer on Nixon, The Cartoon Presidency.* New York: Random House, n.d. (ca. 1973).

Fischetti, John. *Zinga Zinga Za!* Chicago: Follett, 1973.

Fitzpatrick, Daniel. *As I Saw It.* New York: Simon and Schuster, 1953.

Fleming, E. McClury. "Symbols of the United States from Indian Queen to Uncle Sam," In Ray Brown et al, eds., *Frontiers of American Culture.* West Lafayette, Ind.: Purdue University Press, 1968.

Flower, B.O. "Homer Davenport: A Cartoonist Dominated by Moral Ideals." *Arena* 34 (July 1905): pp. 58-69.

Foreign Policy Association. *A Cartoon History of United States Foreign Policy.* New York: Vintage Books, 1967.

Fredericks, Peirce, ed. *The People's Choice, The Issues of the Campaign as Seen by the Nation's Best Political Cartoonists,* New York: Dodd Mead and Co., 1956.

Friers, Rowell. *Riotous Living.* Belfast: Blackstaff Press, 1971.

—— . *Pig in the Parlor.* Belfast: Blackstaff Press, 1973.

Furniss, Harry. *The Confessions of a Caricaturist.* 2 Vols. New York: Harper and Brothers, 1902).

Garlin Sender, ed. *Red Cartoons Reprinted from the Daily Worker,* New York : Comprodaly Publishing Co., 1929.

Garrison, Lloyd McK. The Work of a Great Cartoonist" (Francis G. Attwood).

Cosmopolitan 29 (September 1900): pp. 550-60.

Geipel, John. *The Cartoon, A Short History of Graphic Comedy and Satire.* London: David and Charles, 1972.

Getlein, Frank, and Getlein, Dorothy. *The Bite of the Print.* New York: Bramhall House, 1963.

George, M. Dorothy. *English Political Caricature.* 2 vols. *(to 1792; 1793-1832).* Oxford: Oxford University Press, 1954, 1959.

――― . *Hogarth to Cruickshank: Social Change in Graphic Satire.* New York: Walker and Co., 1967.

Giles. *Sunday Express and Daily Express Cartoons.* London: The Daily Express, annual collection beginning 1957.

Gombrich, E.H. *Meditations on a Hobby Horse.* London: Phaedon, 1963; reprinted 1965.

Goodrich, Lloyd. *Five Paintings from Thomas Nast's Grand Caricaturama.* New York: The Swann Collection of Caricature and Cartoon, 1970.

Gould, Francis Carruthers. *Political Caricatures.* London: Westminster Gazette. annual vol. of caricatures published from 1895 to 1906.

Grasten, Bent. *Dansk Humor i Streg, Fra til Idag.* Copenhagen: Hans Reitzel, 1962.

Gray, Harold. *Arf! The Life and Hard Times of Little Orphan Annie 1935-1945.* New Rochelle, N.Y.: Arlington House, 1970.

Grego, Joseph. *Rowlandson the Caricaturist.* London: Chatto and Windus, 1880; reissued New York: Collectors Editions, n.d. (ca. 1972).

Gribayedoff, Valerian. "Pictorial Journalism," *Cosmopolitan* 11 (August 1891): pp. 473-81.

Gros, Raymond, ed. *T.R. in Cartoon.* (New York: The Saalfield Publishing Co., 1910).

Grosz, George. *A Little Yes and a Big No, The Autobiography of George Grosz.* New York: The Dial Press, 1946.

Halsey, R.T. Haines. "Impolitical Prints, An Exhibition of Contemporary English Cartoons Relating to the American Revolution". New York Public Library Bulletin, 1939.

Hancock, La Touche. "American Caricature and Comic Art." *The Bookman,* October 1902, pp. 120-21.

Hanfstaengl, Ernst, ed. *Hitler in der Karikatur der Welt.* Berlin: Carl Reutsch, 1933.

――― . *Tat Gegen Tinte, Hitler in der Karikatur der Welt, Neue Folge.* Berlin: Carl Reutsch, 1934.

Hanny. *Looking Backward '16.* St. Joseph, Missouri: *News Press, 1916.*

Harris, Bruce, and Harris, Seena, eds. *Honoré Daumier, Selected Works.* New York: Bounty Books, 1969.

Harvey, Steve. "Kid Granddaddy of Comics and Yellow Journalism." Los Angeles *Times,* Sunday, March 18, 1973, pt. VI, p. 5.

de Haswell, James. *Napoleon III from the Popular Caricatures of the Last Thirty Years.* London: James Camden, n.d. (c.a. 1874).

Haynie, Hugh. *Hugh Haynie: Perspective.* Louisville, Ky.: The *Courier Journal* and the Louisville *Times,* 1974.

Hecht, George, ed. *The War in Cartoons.* New York: Dutton, 1919.

Hess, Stephen, and Kaplan, Milton. *The Ungentlemanly Art*. New York: Macmillan, 1968; rev. ed. 1975.

Hill, Draper. *Fashionable Contrasts; 100 Caricatures by James Gillray*. London: Phaedon Press, 1966.

———. *The Lively Art of J.P. Alley*. Memphis, Tenn.: Brooks Memorial Art Gallery, 1973 (pamphlet).

———. *Mr. Gillray the Caricaturist*. London: Phaidon, 1965.

———. *What Fools We Mortals Be!* A Study of the Work of Joseph Keppler, Founder of Puck. Bachelor thesis, Harvard College, 1957

———. ed., *The Satirical Etchings of James Gillray*. New York: Dover Publications, 1976.

Hillier, Bevis. *Cartoons and Caricatures*. London: Dutton Paperback, 1970.

Hirschfeld, Al. *The World of Hirschfeld*, New York: Harry N. Abrams, n.d. (1970?).

Hopkins, Livingston. *On the Hop!* Sidney, Australia: *The Bulletin* Newspaper Co., 1904.

Ingrams, Richard, ed. *The Life and Times of Private Eye, 1961-1971*. London: Allen Lane, Penguin Books, 1971.

Ivins, William M., Jr. *Prints and Visual Communication*. London: Routledge and Kegan Paul, Ltd. 1935, reprinted Cambridge, Mass.: The M.I.T. Press, paperback.

Jackson, J.H. *Through Jackson's Eyes*. Capetown and Pretoria: Citadel Press, 1961.

Johnson, Gerald W. *The Lines are Drawn*. Philadelphia: J.B. Lippincott, 1958.

Johnson, Herbert. *Cartoons*, Philadelphia: Lippincott, 1936.

Jones, Michael Wynn, ed. *The Cartoon History of Britain*. London: Tom Stacey, 1971.

——— ,ed. *The Cartoon History of the American Revolution*. New York: G.P. Putnam's Sons, 1975.

——— ,ed. *A Cartoon History of the Monarchy*. London: MacMillan, 1978.

Judy. *The Right Hon. W.E. Gladstone from Judy's Point of View*. London: The Judy Office, 1880.

Kahn, E.J. "Ooff! (Sob) eep! (gulp) Zowie!" *New Yorker*. November 29, 1947. pp. 45-58 and December 6, 1947, pp. 46-50.

Keller, Morton. *The Art and Politics of Thomas Nast*. New York: Oxford University Press, 1968.

Kelly, Walt, Jr. *Ten Ever-Lovin' Blue-Eyed Years with Pogo*. New York: Simon and Schuster, 1959.

Kem. *Toy Titans, Political Cartoons and Socio-Caricatures*. London: Arthur Barker, 1937.

Lyon, Peter. "The World of Herblock". *Holiday Magazine* 31 (April 1962) : 118 ff.

McCutcheon, John T. *Cartoons by McCutcheon*. Chicago : A.C. McClung, 1903.

———. *Bird Center Cartoons*. Chicago : A.C. McClung, 1904.

———. *The Cartoons That Made Prince Henry Famous*. Chicago : Chicago Herald Record, 1903.

———. *Drawn From Memory*. Indianapolis, Ind.: Bobbs-Merrill, 1950.

———. *The Mysterious Stranger and Other Cartoons*. New York : McClure, Phillips and Co., 1905.

———. et al. *War Cartoons Reproduced from the Chicago Tribune (December 8, 1941-September 28, 1942)*. Chicago : Chicago Tribune, n.d. (ca. 1943).

McDougall, Walt. *This Is the Life!* New York: Knopf, 1926.

MacNelly, Jeff. *MacNelly, The Pulitzer Prize Winning Cartoonist.* Richmond Va.: The Westover Publishing Co., 1972.

Macpherson, Duncan. *Cartoons by Duncan Macpherson.* Toronto : Toronto *Star,* annual vol. beginning 1960.

Manning, Reg. *Little Itchy Itchy and Other Cartoons.* New York : J.J. Augustin Publishers, 1944.

Maremma, T. "Who Is This Crumb? Underground Cartoons of the Late Sixties," New York *Times Magazine,* October 1, 1972, pp. 12-13.

Martin, Ben. *John Brown's Body.* New York : Vanguard, 1939.

Marzio, Peter C. *Do It the Hard Way, Rube Goldberg and Modern Times.* *Washington D.C.:* The Smithsonian Institution, 1970.

Mathmore, J.C., and Coons H. "Fighting Funnies, Our Comic Strips Have Marched Off to War," *Colliers,* January 29, 1944, pp 24 ff.

Matthews, Albert. "Brother Jonathan," Transactions 1900-1902. *The Colonial Society of Massachusetts.* Boston : C.S.M., 1950.
———— , "Uncle Sam." *Proceedings of the American Antiquarian Society,* n.s. 19 (April 15, 1907-April 21, 1909. Worcester, Mass., 1909, pp 21-25.

Matthews, Roy. "Spy" (Sir Leslie Ward), *British History Illustrated* 3 (June-July 1976) : pp. 50-57.

Mauldin, Bill. *Up Front.* New York : The World Publishing Co., 1945.
———— . *Back Home.* New York : William Sloane Associates, 1947.
———— . *Whats Got Your Back up?* New York : Harper and Row, 1961.
———— . *I've Decided I Want My Seat Back.* New York : Harper and Row, 1965.
———— . *The Brass Ring.* New York : W.W. Norton, 1971.
———— . "Evolution of a Dove; Ain't Gonna Cover War No More," *The New Republic,* February 10, 1973, pp. 18-20.

Maurice, Arthur B. "Thomas Nast and His Cartoons," *Bookman,* March 1902, pp. 19-25.

Mayer, Henry (Hy). *Fantasies in Ha! Ha!* New York: Mayer, 1900.

Merritt, Richard L. *Symbols of American Community.* New Haven, Conn.: Yale University Press, 1966.

Milenkovitch, Michael M. *The View from Red Square; A Critique of Cartoons from Pravda and Izvestia, 1947-1964.* New York : Hobbs, Dorman, and Co., 1966.

Mitchell, J.A. "Contemporary American Caricature." *Scribner's Magazine* 6 (1889) : p. 729.

Morgan, Matt, and others. *The American War Cartoons.* London : Chatto and Windus, 1874.

Mott, Frank Luther. *A History of American Magazines,* 4 Vols. Cambridge, Mass. Harvard University Press, 1938-57.

Murrell, William. "Cartooning in Wartime America," *Art News* 42 (April 1-14, 1943) : pp. 8-15 ff.
———— . *A History of American Graphic Humor,* 2 vols. New York : Whitney Museum, 1933, 1938, reissued New York : Cooper Square Publishers, 1967.
———— . "Rise and Fall of Cartoon Symbols." *The American Scholar* (Summer 1935), pp. 206-13.

Nebiolo, Gino, and Wilkinson Endymion, eds. *The People's Comic Book : Red Women's Detachment, Hot on the Trail and Other Chinese Comics.* New York : Anchor, Doubleday and Co., 1973.

Nelson, Roy Paul. *Fell's Guide to the Art of Cartooning.* New York : Frederick Fell, 1962.

———. "What the — ?!! What's happening to the comics? Biff! Pow! 2 KO's Show Trend," Los Angeles *Times,* Sunday, March 18, 1973, pt. VI, p. 4.

Nelson, William. *Out of the Crocodile's Mouth.* Washington, D.C.: Public Affairs Press, 1949.

Neuberger, Richard. "Hoover Is in the Funnies, " *The New Republic,* July 11, 1934. pp. 234-35.

Nevins, Allan. "Let's Disown Uncle Sam" New York *Times Magazine* (April 12, 1959) p. 12f.

———. and Weitenkampf, Frank, *A Century of Political Cartoons.* New York : Scribners, 1944.

Novick, Julius. "Jules Feiffer and the Almost-In Group," *Harpers,* Sept. 1961, pp. 58-62.

Oistros. *Truffle-Eater, Pretty Stories and Funny Pictures.* London : Arthur Barker, n.d. ca. 1933).

Oliphant, Pat. *The Oliphant Book, A Cartoon History of Our Times.* New York : Simon and Schuster, 1969.

———. *Four More Years.* New York : Simon and Schuster, 1973.

O'Neil, William L, ed. *Echoes of Revolt : The Masses 1911-1917* Chicago : Quadrangle, 1966.

Osborn, R. *War Is No Damn Good.* Garden City, N.Y.: Doubleday, 1946.

Paine, Albert Bigelow. *Th. Nast, His Period and His Pictures.* New York : Pearson Publishing Co., 1904; reissued, Gloucester, Mass.: Peter Smith, 1967.

Parton, James. *Caricature and Other Comic Art.* New York : Harper and Brothers, 1878.

Paston, George. *Social Caricature in the Eighteenth Century,* London, 1905; reissued New York : Benjamin Blom, 1968.

Petersen, Robert Storm. *Storm P.* Copenhagen : Carit Andersen's Forlag, 1942.

Peterson, William J., ed. "A Treasury of Ding" (Jay N. "Ding" Darling). *The Palimpsest,* monthly journal of the State Historical Society of Iowa, March 1972, pp. 81-177.

Physick, John, *The Duke of Wellington in Caricature* (esp. W.H. Heath — "Peter Pry"). London : Her Majesty's Stationary Office, 1965.

Press, Charles. "The Georgian Political Cartoon and Democratic Government." *Comparative Studies in Society and History* 19 (1977) pp. 216-38.

Punch. *Cartoons from Punch.* 4 vols. London : Bradbury and Agnew, 1906.

Raemaekers, Louis. *America in the War.* New York : Century, 1918.

Rajski, Raymond B., ed. *A Nation Grieved, The Kennedy Assassination in Editorial Cartoons.* Rutland, Vt.: Charles E. Tuttle Co., 1967.

Redfield, A. *The Ruling Claws.* New York : The Daily Worker, 1935.

Robinson, Boardman. *Cartoons on the War.* New York : Dutton, 1915.

———. *93 Drawings.* Colorado Springs, Col.: Colorado Springs Fine Art Center, 1937.

Rogers, William A. *America's Black and White Book: One Hundred Pictured Reasons Why We Are at War.* New York : Cupples and Leon, 1917.

———. *Hits at Politics.* New York : R.H. Russell, 1899.

Rogers, W.G. *Mightier Than the Sword.* New York : Harcourt, Brace and World, 1969.

Rosenblum, Sig. and Charles Antin, eds., *LBJ Lampooned, Cartoon Criticism of*

Lyndon Baines Johnson: (New York : Cobblehill Press, 1968.) Introduction by Jules Feiffer.

Rourke, Constance. *American Humor, A Study of National Character.* New York : Harcourt Brace and Co., 1931, reissued by Anchor Doubleday, n.d.

Russell, Ruth. "Orr-Cartoonist." *The Literary Digest,* May 30, 1925, p.36.

St. Hill, Thomas Nast. *Thomas Nast's Christmas Drawings for the Human Race.* London : Harper and Row, 1971.

―――― *Thomas Nast, Cartoons and Illustrations.* New York : Dover, 1974.

St. Stephens Review. *The Rake's Progress and Other Political Cartoons Reprinted from St. Stephen's Review.* London : The Conservative Press Co. Ltd., 1884.

Sadecky, Petr. *Octobriana and the Russian Underground.* New York : Harper and Row, 1971.

Sanders, Bill. *Run for the Oval Room . . . they can't corner us there!* (Milwaukee, Wis.: Alpha Press, 1974.

Sarzano, Frances. *Sir John Tenniel.* London : Art and Technics, 1948.

Saunders, John Monk. "This Cartoonist Gives Us a Look at Ourselves" (H.T. Webster). *American Magazine* 98 (September 1924): p. 50 ff.

Segal, David. "Feiffer, Steinberg and Others, " *Commentary,* November 1961, pp. 431-35.

Shaw, Albert. *Abraham Lincoln, His Path to the Presidency, A Cartoon History,* New York : Review of Reviews, 1929.

―――― . *Abraham Lincoln, The Year of His Election: A Cartoon History* (vol. 2 of the above). New York : Review of Reviews, 1929.

―――― . *A Cartoon History of Roosevelt's Career.* New York : Review of Reviews, 1910.

Sherwood, Margaret. "Uncle Sam", *The Atlantic,* March 1918, pp. 330-33.

Shikes, Ralph E. *The Indignant Eye: The Artist as Social Critic in Prints and Drawings from the Fifteenth Century to Picasso.* Boston : Beacon Press, 1969.

Shoemaker, Vaughn. *Shoemaker,* Chicago : Chicago American, 1966.

―――― . A Series of vols.: *1938 A.D., 1939 A.D., 1940 A.D., '41 and '42 A.D., '43 and '44 A.D., and '45 and '46 A.D.* Chicago : Chicago Daily News, 1939, 1940, 1941, 1943, 1945 and 1947.

Smith, Dorman H. *One Hundred and One Cartoons,* Chicago : Ring, 1936.

Smith, Henry Ladd. "The Two Major Downings : Rivalry in Political Satire," *Journalism Quarterly* 41 (Winter 1964) : pp. 74-78, 127.

Sorel, Edward. *Moon Missing.* New York : Simon and Schuster, 1961.

Spencer, Dick, III. *Pulitzer Prize Cartoons.* Ames, Iowa : Iowa State College Press, 1951.

Stonach, George. *The Gladstone Almanack, 1885.* London : William Blackwood and Sons, 1885.

Streicher, Lawrence H. "On a Theory of Political Caricature," *Comparative Studies in Society and History* 9 (July 1967). pp. 427-45.

―――― . "David Low and the Sociology of Caricature." *Comparative Studies in Society and History* 8 (October 1965) : pp. 1-23.

Strube, Sidney. *Cartoons from the Daily Express.* London : London Express, annual paperback series from 1927 through 1933.

Suares, Jean Claude, ed. *Art of the Times.* New York : Avon Paperbound, 1973.

Swearington, Rodger. *What's So Funny Comrade?* New York : Praeger, 1961.

Szyk, Arthur. *The New Order.* New York : G.P. Putnam's Sons, 1941.

Tempest, Peter. *Soviet Humour : Stories and Cartoons from Crocodile.* London : The Society for Cultural Relations with the U.S.S.R., n.d.

Thurber, James. *The Last Flower, A Parable in Pictures.* New York : Harper, 1939.

Trevelyan, G.M. *The Seven Years of William IV, A Reign Cartooned by John Doyle.* London : Avalon Press and William Heinemann, 1952.

Veth, Cornelius. *Comic Art in England.* London : Edward Goldstein, 1930.

Vincent, Howard P. *Daumier and His World.* Evanston, Ill.: Northwestern University Press, 1968.

Vinson, J. Chal. *Thomas Nast, Political Cartoonist.* Athens, Ga.: University of Georgia Press, 1969.

Walker, Martin, *Daily Sketches, A History of British Twentieth Century Politics,* London : Paladin Granada Books, 1978.

Walsh, Richard, ed. *No Holts Barred.* Melbourne : Sun Books, 1966.
———— . *Gough Syrup.* Melbourne : Sun Books, 1967.
———— . *Gortn the Act.* Melbourne : Sun Books, 1968.

Walsh, William S. *Abraham Lincoln and the London Punch* (John Tenniel). New York : Moffat, Yard and Co., 1909.

Wark, Robert R., ed. *Rowlandson's Drawings for a Four in a Post Chase.* San Marino, Calif.: Huntington Library, 1964.
———— . *Rowlandson's Drawings for the English Dance.* San Marino, Calif.: Huntington Library, 1966.

Washington Evening *Star. The Campaign of 48* Cartoons by Clifford and Jim Berryman and Gib Crochett. Washington D.C.: Washington Star, 1949.
———— . *The Campaign of '52.* Washington, D.C.: Washington Star, 1953.
———— . *Campaigns of '56.* Washington, D.C.: Washington Star, 1957.

Wathur, K. "Bismarck in German Caricature," *Cartoons Magazine* (June and July 1915, pp. 879-88, 117-24.

Weitenkampf, Frank. "American Cartoonists of Today," *Century* 85 (February 1913). pp. 540-52.
———— . *Political Caricature in the United States, In Separately Published Cartoons, An Annotated List.* New York : New York Public Library, 1953, reissued New York : The Arno Press, 1971.
———— . "Uncle Sam Through the Years : A Cartoon Record, Annotated List and Introduction," Unpublished manuscript, New York Public Library, 1949, 24pp.

Werthman, William, and McNutt, W. Stewart. *Canada in Cartoons.* New Brunswick : Brunswick Press, 1967.

Westwood, H.R. *Modern Caricaturists.* London : Lovat Dickson, 1932.

What America Thinks Inc. *What America Thinks, Editorials and Cartoons.* Chicago : What America Thinks Inc., 1941.

White, David Manning, *From Dogpatch to Slobbovia: The World of Li'l Abner.* Boston : Beacon, 1964.

Whitman, Bert. *Here's How, About the Newspaper Cartoon : A Collection of Editorial Cartoons from the Past Decade.* Lodi, Calif.: Lodi Publishing Co., 1968.

Wilson, Rufus Rockwell. *Lincoln in Caricature.* New York : Horizon Press, 1953.

Windsor, H.H. *Cartoons Magazine* 1912-1924.

Wright, Don. *Wright On! A Collection of Political Cartoons.* New York : Simon and Schuster, 1971.

Wright, Grant. *The Art of Caricature.* New York : The Baker Taylor Co. 1904.

Wright, Thomas. *A History of Caricature and Grotesque in Literature and Art.* London, 1865 reissued New York : Frederick Ungar Publishing Co., 1968.

—— . *A Caricature History of the Georges.* London, 1968, reissued New York : Benjamin Blom, n.d. (ca. 1970).

—— : *Historical and Descriptive Account of the Caricature of James Gillray.* New York : Benjamin Blom, reissue of 1851 ed., 1968.

Yonker, Gary. *Prop Art.* New York : Darrien House, 1972).

Young, Art. *Art Young, His Life and Times.* New York : Sheridan House, 1939.

—— . *The Best of Art Young,* New York : Vanguard, 1936.

—— . *On My Way, Being the Book of Art Young in Text and Picture.* New York : Horace Liveright, 1928.

Zigrosser, Carl. *Prints and Drawings of Käthe Kollwitz.* New York : Dover Publications, 1951.

Index

British cartoons: Victorian, 83-106, 340-51; post-World War I, 351-55; Story-book, 339
Broadley, A. M., 374, 380
Brodie, Howard, 13
Brooks, Charles, 32, 206, 325, 326, 371, 374, 377, 380
Brown, Ray, 374, 382
Buchwald, Art, 377
Burck, Jacob, 184, 190, 197, 283, 374, 376, 381
Bush, Charles G., 185, 220, 221, 228, 293
Bushnell, E. A., 278, 297
Butterfield, Roger, 209, 374, 381

Callot, Jacques, 139, 244
Cameron, James, 378, 381
Campbell, Gordon, 375, 381
Campbell, Mary, 375, 381
Canadian cartoons, 358-60
Caniff, Milt, 331, 333
Capp, Al, 17, 186, 331-32, 333, 334, 377, 381
Caran d'Ache, 364
Caricature, political: early examples of, 33-34; first used in political cartoons, 34, modern, 336
Carmon, Walt, 376-81
Carracci, Agostino, Annibale, and Lodovico, 33
Carter, Robert, 294-95
Cartoon, political: authoritarian, 53-56; defined, 11-17; democratic, 56-57; evaluated, 17-26; impact of technology on, 34-49; elements of, 62-78; revolutionary, 112-14; shorthand typology of, 75-78; symbols in, 208-31; totalitarian, 52-53, 180-81; understanding older cartoons, 17-26
Cartoonists, democratic: and cherished communities, 57-62; constraints on by government, 188-91; constraints on by publishers, 184-88; deadline pressures on, 191-93; defending the system, 80-111; general constraints on, 178-81; pressures from other cartoonists, 193-96; rewards and awards, 194-207
Caufman, Sam, Jr., 190
Cesare, Oscar, 141, 162-63, 198, 283, 296, 297, 373, 381
Cham, 364
Chambers, Robert W., 359
Chapin, Will, 278, 279
Charles, William, 214, 234, 243
Chase, John, 22, 195, 196, 374, 381
Christ-Janer, Albert, 376, 381
Clay, E. W., 218, 239, 246
Clark, Kinnaird, 381
Cobb, Ron, 334-35, 377, 381
Coleman, Glen, 183

Collins, John, 358
Comics with politics, 328-35; boxes for the editorial page, 335-39
Conrad, Paul, 135-36, 185, 186, 197, 203, 320, 380, 381
Coons, H., 377, 385
Cooper, Frederic Taber, 374, 381
Cory, J. Campbell, 297, 298, 377, 381
Coupe, W. A., 75, 76, 79, 371, 372, 375, 381
Craiger, J. Sidney, 377
Cranach, Lucas, 36
Crane, Walter, 95, 97, 372
Craven, Thomas, 371, 374, 381
Crawford, Bill, 322
Crawford, Charles, 381
Crockett, Gib, 196, 322
Crosby, Percy, 329-30, 377
Cruikshank, George, 13, 32, 54, 55, 92
Cruikshank, Robert, 87
Cruikshanks, Eveline, 371
Crumb, Robert, 182, 265, 334
Cudlipp, Hugh, 374
Cummings, Michael, 354-55, 356, 378, 381
Currier and Ives, 41, 45, 219, 232, 236-39, 243, 262
Curtis, L. Percy, Jr., 100, 372, 381
Curtis, R. A., 380
Curtis Tom, 322, 323
Cynicus (J. Martin Anderson), 103, 349, 379

Dahl, Francis, 336
Dahl, Robert, 373
Dalrymple, Louis, 255
Danish cartoons, 367
Dannett, Sylvia G. L., 374, 381
Darcy, Tom, 135, 137, 197, 203, 320, 382
Darling, Jay N. "Ding," 32, 60, 61, 62, 78, 79, 141-42, 165, 172, 179, 193, 197, 198, 199, 202, 203, 223, 267, 273, 276-78, 369, 370, 373, 376, 382
Darrow, Whitney, 13
Daumier, Honoré, 25, 45, 65, 114, 120-28, 133, 135, 137, 149-52, 181, 182, 281, 283, 364
Davenport, Homer, 25, 77, 78, 188, 189, 198, 228, 230, 231, 267-70, 292, 353, 382
Davis, Charles Augustus, 218
Davis, Stuart, 183
Day, Robert, 13
de Haswell, James, 373, 383
Dehn, Adolf, 183, 283
DeMar, John L., 228, 377
Dix, Otto, 139-40, 144
Dobbins, Jim, 382
Donahey, James H., 278, 280, 297, 376, 382
Doolittle, Amos, 217, 218, 234

394